Rick Steves'

SCANDINAVIA

2007

W9-COJ-761

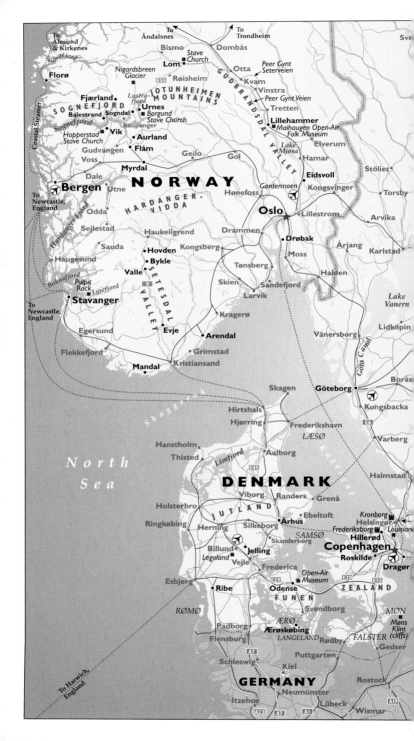

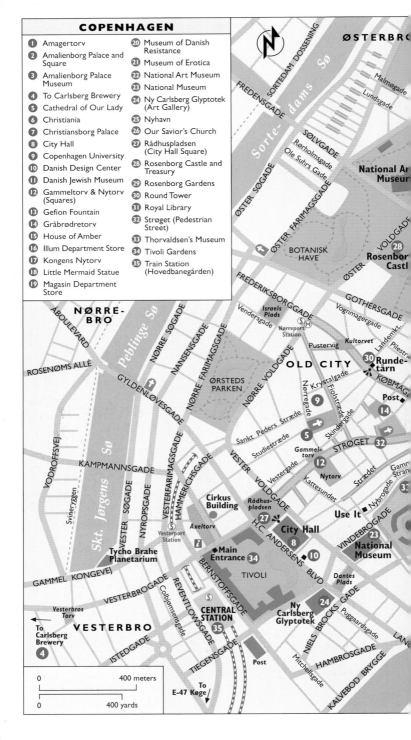

COPENHAGEN

1. Amagertorv
2. Amalienborg Palace and Square
3. Amalienborg Palace Museum
4. To Carlsberg Brewery
5. Cathedral of Our Lady
6. Christiania
7. Christiansborg Palace
8. City Hall
9. Copenhagen University
10. Danish Design Center
11. Danish Jewish Museum
12. Gammeltorv & Nytorv (Squares)
13. Gefion Fountain
14. Gråbrødretorv
15. House of Amber
16. Illum Department Store
17. Kongens Nytorv
18. Little Mermaid Statue
19. Magasin Department Store
20. Museum of Danish Resistance
21. Museum of Erotica
22. National Art Museum
23. National Museum
24. Ny Carlsberg Glyptotek (Art Gallery)
25. Nyhavn
26. Our Savior's Church
27. Rådhuspladsen (City Hall Square)
28. Rosenborg Castle and Treasury
29. Rosenborg Gardens
30. Round Tower
31. Royal Library
32. Strøget (Pedestrian Street)
33. Thorvaldsen's Museum
34. Tivoli Gardens
35. Train Station (Hovedbanegården)

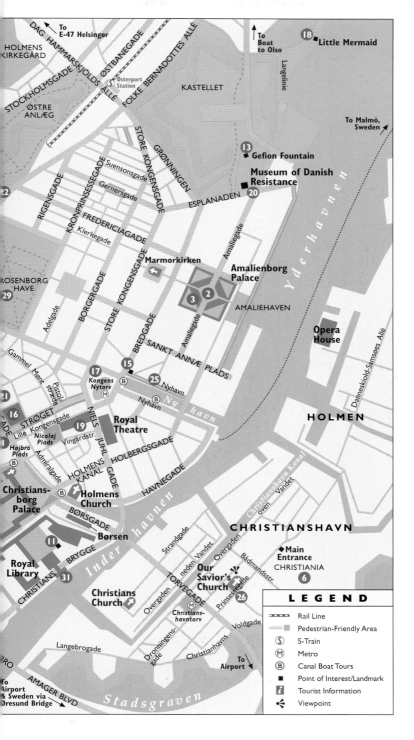

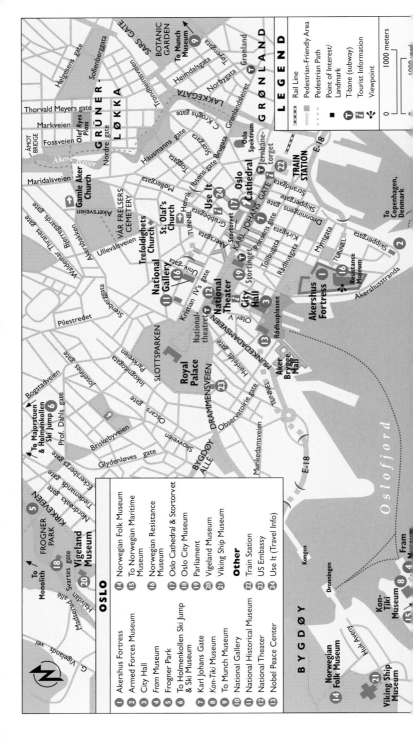

OSLO

1. Akershus Fortress
2. Armed Forces Museum
3. City Hall
4. Fram Museum
5. Frogner Park
6. To Holmenkollen Ski Jump & Ski Museum
7. Karl Johans Gate
8. Kon-Tiki Museum
9. To Munch Museum
10. National Gallery
11. National Historical Museum
12. National Theater
13. Nobel Peace Center
14. Norwegian Folk Museum
15. To Norwegian Maritime Museum
16. Norwegian Resistance Museum
17. Oslo Cathedral & Stortorvet
18. Oslo City Museum
19. Parliament
20. Vigeland Museum
21. Viking Ship Museum

Other
22. Train Station
23. US Embassy
24. Use It (Travel Info)

LEGEND

Rail Line
Pedestrian-Friendly Area
Pedestrian Path
Point of Interest/Landmark
■ Point of Interest/Landmark
T T-bane (subway)
i Tourist Information
Viewpoint

0   1000 meters

BYGDØY

Norwegian Folk Museum

Viking Ship Museum

Kon-Tiki Museum

Fram

Oslofjord

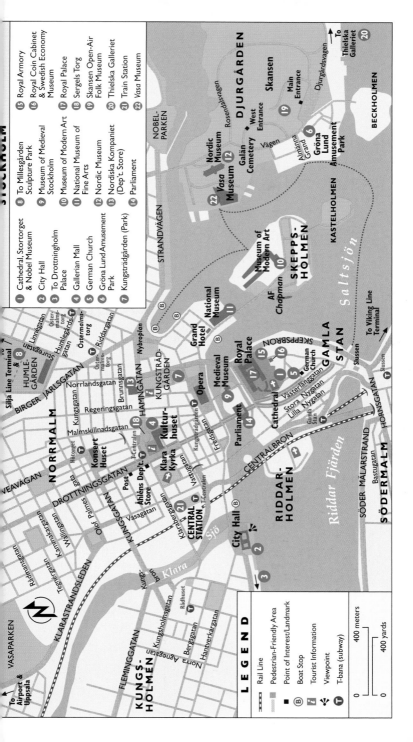

STOCKHOLM

LEGEND

- Rail Line
- Pedestrian-Friendly Area
- ■ Point of Interest/Landmark
- ⒷBoat Stop
- ⓘ Tourist Information
- ❖ Viewpoint
- Ⓣ T-bana (subway)

| 0 | 400 meters |
| 0 | 400 yards |

1. Cathedral, Stortorget & Nobel Museum
2. City Hall
3. To Drottningholm Palace
4. Gallerian Mall
5. German Church
6. Gröna Lund Amusement Park
7. Kungsträdgården (Park)
8. To Millesgården Sculpture Park
9. Museum of Medieval Stockholm
10. Museum of Modern Art
11. National Museum of Fine Arts
12. Nordic Museum
13. Nordiska Kompaniet (Dept. Store)
14. Parliament
15. Royal Armory
16. Royal Coin Cabinet & Swedish Economy Museum
17. Royal Palace
18. Sergels Torg
19. Skansen Open-Air Folk Museum
20. Thielska Galleriet
21. Train Station
22. Vasa Museum

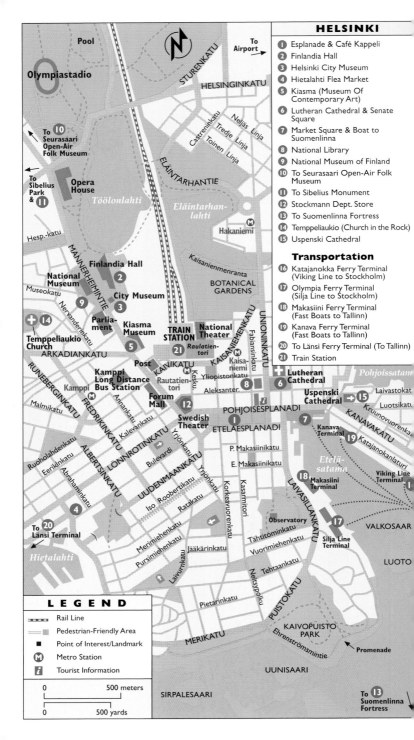

HELSINKI

1. Esplanade & Café Kappeli
2. Finlandia Hall
3. Helsinki City Museum
4. Hietalahti Flea Market
5. Kiasma (Museum Of Contemporary Art)
6. Lutheran Cathedral & Senate Square
7. Market Square & Boat to Suomenlinna
8. National Library
9. National Museum of Finland
10. To Seurasaari Open-Air Folk Museum
11. To Sibelius Monument
12. Stockmann Dept. Store
13. To Suomenlinna Fortress
14. Temppeliaukio (Church in the Rock)
15. Uspenski Cathedral

Transportation

16. Katajanokka Ferry Terminal (Viking Line to Stockholm)
17. Olympia Ferry Terminal (Silja Line to Stockholm)
18. Makasiini Ferry Terminal (Fast Boats to Tallinn)
19. Kanava Ferry Terminal (Fast Boats to Tallinn)
20. To Länsi Ferry Terminal (To Tallinn)
21. Train Station

LEGEND

- ▪▪▪▪ Rail Line
- ▬ ▬ ■ Pedestrian-Friendly Area
- ■ Point of Interest/Landmark
- Ⓜ Metro Station
- 𝒊 Tourist Information

0   500 meters

0   500 yards

Rick Steves'

SCANDINAVIA
2007

AVALON
TRAVEL

CONTENTS

Top Destinations in Scandinavia

INTRODUCTION

Scandinavia—known for its stunning natural beauty, fun-loving cities, trend-setting design, progressive politics, high latitudes, and even higher taxes—is one of Europe's most enjoyable and most interesting corners. A visit here connects you with immigrant roots, modern European values, and the great outdoors like none other. You'll gasp at breathtaking fjords, glide on a cruise ship among picturesque islands, and marvel at the efficiency and livability of its big cities. Yes, Scandinavia is expensive. But, delightfully, the best time to visit—midsummer—is also the best time to get great deals on the fancier hotels.

This book breaks Scandinavia into its top big-city, small-town, and rural attractions. It gives you all the information and opinions necessary to wring the maximum value out of your limited time and money. If you plan a month or less in Scandinavia, this lean and mean little book is all you need.

Experiencing the culture, people, and natural wonders of Scandinavia economically and hassle-free has been my goal for three decades of traveling, guiding tours, and travel writing. With this book, I pass on to you the lessons I've learned, updated for 2007.

Rick Steves' Scandinavia is your smiling Swede, your Nordic navigator, and a tour guide in your pocket. This book is balanced to include a comfortable mix of exciting capital cities and cozy small towns. It covers the predictable biggies and mixes in a healthy dose of Back Door intimacy. Along with seeing Tivoli Gardens, Hans Christian Andersen's house, and *The Little Mermaid,* you'll take a bike tour of a sleepy, remote Danish isle, dock at a time-passed fjord village, and wander among eerie, prehistoric monoliths in Sweden. And for a breezy look at the Baltics, I've added Tallinn, Estonia.

To save time, maximize diversity, and avoid tourist burnout, I've been very selective. We won't cruise both the Geirangerfjord and Sognefjord. Instead, we'll see just the better of the two: Sognefjord.

The best is, of course, only my opinion. But after spending half of my adult life researching Europe, I've developed a sixth sense for what travelers enjoy.

This Information Is Accurate and Up-to-Date

This book is updated every year. Most publishers of guidebooks that cover a country from top to bottom can afford an update only once every two or three years (and, even then, it's often by e-mail or fax). Because this book is selective, covering only the places that I think make the best month of sightseeing, it's easy to update it in person every year.

The prices, hours, and telephone numbers in this book are accurate as of mid-2006. Even with an annual update, things change. Still, if you're traveling with the current edition of this book, you're using the most up-to-date information available in print. For the latest, see www.ricksteves.com/update. Also at our Web site, you'll find a valuable list of reports and experiences—good and bad—from fellow travelers who have used this book (www.ricksteves.com/feedback).

Use this year's edition. If you're packing an old book, you'll understand the seriousness of your mistake...in Scandinavia. Your trip costs about $10 per waking hour. Your time is valuable. This guidebook saves lots of time.

About This Book

This book is organized by destinations. Each of these destinations is a mini-vacation on its own, filled with exciting sights and homey, affordable places to stay. In the following chapters, you'll find these sections:

Planning Your Time offers ideas on how best to use your limited time.

Orientation includes tourist information, public transportation tips, and easy-to-read maps.

Self-Guided Walks takes you through interesting neighborhoods, with a personal tour guide in hand.

Sights provides a succinct overview of Scandinavia's most important sights, with ratings:

▲▲▲—Don't miss.

▲▲—Try hard to see.

▲—Worthwhile if you can make it.

No rating—Worth knowing about.

Sleeping describes my favorite hotels, from budget deals to splurges.

Budget Tips

While Scandinavia is expensive, the transportation passes, groceries, alternative accommodations, and admissions are affordable (about what you'd pay in England or Italy). Being aware of your budget options will save you money.

It's fun to take advantage of midsummer hotel discounts, but keep in mind that these discounts are generally offered only by the more expensive hotels. You'll save much more by staying in private homes, or, cheaper still, in hostels (many hostels have double rooms and great breakfasts).

Have picnics in the park. Quench your thirst for beer in Denmark, where alcohol isn't quite as pricey as it is farther north.

Scanrail passes can make train travel one of your smaller expenses; bus travel is even cheaper—and sometimes faster. At sights, ask about discounted admission costs, as many aren't posted (see "Discounts," page 11).

The great scenery is free. When things are pricey, remind yourself you're not getting less for your travel dollar. Up here there simply aren't any lousy or cheap alternatives to classy, cozy, sleek Scandinavia. Electronic sensors flush youth-hostel toilets and breakfasts are all-you-can-eat.

This book will help you save a shipload of money and days of headaches. Read it carefully. Many of the skills and tricks that are effective in Copenhagen work in Oslo and Stockholm as well.

Eating serves up good-value restaurants, ranging from inexpensive cafés to fancier options.

Transportation Connections lays the groundwork for your smooth arrival and departure, explaining connections by bus, train, and plane.

The **appendix** is a traveler's tool kit, with telephone tips, a climate chart, tips on metric conversion, and a list of festivals.

Browse through this book, choose your favorite destinations, and link them together. Then have a great trip! Traveling like a temporary local, you'll get the absolute most out of every mile, minute, and dollar. As you travel the route I know and love, I'm happy you'll be meeting some of my favorite Scandinavian people.

PLANNING

Trip Costs

Five components make up the cost of your trip: airfare, surface transportation, room and board, sightseeing/entertainment, and

Scandinavia's Best Three-Week Trip by Car

Day	Plan	Sleep in
1	Arrive in Copenhagen	Copenhagen
2	Copenhagen	Copenhagen
3	Copenhagen	Copenhagen
4	North Zealand, into Sweden	Växjö
5	Växjö, Kalmar, Glass Country	Kalmar
6	Kalmar to Stockholm	Stockholm
7	Stockholm	Stockholm
8	Stockholm	Boat to Helsinki
9	Helsinki	Boat to Stockholm
10	Uppsala to Oslo	Oslo
11	Oslo	Oslo
12	Oslo	Oslo
13	Lillehammer, Gudbrandsdal Valley	Jotunheimen or Sogndal
14	Jotunheimen Country	Sogndal or Aurland
15	Sognefjord, Norway in a Nutshell	Bergen
16	Bergen	Bergen
17	Long drive south, Setesdal Valley	Kristiansand
18	Jutland, Århus, Legoland	Århus/Billund
19	Jutland to Ærø	Ærøskøbing
20	Ærø	Ærøskøbing
21	Odense, Roskilde	Copenhagen

Flying "open jaw" into Copenhagen and home from Bergen (with a likely transfer in Copenhagen) can be wonderfully efficient; if you opt for this, you can see Jutland and Ærø sights near Copenhagen at the beginning of your trip. Otherwise, it's about 20 hours by train from Bergen to Copenhagen (transfer in Oslo).

shopping and miscellany.

Airfare: Don't try to sort through the mess. Find and use a good travel agent. A basic round-trip flight from the US to Copenhagen will cost $700–1,300 (cheaper in winter), depending on where you fly from and when. Consider saving time and money in Europe by flying "open jaw" (for instance, flying into Copenhagen and out of Bergen).

Surface Transportation: For a three-week whirlwind trip of all my recommended destinations, allow $660 per person for public transportation. This pays for a second-class 21-day Scanrail pass (which also covers 50 percent of the boat fare between Stockholm and Helsinki), plus extra boat rides that aren't covered by the pass (such as Helsinki–Tallinn and Tallinn–Stockholm). By car, figure

about $850 per person: $750 per person (based on two people sharing car and related expenses) for a three-week car rental, tolls, gas, and insurance, plus a minimum of about $170 per person for the round-trip boat fare between Stockholm and Helsinki. Ferrying to and from Tallinn will add another $100. Car rental is usually cheapest if arranged from the US. Consider flying. Hopping on a plane to zip from Tallinn (Estonia) to Copenhagen (Denmark) in an hour can be an excellent time-saver.

Room and Board: You can eat and sleep well in Scandinavia for $100 a day per person for room and board. A $100-a-day budget allows $10 for lunch, $20 for dinner, and $70 for lodging (based on two people splitting the cost of a $140 double room that includes breakfast). Students and tightwads can do it on $55 ($30 per hostel bed, $25 for groceries and snacks).

Sightseeing and Entertainment: In big cities, figure $5–13 per major sight (Oslo's *Kon-Tiki* Museum-$7, Copenhagen's Tivoli Gardens-$12), $3 for minor ones (climbing towers), and $25 for splurge experiences (e.g., folk concerts, bus tours, and fjord cruises). The major cities have cards giving you a 24-hour free run of the public transit system and entrance to all the sights for about $35/day. An overall average of $20 per day works for most people. Don't skimp here. After all, this category is the driving force behind your trip—you came to sightsee, enjoy, and experience Scandinavia.

Shopping and Miscellany: Shopping can brutalize your budget in Scandinavia. Good budget travelers find that this category has little to do with assembling a trip full of lifelong and wonderful memories. (But if you're a dedicated shopper, see "VAT Refunds and Customs Regulations," page 15.)

When to Go

Summer is a great time to go. Scandinavia bustles and glistens under the July and August sun; it's the height of the tourist season, when all the sightseeing attractions are open and in full swing. In many cases, things don't kick into gear until midsummer—about June 20—when Scandinavian schools let out. Most local industries take July off, and the British and southern Europeans tend to visit Scandinavia in August. You'll notice crowds during these times, but up here "crowds" mean fun and action rather than congestion. Things quiet down when the local kids go back to school, about August 20.

"Shoulder-season" travel—in late May, early June, and September—lacks the vitality of summer but offers good weather and minimal crowds.

Winter is a bad time to explore Scandinavia. Like a bear, Scandinavia's metabolism goes down and many sights and accommodations are closed or open on a limited schedule. Business travelers drive hotel prices way up. Winter weather can be cold and dreary, and nighttime will draw the shades on your sightseeing well before dinner.

Sightseeing Priorities

Depending on the length of your trip, and taking geographic proximity into account, here are my recommended priorities:

4 days:	Copenhagen, Stockholm (connected by a 5.5-hour express train)
6 days, add:	Oslo
8 days, add:	Norway in a Nutshell fjord trip, Bergen
10 days, add:	Overnight cruise from Stockholm to Helsinki—and slow down

Scandinavia's Best Three-Week Trip by Train

Day	Plan	Sleep in
1	Arrive in Copenhagen	Copenhagen
2	Copenhagen	Copenhagen
3	Copenhagen	Copenhagen
4	Roskilde, Odense, Ærø	Ærøskøbing
5	Ærø	Ærøskøbing
6	Ærø to Kalmar	Kalmar
7	Kalmar	Kalmar
8	Kalmar, early train to Stockholm	Stockholm
9	Stockholm	Stockholm
10	Stockholm, night boat to Helsinki	boat
11	Helsinki	Helsinki
12	Helsinki, jet boat to Tallinn	Tallinn
13	Tallinn, night boat to Stockholm	boat
14	Stockholm, afternoon train to Oslo	Oslo
15	Oslo	Oslo
16	Oslo	Oslo
17	Train to Aurland	Aurland
18	Aurland to Bergen via fjord cruise	Bergen
19	Bergen	Bergen
20	Free day: more fjords, Århus, resting, or whatever	
21	Trip over	

If you want to see Legoland (near Billund) and the "bog man" (in Århus), visit these from Odense (closer) or Copenhagen.

14 days, add: Ærø, Odense, Roskilde, Frederiksborg (all in Denmark)
17 days, add: Jutland (Denmark), Kalmar (Sweden)
21 days, add: Tallinn (Estonia) and more time in capitals
24 days, add: More Norwegian countryside

Travel Smart

Your trip to Scandinavia is like a complex play—easier to follow and really appreciate on a second viewing. While no one does the same trip twice to gain that advantage, reading this book in its entirety before your trip accomplishes much the same thing.

Reread this book as you travel, and visit local tourist information offices. Upon arrival in a new town, lay the groundwork for a smooth departure; write down the schedule for the train or bus you'll take when you depart. Buy a phone card or carry a mobile phone, and use it for reservations and confirmations—take advantage of the Scandinavians' incredible proficiency in English.

Design an itinerary that enables you to visit the sights at the best possible times. As you read through this book, make note of festivals, colorful market days, and days when sights are closed. Saturday morning feels like any bustling weekday morning, but at lunchtime, many shops close down through Sunday. Sundays have pros and cons, as they do for travelers in the US (special events, limited hours, shops and banks closed, limited public transportation, no rush hours). Popular places are even more popular on weekends. Many sights are closed on Monday.

Plan ahead for banking, laundry, Internet stops, and picnics. To maximize rootedness, minimize one-night stands. Mix intense and relaxed periods, villages and cities, fjords and museums. Every trip (and every traveler) needs at least a few slack days. Pace yourself. Assume you will return.

Enjoy the friendliness of the local people. Ask questions. Most locals are eager to point you in their idea of the right direction. Wear your money belt, pack along a pocket-size notebook to organize your thoughts, and practice the virtue of simplicity. Those who expect to travel smart, do.

RESOURCES
Tourist Information Offices
In the US
The Scandinavian Tourist Board's US office is a wealth of information. Before your trip, get the free general information packet and request any specifics you want (such as regional and city maps and festival schedules). Call 212/885-9700 or visit www.goscandinavia .com (info@goscandinavia.com).

In Scandinavia
Your best first stop in any new city is the tourist information office (abbreviated in this book as **TI**). Throughout Scandinavia, you'll find TIs are usually well-organized and all staff speak English. Try to arrive before the TI closes, and take full advantage of their help. Have a list of questions ready, and pick up maps, brochures, and walking-tour information. If you're arriving late, telephone ahead (and try to get a map for your next destination from a TI in the town you're leaving). Important: Each big city publishes a *This Week In...* guide (to Copenhagen, Stockholm, Oslo, Bergen, Helsinki, Århus, and Tallinn). These are free, found all over town, and packed with all the tedious details about each city (24-hour pharmacy, embassies, tram/bus fares, restaurants, sights with hours/admissions/phone numbers), plus a useful calendar of events and a map of the town center.

Begin Your Trip at www.ricksteves.com

At our travel Web site, you'll find a wealth of **free information** on European destinations, including fresh monthly news and helpful tips from thousands of fellow travelers.

Our online Travel Store offers travel bags and accessories specially designed by Rick Steves to help you travel smarter and lighter. These include Rick's popular carry-on bags (wheeled and rucksack versions), money belts, totes, toiletries kits, adapters, other accessories, and a wide selection of guidebooks, planning maps, and DVDs.

Choosing the right railpass for your trip—amidst hundreds of options—can drive you nutty. We'll help you choose the best pass for your needs, plus give you a bunch of free extras.

Travel agents will tell you about mainstream tours of Europe, but they won't tell you about **Rick Steves' tours.** Rick Steves' Europe Through the Back Door travel company offers more than two dozen itineraries and 400+ departures reaching the best destinations in this book...and beyond. You'll enjoy great guides, a fun bunch of travel partners (with small groups of generally around 25), and plenty of room to spread out in a big, comfy bus. You'll find European adventures to fit every vacation length. To get our Tour Catalog and a free *Rick Steves Tour Experience* DVD (filmed on location during an actual tour), visit www.ricksteves.com.

While the TIs offer room-finding services, they're a good deal only if you're in search of summer and weekend deals on business hotels. The TIs can help you with small pensions and private homes, but you'll save both yourself and your host money by going direct with the listings in this book.

Rick Steves' Guidebooks, Public Television Show, and Radio Show

With the help of my staff, I produce materials to help you plan your trip and travel smoothly.

Guidebooks: This book is one of a series of 30+ books on European travel that includes country guidebooks, city and regional guidebooks, and my budget-travel skills handbook, *Rick Steves' Europe Through the Back Door.* All are annually updated. My phrase books—for Italian, French, German, Spanish, and Portuguese—are practical and budget-oriented. My other books include *Europe 101* (a crash course on art and history), *European Christmas* (on traditional and modern-day celebrations, including Norway's), and *Postcards from Europe* (a fun memoir of my travels over 25 years). For a complete list of my books, see the inside of the last page of this book.

Public Television and Radio Shows: My television series, *Rick Steves' Europe,* covers European destinations. My weekly public radio show, *Travel with Rick Steves,* features interviews with travel experts from around the world. All the TV scripts and radio shows are at www.ricksteves.com. Listen to the shows at any time, or download them onto your MP3 player to take along on your trip.

Other Guidebooks

Especially if you're traveling beyond my recommended destinations, you may want some supplemental travel information. When you consider the improvements they'll make in your $3,000 vacation, $30 for extra maps and books is money well spent. Especially for several people traveling by car, the weight and expense are negligible. One good tip can save the price of an extra guidebook.

Lonely Planet's *Scandinavian Europe* is thorough, well-researched, and packed with good maps and hotel recommendations for low- to moderate-budget travelers. The similar *Rough Guide to Scandinavia* is written by insightful British researchers.

Students and vagabonds like the highly opinionated *Let's Go: Western Europe,* which includes some coverage of Scandinavia (updated by Harvard students, has thorough hostel listings). *Let's Go* is best for backpackers who have railpasses and are interested in the youth and nightlife scene.

For Estonia, consider the *Bradt Guide to Estonia* (published by Globe Pequot Press).

Note that none of the above-mentioned books are updated annually; check the publication date before you buy.

Maps

The black-and-white maps in this book, drawn by Dave Hoerlein, are concise and simple. Dave, who is well-traveled in Scandinavia, has designed the maps to help you locate recommended places and get to local TIs, where you can pick up a more in-depth map (usually free) of the city or region.

Train travelers can use a simple rail map (such as the one that comes with your train pass). But drivers shouldn't skimp on maps—get one good overall road map for Scandinavia (either the Michelin *Scandinavia* or the Kummerly & Frey *Southern Scandinavia* 1:1,000,000 edition). The Collins Road Atlas is also good. The only detailed map worth considering is the *Southern Norway-North* (Sør Norge-nord, 1:325,000) by Cappelens Kart ($15 in Scandinavian bookstores).

PRACTICALITIES

Red Tape: Traveling throughout this region requires only a passport—no shots and no visas. It's a good idea to pack a photocopy of your passport in your luggage in case the original is lost or stolen. Border crossings between Norway, Sweden, Denmark, and Finland are a wave-through. Getting into and out of Estonia, even though it's in the European Union, takes a little longer, but still goes relatively quickly. When you change countries, you change money, phone cards, and postage stamps.

Time: Norway, Sweden, and Denmark, which share the same time zone as continental Europe, are six/nine hours ahead of the East/West Coasts of the US. Finland and Estonia are one hour ahead of continental Europe.

In Scandinavia—and in this book—you'll be using the 24-hour clock. It's the same through 12:00 noon, then keep going—13:00, 14:00, and so on. For anything past 12, subtract 12 and add p.m. (14:00 is 2:00 p.m.).

Discounts: I have not listed special age-based discounts in this book. But in keeping with its liberal orientation, Scandinavia is Europe's most generous corner when it comes to youth, student, senior, and family discounts. If you are any of the above, always mention it. Students should travel with an ISIC (International Student Identity Card, normally available at university foreign-study offices in North America; www.isic.org). Spouses sometimes pay half price when doing things as a couple. Seniors should ask about senior discounts. Children usually sleep and sightsee for half price or for free.

Metric: Get used to metric. A liter is about a quart (4 quarts to a gallon). A kilometer is six-tenths of a mile. I figure kilometers to miles by cutting them in half and adding back 10 percent of the original (120 km: 60 + 12 = 72 miles, 300 km: 150 + 30 = 180 miles).

Watt's Up? If you're bringing electrical gear, you'll need a two-prong adapter plug (sold cheap at travel stores in the US). You may also need a converter to deal with the increased voltage. Travel appliances often have convenient, built-in converters; look for a voltage switch marked 120V (US) and 240V (Europe).

News: Americans keep in touch in Europe with the *International Herald Tribune* (published almost daily via satellite). Every Tuesday, the European editions of *Time* and *Newsweek* hit the stands with articles of particular interest to travelers in Europe. Sports addicts can get their fix from *USA Today*. Good Web sites include www.europeantimes.com and http://news.bbc.co.uk. Many hotels have CNN or BBC television channels.

MONEY

Exchange Rates

I've priced things in local currencies throughout the book.

$1 equals about...
6 Danish kroner (1 krone equals about $0.17)
6.5 Norwegian kroner (1 krone equals about $0.15)
7 Swedish kronor (1 krona equals about $0.14)
0.85 euro in Finland (€1 equals about $1.20)
13 Estonian krooni (1 kroon equals about $0.08)

In Scandinavia, kroner are decimalized: 100 øre = 1 krone. Kroner from one Scandinavian country are not accepted in the next (except at foreign-exchange services and banks, and then only bills).

Standard abbreviations are Danish krone, DKK; Swedish krona, SEK; and Norwegian kroner, NOK. I'll keep it simple. For all three countries, I'll use the kroner abbreviation "kr."

The exchange rates for Norway and Denmark are nearly the same. To roughly translate Danish and Norwegian prices into US dollars, divide by 6 (e.g., 100 kr = about $16). In Sweden, divide prices by 7 (50 kr = about $7).

Finland's currency is the euro (€). To roughly convert prices in euros to dollars, add 20 percent (€20 = about $24).

Tallinn's kroon, officially abbreviated as EEK, appears as "kr" in this book. To roughly convert prices from krooni into dollars, drop the last two digits and multiply by eight (500 kr = about $40; 1,255 kr = about $96). Anything under 100 kr is less than $8.

Banking

Bring plastic (ATM, debit, or credit cards) along with several hundred dollars in hard cash as an emergency backup. Traveler's checks are a waste of time (waiting at banks) and a waste of money (paying to purchase and then cash checks).

Before you go, verify with your bank that your card will work. Also inquire about "international transaction" fees (which can be up to $5 per transaction). Alert your bank that you'll be making withdrawals in Europe; otherwise, the bank may not approve transactions if they perceive unusual spending patterns. Bring an extra card in case one gets demagnetized or gobbled up by a temperamental machine.

The best and easiest way to get cash is to use the readily available, easy-to-use ATMs (with English instructions). To withdraw cash, you'll need a card that can withdraw money from your bank account, plus a PIN code (numbers only, no letters on European keypads).

Just like at home, credit or debit cards work easily at larger hotels, restaurants, and shops. Visa and MasterCard are more commonly accepted than American Express. Smart travelers function with plastic and cash. Smaller businesses prefer—and sometimes require—payment in hard kroner rather than plastic. If you have lots of large bills, break them for free at a bank, especially if you like shopping at mom-and-pop places; they rarely have huge amounts of change.

In Denmark, many places charge a fee for using a credit card, so it's a good idea to ask before using your card. These fees aren't the only reason you should keep plenty of cash in your money belt: Many Danish businesses, even large ones, do not accept foreign-issued credit cards at all.

Banking in Scandinavia is straightforward, and exchange rates are nearly standard. Buy and sell rates are within about 2 percent of each other. If you must bring traveler's checks, get them in large denominations because bank fees are very stiff and can be per check rather than transaction. (In Norway, some banks charge 1 or 2 percent rather than per check.) American Express offices in each capital change AmEx checks (and sometimes other brands as well) for no extra fee. Even with their worse-than-banks' exchange rates, AmEx can save you money if you're changing less than $1,000. Post offices, which have long hours, decent rates, and smaller fees, can be a good place to change money.

Bring some $20 American bills along for those times when you need just a little more local cash (e.g., if you're just passing through or about to leave a country). In many cases, small cash exchanges are cheaper outside of banks, at places that offer worse rates but smaller (or no) fees, such as the handy FOREX window at the Copenhagen train station or exchange desks on international boats.

Even in safe, orderly Scandinavia, you should use a money belt (a cloth pouch worn around your waist and tucked under your clothes). Thieves target tourists. A money belt provides peace of mind. You can carry lots of cash safely in a money belt, and given ATM and credit-card fees, you should. Don't be petty about getting money. Withdraw the money you'll need for a country, stuff it in your money belt, and travel!

Tips on Tipping

Tipping in Europe isn't as automatic and generous as it is in the US—but for special service, tips are appreciated, if not expected. As in the US, the proper amount depends on your resources, tipping philosophy, and the circumstance, but some general guidelines apply.

Damage Control for Lost or Stolen Cards

If you lose your credit, debit, or ATM card, you can stop people from using your card by reporting the loss immediately to the respective global customer-assistance centers. If you promptly report your card lost or stolen, typically you won't be held responsible for any unauthorized transactions on your account, although many banks charge a liability fee. Call these 24-hour US numbers collect: Visa (tel. 410/581-9994), MasterCard (tel. 636/722-7111), and American Express (tel. 336/393-1111).

At a minimum, have the following information ready: the name of the financial institution that issued you the card, along with the type of card (classic, platinum). Ideally, you want to plan ahead: Pack photocopies of the backs of your cards (with the collect-call numbers), and write down your card numbers on a separate piece of paper that doesn't have your name on it. Providing the following information will allow a quicker cancellation of your missing card: full card number, whether you are the primary or secondary cardholder, the cardholder's name exactly as printed on the card, billing address, home phone number, circumstances of the loss or theft, and identification verification (such as your birth date, your mother's maiden name, or your Social Security number—memorize this, don't carry a copy). If you are the secondary cardholder, you'll also need to provide the primary cardholder's identification verification details. You can generally receive a temporary card within two or three business days in Europe.

Restaurants: Tipping is an issue only at restaurants that have table service. If you order your food at a counter, don't tip.

Throughout Scandinavia, a service charge is included in your bill, so there's no need to leave an additional tip. In fancier restaurants or for great service, round up the bill (about 5 percent of the total check). It's generally good form to tip about 5 percent at any restaurant in Estonia, where servers earn low wages and rely on tips.

Taxis: To tip the cabbie, round up. For instance, to pay a 85-kr fare, give 90 kr (about 5 percent). If the cabbie hauls your bags and zips you to the airport to help you catch your flight, you might want to toss in a little more. But if you feel like you're being driven in circles or otherwise ripped off, skip the tip.

Hotels: I don't tip at hotels, but if you do, give the porter a few kroner for carrying your luggage.

When in doubt, ask: If you're not sure whether (or how much) to tip for a service, ask your hotelier or the tourist information office; they'll fill you in on how it's done on their turf.

VAT Refunds and Customs Regulations

Wrapped into the purchase price of your Scandinavian souvenirs is a Value Added Tax (VAT) of 20–25 percent (among the highest rates in Europe). You're entitled to get most of that tax back if you make a purchase of a certain amount ($50 in Denmark, $48 in Finland and Norway, $25 in Sweden, and $210 in Estonia) at a store that participates in the VAT refund scheme. (In Denmark, for instance, look for the Danish Tax-Free Shopping emblem.) VAT is called MVA in Norway and MOMS in Denmark, Finland, and Sweden. Note that you can't get refunds on meals, hotel stays, or transportation in Scandinavia.

Personally, I've never felt that VAT refunds are worth the hassle, but if you do, here's the scoop.

If you're lucky, the merchant will subtract the tax when you make your purchase (this is more likely to occur if the store ships the goods to your home). Otherwise, you'll need to do all this:

• **Get the paperwork.** Have the merchant completely fill out the necessary refund document, called a "cheque." You'll have to present your passport at the store.

• **Get your stamp at the airport or border.** If you've made purchases in Denmark, Finland, Sweden, and/or Estonia, get your cheque(s) stamped at your last stop in the European Union by the customs agent who deals with VAT refunds. If you've shopped hard in Norway (a non-EU country), get your cheque(s) stamped at the border or at your point of departure from Norway.

It's best to keep your purchases in your carry-on for viewing, but if they're too large or dangerous (such as knives) to carry on, then track down the proper customs agent to inspect them before you check your bag. You're not supposed to use your purchased goods before you leave. If you show up at customs wearing your new clogs, officials might look the other way—or deny you a refund.

• **Collect your refund.** To collect your refund, you'll need to return your stamped documents to the retailer or its representative. Many merchants work with a service such as Global Refund or Premier Tax Free, which have offices at major airports, ports, or border crossings. These services, which extract a 4 percent fee, can refund your money immediately in your currency of choice or credit your card (within two billing cycles). If you have to deal directly with the retailer, mail the store your stamped documents and then wait. It could take months.

Customs Regulations: You can take home $800 in souvenirs per person duty-free. The next $1,000 is taxed at a flat 3 percent. After that, you pay the individual item's duty rate. You can also bring in duty-free a liter of alcohol (slightly more than a standard-size bottle of wine), a carton of cigarettes, and up to 100 cigars. As for food, anything in cans or sealed jars is acceptable. Don't bring home meat (even if it's dried and cured), cheeses, or fresh fruits and veggies. To check customs rules and duty rates, visit www .customs.gov.

TRANSPORTATION

Getting to Scandinavia

Copenhagen is usually the most direct and least expensive Scandinavian capital to fly into from the US (though Stockholm, Oslo, and Helsinki are easy to reach via Icelandair from the East Coast). Copenhagen is also Europe's gateway to Scandinavia from points south. There are often cheaper flights from the US into Frankfurt and Amsterdam than into Copenhagen, but it's a long, rather dull, one-day drive (with a 2-hour, $70-per-car ferry crossing at Puttgarden, Germany). By train, the trip is an easy overnight ride from Amsterdam, Paris, or Frankfurt. The trip ($150–200) is covered if you have the comprehensive Eurailpass or a railpass covering the particular countries.

Another option is flying into London and then hopping to Copenhagen on a low-cost, no-frills airline, such as bmi (British Midland, www.flybmi.com), easyJet (www.easyjet.com), or Ryanair (www.ryanair.com).

Cheap Flights Within Scandinavia

This book covers far-flung destinations separated by vast stretches of mountains and water. While boats and trains are more romantic, cheap flights can provide an affordable and efficient way to connect the dots on a Scandinavian itinerary.

Several new budget airlines have cropped up in the last few years. Most of these airlines offer flights both within Nordic Europe and to destinations all over the Continent and beyond.

SAS, the region's dominant airline, operates a low-cost subsidiary called Snowflake, with hubs in Stockholm and Copenhagen (www.flysnowflake.com). SAS also has a Finnish subsidiary called Blue1 (hubs in Helsinki and Stockholm, www .blue1.com).

Other options are the Swedish airlines FlyNordic (hub in Stockholm, www.flynordic.com) and FlyMe (hubs in Göteborg and Stockholm, www.flyme.com); Norwegian Airlines (hubs in Oslo and Bergen, www.norwegian.no); the Denmark-based Sterling (specializes in connecting Scandinavian capitals such as Oslo and Copenhagen with sunny destinations in southern Europe, www.sterlingticket.com); and Tallinn-based Estonian Air (www.estonian-air.com).

Public Transportation

As with all no-frills airlines, be aware of trade-offs for cheap flights: minimal customer service, non-refundable tickets, and strict restrictions on the amount of baggage you're allowed to check without paying extra.

As you decide on how to get around, remember that one advantage of a night train is that it saves you the cost of a hotel room, which can be substantial in expensive Scandinavia. Night boats (such as between Stockholm and Tallinn) can be more pricey, so a cheap flight can save you a boatload of time and money.

Railpasses

Prices listed are for 2006. My free Rick Steves' *Guide to Eurail Passes* has the latest prices and details (and easy online ordering) at www.ricksteves.com/rail. Prices subject to change.

Note that senior rates are for those aged 60 and up, and youth prices apply to those under age 26.

SCANRAIL PASS

	2nd Cl. Adult	2nd Cl. Senior	2nd Cl. Youth
5 days in 2 months	$310	$273	$215
8 days in 2 months	375	331	259
10 days in 2 months	416	368	289
21 consecutive days	481	423	336

Trolls 4–11 half adult fare; under 4 free. Covers Denmark, Norway, Sweden, and Finland.

FINNRAIL PASS

	1st Class	2nd Class
3 days in 1 month	$237	$159
5 days in 1 month	318	212
10 days in 1 month	431	286

Kids 6–16 half price when accompanied by parent; under 6 free.

NORWAY PASS

	Adult 2nd Cl.	Senior 2nd Cl.	Youth 2nd Cl.
3 days in 1 month	$227	$193	$169
Extra rail days (max 5)	41	35	32

Kids 4–15 half adult fare; under 4 free. Not valid on Airport Express.

Map key:

Approximate point-to-point one-way second-class rail fares in US dollars. First class costs 50 percent more. Add up fares for your itinerary to see whether a railpass will save you money.

SWEDEN PASS

	Adult 1st Cl.	Adult 2nd Cl.	Senior 1st Cl.	Senior 2nd Cl.	Youth 1st Cl.	Youth 2nd Cl.
3 days in 1 month	$305	$232	$259	$197	$214	$163
Extra rail days (max 5)	36	28	31	25	25	19

Kids 4-15 half adult fare; under 4 free.

DENMARK PASS

	Adult 1st Cl.	Adult 2nd Cl.	Saver 1st Cl.	Saver 2nd Cl.	Youth 2nd Cl.
3 days in 1 month	$116	$77	$103	$64	$51
7 days in 1 month	181	116	155	103	90

"Saver" prices are per person for two or more people traveling together. Kids 4-11 approximately half adult or Saver fare; under 4 free.

SELECTPASS

This pass covers travel in three adjacent countries. Please visit **www.ricksteves.com/rail** for four- and five-country options.

	Individual 1st Class	Saver 1st Class	Youth 2nd Class
5 days in 2 months	$383	$325	$249
6 days in 2 months	423	360	275
8 days in 2 months	503	428	325
10 days in 2 months	580	493	375

"Saver" prices are per person for two or more people traveling together. Kids 4–11 pay half of adult individual or Saver fare; under 4 free.

SCANRAIL & DRIVE PASS

Any 5 rail days and 2 car days in 2 months.

Car Category	2nd Class	Extra Car Day
Economy	$360	$59
Compact	375	69
Intermediate	385	79

No extra rail days. Price per person, two traveling together. To order Rail & Drive passes, call your travel agent, or Rail Europe at 800-438-7245. *This pass is not sold by Europe Through the Back Door.*

By Car, Train, or Bus?

While a car gives you the ultimate in mobility and freedom, enables you to search for hotels more easily, and carries your bags for you, the train zips you effortlessly and scenically from city to city, usually dropping you in the center and near the tourist office. Cars are great in the countryside but an expensive headache in big cities. Three or four people travel cheaper by car. With a few exceptions, trains cover my recommended destinations wonderfully. Pick up train schedules from stations as you go. To study ahead on the Web, check http://bahn.hafas.de/bin/query.exe/en (Germany's excellent Europe-wide timetable). The local train companies also have their own sites with fare and timetable information, and even online booking in English; see http://dsb.dk or www.rejseplanen .dk (Denmark), www.vr.fi (Finland), www.nsb.no (Norway), and www.sj.se (Sweden).

Don't overlook long-distance buses, which are usually slower but have considerably cheaper and more predictable fares than trains. (In Denmark, however, the train system is excellent and nearly always the better option.) On certain routes, such as between Stockholm and Oslo, the bus is both cheaper and can be slightly faster than the train. Scandinavia's big bus carriers are Sweden's Swebus (www.swebusexpress.se), Norway's Nor-Way Bussekspress (www.nor-way.no), Denmark's public buses (www.rejseplanen.dk), and Finland's Matkahuolto (www.matkahuolto.fi).

Trains

One of the great Nordic bargains, the Scanrail pass is your best railpass deal for a trip limited to Scandinavia. Those sold in the US are listed on page 18. More restrictive 5-days-out-of-15 or 21-consecutive-day variations are also available for a similar price at any major train station in Scandinavia (www.scanrail.com). Although Scanrail passes are available only for second-class seats, Scandinavian second class is plenty comfortable. Some trains, including those that cover part of the popular Norway in a Nutshell route (see page 188), do not offer first class.

If your trip extends south of Scandinavia, consider the flexible Eurail Selectpass (see prices on page 19), which allows you to choose three, four, or five adjoining countries connected by land or ferry (for instance, Germany–Sweden–Finland). A more expensive Eurailpass is a good value only for those spending more time throughout Europe. A three-week first-class Eurailpass costs $785 (or $668 apiece for a Eurail Saverpass, if you travel with a companion).

Railpasses give you free or discounted use of many boats (such as Stockholm to Finland) and cover almost all trains in the region (though you'll need 50-kr reservations for long rides and express trains, plus a 120-kr supplement for Norway's Myrdal–Flåm ride—part of the Norway in a Nutshell route).

A Scanrail 'n' Drive pass offers a flexible way to mix rail and car rental, and is handy if you plan to explore Sweden's Glass Country or the Norwegian mountains and fjords. However, if you're planning on using a car more than two days in a row, you're probably better off renting a car rather than getting a pass.

Consider the efficiency of night travel. A bed in a compartment on a night train is a good value in Scandinavia. Beyond the cost of your first- or second-class ticket or pass, you'll pay about $25 for a bed in a triple, $40 for a bed in a double, or $100 for a single.

Car Rental and Leasing

Car rental is usually cheapest when arranged in advance from home. Call various companies, look online, or arrange a rental through your hometown travel agent, who can help you out if anything goes wrong during your trip. Each major rental agency has an office in the Copenhagen airport. Rent by the week with unlimited mileage. (For longer trips, consider leasing; see below.) Auto Europe is one of many good companies (www.autoeurope.com).

Expect to pay about $750 per person (based on two people sharing the car) for a small economy car for three weeks with unlimited mileage, including gas, parking, and insurance. I normally rent a small, inexpensive model like a Ford Fiesta. For a

STOP AND LEARN THESE ROAD SIGNS

Speed Limit (km/hr) — Yield — No Passing — End of No Passing Zone

One Way — Intersection — Main Road — Freeway

Danger — No Entry — No Entry for cars — All Vehicles Prohibited

Parking — No Parking — Customs — Peace

bigger, roomier, more powerful but still inexpensive car, move up to a Ford Focus or VW Polo. Always keep your receipts in case any questions arise about your billing.

Insurance: For peace of mind, I spring for the Collision Damage Waiver insurance (CDW, about $15–25 per day), which limits my financial responsibility in case of an accident. Unfortunately, CDW now has a high deductible hovering at about $1,200. When you pick up your car, many car-rental companies will try to sell you "super CDW" at an additional cost of $10–20 per day to lower the deductible to zero.

As an alternative, some credit cards offer zero-deductible collision coverage (similar to CDW) for no charge to their customers. Quiz your credit-card company on the worst-case scenario. You have to choose either the coverage offered by your car-rental company or by your credit-card company. This means that if you go with the credit-card coverage, you'll have to decline the CDW offered by the car-rental company. In this situation, some car-rental companies put a hold on your credit card for the amount of the full deductible (which can equal the value of the car). This is bad news if your credit limit is low—particularly if you plan on using that card for other purchases during your trip.

Another option is to buy CDW insurance from Travel Guard ($9/day plus a one-time $3 service fee covers you up to $35,000, $250 deductible, US tel. 800-826-4919, www.travelguard.com). It's valid throughout Europe, but some car-rental companies refuse to honor it, especially in Italy and the Republic of Ireland. Oddly, residents of some states (including Washington) are not allowed to buy this coverage.

In summary, buying CDW from the car-rental company— along with the supplemental insurance to buy down the deductible, if you choose—is the easiest but priciest option. Using the coverage that comes with your credit card is cheaper, but can involve more hassle. If you're taking a short trip, an easy solution is to buy Travel Guard's very affordable CDW.

Driving in Scandinavia: Distance and Time

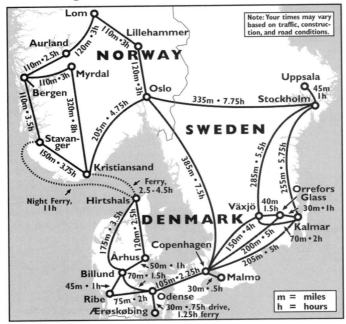

Leasing: For trips of about 17 days or more, leasing is the best way to go. By technically buying and then selling back the car, you save lots of money on tax and insurance. Leasing provides you with a brand-new car with unlimited mileage and a 24-hour emergency assistance program. Car leases must be arranged from the US. One of many reliable companies that offers lease packages is Europe by Car (US tel. 800-223-1516, www.europebycar.com).

Driving

Except for the dangers posed by the scenic distractions and moose crossings, Scandinavia is a great place to drive. Your American license is accepted. Gas is expensive—more than $5 per gallon—and if you use your credit card to pay for it, you may need to enter your card's PIN code, so memorize it before you go. Roads are good (though nerve-rackingly skinny in western Norway). Traffic is generally sparse, and drivers are sober and civil. Signs and road maps are excellent. Local road etiquette is similar to that in the US. Use your headlights day and night; it's required in most of Scandinavia. Seat belts are mandatory. Bikes tend to whiz by close and quiet, so be on guard.

There are plenty of good facilities, gas stations, and scenic

One Region, Different Countries

Scandinavia is Western Europe's least populated, most literate, most prosperous, most demographically homogeneous, most highly taxed, most socialistic, and least churchgoing corner. While the state religion is Lutheranism, only a small percentage of Scandinavians actually attends church other than at Easter or Christmas.

Denmark, Norway, and Sweden are each constitutional monarchies with a royal family that knows how to stay out of the tabloids and work with the parliaments. Scandinavia is the home of cradle-to-grave security and, consequently, residents (and visitors) pay hefty taxes. Blessed with pristine natural surroundings, the Scandinavians are environmentalists (except for the Norwegians' stubborn appetite for whaling). The region is also a leader in progressive lifestyles. More than half the couples in Denmark are "married" only because they've lived together for so long and have children.

Denmark, packing five million fun-loving Danes into a flatland the size of Switzerland, is the most densely populated Scandinavian country. Sweden, the size of California, has 8.5 million people; and 4.2 million Norwegians stretch out in vast yet skinny Norway. Oslo is as far from the northern tip of Norway as it is from Rome.

rest stops. Snow is a serious problem off-season in the mountains. Parking on the street is a headache only in major cities, where expensive garages are safe and plentiful. Denmark uses a parking windshield-clock disk (free at TIs, post offices, and newsstands; set it when you arrive and be back before your posted time limit is up). Even in the Nordic countries, thieves break into cars. Park carefully, use the trunk, and show no valuables. Never drink and drive. Even one drink can get a driver into serious trouble.

As you navigate, you'll find town signs followed by the letters *N, S, Ø* (Ö in Sweden), *V,* or *C.* These stand for north *(nord),* south *(sud),* east *(øst),* west *(vest),* and center *(centrum),* respectively; understanding them will save you lots of wrong exits. Due to recent changes, many maps have the wrong road numbers. It's safest to navigate by town names.

COMMUNICATING

The Language Barrier

In Scandinavia, English is all you need. These days every well-educated person seems to speak English. Still, knowing the key words is good style and helpful.

A few words you'll see and hear a lot (these are all in Norwegian; the Danish and Swedish versions differ slightly): *takk* (thanks), *gammel* (old), *lille* (small), *stor* (big), *slot* (palace), *fart* (trip), *centrum* (center), *gate* (street), *øl* (beer), *forbudt* (not allowed), and *udsalg*, *salg*, or *rea* (sale).

Each country has its own language. Danish, Norwegian, and Swedish are so closely related that locals can laugh at each other's TV comedies. The languages are similar to English but with a few letters we don't have (Æ, Ø, Ö, Å, Ä). These letters barely affect pronunciation, but do affect alphabetizing. If you can't find, say, Århus in a map index, look after Z. Finnish and Estonian are vastly different from the other Scandinavian languages and English; in fact, Finnish has more in common with Hungarian than Swedish (see page 328).

Telephones

Smart travelers learn the phone system and use it daily to reserve or reconfirm rooms, get tourist information, reserve restaurants, confirm tour times, or phone home.

Types of Phones

You'll encounter various kinds of phones in Scandinavia.

• **Public pay phones** usually accept insertable phone cards instead of coins. To make a call, simply take the phone off the hook, insert the prepaid card, wait for a dial tone, and dial away. The price of the call (local or international) is automatically deducted while you talk. You can also use an international phone card to make calls from pay phones that take coins or insertable cards. For details on the different phone cards, see below.

• **Hotel room phones** are fairly cheap for local calls, but pricey for international calls, unless you use an international phone card (see below).

• **American mobile phones** work in Europe if they're GSM-enabled, tri-band (or quad-band), and on a calling plan that includes international calls. For example, with a T-Mobile phone, you can roam using your home number, and pay $1–2 per minute for making or receiving calls.

• Some travelers buy a **European mobile phone** in Europe. For about $125, you can get a phone that will work in most countries once you pick up the necessary chip (about $30) per country. Or you can buy a cheaper "locked" phone that only works with a SIM card from the country where you purchased it (about $100, includes $20 worth of calls). If you're interested, stop by any European shop that sells mobile phones; you'll see prominent store window displays. You aren't required to (and shouldn't) buy a monthly contract—buy prepaid calling time instead (as you use it up, buy additional minutes at newsstands or mobile-phone shops). If you're on a budget, skip mobile phones and use phone cards instead.

Paying for Calls

You can spend a fortune making phone calls in Scandinavia...but why would you? Here's the skinny on different ways to pay, including the best deals.

• Scandinavian **phone cards** come in two types: phone cards that you insert into a pay phone (best for local calls or quick international calls), and phone cards that come with a dial-up code and can be used from almost any phone (best for international calls).

Insertable phone cards are a convenient way to pay for calls from public pay phones (see previous page). Each country's telephone company sells a basic phone card (usually in denominations of roughly $5 and $10), good for use only in that country's phone booths. You can buy phone cards at the post office, newsstands, and tobacco shops.

International phone cards, which are not inserted, can be used from almost any phone, even from the one in your hotel room. Dial the toll-free number listed on the card, and you'll reach an automated operator. When prompted, dial in a code number, also written on the card. A voice tells you how much is left in your account. Then dial your number. The card is good for local, long-distance, or international calls.

Calls to the US cost about $1 for 10 minutes. Cards, offered in denominations of $5 and $10, are sold at small newsstand kiosks and hole-in-the-wall long-distance phone shops. Because there are so many brand names, simply ask for an international telephone card and tell the vendor where you'll be making most calls ("to America"), and he'll select the brand with the best deal. Get small denominations in case the card is a dud.

Beware: Most merchants promise that the cards work throughout Scandinavia (because each card has local access numbers for each country), but often they don't work in neighboring countries, and you're stuck with extra minutes that you can't use. The Go Bananas card is more reliable than most—it's good in Denmark, Norway, Sweden, and Germany. Unfortunately, it can be difficult to find international phone cards in Finland.

• **Dialing direct from your hotel room** without using an international phone card is a terrible rip-off for international calls. (If you must dial direct from your hotel room phone, first ask how much you'll be charged.) Keep in mind that you might have to pay for local and occasionally even toll-free calls.

• **Receiving calls in your hotel room** is often the cheapest way to keep in touch with the folks back home, especially if your family has an inexpensive way to call you (either a good deal on their long-distance plan or a prepaid calling card with good rates to Europe). Give them a list of your hotels' phone numbers before you go. As you travel, send your family an e-mail or make a quick pay phone call to set up a time for them to call you, and then wait for the ring.

• **VoIP (Voice over Internet Protocol),** which is an option only for those traveling with a laptop computer, allows VoIP users to talk with each other for free via their computers over a fast Internet connection. Look into Skype (www.skype.com) and Google Talk (www.google.com/talk).

• **US calling cards** (such as the ones offered by AT&T, MCI, or Sprint) are the worst option. You'll nearly always save a lot of money by paying with a phone card.

How to Dial

Calling from the US to Scandinavia, or vice versa, is simple—once you break the code. The European calling chart on page 396 will walk you through it. Remember that Norwegian, Swedish, and Danish time is six/nine hours ahead of the East/West Coasts of the US, while Finnish and Estonian time is seven/ten hours ahead.

Dialing Domestic Calls: In Denmark, Estonia, and Norway, which don't use area codes, just dial local numbers direct from anywhere in the country. For example, to call one of my recommended Copenhagen hotels from anywhere in Denmark (including Copenhagen), simply dial its local number (33 13 19 13). Sweden and Finland do have area codes (like we do in the US). When making long-distance calls within Sweden or Finland, include the entire area code (which starts with a zero); when making local calls, omit the area code. So, to call one of my recommended Stockholm hotels from anywhere in Sweden outside of Stockholm, dial 08 (Stockholm's area code), then the local number, 723-7250. To call the same hotel from Stockholm's train station, just dial 723-7250 (without the area code).

Dialing International Calls: To make an international call to a Scandinavian country, you'll need to:

• Dial the international access code (011 if calling from the US or Canada, 00 from Europe—except in Finland, which uses 999 or another 900 number depending on the phone service you're using).

• Dial the country code of the country you're calling. For a list of country codes, see the appendix.

• If you're calling Denmark, Estonia, or Norway (which don't use area codes), simply dial the rest of the number. If you're calling Sweden or Finland (which use area codes), dial the rest of the number, omitting the initial zero.

To call the Copenhagen hotel from the US, dial 011 (US international access code), 45 (Denmark's country code), then 33 13 19 13 (local number). To call the Stockholm hotel from the US, dial 011 (US international access code), 46 (Sweden's country code), 8 (Stockholm's area code is 08, but you drop the initial zero), then 723-7250 (local number).

To call my office in Edmonds from anywhere in Europe, I dial 00 (Europe's international access code), 1 (US country code), 425 (Edmonds' area code), and 771-8303.

E-mail and Mail

E-mail: Many travelers set up a free e-mail account with Yahoo, Microsoft (Hotmail), or Google (Gmail). E-mail use among Scandinavian hoteliers is quite common. Internet cafés and little hole-in-the-wall Internet-access shops (offering a few computers, no food, and cheap prices) are popular in most cities. More and more hotels now offer Internet access in their lobbies for guests, and some even have Wi-Fi wireless connections for travelers with laptop computers. Ask if your hotel has access. If it doesn't, your hotelier will direct you to the nearest place to get online.

Mail: While you can arrange for mail delivery to your hotel (allow 10 days for a letter to arrive), phoning and e-mailing are so easy that I've dispensed with mail stops altogether.

SLEEPING

For each destination, I recommend the best accommodations values, from $15 bunk beds to $200 doubles. An overall average of $80 per night in humble doubles is possible using this book's listings. I like small, central, clean, traditional, friendly places that aren't listed in other guidebooks. Most places listed meet five of these six virtues. For smart use of your time, I favor hotels and restaurants handy to your sightseeing activities and public transportation.

Room-finding services offered by tourist information offices, if you have no place in mind, can be worth the booking fee (about $8). Be very clear about what you want. (Mention if you have sheets or a sleeping bag, whether you will take a twin or double, if a bathroom down the hall is acceptable, and so on.) They know the hotel quirks and private-room scene better than anybody. Official "rack rates" (the highest rates a hotel charges) are often misleading; they omit cheaper oddball rooms and special clearance deals.

To save money, bring your own sheet or sleeping bag and offer to provide it in low-priced establishments. This can save $10 per person per night, especially in rural areas. Families can get a price break; normally a child can sleep free or for very little in Mom and Dad's room.

To get the most sleep for your dollar, pull the dark shades (and even consider bringing your own night shades) to keep out the early-morning sun.

Hotels

Hotels are expensive ($80–200 doubles), with some exceptions. Business-class hotels drop prices to attract tourists with summer rates (late June–early Aug) and weekend rates (Fri, Sat, and sometimes Sun). Some chains such as Thon Hotels in Norway offer 400-kr discounts (about $60) per night if you purchase a 95-kr discount card from them (about $15, see www.skanplus.com). You need to ask about these—receptionists don't volunteer the information.

To sleep in a fancy hotel in a big city, it's cheapest to arrive without a reservation and let the local tourist office book you a room. When a classy, modern $200 place has a $100 summer special that includes two $10 buffet breakfasts, the dumpy $60 hotel room without breakfast becomes less exciting.

There actually are several tiers of rates, including tourist office referral, weekend, summer, summer weekend, and walk-in. Walk-ins at the end of a quiet day can often get a room even below the summer rate. Some hotels also have lower rates for online bookings, so check the Web for deals. Many modern hotels have "combi" rooms (singles with a sofa that turns the room into a perfectly good double), which are cheaper than a full double. Also, many places have low-grade older rooms, considered unacceptable for the general public and often used by workers on weekdays outside of summer. If you're on a budget, ask for cheaper rooms with no windows or no water. And if a hotel is not full, any day can bring out summer discounts.

Be aware that hotel rates in Norway could increase this year over those listed in this book—hoteliers there may decide to pass the cost of a new 8 percent VAT on to hotel guests.

Hostels

Scandinavian hostels, Europe's finest, are open to travelers of all ages. They offer classy facilities, members' kitchens, cheap hot meals (often breakfast buffets), plenty of doubles (for a few extra kroner), and great people experiences. Hostels are also a tremendous source of local and budget travel information. Receptionists will hold a room if you promise to arrive by 18:00. Note that many hostels close in the off-season.

Hosteling only saves money if you come prepared. Buy a hostel membership card before you leave home ($28 a year, free if you're younger than 18 and $15 if you're older than 54; sold at your local student travel office, any hostel office, Hostelling International— US tel. 301/495-1240, or online at www.hiayh.org). Those without

Sleep Code

To help you sort easily through these listings, I've divided the rooms into three categories based on the price for a standard double room with bath:

$$$ **Higher Priced**
$$ **Moderately Priced**
$ **Lower Priced**

To give maximum information with a minimum of space, I use the following code to describe accommodations listed in this book. Prices are listed per room, not per person. When a range of prices is listed for a room, the price fluctuates with room size or season. You can assume a hotel takes credit cards unless you see "cash only" in the listing.

S = Single room (or price for one person in a double).
D = Double or Twin. Double beds are usually big enough for non-romantic couples.
T = Triple (often a double bed with a single bed moved in).
Q = Quad (an extra child's bed is usually cheaper).
b = Private bathroom with toilet and shower or tub.
s = Private shower or tub only (the toilet is down the hall).

English is spoken unless otherwise noted. According to this code, a couple staying at a "Db-995 kr" hotel in Sweden would pay a total of 995 kr (about $140) for a double room with a private bathroom. The hotel accepts credit cards or hard kronor in payment.

---

hostel cards pay about $7-per-night extra. Many hostels in Norway regularly promote non-member prices—if you have a membership card, be sure to ask about a discount. Not all hostels belong to Hostelling International; these private hostels don't require any membership and are more laid-back, but less predictable.

Bring a hosteling sleep sack or bed sheets from home, or else plan on renting them for about $6 per stay. Making your meals in the hostel kitchen is a great way to save money.

You'll find lots of Volvos in hostel parking lots, as Scandinavians know that hostels provide the best (and usually only) $30 beds in town. Hosteling is ideal for families who fit into two sets of bunk beds (4-bed rooms, kitchens, washing machines, discount family memberships). Pick up each country's free hostel directory at any hostel or TI.

Private Rooms

Throughout Scandinavia, people rent out rooms in their homes to travelers for about $50 per double (or about $75 for a double with private bath). While some put out a *Værelse, Rom, Rum,* or *Hus Rum* sign, most operate solely through the local TI (which occasionally keeps these B&Bs a secret until all hotel rooms are taken). You'll get your own key to a clean, comfortable, but usually simple private room (sometimes without a sink), with free access to the family shower and WC (unless the room has a private bath). Booking direct saves both you and your host the cut the TI takes. The TIs are very protective of their lists. If you enjoy a big-city private home that would like to be listed in this book, I'd love to hear from you.

Camping

Scandinavian campgrounds are practical, comfortable, and cheap (about $6–7 per person with camping card, available on the spot). The national tourist office has a fine brochure/map listing all their campgrounds. This is the middle-class Scandinavian family way to travel: safe, great social fun, and no reservation problems.

Most campgrounds provide **huts** *(hytter)* for wanna-be campers with no gear. Huts normally sleep four to six in bunk beds, come with blankets and a kitchenette, and charge one fee (about 300 kr or $50, plus extra if you need sheets). Because locals typically move in for a week or two, many campground huts are booked for summer long in advance. If you're driving late with no place to stay, find a campground and try to grab a hut.

Making Reservations

You can do this entire trip easily without reservations during most of the year (except, for instance, in the capitals during conventions—early June is packed in Oslo and Stockholm). Still, given the high stakes, erratic accommodations values, and the quality of the gems I've found for this book, I'd recommend booking rooms in advance (by e-mail or phone).

If you want maximum flexibility, phone between 9:00 and 10:00 on the day you plan to arrive, when the hotelier knows who'll be checking out and just which rooms will be available. Some hotel receptionists will trust you and hold a room until 16:00 without a deposit, while others will ask for a credit card number. *Honor your reservations or cancel by phone. Trusting people to show up is a hugely stressful issue and a financial risk for hotel owners.* I promised the owners of the places I list that you will be reliable when you make a telephone reservation; please don't let them (or me) down. Long distance is cheap and easy from public phone booths. Being a little late is no problem if you are in telephone contact. Don't needlessly confirm rooms through the tourist office; they'll take a commission.

If you want to nail down your itinerary in advance, you can make reservations from home or while on the road. To reserve a room, e-mail, call, or fax the hotel. Phone and fax costs are reasonable, e-mail is a steal, and simple English is fine. To fax, use the form in the appendix (also online at www.ricksteves.com /reservation). In Europe, dates are written as day/month/year, so a two-night stay in August would be "2 nights, 16/8/07 to 18/8/07." (European hotel jargon includes your day of departure.) You'll often receive a response back from the hotel requesting one night's deposit. Faxing your card number (rather than e-mailing it) keeps it private, safer, and out of cyberspace. If you do reserve with a credit card, you can pay with your card or cash when you arrive; if you don't show up, you'll be billed for one night. Reconfirm your reservations a day or two in advance for safety.

If you receive a response from the hotel stating its rates and room availability, it's not necessarily a confirmation. You must confirm that you indeed want a room at the given rate for the agreed-upon dates. (Don't assume you can extend your stay upon arrival; take the time to consider in advance how long you'll stay.)

EATING

Breakfast

Hotel breakfasts are a huge and filling buffet, generally included but occasionally a $10-or-so option. This features fruit, cereal, and various milks (*skummet* is skim, *lett* is low-fat, *sød* or *hel* is whole, *filmjölk* is buttermilk). Grab a drinkable yogurt and go local by pouring it in the bowl and sprinkling your cereal over it. The great selection of breads and crackers comes with jam, butter *(smør)*, margarine (same word), and cheese. And you'll get cold cuts, pickled herring, caviar paste (in a squeeze tube), and boiled eggs (*bløt* is soft-boiled, *kokt* is hard-boiled); use the plastic egg cups and small spoons provided to eat your soft-boiled egg Scandinavian-style.

The brown cheese with the texture of earwax and a slightly sweet taste is made from boiled-down whey (the liquid by-product of cheese-making). In Norway, it's called goat cheese *(geitost)*, but only cheese labeled *ekte* (genuine) is really made from goat's milk. Try to develop a taste for this odd but tasty cheese, because you'll see it everywhere. Swedes prefer a spreadable variety, called *messmör*.

For beverages, it's orange juice (the word for orange is *appelsin*, so OJ is AJ) and coffee or tea. Coffee addicts can buy a thermos and get it filled in most hotels and hostels for $3 or $4. While it is bad form to take freebies from the breakfast buffet to eat later, many hotels will provide you with wax paper and a plastic bag to pack yourself a lunch, legitimately, for $6–7. Ask for a *matpakke*.

If you skip your hotel's breakfast, you can visit a bakery to get a sandwich and cup of coffee. Bakeries have wonderful inexpensive pastries. The only cheap breakfast is the one you make yourself. Many simple accommodations provide kitchenettes or at least coffeepots with heated bases.

Lunch

Many restaurants offer cheap daily lunch specials *(dagens rett)* and buffets for office workers. Scandinavians, not big on lunch, often just grab a sandwich *(smørrebrød)* and a cup of coffee at their work desk.

Especially in Denmark, you'll find *smørrebrød* shops turning sandwiches into an art form. These open-face delights taste as good as they look. My favorite is the one piled high with *rejer* (shrimp). The roast beef is good, too. Shops will wrap sandwiches up for a perfect picnic in a nearby park.

If you want to enjoy a combination of picnics and restaurant meals on your trip, you'll save money by eating in restaurants at lunch (when there's usually a special and food is generally cheaper) and picnicking for dinner.

Picnics

Scandinavia has colorful markets and economical supermarkets. Picnic-friendly mini-markets at gas and train stations are open late. Samples of picnic treats: *Wasa* cracker bread (Sport is my favorite; Ideal *flatbrød* is ideal for munchies), packaged meat and cheese, brown goat cheese *(geitost)*, drinkable yogurt, freshly cooked or smoked fish from markets, fresh fruit and vegetables, lingonberries, squeeze tubes of mustard and sandwich spreads  (shrimp, caviar), rye bread, and boxes of juice and milk. Grocery stores sell a cheap, light breakfast: a handy yogurt with cereal and a spoon. Most places offer cheap ready-made sandwiches. If you're bored with sandwiches, some groceries and most delis have hot chicken, salads by the portion, and picnic portables.

Dinner

The large meal of the Nordic day is an early dinner. Most Scandinavians eat dinner at home, and restaurant dinners are expensive treats. Alternate between picnic dinners (outside or in your hotel or hostel), cheap, forgettable, but filling cafeteria or fast-food dinners ($10), and atmospheric, carefully chosen restaurants popular with locals ($25). One main course and two salads or soups fill up two travelers without emptying their pocketbooks. If potatoes came with your main dish, most servers are happy to give you a second helping. Booze is pricey: A beer costs $8 in Oslo. Water is served free with an understanding smile at most restaurants (though in Denmark, there is a charge for water if you don't order another beverage).

In Scandinavia, a $15 meal in a restaurant is not that much more than a $10 American meal, since tax and tip are included in the menu price.

Most Scandinavian nations have one inedible dish that is cherished with a perverse but patriotic sentimentality. These dishes, which often originated during a famine, now remind the young of their ancestors' suffering. Norway's penitential food, *lutefisk* (dried cod marinated for days in lye and water), is used for Christmas and for jokes.

Smörgåsbord

Seek out a Scandinavian feast, the *smörgåsbord* (known in Denmark and Norway as the *store koldt bord*), at least once during your trip. This all-you-can-eat buffet allows you to sample the culinary delights of the Nordic lands. For a seven-step Swedish smörgåsbord plan, see page 303.

Resist the urge to pile everything on your plate at once, as many Americans do, "Royal Fork" style. Instead, watch the locals. Take your time and dine in stages. Dirty lots of dishes.

Your first course is fish. Start with *sild* (pickled herring) on a slice of dense rye bread called *rugbrød*. Then maybe *gravad laks* (smoked salmon) with caviar on the side. Wash it down with beer or an ice-cold shot of *akvavit* (see "Drinking," below). *"Skål!"* (pronounced "skole") means "Cheers!"

Then get a new plate and move on to the main course of fish, chicken, or another meat, often accompanied by potatoes. The seafood is usually wonderful.

Next comes the cheese and fruit course with *franskbrød* white bread. Try creamy Havarti, blue Castello (a soft, mild blue cheese), and, in Norwegian buffets, goat cheese. The whole affair is topped off with a dessert (see "Dessert," below) and coffee.

You'll find these buffets for lunch and dinner; lunch is usually cheaper. Some good places for a Nordic buffet include Stockholm's Grand Hotel (see page 302) and on the boats between Copenhagen and Oslo and between Stockholm and Helsinki or Tallinn. Note that many hotels offer a mini-version of the feast mentioned above.

Drinking

Purchasing wine, beer, and spirits in Scandinavia can put a dent in your vacation budget. In **Sweden** and **Norway,** spirits, wine, and strong beer (more than 3.5 percent alcohol) are sold in state-run liquor stores: Systembolaget in Sweden, and Vinmonopolet in Norway. (Rumor has it, though, that Sweden will soon liberalize its booze sales.) Buying a beer or glass of wine in a bar or restaurant in Sweden or Norway is particularly expensive. Therefore, many Scandinavians will have a drink or a glass of wine at home (or in their hotel room) before going out, then limit themselves to one or two glasses at the restaurant. If taking an overnight cruise during your trip, you can get a good deal on a bottle of wine or spirits in the on-board duty free shop. Liquor laws are much more relaxed in **Denmark,** where you can buy wine, beer, and spirits at any supermarket or corner store. Prices are a bit lower as well. Public drinking is acceptable in Denmark, while it is illegal (although often done) in Norway and Sweden.

Some local specialties are *Akvavit* (Norway, Sweden, and Denmark), a strong spirit distilled from potatoes and flavored with anise, caraway, or other herbs and spices; *Lakka* (Norway, Sweden, and Finland), a syrupy-sweet liqueur made from cloud-berries, the small orange berries grown in the Arctic; *Salmiakka* (Finland, Norway, and Denmark), a nearly black licorice-flavored liqueur; and *Gammel Dansk* (Denmark), Danish bitters for the adventurous.

Dessert

Scandinavians love sweets. A meal is not complete without a little treat and a cup of coffee at the end. Bakeries *(konditori)* fill their window cases with all varieties of cakes, tarts, cookies, and pastries. The most popular ingredients are marzipan, almonds, hazelnuts, chocolate, and fresh berries. Many cakes are covered with entire sheets of solid marzipan. To find the neighborhood bakery, just look for a golden pretzel hanging above the door or windows.

Scandinavian chocolate is some of the best in Europe. In Denmark, seek out Anthon Berg's dark chocolate and marzipan treats as well as Toms' chocolate-covered caramels (Toms Guld are the best). Sweden's biggest chocolate producer, Maribou, makes huge bars of solid milk chocolate, as well as some with dried fruits or nuts. *Daim* are milk chocolate-covered hard toffees, sold in a variety of sizes, from large bars to bite-size pieces, all in bright-red wrappers. The Freia company, Norway's chocolate goddess (named for the Norse goddess Freya), makes a wonderful assortment of delights, from *Et lite stykke Norge* ("A little piece of Norway"—bars of creamy milk chocolate wrapped in pale-yellow paper) and *Smil* (chocolate-covered soft caramels sold in rolls) to *Firkløver* (bars of

How Was Your Trip?

Were your travels fun, smooth, and meaningful? If you'd like to share your tips, concerns, and discoveries, please fill out the survey at www.ricksteves.com/feedback or e-mail me at rick @ricksteves.com. I personally read and value your feedback. Thanks in advance—it helps a lot.

milk chocolate with hazelnuts). For those who can't decide on one type, the company sells bags of assorted chocolates called *Twist* and red gift boxes of chocolates called *Kong Haakon*, named after Norway's first king.

While chocolate rules, licorice and gummy candies are also popular. Black licorice *(lakrits)* is at its best here, except for *salt lakrits* (salty licorice), which is not for the timid. Black licorice flavors everything from ice cream to chewing gum to liqueur (see "Drinking," above). Throughout Scandinavia, you'll find stores selling all varieties of candy in bulk. Fill your bag with a variety of candies and pay by the gram. Look around at the customers in these stores...they aren't all children.

TRAVELING AS A TEMPORARY LOCAL

We travel all the way to Scandinavia to enjoy differences—to become temporary locals. You'll experience frustrations. Certain truths that we find "God-given" or "self-evident," such as cold beer, ice in drinks, and bottomless cups of coffee, are suddenly not so true. One of the beauties of travel is the opportunity to see that there are logical, civil, and even better alternatives. While the materialistic culture of the US is sneaking into these countries, simplicity has yet to become subversive. Scandinavians are into "sustainable affluence." They have experimented aggressively in the area of social welfare—with mixed results. Travel in high-tax/high government–service Scandinavia can rattle capitalist Americans. The people seem so happy and the society seems so genteel. Fit in, don't look for things American on the other side of the Atlantic, and you're sure to enjoy some thought-provoking stimulation and a full dose of Scandinavian hospitality.

If there is a negative aspect to the image Europeans have of Americans, it is that we are big, aggressive, impolite, rich, loud, and a bit naive. Americans tend to be noisy in public places, such as restaurants and trains. Our raised voices can demolish Europe's reserved ambience. Talk softly. While Europeans look bemusedly at some of our Yankee excesses—and worriedly at others—they nearly always grant us individual travelers all the warmth we deserve.

Judging from all the happy postcards I receive from travelers who have used this book, it's safe to assume you'll enjoy a great, affordable vacation—with the finesse of an independent, experienced traveler. Thanks, and happy travels!

BACK DOOR TRAVEL PHILOSOPHY
From *Rick Steves' Europe Through the Back Door*

Travel is intensified living—maximum thrills per minute and one of the last great sources of legal adventure. Travel is freedom. It's recess, and we need it.

Experiencing the real Europe requires catching it by surprise, going casual..."Through the Back Door."

Affording travel is a matter of priorities. (Make do with the old car.) You can travel—simply, safely, and comfortably—anywhere in Europe for $100 a day plus transportation costs. In many ways, spending more money only builds a thicker wall between you and what you came to see. Europe is a cultural carnival, and, time after time, you'll find that its best acts are free and the best seats are the cheap ones.

A tight budget forces you to travel close to the ground, meeting and communicating with the people, not relying on service with a purchased smile. Never sacrifice sleep, nutrition, safety, or cleanliness in the name of budget. Simply enjoy the local-style alternatives to expensive hotels and restaurants.

Extroverts have more fun. If your trip is low on magic moments, kick yourself and make things happen. If you don't enjoy a place, maybe you don't know enough about it. Seek the truth. Recognize tourist traps. Give a culture the benefit of your open mind. See things as different but not better or worse. Any culture has much to share.

Of course, travel, like the world, is a series of hills and valleys. Be fanatically positive and militantly optimistic. If something's not to your liking, change your liking. Travel is addictive. It can make you a happier American as well as a citizen of the world. Our earth is home to six and a half billion equally precious people. It's humbling to travel and find that people don't envy Americans. Europeans like us, but, with all due respect, they wouldn't trade passports.

Globe-trotting destroys ethnocentricity. It helps you understand and appreciate different cultures. Regrettably, there are forces in our society that want you dumbed down for their convenience. Don't let it happen. Thoughtful travel engages you with the world—more important than ever these days. Travel changes people. It broadens perspectives and teaches new ways to measure quality of life. Rather than fear the diversity on this planet, travelers celebrate it. Many travelers toss aside their hometown blinders. Their prized souvenirs are the strands of different cultures they decide to knit into their own character. The world is a cultural yarn shop, and Back Door travelers are weaving the ultimate tapestry. Join in!

DENMARK

DENMARK

(Danmark)

Denmark is by far the smallest of the Scandinavian countries, but in the 16th century, it was the largest; at one time Denmark ruled all of Norway and the three southern provinces of Sweden. Danes are proud of their mighty history and are the first to remind you that they were a lot bigger and a lot stronger in the good old days.

In the 10th century, before its heyday as a Scan-superpower, Denmark was, like Norway and Sweden, home to the Vikings. More than anything else, these fierce warriors were known for their great shipbuilding, which enabled them to travel far. Denmark's Vikings traveled west to Great Britain and Ireland (where they founded Dublin), bringing back many influences to Denmark, including Christianity.

Denmark consists of many islands and a peninsula (Jutland) that juts up from northern Germany, along with Greenland and the Faroe Islands. The two main islands are Zealand, where Copenhagen is located, and Funen, where H. C. Andersen was born. Out of the hundreds of smaller islands, ship-in-bottle cute Æro is my favorite. Danes like to say you can stand on a beer crate anywhere in the country and see the sea, and in fact, no part of the country is more than 30 miles from the ocean. The Danish landscape is gentle compared to the dramatic fjords, mountains, and vast

lakes of other Scandinavian nations. Denmark's highest point in Jutland is only 560 feet above sea level. In contrast to the rest of Scandinavia, much of Denmark is arable. The landscape consists of rolling hills, small thatched-roof farmhouses, beech forests, and whitewashed churches with characteristic stairstep gables.

Like the other Scandinavian countries, Denmark is predominantly Lutheran, but only a small minority attends church

Denmark

regularly. The majority are ethnic Danes, and many but certainly not all of them have the stereotypical blond hair and blue eyes. Two out of three Danes have last names ending in "-sen." The assimilation of ethnic groups into this homogeneous society, which began in earnest in the 1980s, is a source of some controversy. But in general most Danes have a live-and-let-live attitude and enjoy one of the highest standards of living in the world. Taxes are high in this welfare state, but education is free and the medical care highly subsidized. Generous maternity leave extends to both men and women.

Denmark, one of the most environmentally conscious European countries, is a front-runner in renewable energy, recycling, and organic farming. You'll see lots of modern windmills dotting the countryside. Lacking other sources of power, wind power accounts for 20 percent of Denmark's energy today, with a

Denmark Almanac

Official Name: Kongeriget Danmark—the Kingdom of Denmark—or simply Denmark.

Population: Denmark's 5.4 million people are mainly of Scandinavian descent, with immigrants—mostly German, Turkish, Iranian, and Somali—making up 8 percent of the population. Greenland is home to the indigenous Inuit, and the Faroe Islands to people of Nordic heritage. Most Danes speak both Danish and English, with a small minority speaking German, Inuit, or Faroese. The population is 95 percent Evangelical Lutheran, 3 percent other Protestant and Roman Catholic, and 2 percent Muslim.

Latitude and Longitude: 56°N and 10°E, similar latitude to northern Alberta, Canada.

Area: 16,600 square miles, roughly twice the size of Massachusetts.

Geography: Denmark includes the Jutland peninsula in northern Europe between the North Sea and the Baltic Sea, and shares a 42-mile border with Germany. In addition to Greenland and the Faroe Islands, Denmark also encompasses 400 islands (78 of which are inhabited). Altogether Denmark has 4,544 miles of coastline. The mainland is mostly flat, and nearly two-thirds of the land is cultivated.

Biggest Cities: Denmark's capital city, Copenhagen (pop. one million), is located on the island of Zealand. Århus (on the mainland) has 300,000 and Odense (on Fyn) has 186,000.

Economy: Denmark's modern economy continues to grow, with a Gross Domestic Product of $188 billion. Denmark's top exports include pharmaceuticals, oil, machinery, and food products. It is also one of the world's leaders in exports of wind turbine technology. The GDP per capita is $34,600.

Currency: Six Danish kroner (kr) = about $1.

Government: Denmark is a constitutional monarchy. Queen Margrethe II is the head of state, but the head of government is the prime minister, a post held since November 2001 by Anders Fogh Rasmussen. The 179-member parliament (Folketinget) is elected every four years.

Flag: The Danish flag is red with a white cross.

The Average Dane: The average Dane is 40 years old, has 1.74 children, and will live to be 78. About 70 percent of Danish women are employed outside the home. About 59 percent own a home or apartment, 92 percent own a DVD player, and 73 percent have Internet access.

goal of 50 percent by 2030. Half of all waste is recycled. In grocery stores, organic products are shelved right alongside nonorganic ones—for the same price.

Denmark's Queen Margrethe II is a very popular and talented woman who along with her royal duties has designed coins, stamps, and book illustrations. Danes gather around the TV on New Year's Eve to hear her annual speech to the nation, and flock to the Royal Palace in Copenhagen on April 16 to sing her "Happy Birthday." Her son, Crown Prince Frederik, recently married Australian Mary Donaldson—their son Christian's birth in 2005 was cause for a national celebration. The Danes are proud of their royal family and of the flag, a white cross on a red background. Legend says it fell from the sky during a 13th-century battle in Estonia, making it Europe's oldest continuously used flag. You'll see it everywhere, decorating cakes, on clothing or fluttering in the breeze atop government buildings. It's as much a decorative symbol as a patriotic one.

From an early age, Danes develop a passion for soccer. You may see red-and-white-clad fans singing on their way to a match. Despite the country's small size, the Danish national team does well in international competition. Other popular sports include sailing, cycling, badminton, and team handball.

Although the Danish language, with its three extra vowels (Æ, Ø and Å), is notoriously difficult for foreigners to pronounce, luckily for us almost everyone also speaks English. Danes have playful fun teasing tourists who make the brave attempt to say Danish words. The most notorious phrase, *rød grød med fløde* (a delightful red fruit porridge topped with cream) is nearly impossible for a non-Dane to pronounce. Ask a local to help you.

Sample Denmark's sweet treats at one of the many bakeries you'll see. The pastries that we call "Danish" in the US are called *wienerbrød* in Denmark. Bakeries line their display cases with several varieties of *wienerbrød* and other delectable sweets. Try *kringle*, *snegle*, or *Napoleonshatte* or find your own favorite. Chances are it will be easier to enjoy than pronounce!

Two important words to know are *skål* (cheers, a ritual always done with serious eye contact), and *hyggelig* (pronounced HEW-glee), meaning warm and cozy. Danes treat their home like a sanctuary and spend a great deal of time improving their gardens and houses—inside and out. Cozying up one's personal space (a national obsession) is something the Danes do best. If you have the opportunity, have some Danes adopt you while you are in Denmark so you can enjoy their warm hospitality.

Heaven to a Dane is returning home after a walk in a beloved beech forest to enjoy open-faced sandwiches washed down with beer among good friends. Around the *hyggelig* candlelit table there will be a spirited discussion of the issues of the day, plenty of laughter, and probably a few good-natured jokes about the Swedes or Norwegians. *Skål!*

COPENHAGEN

(København)

Copenhagen, Denmark's capital, is the gateway to Scandinavia. And now that the Øresund Bridge connects Sweden and Denmark (creating the region's largest metropolitan area), Copenhagen is energized and ready to dethrone Stockholm as Scandinavia's powerhouse city. A busy day cruising the canals, wandering through the palace, and taking an old-town walk will give you your historical bearings. Then, after another day strolling the Strøget (Europe's first and greatest pedestrian shopping mall), biking the canals, and sampling the Danish good life, you'll feel right at home. Copenhagen is Scandinavia's cheapest and most fun-loving capital. So live it up.

Planning Your Time

A first visit deserves a minimum of two days.

Day 1: Catch a 10:30 city walking tour (departs from TI May–Sept daily except Sun; see "Tours," below). After lunch at Riz-Raz, visit the Use It information center and catch the relaxing canal-boat tour out to *The Little Mermaid* and back. Enjoy the rest of the afternoon tracing Denmark's cultural roots in the National Museum (touring the Victorian Apartment, if possible) and visiting the Ny Carlsberg Glyptotek art gallery or the National Art Museum (Impressionists and Danish artists). Spend the evening strolling the Strøget (follow my self-guided walk, described on page 56).

Day 2: At 10:00, go Neoclassical at Thorvaldsen's Museum (closed Mon). At 11:00, take the 50-minute guided tour of Denmark's royal Christiansborg Palace (daily May–Sept). After a *smørrebrød* lunch in a park, spend the afternoon seeing the

Rosenborg Castle/crown jewels and the Museum of Danish Resistance. Spend the evening at Tivoli Gardens.

Christiania—the hippie squatters' community—is not for everyone. But if you're intrigued by alternative lifestyles, or simply want a break from the museums, consider a visit. In the above itinerary, it fits well in place of the art museums on the afternoon of Day 1, or instead of Thorvaldsen's Museum and Christiansborg Palace on the morning of Day 2. Christiania, with plenty of opportunities to sample tasty, inexpensive, mostly organic food, is a fine place for lunch or dinner.

Remember the efficiency of sleeping while traveling in and out of town. Consider taking an overnight train (via Malmö) to Stockholm or Oslo, or cruise up to Oslo on a night boat. Kamikaze sightseers see Copenhagen as a useful Scandinavian bottleneck. They sleep in and out heading north into Scandinavia, and in and out heading south at the end of their Scandinavian travels, with two days and no nights in Copenhagen (you can check your bag and take a shower at the train station). Considering the joy of Oslo and Stockholm, this isn't all that crazy if you have limited time and can sleep soundly on a moving train.

ORIENTATION

For most visitors, the core of Copenhagen is the axis formed by the train station, Tivoli Gardens, Rådhuspladsen (City Hall Square), and the Strøget pedestrian street, ending at the colorful old Nyhavn sailors' harbor. Bubbling with street life, colorful pedestrian zones, and most of the city's sightseeing, this main drag is fun (and most of it is covered by my self-guided walk on page 56). But also be sure to get off the Strøget and explore.

By doing things by bike or on foot, you'll stumble onto some charming bits of Copenhagen that many miss. I rent a bike for my entire visit (for about the cost of a single cab ride per day) and park it safely in my hotel courtyard. I get anywhere in the town center literally faster than by taxi. The city is an absolute delight by bike.

Outside of the old city center, there are three areas of interest to tourists:

1. To the north are Rosenborg Castle and the *Little Mermaid* area (Amalienborg Palace and Museum of Danish Resistance).

2. To the east is the island of Amager (or "Ama'r"), home to the "Little Amsterdam" district of Christianshavn, with many of the city's best B&Bs, and the alternative enclave of Christiania.

3. To the west is Vesterbro, a young and trendy part of town with lots of cafés, bars, and boutiques; the picnic-friendly Frederiksberg park; and the Carlsberg Brewery.

The Story of Copenhagen

If you study your map carefully, you can read the history of Copenhagen into today's street plan. København (literally, "Merchants' Harbor") was born on the little island of Slotsholmen—today home of the Christiansborg Palace—in 1167. What was Copenhagen's medieval moat is now a string of pleasant lakes and parks, including Tivoli Gardens. You can still make out some of the zigzag pattern of the moats and ramparts in the city's greenbelt.

Many of these fortifications—and several other landmarks—were built by Denmark's most memorable king. You need to remember one character in Copenhagen's history: Christian IV. Ruling from 1588 to 1648, he was Denmark's Renaissance king and a royal party animal (see sidebar on page 73). The personal energy of this "Builder King" sparked a Golden Age when Copenhagen prospered and many of the city's grandest buildings were erected. In the 17th century, Christian IV extended the city fortifications to the north, doubling the size of the city, while adding a grid plan of streets and his Rosenborg Castle. This old "new town" has the Amalienborg Palace and *The Little Mermaid*.

In 1850, Copenhagen's 140,000 residents all lived within this defensive system. Building in the no-man's-land outside the walls was only allowed with the understanding that in the event of an attack, you'd burn your dwellings to clear the way for a good defense.

Most of the city's historic buildings still in existence were built within the medieval walls, but conditions became too crowded, and outbreaks of disease forced Copenhagen to spread outside the walls. Ultimately those walls were torn down and replaced with "rampart streets" that define today's city center: Vestervoldgade (literally, "West Rampart Street"), Nørrevoldgade ("North"), and Østervoldgade ("East"). The fourth side is the harbor and the island of Slotsholmen, where København was born.

All of these sights are walkable from the Strøget, but taking a bike, bus, or taxi is more efficient.

Tourist Information

Copenhagen This Week is a free, handy, and misnamed monthly guide to the city, worth reading for its good maps, museum hours with telephone numbers, sightseeing tour ideas, shopping suggestions, and calendar of events, including free English tours and concerts (online at www.ctw.dk). This is *the* essential listing of everything in town, and it's always the most up-to-date information

Copenhagen Overview

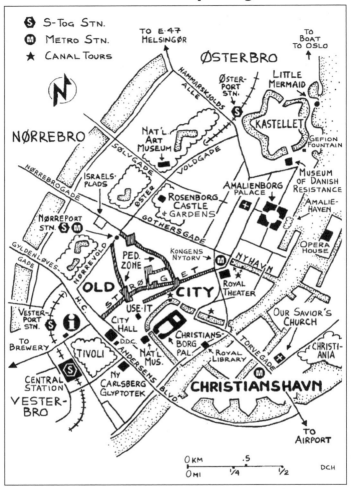

in print. While the "TIs" are really just an advertising agency (see below), you should be ready to roll with a map and *Copenhagen This Week*—both free and available at TIs and most hotels. The Danish Tourist Board's Web site also has a wealth of information on activities and events in Copenhagen (www.visitdenmark.com).

Copenhagen Right Now, as the tourist office is called, is a for-profit company. This colors the advice and information it provides. Mindful of this, drop by to get a city map and *Copenhagen This Week*, browse the racks of brochures, and get your questions answered (July–Aug Mon–Sat 9:00–20:00, Sun 9:00–18:00;

May–June Mon–Sat 9:00–18:00, closed Sun; Sept–April Mon–Fri 9:00–16:00, Sat 9:00–14:00, closed Sun; across from train station at Vesterbrogade 4A, tel. 70 22 24 42, www.visitcopenhagen.dk). They also book their recommended rooms for a 30-kr fee at the desk or from self-service computers. The TI only posts information from outfits that pay for the shelf space. You'll find this week's entertainment program for Tivoli on posts outside Tivoli's main entrance (around the corner from the TI).

Use It is a better information service (10-min walk from train station). Government-sponsored, it caters to Copenhagen's young but welcomes budget travelers of any age. It's a friendly, driven-to-help, energetic, no-nonsense source of information, offering free Internet access and free short-term luggage lockers. While they do not offer a room-booking service, they have a computer available and dedicated to accommodations listings. Their free annual *Playtime* publication has Back Door–style articles on Copenhagen and the Danish culture, special budget tips, and self-guided tours. Read it! To get from the train station to Use It, head down the Strøget, then turn right on Rådhusstræde and walk for three blocks—past Gammeltorv and Nytorv—to #13 (mid-June–mid-Sept daily 9:00–19:00; mid-Sept–mid-June Mon–Wed 11:00–16:00, Thu 11:00–18:00, Fri 11:00–14:00, closed Sat–Sun; tel. 33 73 06 20, www.useit.dk).

The **Copenhagen Card,** which includes free entry to many of the city's sights and all local transportation, can save you some money if you're sightseeing like crazy (199 kr/24 hrs, 429/72 hrs, sold at Copenhagen Right Now, airport TI, and some hotels).

Arrival in Copenhagen
By Train
The main train station is called Hovedbanegården (HOETH-bahn-gorn). It's a temple of travel and a hive of travel-related activity, offering lockers (25–35 kr/day), a checkroom (*garderobe*, 30–40 kr/day per backpack, Mon–Sat 5:30–24:00, Sun 6:00–24:00), a post office (Mon–Fri 8:00–21:00, Sat 10:00–16:00, Sun 10:00–16:00), 24-hour thievery, and the best bike-rental shop in town (see "Getting Around Copenhagen," page 51).

The station has ATMs and Forex exchange desks with long hours (the least expensive place in town to change money, daily 8:00–21:00). Showers for 15 kr are available in the public rest rooms at the back of the station. As you explore, notice how the classical music effectively keeps the junkies away from the back door.

While you're in the station, you can plan for your departure by reserving your overnight train seat or *couchette* at the *Billetsalg* office (daily 9:30–18:00). Some international rides and high-speed InterCity trains require reservations (usually 25–55 kr). The

Kviksalg office sells tickets within Denmark (plus the regional train to Malmö, Sweden). This "quick sale" office will also help you with reservations for international trips if the *Billetsalg* office is closed, and you're departing by train within one hour or early the next day (daily 5:45–23:30).

To get from the train station to the recommended Christians-havn B&Bs, catch bus #2A or #48 (18 kr, 4/hr, in front of station on near side of Bernstorffsgade; with your back to the station, take the bus heading to the right; get off at stop just after *Knippelsbro*—Knippels Bridge). Note the time the bus departs, and while you're waiting, stop by the TI across the street to pick up a free Copenhagen city map that shows bus routes. A taxi to Christianshavn costs about 120 kr.

By Plane

Kastrup, Copenhagen's international airport, is a traveler's dream, with a TI, baggage check, bank, ATMs, post office, shopping mall, grocery store, and bakery. You can use dollars or euros at the airport, but you'll get change back in kroner (airport info tel. 32 47 47 47, www.cph.dk; SAS info tel. 70 10 20 00).

Getting Downtown from the Airport: Taxis are fast, civil, accept credit cards, and, at about 225 kr to the town center, are a reasonable deal for foursomes. The slick and easy Air Rail train links the airport with the central train station, as well as the Nørreport station (27 kr, 3/hr, 12 min). City bus #250S gets you downtown to the Rådhuspladsen (City Hall Square, near the train station) in 30 minutes for 27 kr (6/hr, across the street and to the right as you exit airport).

Getting to Christianshavn from the Airport: Hop on bus #250S, ask for Christianshavn, and the driver will show you where to transfer to #2A, which takes you right through the middle of Christianshavn (34 kr, pay driver, 30 min). Or you could take the DSB S-tog (see "Getting Around Copenhagen," below) to Nørreport, then change to the Metro for Christianshavn (same 36-kr ticket works for entire trip). In a few years, the Metro will connect the airport and Christianshavn directly in 10 minutes.

Helpful Hints

Emergencies: Dial 112 and specify fire, police, or ambulance. Emergency calls from public phones are free.

US Embassy: It's at Dag Hammerskjölds Alle 24 (tel. 35 55 31 44).

Pharmacy: Steno Apotek is across from the train station (open 24 hours daily, Vesterbrogade 6c, tel. 33 14 82 66).

Telephones: Use the telephone liberally. Everyone speaks English, and *Copenhagen This Week* and this book list phone numbers for everything you'll be doing. All telephone numbers in

Denmark are eight digits, and there are no area codes. Calls anywhere in Denmark are cheap; calls to Norway and Sweden cost 6 kr per minute from a booth (half that from a private home). Get a phone card (sold at newsstands, starting at 30 kr). To make inexpensive international calls, buy an international phone card (7-Eleven stores give you a receipt that acts as the calling card, with English instructions and your pin code). The Go Bananas and Global Passport cards are particularly reliable (sold at kiosks for 100 kr—giving you more than 200 minutes of talk time to the US; the Go Bananas card also works in Germany, Denmark, Sweden, and Norway).

Internet Access: Boom Town, next to the TI on Vesterbrogade, is open all day, every day except Christmas (30 kr/hr, 20 kr minimum). Internet access is available for free at **Use It** (described under "Tourist Information," above; 30-min limit if there's a wait).

Ferries: Book any ferries now that you plan to take later in Scandinavia. Visit a travel agent or call direct. For the Copenhagen–Oslo ferry described on page 94, call **DFDS** (Mon–Fri 8:30–18:00, Sat–Sun 9:00–17:00, tel. 33 42 30 00, www.dfdsseaways.com) or visit the **DSB Resjebureau** at the main train station. For the cruise from Stockholm to Helsinki described on page 330, call **Silja Line** (tel. 96 20 32 00, www .silja.com). With the Øresund Bridge linking Denmark to Sweden, you'll no longer need to use a ferry.

Jazz Festival: The Copenhagen Jazz Festival—10 days starting the first Friday in July (July 6–15 in 2007)—puts the town in a rollicking slide-trombone mood. The Danes are Europe's jazz enthusiasts, and this music festival fills the town with happiness. The TI prints up an extensive listing of each year's festival events, or get the latest at www.jazzfestival.dk. There's also an autumn jazz festival the first week of November.

Getting Around Copenhagen

By Bus, S-tog, and Metro: It's easy to navigate Copenhagen with its fine buses, Metro, and S-tog (a suburban train system with stops in the city; Eurail valid on S-tog). An 18-kr two-zone ticket (pay as you board buses, buy from station ticket offices or vending machines for the Metro) gets you an hour's travel within the center. Consider the blue two-zone *klippekort* (115 kr for 10 1-hr rides), the 24-hour pass (105 kr, validate by stamping in yellow machine on bus or at station), or the seven-day pass (190 kr and a good value for extended stays). All passes are sold at stations, the TI, 7-Elevens, and other kiosks. Assume you'll be within the middle two zones. Buses go every five to eight minutes during daytime hours. Bus drivers are patient, have change, and speak English. City maps

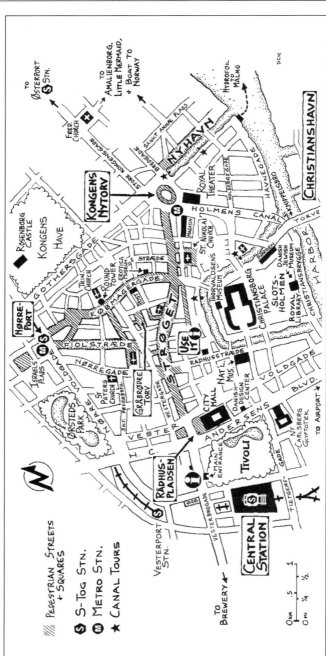

Copenhagen

list bus and subway routes. Locals are usually friendly and helpful. The HUR Kundecenter, the big, black building on Rådhuspladsen (City Hall Square), is very helpful and has a fine, free map showing all the bus routes (daily 9:00–19:00, tel. 36 13 14 15).

Copenhagen's super-futuristic Metro line connects the residential Frederiksberg and Amager neighborhoods (including Christianshavn) with downtown: Kongens Nytorv (near Nyhavn and the north end of the Strøget) and Nørreport (two stops on S-tog to main train station). Eventually the Metro will run to the airport and on to Ørestad, the industrial and business center created after the Øresund Bridge was built between Denmark and Sweden (for the latest, see www.m.dk).

By Bus Tour: Open Top Tour buses do a hop-on, hop-off one-hour circle connecting the city's top sights (for details, see "Tours," page 55).

By Taxi: Taxis are plentiful, easy to call or flag down, and pricey (23-kr pickup charge, and then 10 kr per kilometer; more in the evening, early morning, and weekends; credit cards accepted). For a short ride, four people spend about the same by taxi as by bus (for example, 120 kr from train station to recommended Christianshavn B&Bs). Calling 35 35 35 35 will get you a taxi within minutes...with the meter already way up there.

By Bike: Cyclists see more, save time and money, and really feel like locals. **Cykelcenter** rents good bikes at the main train station (95 kr/24 hrs, cheaper for longer periods if paid in advance, Mon–Fri 8:00–17:30, Sat 9:00–13:00, July–Aug open Sun 10:00–13:00, otherwise closed Sun, helmets-20 kr, tel. 33 33 86 13). Cykel-center also has a shop at the Østerport S-tog station (same prices, Mon–Fri 8:00–18:00, Sat 9:00–13:00, closed Sun, tel. 33 33 85 13).

Free Bikes: From May through November, 2,400 clunky but practical little bikes are scattered around the old-town center (basically the terrain covered in the Copenhagen map in this chapter). Simply locate one of the 110 racks, unlock a bike by popping a 20-kr coin into the handlebar, and pedal away. When you're done, plug your bike back into any other rack and your deposit coin will pop back out (if you can't find a rack, just abandon your bike and someone will take it back and pocket your coin). These simple bikes come with theft-proof parts (unusable on regular bikes) and—they claim—computer tracer chips embedded in them so that bike patrols can retrieve strays. These are funded by advertisements

painted on the wheels and by a progressive electorate.

Copenhagen's radical city-bike program is a clever idea, but in practice, it doesn't work great for sightseers. It's hard to find bikes in working order, and when you get to the sight and park your bike, it'll be gone by the time you're ready to pedal on. (The 20-kr deposit coin acts as an incentive for any kid or homeless person to pick up city bikes not plugged back into their special racks.) Use the free bikes for a one-way pedal here and there. For efficiency, pay to rent one.

TOURS

▲▲▲**Walking Tours**—Copenhagen is an ideal city to get to know by foot. You have two good options.

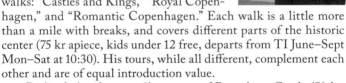

Richard Karpen's Tours: Once upon a time, American Richard Karpen visited Copenhagen and fell in love with the city (and one of its women). Now, dressed as Hans Christian Andersen, he leads daily 90-minute tours that wander in and out of buildings, courtyards, backstreets, and unusual parts of the old town. Along the way, he gives insightful and humorous background on the history and culture of Denmark, Copenhagen, and the Danes.

Richard offers three entertaining walks: "Castles and Kings," "Royal Copenhagen," and "Romantic Copenhagen." Each walk is a little more than a mile with breaks, and covers different parts of the historic center (75 kr apiece, kids under 12 free, departs from TI June–Sept Mon–Sat at 10:30). His tours, while all different, complement each other and are of equal introduction value.

Richard also does excellent tours of Rosenborg Castle (50 kr, doesn't include castle entry, Mon and Thu at 13:30, 90 min, led by dapper Renaissance "Sir Richard," meet outside castle ticket office). No reservations are needed for Richard's tours—just show up.

For details, pick up Richard's schedule in *Copenhagen This Week*, at the TI, or see www.copenhagenwalks.com.

Copenhagen History Tours: Christian Donatzky, a charming young Dane with a master's degree in history, runs three walking tours. On Friday at 14:00, the "Reformed Copenhagen" tour covers Copenhagen from 1400–1600—the era before, during, and after the Protestant Reformation. On Saturday at 10:00, the "The King's Copenhagen" tour focuses on 1600–1800, when Copenhagen became an international business center. On Sunday at 10:00 is the "Hans Christian Andersen's Copenhagen" tour (1800–2000), set in a time when Denmark turned democratic. The tours are thoughtfully designed, and those with a serious interest in Danish history find them time well spent (75 kr, approximately 90 min each in small groups, tours run Feb–Nov, depart from statue of Bishop Absalon on Højbro Plads between Strøget and Christiansborg Palace, no advance booking necessary, tel. 28 49 44 35, www.historytours.dk).

▲▲**Canal and Harbor Cruises**—Two companies offer essentially the same live, three-language, 50-minute tours through the city canals. Both boats leave at least twice an hour from Nyhavn and Christiansborg Palace, cruise around the palace and Christianshavn area, and then proceed into the wide-open harbor. It's a relaxing way to see *The Little Mermaid* and munch on a lazy picnic during the slow-moving narration.

The inexpensive **Netto-Bådene** cruises cost only half the price of their rival. Go with Netto; there's no reason to pay double (30 kr, mid-March–mid-Oct daily 10:00–17:00, later in summer, sign at dock shows next departure, 2–5/hr, dress warmly—boats are open-top until Sept, tel. 32 54 41 02, www.havnerundfart .dk). The pricier option, **DFDS Canal Tours,** does the same tour for 60 kr (daily April–mid-Oct 10:00–17:00, until 19:30 late June–late Aug, mid-Oct–mid-Dec 10:00–15:00, tel. 33 93 42 60). In summer, DFDS also runs unguided hop-on, hop-off "water bus" tours (50

kr, late-May–Aug daily 10:15–16:45) and two-hour evening **jazz cruises** (see "Nightlife," page 81).

Don't mix up the cheaper Netto and pricier DFDS boats: At Nyhavn, the Netto dock is midway down the canal (on the city side), while the DFDS dock is at the head of the canal. At Christiansborg Palace, the Netto boats leave from Holmen's Bridge in front of the palace, while DFDS boats depart from Gammel Strand, 200 yards away.

Bus Tours—A variety of guided bus tours depart from Rådhuspladsen in front of the Palace Hotel. The hop-on, hop-off **Open Top Tour** does the basic one-hour circle of the city sights—Tivoli Gardens, the royal Christiansborg Palace, National Museum, *The Little Mermaid,* Rosenborg Castle, Nyhavn sailors' quarter, and more—with recorded narration (120 kr, 2/hr, 150 kr for access to all 3 tour lines, ticket good for 48 hrs, April–Oct daily 9:30–17:00; you can get off, see a sight, and catch a later bus; bus departs City Hall below the *Lur Blowers* statue—to the left of City Hall—or at many other stops throughout city, pay driver, run by Copenhagen Excursions, tel. 32 66 00 00, www.sightseeing.dk).

The same company also runs jaunts into the countryside, with themes such as Vikings, castles, and Hamlet.

Bike Tours—**City Safari** offers three-hour guided bike tours of Copenhagen with a little history (250 kr, includes bike, in English and Danish as needed but generally at 10:00 and 13:30, pre-book by e-mail or phone, then show up 10 min in advance at Danish Center for Architecture, Gammel Dok Storehouse, Strandgade 27B, tel. 33 23 94 90, www.citysafari.dk, basictours@citysafari.dk, or ask at Use It).

SELF-GUIDED WALK

Strøget and Copenhagen's Heart and Soul

Start from **Rådhuspladsen** (City Hall Square), the bustling heart of Copenhagen, dominated by the tower of the City Hall. This was Copenhagen's fortified west end. For 700 years, Copenhagen was contained within its walls. In the mid-1800s, 140,000 people were packed inside. The overcrowding led to hygiene problems. (A cholera outbreak killed 5,000.) It was clear: The walls needed to come down...and they did.

In 1843, magazine publisher Georg Carstensen convinced the king to let him build a pleasure garden outside the walls of crowded Copenhagen. The king quickly agreed, knowing that happy people care less about fighting for democracy. **Tivoli Gardens** became Europe's first great public amusement park. When the train lines came, the station was placed just beyond Tivoli. Those formidable walls faded away, surviving only in echoes—a circular series of roads and remnants of moats, now people-friendly city lakes (see page 47).

The **City Hall,** or Rådhus, is worth a visit (described on page 67). Old **Hans Christian Andersen** sits to the right of City Hall, almost begging to be in another photo (as he used to in real life). Climb onto his well-worn knee. (While up there, you might take off your shirt for a racy photo, as many Danes enjoy doing.)

On a pedestal left of City Hall, note the *Lur Blowers* **sculpture** honoring the earliest warrior Danes. The *lur* is a horn that was used 3,500 years ago. The ancient originals, which still play, are displayed in the National Museum. (City tour buses leave from below these Vikings.)

The golden **weather girls** high up on the tower (marked *Philips* in blue) opposite the Strøget's entrance indicate the weather: on a bike (fair weather) or with an umbrella. These two have been called the only women in Copenhagen you can trust, but for years they've been stuck in the almost-sunny mode...with the bike just peeking out. Notice that the red temperature dots only go to 28 degrees Celsius (that's 82 degrees Fahrenheit).

Hans Christian Andersen
(1805–1875)

The author of such classic fairy tales as *The Ugly Duckling* was an ugly duckling himself—a misfit who blossomed. Hans

Christian Andersen (called H. C., pronounced "hoe see" by the Danes) was born to a poor shoemaker in Odense. As a child he was gangly, high-strung, and effeminate. He avoided school because the kids laughed at him, so he spent his time in a fantasy world of books and plays. When his father died, the 11-year-old was on his own, forced into manual labor. He moved to Copenhagen and worked as a boy soprano for the Royal Theater. When his voice changed, the director encouraged him to return to school. He dutifully attended—a teenager among boys—and went on to the university.

After graduation, Andersen toured Europe, the first of many trips he'd make and write about. Still in his twenties, he published an (obviously autobiographical) novel, *The Improvisatore,* about a poor young man who comes into his own while traveling in Italy. The novel launched his writing career, and soon he was hobnobbing with the international crowd—Charles Dickens, Victor Hugo, Franz Liszt, Richard Wagner, Henrik Ibsen, and Edvard Grieg.

Though he wrote novels, plays, and travel literature, it was his fairy tales that made him famous in Denmark and abroad, including *The Ugly Duckling, The Emperor's New Clothes, The Princess and the Pea, The Little Mermaid,* and *The Red Shoes.* They made him Denmark's best-known author, the "Danish Charles Dickens." Some stories are based on earlier folk tales, and others came straight from his inventive mind, all written in conversational language.

The tales appeal to children and adults alike. They're full of magic and touch on strong, universal emotions—the pain of being different, the joy of self-discovery, and the struggle to fit in. The ugly duckling, for example, is teased by his fellow ducks before he finally discovers his true identity as a beautiful swan. In *The Emperor's New Clothes*, a boy is derided by everyone for speaking the simple, self-evident truth that the emperor is fooling himself.

By the time of his death, the poor shoemaker's son was wealthy, cultured, and had been knighted. His rise through traditional class barriers mirrors the social progress of the 19th century.

Self-Guided Walk: Strøget and Copenhagen's Heart and Soul

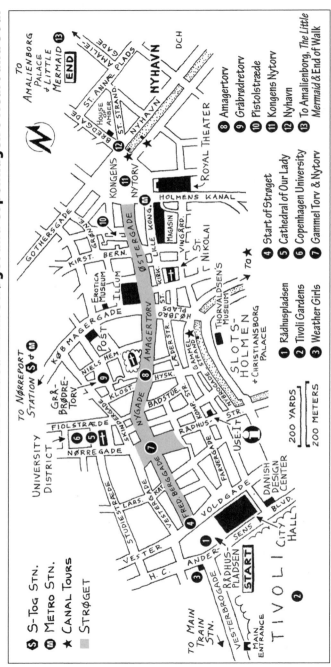

Legend:
- **S** S-Tog Stn.
- **M** Metro Stn.
- ★ Canal Tours
- Strøget

1. Rådhuspladsen
2. Tivoli Gardens
3. Weather Girls
4. Start of Strøget
5. Cathedral of Our Lady
6. Copenhagen University
7. Gammel Torv & Nytorv
8. Amagertorv
9. Gråbrødretorv
10. Pistolstræde
11. Kongens Nytorv
12. Nyhavn
13. To Amalienborg, The Little Mermaid & End of Walk

Here, in the traffic hub of this huge city, you'll notice...not many cars. Denmark's 180 percent tax on car purchases makes the bus or bike a sweeter option.

The **SAS building** is Copenhagen's only skyscraper. Locals say it seems so tall because the clouds hang so low. When it was built in 1960, Copenhageners took one look and decided—that's enough of a skyline.

The American trio of Burger King, 7-Eleven, and KFC marks the start of the otherwise charming **Strøget**. Finished in 1962, Copenhagen's experimental, tremendously successful, and most-copied pedestrian shopping mall is a string of lively (and individually named) streets and lovely squares that bunny-hop through the old town from City Hall to the Nyhavn quarter, a 20-minute stroll away.

As you wander down this street, remember that the commercial focus of a historic street like Strøget drives up the land value, which generally trashes the charm and tears down the old buildings. Look above the modern window displays and street-level advertising to discover bits of 19th-century character that still survive. While Strøget has become hamburgerized, historic bits and attractive pieces of old Copenhagen are just off this commercial cancan.

Copenhagen was fortified around large mansions with expansive **courtyards.** As the population grew, the walls constricted the city's physical size. These courtyards were gradually filled with higgledy-piggledy secondary buildings. Today throughout the old center, you can step off a busy pedestrian mall and back in time into these characteristic half-timbered time-warps. Replace the parked car with a tired horse, replace the bikes with a line of outhouses, and you are in 19th-century Copenhagen. If you see an open door, you're welcome to discreetly wander in and look around. Don't miss the courtyards of Copenhagen.

After one block (at Kattesundet), make a side-trip three blocks left into Copenhagen's colorful **university district.** Formerly the old brothel neighborhood, later the heart of Copenhagen's hippie community in the 1960s, today this "Latin Quarter" is Soho chic.

At Sankt Peders Stræde, turn right and walk to the end of the street. On your right is the big Neoclassical **Cathedral of Our Lady** (Vor Frue Kirche). Stand across the street from its facade. The Reformation Memorial celebrates the date Denmark broke from the Roman Catholic Church and became Lutheran (1536). Walk around and study the reliefs of great Danish reformers protesting from their pulpits. The relief facing the church shows King Christian III, who, after being influenced by Luther in his German travels (and realizing the advantages of being the head of his own state church), oversaw the town council meeting that decided on this break. Because of 1536, there's no Mary in the Cathedral of Our Lady.

The cathedral's **facade** is a Greek temple. (To the right in the distance, notice more Neoclassicism—the law courts.) You can see why Golden Age Copenhagen (early 1800s) fancied itself a Nordic Athens. Old Testament figures (King David and Moses) flank the cathedral's entryway. Above, John the Baptist stands where you'd expect to see Greek gods. He invites you in...to the New Testament.

Enter the cathedral—a world of Neoclassical serenity (free, open daily 8:00–17:00). This pagan temple now houses Christianity. The nave is lined by the 12 apostles (all clad in Roman togas—masterpieces by the great Danish sculptor Bertel Thorvaldsen). They lead to a statue of the risen Christ, standing where the statue of Caesar would have been. Rather than wearing an imperial toga, Jesus wears his burial shroud and says, "Come to me." The marvelous acoustics are demonstrated in free organ concerts each Saturday at noon. This is where Copenhagen gathers for extraordinary events. After September 11, 2001, the queen, her government, and the entire diplomatic core held a memorial service here.

Head back outside. If you face the facade and look to the left, you'll see **Copenhagen University**—home of 30,000 students. The king founded this university in the 17th century to stop the Danish brain drain to Paris. Today tuition is free (but room, board, and beer are not). Locals say it's easy to get in, but, given the wonderful lifestyle, very hard to get out.

Step up the middle steps of the university's big building and enter a colorful lobby, starring Athena and Apollo. The frescoes celebrate high thinking, with themes such as the triumph of wisdom over barbarism. Notice how harmoniously the architecture, sculpture, and painting work together. Outside, busts honor great minds from the faculty, including (at the end) Niels Bohr, a professor who won the 1922 Nobel Prize for theoretical physics. He evaded the clutches of the Nazi science labs by fleeing to America in 1943, where he helped develop the atomic bomb.

Rejoin Strøget (down where you saw the law courts) at **Gammeltorv** and **Nytorv** (Old Square and New Square). This was the old town center. In Gammeltorv, the Fountain of Charity (Caritas) is named for the figure of Charity on top. It has provided drinking water to locals since the early 1600s. Featuring a pregnant woman squirting water from her breasts next to a boy urinating, this was just too much for people of the Victorian age. They corked both figures and raised the statue to what they hoped would be out of view. The Asian-looking kiosk was one of the city's first community telephone centers from the days before phones were privately owned. Look at the reliefs ringing its top: an airplane with bird wings (c. 1900) and two women talking on the newfangled phone. (It was thought business would popularize the telephone, but actually it was women. Now, 100 years later, look at the mobile phones.)

While Gammeltorv was a place of happiness and merriment, Nytorv was a place of severity and judgment. Walk to the small raised area in front of the old, ancient Greek–style former City Hall. Do a 360. The entire square is Neoclassical. Read the old Danish on the City Hall facade: "With Law Shall Man Land Build." Look down at the pavement and read the plaque: "Here stood the town's Kag (whipping post) until 1780." The Restaurant and Café Nytorv on the square is a good option for a traditional Danish lunch (see page 88).

Next, walk down the next stretch of the Strøget, **Amagertorv** (prime real estate for talented street entertainers and pickpockets), past the Gad Bookstore and its excellent selection of English-language guidebooks and cookbooks, to the stately brick Holy Ghost church. The fine spire is typical of old Danish churches. Under the stepped gable was a medieval hospital run by monks.

A block behind the church (walk down Valkendorfsgade and through a passage under the rust-colored building at #32) is the leafy and caffeine-stained **Gråbrødretorv.** This "Grey Friars' Square," surrounded by fine old buildings, is a popular place for an outdoor meal or drink in the summer. At the end of the square, the street Niels Hemmingsens Gade returns (past the Copenhagen Jazz House, a good place for live music nightly—see page 81) to Strøget. Continue down the pedestrian street, with its fine inlaid Italian granite stonework, to the next square with the stork fountain (actually a heron). The Victorian WCs here (steps down from fountain, 2 kr) are a delight.

Amagertorv is a highlight for shoppers. A line of Royal Copenhagen stores here sell porcelain (with demos), glassware, jewelry, and silverware. Illums Bolighus is known for modern design (Mon–Thu, 10:00–19:00, Fri 10:00–20:00, Sat 9:00–17:00, closed Sun, shorter hours off-season). From here, you can see the imposing Parliament building, Christiansborg Palace, and an equestrian statue of Bishop Absalon, the city's founder (canal boat tours depart nearby). A block toward the canal, running parallel to Strøget, starts Strædet, which is a second Strøget featuring cafés, antique shops, and no fast food. North of Amagertorv, a broad pedestrian mall, Købmagergade, leads past the Museum of Erotica to Christian IV's Round Tower and the Latin Quarter (university district). Café Norden overlooks the fountain—a smoky but good place for a coffee with a view. The second floor offers the best vantage point.

The final stretch of Strøget leads to **Pistolstræde** (leading off

Copenhagen at a Glance

▲▲▲**Tivoli Gardens** Copenhagen's classic amusement park, with rides, music, food, and other fun. **Hours:** Mid-April–late Sept daily 11:00–23:00, later on Fri–Sat and in summer, also open daily 11:00–22:00 for a week in Oct and mid-Nov–Christmas.

▲▲▲**National Museum** History of Danish civilization with tour-able 19th-century Victorian Apartment. **Hours:** Museum Tue–Sun 10:00–17:00, closed Mon; Victorian Apartment tours June–Sept Sat at 11:00.

▲▲▲**Rosenborg Castle and Treasury** Renaissance castle of larger-than-life "warrior king" Christian IV; castle closed until 2008, but treasury still open. **Hours:** June–Sept daily 10:00–17:00; May and Oct daily 10:00–16:00; Nov–April Tue–Sun 11:00–14:00, closed Mon.

▲▲▲**Christiania** Colorful counterculture squatters' colony. **Hours:** Always open.

▲▲**Christiansborg Palace** Royal reception rooms with dazzling tapestries. **Hours:** Visit only with tour, May–Sept daily at 11:00, 13:00, and 15:00; Oct–April Tue–Sun at 15:00, closed Mon.

▲▲**Museum of Danish Resistance** Chronicle of Denmark's struggle against the Nazis. **Hours:** May–Sept Tue–Sat 10:00–16:00, Sun 10:00–17:00, closed Mon; Oct–April Tue–Sat 10:00–15:00, Sun 10:00–16:00, closed Mon.

▲**City Hall** Copenhagen's landmark, packed with Danish history

Strøget to the left from Østergade at #24), a cute lane of shops in restored 18th-century buildings. Wander back into the half-timbered section. The bakery has a rack of tourist fliers, including the very handy-for-shoppers *Local Life*, which highlights small specialty shops in the area.

Continuing along Strøget, you'll pass McDonald's (good view from top floor) and major department stores (Illum and Magasin—see "Shopping," page 80) to Kongens Nytorv.

Kongens Nytorv, the biggest square in town, is home to the Royal Theater, French embassy, and venerable Hotel d'Angleterre. The statue in the middle of the square celebrates Christian V, who, in the 1670s, enlarged Copenhagen by adding this "King's New Square." The entire center is a fun skating rink for three months each winter.

and symbolism and topped with a tower. **Hours:** Mon–Fri 7:45–17:00, open Sat only for tours, closed Sun.

▲**Ny Carlsberg Glyptotek** Scandinavia's top art gallery, featuring Egyptians, Greeks, Etruscans, French, and Danes. **Hours:** Tue–Sun 10:00–16:00, closed Mon.

▲**Thorvaldsen's Museum** Works of the Danish Neoclassical sculptor. **Hours:** Tue–Sun 10:00–17:00, closed Mon.

▲**Danish Jewish Museum** Exhibit tracing the 400-year history of Danish Jews, in a unique building by American architect Daniel Libeskind. **Hours:** June–Aug Tue–Sun 10:00–17:00, closed Mon; Sept–May Tue–Fri 13:00–16:00, Sat–Sun 12:00–17:00, closed Mon.

▲**Rosenborg Gardens** Park surrounding Rosenborg Castle, filled with statues and statuesque Danes. **Hours:** Always open.

▲**National Art Museum** Good Danish and Impressionist collections. **Hours:** Tue–Sun 10:00–17:00, Wed until 20:00, closed Mon.

▲**Amalienborg Palace Museum** Quick and intimate look at Denmark's royal family. **Hours:** May–Oct daily 10:00–16:00; Nov–April Tue–Sun 11:00–16:00, closed Mon.

▲**Our Savior's Church** Spiral-spired church with bright Baroque interior. **Hours:** April–Aug Mon–Sat 11:00–16:30, Sun 12:00–16:30, off-season closes at 15:30, spire closed in bad weather and Nov–March.

On the right (just before the Metro station, at #19), **Hviids Vinstue,** the town's oldest wine cellar (from 1723), is a colorful spot for an open-face sandwich and a beer (three sandwiches and a beer for 60 kr at lunchtime). Wander around inside, if only to see the old photos.

Just off Kongens Nytorv (30 yards from Hviids Vinstue) is the entrance to the futuristic Metro. Ride the escalators down and up to see the latest in Metro design (automated cars, no driver...sit in front to watch the tracks coming at you).

Head back up to ground level. Across the square is the trendy harbor of Nyhavn.

Nyhavn is a recently gentrified sailors' quarter. (Hong Kong is the last of the nasty bars from the rough old days.) With its trendy cafés, jazz clubs, and tattoo shops (pop into Tattoo Ole at #17—

fun photos, very traditional), Nyhavn is a wonderful place to hang out. The canal is filled with glamorous old sailboats of all sizes. Any historic sloop is welcome to moor here in Copenhagen's ever-changing boat museum. Hans Christian Andersen lived and wrote his first stories here (in the red double-gabled building on the right at #20). Wander the quay, enjoying the frat-party parade of tattoos (hotter weather reveals more tattoos). Celtic and Nordic mythological designs are in (as is bodybuilding, by the looks of things). The place thrives—with the cheap-beer drinkers dockside and the richer and older ones looking on from comfier cafés.

A note about all this public beer-drinking: There's no more beer consumption here than in the US; it's just out in public. Many young Danes can't afford to drink in a bar, so they "picnic drink" their beers in squares and along canals, spending a quarter of the bar price for a bottle from a nearby kiosk (just past the bridge on the right).

Just past the first bridge, a line of people wait for the best ice cream around—packed into fresh-baked waffles (look through the window to see the waffle iron in action).

Continuing north along the harborside (from end of Nyhavn canal, turn left), you'll stroll a delightful waterfront promenade to the modern fountain of Amaliehaven Park (immediately across the harbor from the new opera house).

The orderly **Amalienborg Palace and Square** is a block inland, behind the fountain. Queen Margrethe II and her family live in the mansion to your immediate left as you enter the square from the harborside. Her son and heir to the throne, Crown Prince Frederik, recently moved into the mansion directly opposite his mother's with his new wife, Australian businesswoman Mary Donaldson, and their young son, Prince Christian. While the guards change with

royal fanfare at noon only when the queen is in residence, they shower every morning. The small Amalienborg Palace Museum offers an intimate look at royal living (see page 72).

From the square, Amaliegade leads north to Kastellet (Citadel) Park and Denmark's fascinating WWII-era Museum

The Little Mermaid

"Far out in the ocean, where the water is as blue as a corn-flower, as clear as crystal, and very, very deep..." there lived a young mermaid. So begins one of Hans Christian Andersen's (1805–1875) best-known stories. The plot line starts much like the Disney children's movie, but it's spiced with poetic description and philosophical dialog about the immortal soul. The tale of unre-quited love mirrors Andersen's own sad love life. He had two major crushes—one of them for the famous opera singer, Jenny Lind—but he was turned down both times, and he never married.

The mermaid's story goes like this: One day, a young mermaid spies a passing ship and falls in love with a handsome human prince. The ship is wrecked in a storm, and she saves the prince's life. To be with the prince, the mermaid asks a sea witch to give her human legs. In exchange, she agrees to give up her voice and the chance of ever returning to the sea. And, the witch tells her, if the prince doesn't marry her, she will immediately die heartbroken and without an immortal soul. The mermaid agrees, and her fish tail becomes a pair of beautiful but painful legs. She woos the prince—who loves her in return—but he eventually marries another. Heartbroken, the mermaid prepares to die. She's given one last chance to save herself, if she kills the prince on his wedding night. She sneaks into the bedchamber with a knife...but can't bear to kill the man she loves. The mermaid throws herself into the sea to die. Suddenly, she's miraculously carried up by the mermaids of the air, who give her an immor-tal soul as a reward her for her long-suffering love.

of Danish Resistance (see page 72). Nearby is the 1908 **Gefion Fountain,** which illustrates the myth of the goddess who was given one night to carve a hunk out of Sweden to make into Denmark's main island, Sjælland (or "Zealand" in English), which you're on. Gefion transformed her four sons into oxen to do the job, and the chunk she removed from Sweden is supposedly today's Vänern, Sweden's largest lake. If you look at a map showing Sweden and Denmark, the island and the lake are, in fact, roughly the same shape.

Beyond the fountain is an Anglican church built of flint, and finally the overrated, overfondled, and overphotographed symbol of Copenhagen, *Den Lille Havfrue—The Little Mermaid.* For the real, non-Disneyfied story, see the sidebar.

Our walking tour is finished. You can get back downtown on foot, by taxi, or on bus #1A, #15, or #19 from Store Kongensgade on the other side of Kastellet Park, or bus #29 from behind the Museum of Danish Resistance on Langelinie street.

SIGHTS

Near the Train Station

Copenhagen's great train station, the Hovedbanegården, is a fascinating mesh of Scandinavian culture and transportation efficiency. Even if you're not a train traveler, check it out (see "Arrival in Copenhagen," page 49). From the station, wonderful sights fan out into the old city. The following attractions are listed roughly in order from the train station to Slotsholmen Island.

▲▲▲**Tivoli Gardens**—The world's grand old amusement park—since 1843—is 20 acres, 110,000 lanterns, and countless ice cream cones of fun. You pay one admission price and find yourself lost in a Hans Christian Andersen wonderland of rides, restaurants, games, marching bands, roulette wheels, and funny mirrors. Tivoli doesn't try to be Disney. It's wonderfully and happily Danish.

Cost, Hours, Location: The park is open every day from mid-April to late September (daily 11:00–23:00, later on Fri–Sat and mid-June–late Aug, 75 kr gets you in, tel. 33 15 10 01, www.tivoli.dk). Rides range in price from 15 to 70 kr (200 kr for all-day pass). All children's amusements are in full swing by 12:00; the rest of the amusements open by 16:30. In winter, Tivoli opens for a week in October, then for a Christmas market with ice skating on Tivoli Lake (daily 11:00–22:00 for week in Oct and mid-Nov–Christmas).

Tivoli is across from the train station. If you're catching an overnight train, this is *the* place to spend your last Copenhagen hours.

Entertainment in Tivoli: Upon arrival (through main entrance, on left in the service center), pick up a map and events schedule. Take a moment to sit down and plan your entertainment for the evening. Events are spread between 15:00 and 23:00; the 19:30 concert in the concert hall can be as little as 50 kr or as much as 500 kr, depending on the performer (box office tel. 33 15 10 12). If the Tivoli Symphony is playing, it's worth paying for. The ticket box office is outside, just to the left of the main entrance (daily 11:00–20:00; if you buy a concert ticket you get into Tivoli for free). You'll also find the daily events schedule on the posts outside the main entrance.

Free concerts, pantomime theater, ballet, acrobats, puppets, and other shows pop up all over the park, and a well-organized visitor can enjoy an exciting evening of entertainment without spending a single krone beyond the entry fee. The children's theater, Valmuen, plays excellent traditional fairy tales nearly every day at 12:00, 13:00, and 14:00. Friday evenings feature a (usually free) rock or pop show at 22:00. A fireworks show occurs nightly in summer except on Fridays. The park is particularly romantic at dusk, when the lights go on.

Eating at Tivoli: Inside the park, expect to pay amusement-park prices for amusement-park-quality food. **Søcafeen,** by the lake, allows picnics if you buy a drink. The *pølse* (sausage) stands are cheap. **Færgekroen** is a good lakeside place for typical Danish food, beer, and an impromptu sing-along with a bunch of drunken Danes. For a cake and coffee, consider the **Viften** café. **Georg,** to the left of the concert hall, has tasty 60-kr sandwiches and 180-kr dinners (which include a glass of wine).

▲City Hall (Rådhus)—This city landmark, between the train station/Tivoli and the Strøget, offers private tours and trips up

its 345-foot-tall tower. It's draped, inside and out, in Danish symbolism. The city's founder, Bishop Absalon, stands over the door. The polar bears climbing on the rooftop symbolize the giant Danish protectorate of Greenland.

Step inside. The lobby has racks of tourist information (city maps and *Copenhagen This Week*). The building was inspired by the City Hall in Siena, Italy (with the necessary addition of a glass roof). Huge functions fill this grand hall (the iron grill in the center of the floor is an elevator for bringing up 1,200 chairs) while the busts of four illustrious local boys—the fairy-tale writer Hans Christian Andersen, the sculptor Bertel Thorvaldsen, the physicist Niels Bohr, and the building's architect Martin Nyrop—look on. Underneath the floor are national archives dating back to 1275, popular with Danes researching their family roots. The City Hall is free and open to the public (Mon–Fri 7:45–17:00, open on Sat only for tours—see below, closed Sun). You can wander throughout the building and into the peaceful garden out back. Guided English-language **tours** get you into more private, official rooms (30 kr, 45 min, year-round

Mon–Fri at 15:00, Sat at 10:00).

Tourists romp (in groups with an escort) up the **tower**'s 300 steps for the best aerial view of Copenhagen (20 kr; June–Sept Mon–Fri at 10:00, 12:00, and 14:00, Sat at 12:00; Oct–May Mon–Sat at 12:00; tel. 33 66 25 82).

Danish Design Center—This center, its building a masterpiece in itself, shows off the best in Danish design as well as top examples from around the world, including architecture, fashion, and graphic arts. A visit to this low-key display case for sleek Scandinavian design offers an interesting glimpse into the culture. The basement showcases the Industrial Design prizewinners from 1965 through 1999, with English descriptions such as, "He taught the materials to do things not even they realized they were able to do" (40 kr, Mon–Fri 10:00–17:00, Wed until 21:00—free after 17:00, Sat–Sun 11:00–16:00, across from Tivoli Gardens and down the street from City Hall at H. C. Andersen Boulevard 27, tel. 33 69 33 69, www .ddc.dk). The boutique next to the ticket counter features three themes: travel light (chic travel accessories and gadgets), modern Danish classics, and books and posters. The café on the main level, under the atrium, serves light lunches (60–100 kr).

▲**Ny Carlsberg Glyptotek**—Scandinavia's top art gallery is an impressive example of what beer money can do. The museum has intoxicating Egyptian, Greek, and Etruscan collections; a fine sample of early 19th-century Danish Golden Age painting (may not be viewable); and a heady, if small, exhibit of 19th-century French paintings (in the new "French Wing," including Géricault, Delacroix, Manet, Impressionists, and Gauguin before and after Tahiti). Linger with marble gods under the palm leaves and glass dome of the very soothing winter garden. Designers, figuring Danes would be more interested in a lush garden than in Classical art, used this wonderful space as leafy bait to cleverly introduce locals to a few Greek and Roman statues. (It works for tourists, too.) One of the original Rodin *Thinker*s (wondering how to scale the Tivoli fence?) is in the museum's backyard (50 kr, free Sun, open Tue–Sun 10:00–16:00, closed Mon, classy cafeteria under palms, behind Tivoli at Dantes Plads 7, tel. 33 41 81 41, www .glyptoteket.dk).

▲▲▲**National Museum**—Focus on the excellent and curiously enjoyable Danish collection, which traces this civilization from its ancient beginnings. Exhibits are laid out chronologically and described in English. Pick up the museum map. The 25-kr audioguide describes the highlights but adds little to the printed descriptions you'll find inside. The prehistory exhibit, which has oak coffins with still-clothed skeletons from 1300 B.C., is currently under renovation until 2008. So we'll skip ahead 8,000 years. Start in the room just past the lockers, filled with late Bronze Age artifacts, still-playable *lur* horns, and horned helmets. Contrary to popular belief (and countless tourist shops), these helmets were not worn by the Vikings. It was their Bronze Age predecessors who wore them, for ceremonial purposes, a couple thousand years earlier. Continue to the exhibit to your left, and head into the Iron Age. There you'll find the 2,000-year-old Gundestrup Cauldron of art-textbook fame, lots of Viking stuff, and a bitchin' collection of well-translated rune stones. Then go upstairs, find Room 101, and carry on to find fascinating material on the Reformation, an exhibit on everyday town life in the 16th and 17th centuries, and, in Room 126, a unique "cylinder perspective" of the noble family (from 1656) and two peep shows. The next floor takes you into modern times, with historic toys and a slice-of-Danish-life 1600–2000 gallery where you'll see everything from rifles and old bras to early jukeboxes. Capping off the collection is a stall that, until recently, was used for selling marijuana in the squatters' community of Christiania (free, Tue–Sun 10:00–17:00, closed Mon, mandatory bag check—10-kr coin deposit, enter at Ny Vestergade 10, tel. 33 13 44 11, www.nationalmuseet.dk). The nice café overlooking the entry hall is ideal for a light 40–90-kr lunch, coffee and pastry, or an over-the-top Sunday brunch for 135 kr (Sun 9:00–15:00).

▲**National Museum's Victorian Apartment**—The National Museum (listed above) inherited an incredible Victorian apartment just around the corner, a tour of which is included with your admission. The wealthy Christensen family managed to keep its plush living quarters a 19th-century time capsule until the granddaughters passed away in 1963. Since then, it's been part of the National Museum, with all but two of its rooms looking like they did around 1890. Visit it if the tour schedule works for you (45-min tours leave from museum reception desk Sat at 11:00 June–Sept).

On Slotsholmen Island

This island, where Copenhagen began in the 12th century, is a short walk from the train station and Tivoli, just across the bridge from the National Museum. It's dominated by Christiansborg Palace and several other royal and governmental buildings.

▲▲**Christiansborg Palace**—A complex of government buildings stands on the ruins of Copenhagen's original 12th-century fortress: the Parliament, Supreme Court, prime minister's office, royal reception rooms, royal library, several museums, and the royal stables.

Although the current palace dates only from 1928 and the royal family moved out 200 years ago, the building is the sixth to stand here in 800 years and is rich with tradition. The information-packed 50-minute English tours of the royal reception rooms are excellent.

As you slip-slide on protect-the-floor slippers through 22 rooms, you'll gain a good feel for Danish history, royalty, and politics. (For instance, the family portrait of King Christian IX shows why he's called the "father-in-law of Europe"—his children eventually became or married royalty in Denmark, Russia, Greece, Britain, France, Germany, and Norway.) The highlight is the dazzling set of modern tapestries—Danish-designed but Gobelin-made in Paris. This gift, given to the queen on her 60th birthday in 2000, celebrates 1,000 years of Danish history with wild wall-hangings from the Viking age to our chaotic times (admission by 60-kr tour only; May–Sept daily at 11:00, 13:00, and 15:00; Oct–April Tue–Sun at 15:00, closed Mon; from equestrian statue in front, go through wooden door, past entrance to Christiansborg Castle ruins, into courtyard, and up stairs on right; tel. 33 92 64 92).

Christiansborg Castle Ruins—An exhibit in the scant remains of the first fortress built by Bishop Absalon, the 12th-century founder of Copenhagen, lies under the palace. There's precious little to see, but it's old and well described (40 kr, good 1-kr guide; May–Sept daily 10:00–16:00; Oct–April Tue–Sun 10:00–15:30, closed Mon).

▲**Thorvaldsen's Museum**—This museum, which has some of the best swoon-worthy art you'll see anywhere, tells the story and shows the monumental work of the great Danish Neoclassical sculptor Bertel Thorvaldsen (1770–1844). Considered Canova's equal among Neoclassical sculptors, Thorvaldsen spent 40 years in Rome. He was lured home to Copenhagen with the promise to showcase his work in a fine museum—which opened in the revolutionary year of 1848 as Denmark's first public art gallery. The ground floor showcases his statues (pull open the little black "information" cases for descriptions). Upstairs, get into the mind of the artist by perusing his personal possessions and the private collection of paintings from which he drew inspiration (20 kr, free Wed, open Tue–Sun 10:00–17:00, closed Mon, well-described, located in Neoclassical building with colorful walls next to Christiansborg Palace, tel. 33 32 15 32, www.thorvaldsensmuseum.dk).

Royal Library—Copenhagen's "Black Diamond" library is a striking, super-modern building made of shiny black granite, leaning over the harbor at the edge of the palace complex. Wander through the old and new sections, read a magazine, and enjoy a classy—and pricey—lunch (library is free, special exhibitions generally 30 kr, restaurant, café, and library hours: Mon–Fri 10:00–19:00, Sat 10:00–17:00, closed Sun, tel. 33 47 47 47, www.kb.dk).

▲**Danish Jewish Museum (Dansk Jødisk Museum)**—This museum, which opened in 2004 in a striking building by American architect Daniel Libeskind, offers a small but well-exhibited display of 400 years of the life and impact of Jews in Denmark. Libeskind—who created the equally conceptual Jewish Museum in Berlin, and whose design is the basis for re-developing the World Trade Center site in New York City—has literally written Jewish culture into this building. The floor plan, a seemingly random squiggle, is actually in the shape of the Hebrew characters for *Mitzvah*, which loosely translated means "act of kindness."

Be sure to watch the introductory film about the Jews' migration to Denmark. As you tour the collection, the uneven floors and asymmetrical walls give you the feeling that what lies around the corner is completely unknown...much like the life and history of Danish Jews. Another interpretation might be that the uneven floors give you the sense of motion, like waves on the sea—a reminder that despite Nazi occupation in 1943, nearly 7,000 Danish Jews were ferried across the waves by fishermen to safety in neutral Sweden (40 kr; June–Aug Tue–Sun 10:00–17:00, closed Mon; Sept–May Tue–Fri 13:00–16:00, Sat–Sun 12:00–17:00, closed Mon; behind the Royal Library at Proviantpassagen 6, tel. 33 11 22 18, www.jewmus.dk).

Near Strøget

Museum of Erotica—This museum's focus is the love life of *Homo sapiens*. Better than the Amsterdam equivalent, it offers a chance to visit a porn shop and call it a museum. It took some digging, but they've put together a history of sex from Pompeii to the present day. Visitors get a peep into the world of 19th-century Copenhagen prostitutes and a chance to read up on the sex lives of Mussolini, Queen Elizabeth, Charlie Chaplin, and Casanova. After reviewing a lifetime of *Playboy* centerfolds and an entire room filled with Marilyn Monroe, visitors sit down for the arguably artistic experience of watching the "electric *tabernakel*," a dozen silently slamming screens of porn (worth the 109-kr entry fee—or 198 kr for two people—only if fascinated by sex, includes a graphic booklet and "erotic horoscope"; May–Sept daily 10:00–23:00; Oct–April Sun–Thu 11:00–20:00, Fri–Sat 10:00–22:00; a block north of Strøget at Købmagergade 24, tel. 33 12 03 11, www.museumerotica.dk).

Copenhagen's dreary little red light district along Istedgade behind the train station has withered away to almost nothing. If you came to Copenhagen to sightsee sex...it's in the museum.

Round Tower—Built in 1642 by Christian IV, the tower connects a church, library, and observatory (the oldest functioning observatory in Europe) with a ramp that spirals up to a fine view of Copenhagen (25 kr, nothing to see inside but the ramp and the view; June–Aug Mon–Sat 10:00–20:00, Sun 12:00–20:00; Sept–May Mon–Sat 10:00–17:00, Sun 12:00–17:00; just off Strøget on Købmagergade).

Amalienborg Palace and Nearby

For a lot more information on this palace and nearby attractions, including the famous *Little Mermaid* statue, see the end of my self-guided walk (page 64).

▲**Amalienborg Palace Museum**—While Queen Margrethe II and her family live quite privately in one of the four mansions that make up the palace complex, another mansion has been open to the public since 1994. It displays the private studies of four kings of the House of Glucksborg, who ruled 1863–1972. Your visit is short—

six or eight rooms on one floor, but it affords an intimate and unique peek into Denmark's royal family (50 kr; May–Oct daily 10:00–16:00; Nov–April Tue–Sun 11:00–16:00, closed Mon; enter on side of palace square farthest from the harbor, tel. 33 12 08 08).

Amalienborg Palace Changing of the Guard—This noontime event is boring in the summer, when the queen is not in residence—the guards just change places.

▲▲**Museum of Danish Resistance (Frihedsmuseet)**—The compelling story of Denmark's heroic Nazi-resistance struggle (1940–1945) is well explained in English, from Himmler's eye patch to fascinating tricks of creative sabotage (free; open May–Sept Tue–Sat 10:00–16:00, Sun 10:00–17:00, closed Mon; Oct–April Tue–Sat 10:00–15:00, Sun 10:00–16:00, closed Mon; guided tours at 14:00 Tue, Thu, and Sun in the summer; on Churchillparken between Amalienborg Palace and *The Little Mermaid,* bus #26 from Langelinie or bus #1, #1A, #19, or #29 from farther away, tel. 33 13 77 14, www.frihedsmuseet.dk).

Rosenborg Castle and Nearby

▲▲▲**Rosenborg Castle (Rosenborg Slot) and Treasury**—This finely furnished Dutch Renaissance–style castle was built by Christian IV in the early 1600s as a summer residence. Rosenborg was his favorite residence, and where he chose to die. Open to the public since 1838, it houses the Danish crown jewels and 500 years of royal knickknacks. Much of the castle will be closed for renovation until spring of 2008, but the treasury, along with the collections of weapons and ivory in the basement, will

Christian IV
(1577–1648)

Christian IV was dynamism in the flesh, a true Renaissance guy who spoke five languages and governed well. In the 60 years of his rule over Denmark (and Norway), the size of Copenhagen doubled, the Danish navy tripled, and the Danish colonial empire got its start.

Because 3,000 of the king's handwritten letters survive, we know a lot about him. He lived life with unusual vigor—and without a lot of self-control. Locals love to tell stories about their beloved king, whose drinking was legendary. When he was famously wounded by shrapnel in a sea battle with Sweden, he lost an eye. No problem for the warrior king with a knack for heroic publicity stunts: When the shrapnel bits were taken out of his eye and forehead, he had them made into earrings. Christian lived to be 70 and fathered 26 children (with two wives and one mistress).

remain open. Possibly a room or two of Christian IV's living quarters will stay open as well.

Cost, Hours, Location: 50 kr, 65 kr when special exhibits are on; June–Sept daily 10:00–17:00; May and Oct daily 10:00–16:00; Nov–April Tue–Sun 11:00–14:00, closed Mon; S-tog: Nørreport, tel. 33 15 32 86, www.rosenborgslot.dk.

Tours: Richard Karpen leads fascinating 90-minute tours in princely garb (June–Sept Mon and Thu at 13:30, 50 kr plus your entrance fee, see "Tours" on page 54). Or take the following self-guided tour through the treasury that I've woven together from the highlights of Richard's walk.

◒ Self-Guided Tour: Head for the basement, which contains the **Royal Danish Treasury.** The palace was a royal residence for a century and has been the royal vault right up until today. As you enter, peek into the royal **wine cellar,** with thousand-liter barrels, to the right of the ticket checker. Then continue into the treasury.

The diamond- and pearl-studded **saddles** were Christian IV's—the first for his coronation, the second for his son's wedding. When his kingdom was nearly bankrupt, Christian had these constructed lavishly—complete with solid-gold spurs—to impress visiting dignitaries and bolster Denmark's credit rating.

The next case displays **tankards.** Danes were always big drinkers, and to drink in the top style, a king had narwhal steins (#4030 and #4031). Note the fancy Greenland Inuit (Eskimo) on the lid. The case is filled with exquisitely carved ivory.

Next case: What's with the mooning snuffbox (#4063)? Also,

check out the amorous whistle (#4064).

Case in corner: The 18th century was the age of **brooches.** Many of these are made of freshwater pearls. Find the fancy combination toothpick and ear spoon (#1140). A queen was caught having an affair after 22 years of royal marriage. Her king gave her a special present: a golden ring—showing the hand of his promiscuous queen shaking hands with a penis (#4146).

Step downstairs, away from all this silliness. Passing through the serious vault door, you come face-to-face with a big, jeweled **sword.** The tall, two-handed, 16th-century coronation sword was drawn by the new king, who cut crosses in the air in four directions, symbolically promising to defend the realm from all attacks. The cases surrounding the sword contain everyday items used by the king (all solid gold, of course). What looks like a trophy case of gold records is actually a collection of dinner plates with amber centers (#5032).

Go down the steps. In the center case is Christian IV's **coronation crown** (from 1596, seven pounds of gold and precious stones, #1524), which some consider to be the finest Renaissance crown in Europe. Its 12 gables radiate symbolism. Find the symbols of justice (sword and scales), fortitude (a woman on a lion with a sword), and charity (a woman nursing—meaning the king will love God and his people as a mother loves her child). The pelican, which famously pecks its own flesh to feed its children, symbolizes God sacrificing his son, just as the king would make great sacrifices for his people. Climb the footstool to look inside—it's as exquisite as the outside. The shields of various Danish provinces remind the king that he's surrounded by his realms.

Circling the cases along the wall (right to left), notice the fine enameled lady's goblet with traits of a good woman spelled out in Latin (#5128); above that, an exquisite prayer book (with handwritten favorite prayers, #5134); the big solid-gold baptismal basin (#5262) hanging above tiny boxes that contained the royal children's umbilical chords (handy for protection later in life, #5272); and royal writing sets with wax, seals, pens, and ink (#5320).

Go down a few more steps into the lowest level of the treasury and last room. The two **crowns** in the center cases are more modern (from 1670), lighter, and more practical—just gold and diamonds without all the symbolism. The king's is only four pounds, the queen's a mere two.

The cases along the walls show off the **crown jewels.** These were made in 1840 of diamonds, emeralds, rubies, and pearls from earlier royal jewelry. The saber (#5540) shows emblems of the realm's 19 provinces. The sumptuous pendant features a 19-carat diamond cut (like its neighbors) in the 58-facet "brilliant" style for maximum reflection. Imagine these on the dance floor. The painting shows the coronation of Christian VIII at Frederiksborg Chapel in 1840. The crown jewels are still worn by the queen on special occasions several times a year.

▲**Rosenborg Gardens**—Rosenborg Castle is surrounded by the royal pleasure gardens and, on sunny days, a minefield of sunbathing Danish beauties and picnickers. While "ethnic Danes" grab the shade, the rest of the Danes worship the sun. When the royal family is in residence, there's a daily changing-of-the-guard mini-parade from the Royal Guard's barracks adjoining Rosenborg Castle (at 11:30) to Amalienborg Castle (at 12:00). The Queen's Rose Garden (across the moat from the palace) is a royal place for a picnic (cheap open-face sandwiches to go at Sos's Smørrebrød, nearby at the corner of Borgergade and Dronningens Tværgade, Mon–Fri 8:00–14:00, closed Sat–Sun). The fine statue of Hans Christian Andersen in the park—erected while he was still alive (and approved by him)—is meant to symbolize how his stories had a message even for adults.

▲**National Art Museum (Statens Museum for Kunst)**—This museum fills an impressive building with Danish and European paintings from the 14th century through today. Of most interest is the Danish Golden Age of paintings, and those from the late 19th and early 20th centuries. Its collection of early French Modernism is impressive (with works by Matisse, Picasso, Braque, and more). It's complemented with works by Danish artists, who, inspired by the French avant-garde, introduced new, radical forms and colors to Scandinavian art. Make a point to meet the "Skagen" artists. They gathered in the fishing village of Skagen on the northern tip of Denmark, surrounded by the sea and strong light, and painted heroic folk fishermen themes in the late 1800s (free for the collection, 70 kr for special exhibitions, Tue–Sun 10:00–17:00, Wed until 20:00, closed Mon, Sølvgade 48, tel. 33 74 84 94, www.smk.dk).

Christiania

If you're interested in visiting a free-wheeling community of alternative living, Christiania is a ▲▲▲ sight.

In 1971, the original 700 Christianians established squatters' rights in an abandoned military barracks just a 10-minute walk from the Danish parliament building. A generation later, this "free city" still stands—an ultra-human mishmash of idealists, hippies, potheads, non-materialists, and happy children (600 adults, 200 kids, 200 cats, 200 dogs, 2 parrots, and 17 horses). There are even a

Christiania

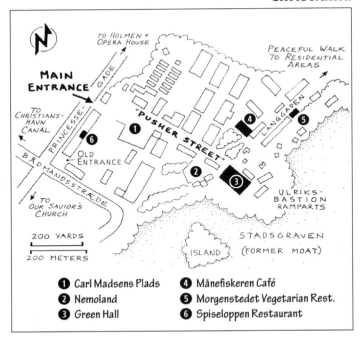

1 Carl Madsens Plads
2 Nemoland
3 Green Hall
4 Månefiskeren Café
5 Morgenstedet Vegetarian Rest.
6 Spiseloppen Restaurant

handful of Willie Nelson–type seniors among the 180 remaining here from the original takeover. And an amazing thing has happened: The place has become the third-most-visited sight among tourists in Copenhagen. Move over, *Little Mermaid.*

"Pusher Street" (named for the former sale of soft drugs here) is Christiania's main drag. Get beyond this touristy side of Christiania, and you'll find a fascinating, ramshackle world of moats and earthen ramparts, alternative housing, cozy tea houses, carpenter shops, hippie villas, children's playgrounds, peaceful lanes, and people who believe that "to be normal is to be in a straightjacket." Be careful to distinguish between real Christianians and Christiania's motley guests—drunks (mostly from other countries) who hang out here in the summer for the freedom. Part of the original charter guaranteed that the community would stay open to the public.

The Community: Christiania is broken into 14 administrative neighborhoods on a former military base. The land is still owned by Denmark's Ministry of Defense. Locals build their homes but don't own the land; there's no buying or selling of property. When someone moves out, the community decides who will be invited in to replace that person. A third of the adult population works on the outside, a third works on the inside, and a third doesn't work much at all. There are nine rules: no cars, no hard drugs, no guns, no explosives, and so on. The Christiania flag is red and yellow because when the original hippies took over, they found a lot of red and yellow paint on site. The three yellow dots in the flag are from the three "i"s in Christiania.

The community pays the city about $1 million a year for utilities and has about $1 million a year more to run its local affairs. A few "luxury hippies" have oil heat, but most use wood or gas. The ground here was poisoned by its days as a military base, so nothing is grown in Christiania. The community has one mailing address (for 25 kr/month, you can receive mail here). A phone chain provides a system of communal security (they have had bad experiences calling the police). Each September 26, the day those first squatters took over the barracks here in 1971, Christiania has a big birthday bash.

Tourists are entirely welcome here, because they've become a major part of the economy. Visitors react in very different ways to the place. Some see dogs, dirt, and dazed people. Others see a haven of peace, freedom, and no taboos. Locals will remind judgmental Americans (whose country incarcerates more than a quarter of the world's prison inmates) that a society must make the choice: Allow for alternative lifestyles...or build more prisons.

Even since its inception, Christiania has been a political hot potato. No one in the Danish establishment wanted it. And no one had the nerve to mash it. In the last decade, Christiania has connected better with the rest of society—paying its utilities and taxes, and so on. But since taking over in 2001, Denmark's conservative government (with pressure from the US) has vowed to "normalize" Christiania, and in recent years police have regularly conducted raids on pot sellers. There's talk about developing posh apartments to replace existing residences, according to one government plan. But Christiania has a legal team, and litigation will likely drag on for many years.

Many predict that Christianians will withstand the government's challenge, as they have in years past. The community, which also calls itself Freetown, fended off a similar attempt in 1976 with the help of fervent supporters from around Europe. *Bevar Christiania*—"Save Christiania"—banners fly everywhere, and locals are confident that their free way of life will survive. As history has shown, the challenge may just make this hippie haven a bit stronger.

Orientation Tour: Passing under the gate, take Pusher Street directly into the community. The first square—a kind of market square (souvenirs and marijuana-related stuff)—is named Carl Madsens Plads, honoring the lawyer who took the squatters' case to the Danish supreme court in 1976 and won. Beyond that is Nemoland (a food circus, on the right). A huge warehouse called the Green Hall (Den Gronne Hal) is a recycling center (where people get most of their building material) that does double duty at night as a concert hall and as a place where children work on crafts. On the left, a lane leads to the Månefiskeren café, and beyond that, to the Morgenstedet vegetarian restaurant. Going straight on Pusher Street takes you to the ramparts that overlook the lake. A walk or bike ride through Christiania is a great way to see how this community lives. (When you leave, look up—the sign above the gate says, "You are entering the EU.")

Smoking Marijuana: Pusher Street was once lined with stalls selling marijuana, joints, and hash. Residents intentionally destroyed the stalls in 2004 to reduce the risk of Christiania being disbanded by the government. (One stall was spared, and is on display at the National Museum—see page 68.) Walking along Pusher Street today, you may witness policemen or covert deals being made—but never at the same time. You may also notice wafts of marijuana smoke and whispered offers of "hash" during your visit. However, purchasing and smoking may buy you more

time in Denmark than you'd planned—possession of marijuana is illegal.

About hard drugs: For the first few years, junkies were tolerated. But that led to violence and polluted the mellow ambience residents envisioned. In 1979, the junkies were expelled—an epic confrontation in the community's folk history now—and since then the symbol of a fist breaking a syringe is as prevalent as the leafy marijuana icon. Hard drugs are emphatically forbidden in Christiania.

Eating in Christiania: The people of Christiania appreciate good food and count on tourism as a big part of their economy. Consequently, there are plenty of decent eateries. Most of the restaurants are closed on Monday (the community's weekly holiday). **Pusher Street** has a few grungy but tasty falafel stands. **Nemoland** is a fun collection of stands peddling Thai food and fast hippie food with great tented outdoor seating. Its stay-a-while atmosphere comes with backgammon, foosball, bakery goods, and fine views from the ramparts. **Morgenstedet** is a good, cheap vegetarian café (60-kr meals, Tue–Sun 12:00–21:00, closed Mon, left after Pusher Street). **Månefiskeren** (literally "Moonfisher Bar") looks like a Brueghel painting—from 2007—with billiards, chess, light meals, and drinks. **Spiseloppen** is *the* classy, good-enough-for-Republicans restaurant in the community (closed Mon, described on page 93).

Hours and Tours: Christiania is open all the time (main entrance is down Prinsessegade behind the Our Savior's Church spiral tower in Christianshavn). You're welcome to snap photos, but ask residents before you photograph them. Guided tours leave from the front entrance of Christiania at 15:00 (just show up, 30 kr, 90 min, daily late June–Aug, Sat–Sun rest of year, in English and Danish).

Near Christiania, in Christianshavn

▲**Our Savior's Church (Vor Frelsers Kirke)**—The church's bright Baroque interior (1696), with its pipe organ supported by the royal elephants, is worth a look (free, helpful English flier, April–Aug Mon–Sat 11:00–16:30, Sun 12:00–16:30, off-season closes at 15:30, bus #2A, #8, #19, or Metro: Christianshavn, Sankt Annægade 29, tel. 32 57 27 98). You can climb the unique spiral spire for great views of the city and of the Christiania commune below (20 kr, 400 steps, 311 feet high, closed in bad weather and Nov–March).

Greater Copenhagen

Carlsberg Brewery—Denmark's beloved source of legal intoxicants, Carlsberg welcomes you to its Visitors Center for a self-guided tour and a half-liter of beer (40 kr, Tue–Sun 10:00–16:00, closed Mon, last entry 1 hour before closing, bus #18, #26, or #6A, enter at Gamle Carlsbergvej 11 around corner from brewery entrance, tel. 33 27 13 14).

Open-Air Folk Museum (Frilandsmuseet)—This park is filled with traditional Danish architecture and folk culture (free, open mid-April–Oct Tue–Sun 10:00–17:00, closed Mon and Nov–mid-April, outside of town in the suburb of Lyngby, S-tog: Sorgenfri and 10-min walk to Kongevejen 100, tel. 33 13 44 11).

Bakken—Danes gather at Copenhagen's *other* great amusement park, Bakken (free; late June–mid-Aug daily 12:00–24:00, shorter hours April–late June and mid-Aug–mid-Sept; closed mid-Sept–March; S-tog: Klampenborg, then walk 10 min through the woods; tel. 39 63 73 00, www.bakken.dk).

Dragør—If you don't have time to get to the idyllic island of Ærø (see Central Denmark chapter), consider a trip a few minutes out of Copenhagen to the fishing village of Dragør (bus #250S or #5A from station five stops to Sundbyvesterplads, where you'll change to #350A). For information, see www.dragoer-information.dk.

SHOPPING

Shops are generally open Monday through Friday from 10:00 to 19:00 and Saturday from 9:00 to 16:00 (closed Sun). While the big department stores dominate the scene, many locals favor the characteristic, small artisan shops and boutiques that are listed in the *Local Life* flier. You can't get this flier at the TI, but keep your eyes peeled for it (for example, at the bus info center on Rådhuspladsen, or at the Kransekagehuset bakery on Pilestræde just off the Strøget).

Uniquely Danish souvenirs to look for include intricate paper cuttings with idyllic motifs of swans, flowers, or Christmas themes; mobiles with everything from bicycles to Viking ships (look for the quality Flensted brand); and the colorful artwork (posters, postcards, T-shirts, and more) by Danish artist Bo Bendixen.

For a street's worth of shops selling **"Scantiques,"** wander down Ravnsborggade from Nørrebrogade.

Copenhagen's colorful **flea markets** are small but feisty and surprisingly cheap (Sat May–Nov 8:00–14:00 at Israels Plads; Fri and Sat May–Sept 8:00–17:00 along Gammel Strand and on Kongens Nytorv). For other street markets, ask at the TI.

The city's top **department stores** (Illum at Østergade 52; and Magasin at Kongens Nytorv 13) offer a good, if expensive, look at today's Denmark. Both are on Strøget and have fine cafeterias on their top floors. The department stores and the Politiken Bookstore on Rådhuspladsen have a good selection of maps and English travel guides.

Shoppers who like jewelry look for amber, known as "gold of the North." Globs of this petrified sap wash up on the shores of all the Baltic countries. **House of Amber** has a shop and a tiny two-room museum with about 50 examples of prehistoric insects trapped in the amber (remember *Jurassic Park*?) under magnifying glasses (25 kr, daily 10:00–18:00, 50 yards off Nyhavn at Kongens Nytorv 2; 4 other locations sell amber, but only the Nyhavn location houses a museum as well).

If you buy anything substantial (more than 300 kr, about $50) from a shop displaying the **Danish Tax-Free Shopping** emblem, you can get a refund of the Value Added Tax, roughly 20 to 25 percent of the purchase price (VAT is "MOMS" in Danish). If you have your purchase mailed, the tax can be deducted from your bill. For details, call 32 52 55 66, and see "VAT Refunds and Customs Regulations" on page 15.

NIGHTLIFE

For the latest on the city's hopping jazz scene, inquire at the TI, study your *Copenhagen This Week* booklet, or pick up the "alternative" *Playtime* magazine at Use It. To locate the following places, see the map on page 90. **Copenhagen Jazz House** is a good bet for live jazz (about 80–125 kr, Tue–Thu and Sun at 20:30, Fri–Sat at 21:30, closed Mon, Niels Hemmingsensgade 10, tel. 33 15 26 00 for the schedule in Danish, www.jazzhouse.dk). For blues, try the **Mojo Blues Bar** (60 kr Fri–Sat, otherwise no cover, nightly 20:00–5:00, music starts at 22:00, Løngangsstræde 21c, tel. 33 11 64 53). **Christiania** always seems to have something musical going on after dark. **Tivoli** has evening entertainment daily from mid–April through mid–September until 23:00 (see page 66).

DFDS Canal Tours offers two-hour **jazz cruises** along the canals of Copenhagen. You can bring a picnic dinner and drinks on board and enjoy a lively night on the water surrounded by Danes (120 kr, April–Sept Thu at 18:00, Oct–Dec Sun at 15:00, no tours Jan–March; departs from DFDS dock at Nyhavn, tel. 32 96 30 00). Call to reserve on July and August evenings; otherwise try arriving 20 to 30 minutes in advance.

SLEEPING

I've listed a few big business-class hotels, the best budget hotels in the center, cheap rooms in private homes in great neighborhoods an easy bus ride from the station, and a few backpacker dorm options.

Big Copenhagen hotels have an exasperating pricing policy.

Sleep Code

(6 kr = about $1, country code: 45)
S = Single, **D** = Double/Twin, **T** = Triple, **Q** = Quad, **b** = bathroom, **s** = shower. Breakfast is generally included at hotels but not at private rooms or hostels. Unless otherwise noted, credit cards are accepted. Everybody speaks English.

To help you sort easily through these listings, I've divided the rooms into three categories, based on the highest rack-rate price for a standard double room with bath during high season:

$$$ **Higher Priced**—Most rooms 1,000 kr or more.
  $$ **Moderately Priced**—Most rooms between
                600–1,000 kr.
    $ **Lower Priced**—Most rooms 600 kr or less.

Their high rack rates are actually charged only about 20 or 30 days a year (unless you book in advance and don't know better). Hotels are swamped at certain times and need to keep their gouging options open. Therefore, you'll need to check their Web site for deals or be bold enough to simply show up and use the TI self-service booking system to find yourself a room on their push list. The TI swears that, except for maybe 10 days a year, you can land yourself a deeply discounted room in a three- or four-star business-class hotel in the center. That means a 1,400-kr double with American-style comfort for about 800 kr, including a big buffet breakfast.

Hotels in Central Copenhagen

Prices include breakfast unless noted otherwise. All of these hotels are big and modern, with elevators and non-smoking rooms upon request, and all accept credit cards. Beware: Many hotels have rip-off phone rates even for local calls. The Mayfair and Ibis hotels are big and soulless. The rest are smaller, cheaper, and more characteristic.

$$$ **Ibsens Hotel** is an elegant 118-room hotel in a charming neighborhood away from the main train station commotion and a short walk from the old center (Sb-1,085–1,185 kr, Db-1,270–1,460 kr, discounted rooms available May–June and Aug–Sept—ask about these and other discounts when booking or check their Web site for the latest offers, Vendersgade 23, S-tog: Nørreport, tel. 33 13 19 13, fax 33 13 19 16, www.ibsenshotel.dk, hotel@ibsenshotel.dk).

$$$ **Hotel Mayfair** is a comfortable but sterile place on a quiet street three blocks behind the station (rack rates: Sb-1,430 kr, Db-1,530 kr; but Db often go for 800–900 kr at the last minute, a half block away from busy Vesterbrogade at Helgolandsgade 3, tel. 70 12 17 00, fax 33 23 96 86, www.choicehotels.dk, cc.mayfair @choice.dk).

$$$ **Carlton** and **Bertrams** are two boutique hotels (owned by Hotel Guldsmeden) in the trendy Vesterbro district. They feel more like B&Bs than hotels, offering comfortable, well-appointed rooms and serving an abundant organic breakfast buffet. Although both hotels are on busy Vesterbrogade, between Frederiksberg park and the central train station, most rooms are clustered around quiet courtyards (Carlton: Sb-1,095 kr, Db-1,395 kr, Vesterbrogade 66; Bertrams: Sb-1,195 kr, Db-1,495 kr, Vesterbrogade 107; both offer a 20 percent discount at certain times of the year with this book in 2007, same contact info: tel. 33 22 15 00, fax 33 22 15 55, www.hotelguldsmeden.dk, reception@hotelguldsmeden.dk). In May, 2007, the same owners will open a third hotel, **Axel**, at Helgolandsgade 7, a block behind the train station (see Web site for details).

Copenhagen Hotels

S S-Tog Stn.
M Metro Stn.
★ Canal Tours

0 km   .5
0 mi   ¼   ½

TO E·47
HELSINGØR

TO BOAT
TO OSLO

ØSTERBRO

ØSTERPORT
STN.

LITTLE
MERMAID

HAMMARSKJØLDS ALLE

KASTELLET

NØRREBRO

GEFION
FOUNTAIN

NAT'L
ART
MUSEUM

SØLVGADE

VOLDGADE

MUSEUM
OF DANISH
RESISTANCE

ISRAELS-
PLADS

NØRREBROGADE

ØSTER

AMALIENBORG
PALACE

AMALIE-
HAVEN

ROSENBORG
CASTLE
& GARDENS

NØRREPORT
STN.

GOTHERSGADE

DE LA COUR

OPERA
HOUSE

TO
8

GYLDENLØVES
GADE

NØRREVOLD

PED.
ZONE

KONGENS
NYTORV

NYHAVN

TO
7

H.C.

OLD   CITY

STRØGET

ROYAL
THEATER

VESTER-
PORT
STN.

USE·IT

CITY
HALL

OUR SAVIOR'S
CHURCH

TO
BREWERY

DDC.

CHRISTIANS-
BORG
PAL.

TORVE GADE

CHRISTIANIA

TIVOLI

ANDERSENS BLVD.

NAT'L
MUS.

ROYAL
LIBRARY

CENTRAL
STATION

NY
CARLSBERG
GLYPTOTEK

CHRISTIANSHAVN

VESTER-
BRO

TO
AIRPORT

DCH

1 Ibsens Hotel

2 Hotels Mayfair, Nebo, Axel
& Ibis Star

3 To Hotels Carlton & Bertrams
& YMCA/YWCA

4 Hotel Bethel Sømandshjem

5 Hotel Jørgensen

6 Cab-Inn City

7 To Cab-Inn Copenhagen Express

8 To Cab-Inn Scandinavia

9 De la Cour & Voutsinos Rooms

10 Danhostel Copenhagen City

11 To Danhostel Copenhagen
Amager

12 Sleep-in Green

$$ Ibis Copenhagen Star Hotel, an Ibis chain hotel, has cookie-cutter rooms at reasonable prices in the city center. Their no-nonsense prices vary only with the season; there are no online specials or last-minute deals (April–Dec Sb-625 kr, Db-850 kr; Jan–March Sb-599 kr, Db-649 kr; breakfast-65 kr, Colbjorn-sensgade 13, tel. 33 22 11 00, star@accorhotel.dk).

$$ Hotel Nebo, a secure-feeling refuge with a friendly welcome and comfy, spacious rooms, is a half block from the station on the edge of Copenhagen's red light district (S-360–460 kr, Sb-650 kr, D-650 kr, Db-860–950 kr; the higher prices are for slightly larger rooms, TV; these prices promised with this book through 2007, cheaper Oct–April, extra bed-150 kr, Istedgade 6, tel. 33 21 12 17, fax 33 23 47 74, www.nebo.dk, nebo@email.dk).

$$ Hotel Bethel Sømandshjem is a calm and stately former seamen's hotel facing the boisterous Nyhavn canal and offering 30 somewhat tired rooms at the most reasonable rack rates in town. A third of their rooms are more modern and non-smoking, but the older rooms are a bit more spacious (Sb-595 kr, Db-795 kr, big Db on corner-895 kr, extra bed-150 kr, bus #650S from station or Metro to Kongens Nytorv, facing bridge over the canal at Nyhavn 22, tel. 33 13 03 70, fax 33 15 85 70, www.hotel-bethel.dk, info @hotel-bethel.dk).

$$ Hotel Jørgensen is a friendly little 30-room hotel beautifully located just off Nørreport with some cheap, depressing rooms and some good-value, nicer rooms. While the lounge is classy and welcoming, the halls are a narrow, tangled maze (basic S-475 kr, Sb-575 kr, very basic D-575 kr, more elegant Db-700 kr, Romersgade 11, tel. 33 13 81 86, fax 33 15 51 05, www.hoteljoergensen.dk, hoteljoergensen@mail.dk). They also rent 140–170 kr dorm beds to those under 35 (4–12 beds per room, sheets-30 kr).

A Danish Motel 6

$$ Cab-Inn is a radical innovation: identical, mostly collapsible, tiny but comfy, cruise ship–type staterooms, all bright, molded, and shiny with TV, coffee pot, shower, and toilet. Each room has a single bed that expands into a twin with one or two fold-down bunks on the walls. The staff will hardly give you the time of day, but it's tough to argue with this kind of efficiency (Sb-525 kr, Db-645 kr, Tb-765 kr, Qb-885 kr, breakfast-50 kr, easy parking-60 kr, www.cabinn.dk). There are two nearly identical Cab-Inns in the same neighborhood (a 15-min walk northwest of the station): **Cab-Inn Copenhagen Express** (86 rooms, Danasvej 32–34, tel. 33 21 04 00, fax 33 21 74 09, express@cabinn.com) and **Cab-Inn Scandinavia** (201 rooms, "Commodore" rooms have a real double bed for 100 kr extra, Vodroffsvej 55, tel. 35 36 11 11, fax 35 36 11 14, scandinavia@cabinn.com). A third location can be found just

Christianshavn

- **1** Hollender Rooms
- **2** Chicken's Private Pension
- **3** To Gitte Kongstad Apts.
- **4** Færge Cafeen
- **5** Ravelin Restaurant
- **6** Bastionen & Løven Restaurant
- **7** Lagkagehuset Bakery
- **8** Spicy Kitchen Indian
- **9** Spiseloppen Restaurant

south of Tivoli: **Cab-Inn City** (350 rooms, Mitchellsgade 14, tel. 33 46 16 16, fax 33 46 17 17, city@cabinn.com).

Rooms in Private Homes

Many travelers seem shy about rooms in private homes. Don't be. I almost always sleep in a private home. And, at about 600 kr or so per double, they're a great value. The experience is as private or as social as you want it to be, offering great "at home in Denmark" opportunities in good neighborhoods (in Christianshavn and near Amalienborg Palace) for a third of the price of hotels. You'll get a key and come and go as you like. Always contact your hosts ahead—they book in advance. All speak English and afford a fine peek into Danish domestic life. Rooms generally have no sink. While they usually don't include breakfast, you'll have access to the kitchen. If their rooms are booked up, they can often find you a place with a neighbor. You can trust the quality of their referrals.

If you still can't snare a place, remember that the TI or Use It would love to send you to one from their stable of locals renting out rooms. For more listings, visit www.bbdk.dk.

Private Rooms in Christianshavn

This area is a never-a-dull-moment hodgepodge of the chic, artistic, hippie, and hobo, with historic fixed-up warehouses in the shadow of government ministries. Colorful with shops, cafés, and canals, Christianshavn is an easy 10-minute walk to the center and has good bus connections to the airport and downtown. The bus stop is just outside the 7-Eleven on Torvegade. Take bus #2A or #48 to City Hall or the main train station and #2A (then transfer to #250S) to the airport. The Metro connects Christianshavn and Nørreport (2 stops on S-tog from main train station).

$ **Annette and Rudy Hollender** enjoy sharing their 300-year-old home with my readers. Even with a long and skinny staircase, sinkless rooms, and two rooms sharing one toilet/shower, it's a comfortable and cheery place to call home (S-350 kr, D-500 kr, T-600 kr, cash only, closed Nov–April, half a block off Torvegade at Wildersgade 19, Metro: Christianshavntorv, tel. 32 95 96 22, hollender@city.dk).

$ **Chicken's Private Pension** rents basic rooms in a funky old house, with steep stairs and rustic furniture. It's right on Christianshavn's main drag (S-400 kr, D-550 kr, T-675 kr, Q-800 kr, extra bed-150 kr, kitchen available for breakfast on your own, cash only, Torvegade 36, Metro: Christianshavntorv, tel. 32 95 32 73, www.chickens.dk, morten@chickens.dk, Morton Frederiksen).

Private Rooms South of Christianshavn

$$ **Gitte Kongstad** rents two fun and funky apartments, each taking up an entire spacious floor in her 100-year-old house. You'll have a kitchen, little garden, Internet connection, and your own bike as you settle comfortably far from the big-city intensity (Sb-525 kr, Db-650 kr, extra bed-200 kr, cash only, family-friendly; bus #250S from airport, then transfer to #2A at Kastrup Station; or bus #12 or #2A from train station; just 75 yards from Metro stop: Lergravsparken; Badensgade 2, tel. & fax 32 97 71 97, mobile 21 65 75 22, www.houseofcolors.dk, info@houseofcolors.dk). You'll feel at home here, and the bike ride into town (or to the beach) is a snap.

Private Rooms a Block from Amalienborg Palace

Amaliegade is a stately cobbled street in a quiet neighborhood (a 10-min walk north of Nyhavn and Strøget). You can look out your window and see the palace guard changing. Catch bus #1A or #15 from the station to Fredericiagade.

The following artistic and professional folks each rent out two rooms in their utilitarian, modern, and very Danish flats. Both rent rooms to travelers April–Sept, and include a do-it-yourself breakfast: **$ Puk and Holger De la Cour** (S-400 kr, D-475 kr extra bed-150 kr, cash only, kitchen/lounge available, Amaliegade 34, 4th floor, tel. 33 12 04 68, mobile 23 72 96 45, delacour@mail .dk); and **$ Line** (LEE-nuh) **Voutsinos** (2 double rooms, 1 with queen bed, 1 with 2 large single beds, D-475 kr, includes breakfast, extra bed-150 kr, cash only, family deals, Amaliegade 34, third floor, tel. & fax 33 14 71 42, line.voutsinos@privat.dk).

Hostels

Copenhagen energetically accommodates the young vagabond on a shoestring. The Use It office is your best source of information (see page 49). Each of these places charges about 100 kr per person for a bed and breakfast. Some don't allow sleeping bags, and if you don't have your own hostel sheet, you'll usually have to rent one for about 60 kr. IYHF hostels normally sell non-cardholders a guest pass for 25 kr.

$ Danhostel Copenhagen City is a huge (1,020 beds on 16 stories), clean, modern, non-smoking, official hostel, a 10-minute walk from the train station and Tivoli. Some rooms on higher floors have panoramic views over the city (available on a first-come, first-served basis). This is your best bet for a clean, basic, and inexpensive room in the city center (dorm beds in 4–8-bed rooms with bathrooms-150 kr, Sb/Db-600 kr, sheets and towel-60 kr, breakfast-50 kr, non-members pay extra 35 kr/night, lockers available, kitchen facilities, Internet access, H. C. Andersen Boulevard 50, tel. 33 11 85 85, www.danhostel.dk/copenhagencity, copenhagencity@danhostel.dk).

$ Danhostel Copenhagen Amager, also an official hostel, is on the edge of town (dorm bed-100 kr, D-360 kr, Db-450 kr, T-460 kr, Tb-530 kr, Q-530 kr, Qb-590 kr, non-members pay extra 35 kr/night, sheets-40 kr, breakfast-47 kr, no curfew, excellent facilities, Internet access, self-serve laundry, Vejlands Allé 200, tel. 32 52 29 08, fax 32 52 27 08, www.danhostel.dk/amager, copenhagen @danhostel.dk). To get downtown to the hostel, take the Metro (Metro: Bella Center, then 10-min walk) or a 30-minute bus ride (#250S with change to #100S, direction: Svanmøllen S).

$ The Danish YMCA/YWCA is a big, grungy, central crash pad open in July and August only (dorm bed-90 kr, 4- to 10-bed rooms, sheets-15 kr, breakfast-25 kr, Valdemarsgade 15, 10-min walk from train station or bus #6, tel. 33 31 15 74).

$ Sleep-in Green, the "ecological hostel," is very young, cool, and open mid-April through October (100-kr bunks, organic breakfast-40 kr, in a quiet spot a 15-min walk from center or catch bus #5A from station to Ravnsborggade, off Nørrebrogade at Ravnsborggade 18, tel. 35 37 77 77, www.sleep-in-green.dk).

EATING

Cheap Meals

For a quick lunch, try a *smørrebrød*, a *pølse*, or a picnic. Finish it off with a pastry.

Smørrebrød

Denmark's 300-year-old tradition of open-face sandwiches survives. Find a *smørrebrød* take-out shop and choose two or three that look good (about 10–20 kr each). You'll get them wrapped and ready for a park bench. Add a cold drink, and you have a fine, quick, and very Danish lunch. Tradition calls for three sandwich courses: herring first, then meat, and then cheese. Downtown, you'll find these handy local alternatives to Yankee fast-food chains:

Near Gammeltorv/Nytorv: **Restaurant and Café Nytorv** has pleasant outdoor seating (with indoor tables available nearby) and a great deal on a *smørrebrød* sampler for about 150 kr—perfect for two people to share. This "Copenhagen Plate" gives you a selection of the traditional sandwiches, and extra bread on request. Not sure where to start? Just ask (Mon–Sat 11:30–22:00, Sun 12:00–21:00, Nytorv 15, tel. 33 11 77 06). **Sorgenfri** offers a local experience in a dark, woody spot just off Strøget (daily 11:00–20:30, Brolæggerstræde 8, tel. 33 11 58 80). Or consider **Domhusets Smørrebrød** (Mon–Fri 7:00–14:30, closed Sat–Sun, Kattesundet 18, tel. 33 15 98 98).

Near Kongens Nytorv: Try **Danish Lunch,** a modern setting for this very traditional meal. You can eat inside on (gasp!) paper plates, or, better yet, grab a meal to go and enjoy it on the nearby square (Mon–Fri 8:30–18:00, Sat–Sun 10:00–18:00, at the end of Strøget just before Kongens Nytorv, three *smørrebrød* for about 60 kr).

Near Rosenborg Palace: **Slaget på Kultorvet** is a butcher shop that sells tasty and fresh *smørrebrød* (Mon–Sat 8:00–17:00, closed Sun, Købmagergade on Kultorvet).

The Pølse

The famous Danish hot dog, sold in *pølsevogne* (sausage wagons) throughout the city, is another typically Danish institution that has resisted the onslaught of our global, Styrofoam-packaged, fast-food culture. Study the photo menu for variations. These are fast, cheap, tasty, and, like their American cousins, almost worthless nutritionally. Even so, what the locals call the "dead man's finger" is the dog Danish kids love to bite.

There's more to getting a *pølse* than simply ordering a hot dog.

Employ these handy phrases: *rød* (red, the basic weenie), *medister* (spicy, better quality), *knæk* (short, stubby, tastier than *rød*), *ristet* (fried), *brød* (a bun, usually smaller than the sausage), *svøb* ("swaddled" in bacon), *Fransk* (French style, buried in a long skinny hole in the bun with sauce), and *flottenheimer* (a fat one with onions and sauce). *Sennep* is mustard and *ristet løg* are crispy, fried onions. Wash everything down with a *sodavand* (soda pop).

By hanging around a *pølsevogn,* you can study this institution. Denmark's "cold feet cafés" are a form of social care: People who have difficulty finding jobs are licensed to run these wienermobiles. As they gain seniority, they are promoted to work at more central locations. Danes like to gather here for munchies and *pølsesnak*—the local slang for empty chatter (literally, "sausage talk").

Picnics

Throughout Copenhagen, small delis *(viktualiehandler)* sell fresh bread, tasty pastries, juice, milk, cheese, and yogurt (drinkable, in tall liter boxes). Two of the largest supermarket chains are **Irma** (in arcade on Vesterbrogade next to Tivoli) and **Super Brugsen.** **Netto** is a cut-rate outfit with the cheapest prices.

Pastry

Find your way to the famous Danish pastries by looking for the golden pretzel sign hanging over the door or windows—it's the Danes' age-old symbol for a bakery. Danish pastries, called *wienerbrød* (Vienna bread) in Denmark, are named for the Viennese bakers who brought the art of pastry-making to Denmark, where the Danes say they perfected it. Try these bakeries: **Nansens** (on corner of Nansensgade and Ahlefeldtsgade, near Ibsens Hotel), **Kransekagehuset** (just off Strøget, near Kongens Nytorv at Ny Ostergade 9), and **Lagekagehuset** (on Torvegade in Christianshavn; and next to the TI). For a genteel bit of high-class 1870s Copenhagen, pay a lot for a coffee and a fresh danish at **Conditori La Glace,** just off Strøget at Skoubogade 3.

Dine with the Danes

For a unique experience and a great opportunity to meet locals in their homes, consider having this organization arrange a dinner for you with a Danish family. You get a homey two-course meal with lots of conversation. Some effort is made to match your age and

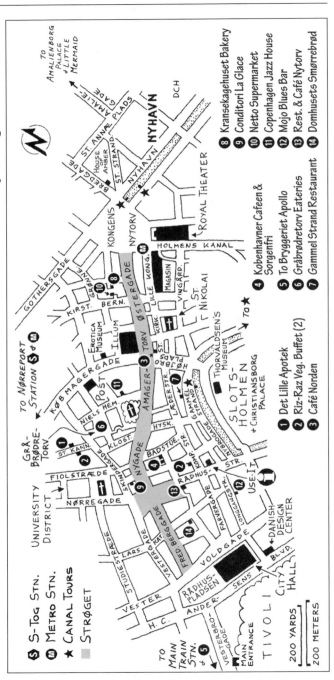

Copenhagen Restaurants

S S-Tog Stn.
M Metro Stn.
★ Canal Tours
Strøget

1 Det Lille Apotek
2 Riz-Raz Veg. Buffet (2)
3 Café Norden
4 Kobenhavner Cafeen & Sorgenfri
5 To Bryggeriet Apollo
6 Gråbrødretorv Eateries
7 Gammel Strand Restaurant
8 Kransekagehuset Bakery
9 Conditori La Glace
10 Netto Supermarket
11 Copenhagen Jazz House
12 Mojo Blues Bar
13 Rest. & Café Nytorv
14 Domhusets Smørrebrød

interests (but not occupations). Book in advance by phone (400 kr per person, reserve at least a day in advance, tel. 26 85 39 61), or book online and save some kroner (150 kr per person, pay your host directly, www.dinewiththedanes.dk).

Restaurants

Due to the high cost of water in Denmark, it's common to be charged for tap water with your meal if you do not order any other beverage. You'll often save money by paying with cash; many Danish restaurants charge a fee for credit-card transactions.

In the Center

Det Lille Apotek (literally, "The Little Pharmacy") is a reasonable, candlelit place. It's been popular with locals for 200 years, and now it's also quite touristy. Their specialty is "Stone Beef," a big slab of tender, raw steak plopped down in front of you on a scalding-hot soapstone. Cut it into smaller pieces and it's cooked within minutes (sandwich lunches, traditional dinners for 120–190 kr nightly from 17:30, just off Strøget, between Frue Church and Round Tower at St. Kannikestræde 15, tel. 33 12 56 06).

Riz-Raz Vegetarian Buffet has two locations in Copenhagen: around the corner from the canal boat rides at Kompagnistræde 20 (tel. 33 15 05 75) and across from Det Lille Apotek at Store Kannikestræde 19 (tel. 33 32 33 45). At both places, you'll find a healthy all-you-can-eat Mediterranean/vegetarian buffet lunch for 59 kr (daily 11:30–16:00) and an even bigger dinner buffet for 69 kr (16:00–24:00). The dinner buffet has to be the best deal in town. The buffet is wonderfully varied and very filling, but they also offer à la carte and meat options for 100–190 kr.

Café Norden, smoky and very Danish with fine pastries, overlooks Amagertorv by the swan fountain. They have good light meals and salads, and great people-watching from window seats on the second floor—order at the bar upstairs (lunch for about 100 kr and 40–50 kr desserts, Østergade 61).

Kobenhavner Cafeen, cozy yet classy, dishes up traditional food at a reasonable price. Their lunch specials are served until 17:00, when the more expensive dinner menu kicks in (daily until 22:00, 2 blocks off Nytorv at Badstuestræde 10, tel. 33 32 80 81).

Bryggeriet Apollo, just outside the main entrance to Tivoli, offers pub atmosphere Danish-style. Beer is brewed on the premises while the kitchen cranks out generous portions of meat-and-potatoes dishes for reasonable prices (80–110-kr lunches and light plates, 150–200-kr dinners, Mon–Sat 11:30–22:00, Sun 15:00–24:00; kitchen closed 14:30–17:00, but beer still served; Vesterbrogade 3, tel. 33 12 33 13). Order a one-liter mug of beer and they take a surprising security deposit.

Gråbrødretorv is perhaps the most popular square in the old center for a meal. It's a food court, especially in good weather. Choose from Greek, Mexican, Danish, or a meal in the old street-car #14.

Department stores serving cheery, reasonable meals in their cafeterias include **Illum** (eat outside at tables along Strøget or head to the elegant glass-domed top floor, Østergade 52) and **Magasin** (Kongens Nytorv 13), which also has a great grocery and deli in the basement.

Gammel Strand, which serves "Danish-inspired French cuisine," is ideal for a dressy splurge in the old center (lunch-100–200 kr, entrées-200–250 kr, three-course meals-350–450 kr, daily 12:00–16:00 & 18:00–22:30 but closes at 22:00 on Sun, reservations wise, across from Canal Tours Copenhagen tour boats at Gammel Strand 42, tel. 33 91 21 21). Outdoor tables enjoy a view of the canal and people strolling by. Indoor tables are white-table-cloth elegant.

In Christianshavn

This neighborhood is so cool, it's worth combining an evening wander with dinner, even if you're not staying here. It's a 10-minute walk across the bridge from the old center, or a three-minute ride on the Metro. Choose one of my listings (for locations, see map on page 85), or simply wander the blocks between Christianshavntorv, the main square, and the Christianshavn Canal—you'll find a number of lively neighborhood pubs and cafés.

Ravelin Restaurant, on a tiny island on the big road 100 yards south of Christianshavn, serves good, traditional Danish food at reasonable prices to happy local crowds. Dine indoors or on the lovely lakeside terrace (smørrebrød-50–80 kr, other lunch dishes-80–100 kr, dinners-140–170 kr, April–mid-Sept daily 11:30–22:00, closed off-season, Torvegade 79, tel. 32 96 20 45).

Bastionen & Løven, at the little windmill (Lille Mølle), serves gourmet Danish: nouveau cuisine from a small but fresh menu, on a Renoir terrace or in its Rembrandt interior. The inside feels like a colonial mansion (65–100-kr lunches, 145–190-kr dinners, three-course meal for 315 kr, daily 10:00–24:00, 150-kr brunch offered Sat–Sun 10:00–14:00, Christianshavn Voldgade 50, walk to end of Torvegade and follow ramparts up to restaurant, at south end of Christianshavn, tel. 32 95 09 40 for reservations indoors).

Færge Cafeen, overlooking a canal, has a cozy and bright interior and canalside outdoor tables. Dine outside and watch the masts sway in the breeze (40–70-kr smørrebrød, 140–170-kr dinners, a traditional Danish plate each night for about 100 kr, Mon–Sat 12:00–22:00, Sun 12:00–16:00, Strandgade 50, tel. 32 54 46 24).

Lagkagehuset, with a big selection of pastries, sandwiches, and excellent fresh-baked bread, is a great place for breakfast (take-out coffee and pastries for 20 kr, Torvegade 45). **Spicy Kitchen** serves cheap and good Indian food (Torvegade 56).

Spiseloppen ("The Flea Eats") is a wonderfully classy place in Christiania. It serves great 140-kr vegetarian meals and 160–220-kr meaty ones by candlelight. It's gourmet anarchy—a good fit for Christiania, the free city/squatter town (Tue–Sun 17:00–22:00, closed Mon, live music Fri and Sat, reservations often necessary on weekends; 3 blocks behind spiral spire of Our Savior's Church, on top floor of old brick warehouse, turn right just inside Christiania's gate, enter the wildly empty warehouse, and climb the graffiti-riddled stairs; tel. 32 57 95 58). Other, less-expensive Christiania eateries are listed on page 78.

Near Nørreport

These places, near the recommended Ibsens and Jørgensens hotels, are all close enough to survey before making a choice.

Café Klimt, which draws a young, hip, but sometimes heavy-smoking crowd, offers omelets, sandwiches, and modern world cuisine (60–150 kr, daily 10:00–24:00, later Fri–Sat, Frederikborggade 29, tel. 33 11 76 70).

Café Marius, with a jazzy elegance, dressy indoor tables, and casual sidewalk seating, is popular for its homemade pasta, hearty burgers, and big salads. Marius is from Chicago, so don't expect traditional Danish here (100–180-kr plates, brunch served daily with American-style pancakes, daily 12:00–23:00, Nørre Farimagsgade 55, tel. 33 11 83 83).

TRANSPORTATION CONNECTIONS

Malmö, Sweden—just a half-hour train trip across the Øresund Bridge from Copenhagen (3/hr)—has become the regional hub for international trains. To reach destinations from Copenhagen such as Stockholm or Berlin, you'll usually have to transfer at the Malmö Central Station; be sure to get off the train at Malmö C (for "Central"). If you get off at Malmö Syd, you'll miss your connection.

From Copenhagen by Train to: Hillerød/Frederiksborg (6/hr, 45 min on S-tog), **Roskilde** (1–3/hr, 30 min), **Humlebæk** (Louisiana modern-art museum; 3/hr, 40 min), **Helsingør** (3/hr, 50 min), **Odense** (2/hr, 1.5–2 hrs), **Ærøskøbing** (5–6/day, 2.75 hrs to Svendborg with a transfer in Odense, then 75-min ferry crossing to Ærøskøbing, see page 119 for info on ferry), **Billund/Legoland** (1–2/hr, train to Vejle, transfer to bus #244, allow 3.5 hrs total), **Århus** (1–2/hr, 3 hrs), **Stockholm** (almost hourly, 5.5 hrs on X2000 high-speed train, most with a transfer at Malmö Central Station, reservation required; see below for night-train option), **Växjö** (5/day, 3 hrs), **Kalmar** (5/day, 4 hrs), **Oslo** (2/day, 8.5 hrs, usually with transfer at Göteborg; see below for night-train option), **Berlin** (4/day, 7–9 hrs, transfer in Hamburg and sometimes Fredericia as well; plus 1 direct night train from Malmö Central, 20:56–6:01), **Amsterdam** (3/day, 11–12 hrs with 2–4 changes, plus 1 night train with change in Duisburg at 6:00), and **Frankfurt/Rhine** (5/day, 8–10 hrs with 1–3 changes, plus 1 direct night train). National train info tel. 70 13 14 15. International train info tel. 70 13 14 16. Cheaper bus trips are listed at Use It (see page 49).

By Night Train to Stockholm and Oslo: There are no direct night trains from Copenhagen to Oslo or Stockholm. However, you can connect to these cities via Malmö, across the Øresund Bridge in Sweden. First take a 30-minute regional train from Copenhagen to **Malmö Central Station**, then transfer to the night train bound for **Stockholm** (22:36–5:55) or **Oslo** (20:36–10:45, may not run in winter). Always confirm schedules locally.

By Bus: Taking the bus to **Stockholm** is cheaper, but more time-consuming, than taking the train (2/day, 9–16 hrs, plus overnight option, www.swebusexpress.se).

Overnight Cruise to Oslo

Luxurious DFDS Seaways cruise ships leave nightly from Copenhagen for Oslo, and from Oslo for Copenhagen. The 16-hour sailings leave at 17:00 and arrive around 9:30 the next day. So you can spend seven hours in Norway's capital and then return to Copenhagen, or take this cruise from Oslo and do Copenhagen as a day trip...or just go one-way in either direction (see page 187 for info on departing from Oslo).

Cabins vary dramatically in price depending on the day and season (most expensive on weekends and late June–mid Aug; cheapest on weekdays and Oct–April). For example, a bed in a two- to four-berth "economy" cabin below the car deck starts at $99 one-way; a two-berth "standard" cabin higher on the ship starts at $149 per person one-way. All cabins have private bathrooms inside.

DFDS Seaways operates two ships on this route—the M.S. *Pearl of Scandinavia* and the M.S. *Crown of Scandinavia*. Both offer all the cruise-ship luxuries: big buffets for breakfast and dinner (at an additional cost), a kids' playroom, pool (indoor on the *Crown*, indoor and outdoor on the *Pearl*), sauna, nightclub, and tax-free shopping (Danish office open Mon–Fri 8:30–17:00, Sat–Sun 9:00–17:00, tel. 33 42 30 00, www.dfdsseaways.com; US tel. 800-533-3755, www.seaeurope.com).

In Copenhagen, the terminal is a short walk north of *The Little*

Mermaid. The terminal is open daily 9:00–17:00 (luggage lockers available). The cruise line operates a shuttle bus, marked *#20E*, from Kongens Nytorv (free for cruise passengers, coordinated with sailing schedule; daily 14:00–16:00, departs every 10–30 min, arrives at the terminal 11 min later). Or take the S-tog from downtown in the direction of Hellerup or Hillerød to the Nordhavn station. Exit the station and cross under the tracks toward the water. Follow the *til Marmokai* signs.

NEAR COPENHAGEN

*Roskilde, Frederiksborg Castle, Karen Blixen Museum,
Louisiana, and Kronborg Castle*

Copenhagen's the star, but there are several worthwhile sights nearby, and the public transportation system makes side-tripping a joy. Visit Roskilde's great Viking ships and royal cathedral. Tour Frederiksborg, Denmark's most spectacular castle, and slide along the cutting edge at Louisiana—a superb art museum with a coastal setting as striking as its art. Blixen fans can get *Out of Africa* at the author's home. At Helsingør, do the dungeons of Kronborg Castle before heading on to Sweden.

Planning Your Time

Roskilde's Viking ships and the Frederiksborg Castle are the area's essential sights. Each one takes a half day, and each one is an easy commute from Copenhagen (30–45-min train ride, then 20-min walk). You'll find fewer tour-bus crowds in the afternoon. While you're in Roskilde, you can also pay your respects to the tombs of the Danish royalty.

If you're choosing between castles, Frederiksborg is the beautiful showpiece, and Kronborg—darker and danker—is more typical of the way most castles really were.

Louisiana is the obvious choice for art-lovers; the Karen Blixen Museum is for her admirers.

By car, you can see these sights on your way into or out of Copenhagen. By train, do day trips from Copenhagen, then sleep to and from Copenhagen while traveling to Oslo (by train or boat) or Stockholm (by train). Consider getting a Copenhagen Card (see page 49), which covers your transportation and admission to (or discounts on) many major sights.

Near Copenhagen

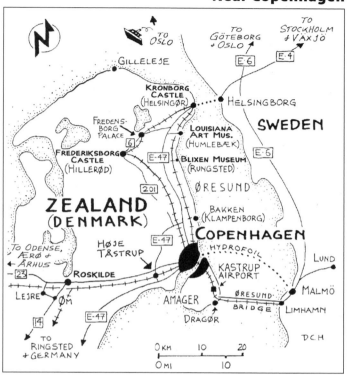

Roskilde

Denmark's roots, both Viking and royal, are on display in Roskilde, a pleasant town 18 miles west of Copenhagen. Eight hundred years ago, Roskilde was the seat of Denmark's royalty—its center of power. Today the town that introduced Christianity to Denmark in A.D. 980 is most famous for hosting northern Europe's biggest annual rock/jazz/folk festival (July 5–8 in 2007, www.roskilde -festival.dk). Wednesday and Saturday are flower/flea/produce market days (8:00–14:00).

Getting There: Roskilde is an easy side-trip from Copenhagen by train (1–3/hr, 30 min).

Tourist Information: Roskilde's TI is helpful (Mon–Thu 9:00–17:00, Fri 9:00–16:00, Sat 10:00–13:00, open 1 hr later late June–Aug, closed Sun, 3 blocks from cathedral, follow signs to *Turistbureau*, tel. 46 31 65 65).

▲▲**Roskilde Cathedral**—Roskilde's imposing 12th-century, twin-spired cathedral houses the tombs of 38 Danish kings and queens (pick up a map as you enter). It's a stately, modern-looking old church with great marblework, paintings (notice the impressive 3-D painting with Christian IV looking like a pirate, in the room behind the small pipe organ), wood carvings in and around the altar, a great 16th-century Baroque organ, and a silly little glockenspiel that plays high above the entrance at the top of every hour (25 kr, good 25-kr guidebook; free tours Mon–Fri at 11:00 at 14:00, Sat at 11:00, and Sun at 14:00; open April–Sept Mon–Fri 9:00–16:45, Sat 9:00–12:00, Sun 13:00–16:45; Oct–March Tue–Sat 10:00–15:45, Sun 12:30–15:45, closed Mon; occasionally closes during the day for baptisms and weddings, tel. 46 31 65 65). From the cathedral, it's a pleasant walk through a park down to the harbor and Viking ships.

▲▲▲**Viking Ship Museum (Vikingeskibshallen)**—*Vik* literally means "shallow inlet," so "Vikings" are people who lived along those inlets. Roskilde—and this award-winning museum—are strategically located along one such inlet. The collection displays five different Viking ships. One boat is like the one Leif Eriksson took to America 1,000 years ago. Another is like those depicted in the Bayeux Tapestry in Normandy, France. These ships were deliberately sunk a thousand years ago to block a nearby harbor and were only recently excavated, preserved, and pieced together. The ships aren't as intact or as ornate as those in Oslo (see page 167), but this museum does a better job of explaining shipbuilding. The English descriptions are excellent—it's the kind of museum where you want to read everything. As you enter, buy the 20-kr guidebook and request the 22-minute English-language movie introduction (80-kr entry, cheaper off-season, daily 10:00–17:00, from station catch bus #607 toward Boserup, 2/hr, 7-min ride, tel. 46 30 02 00, www.vikingeskibsmuseet.dk).

The museum's archaeological workshop lets visitors observe the completed reproduction of a 100-foot-long, eight-man long boat built using ancient techniques (daily 10:00–15:00). They plan to practice sailing it for two years, relearning the techniques. And, in 2007, they'll reconquer Ireland.

Frederiksborg Castle

Frederiksborg Castle, rated ▲▲, is located in the cute town of Hillerød. This grandest castle in Scandinavia is often called the "Danish Versailles." Built from 1602 to 1620, Frederiksborg is the castle of Denmark's King Christian IV. Much of it was reconstructed after an 1859 fire, with the normal Victorian over-the-top flair, by the brewer J. C. Jacobsen and his Carlsberg Foundation.

A museum since 1878, today's castle takes you on a chronological walk through the story of Denmark from 1500 until today
(the third floor covers modern times). Many rooms have a handy
English-language information sheet. The countless musty paintings are a fascinating scrapbook of Danish history.

The traffic-free center of Hillerød is also worth a wander (just
outside the gates of the castle, past the TI).

Getting There: To reach the castle from Copenhagen, take
the S-tog to Hillerød (6/hr, 45 min) and enjoy a pleasant 20-
minute walk or catch bus #701 or #702 (free with S-tog ticket or
Copenhagen Card) from the train station. Drivers will find easy
parking at the castle.

Tourist Information: Pick up a city map and brochures
about the area at Hillerød's TI (Mon–Wed 10:30–16:30, Thu–Fri
10:30–16:30, closed Sat–Sun; inside the library at Christiansgade 1,
tel. 48 24 26 26, www.hillerodturist.dk, turistbureau@c4.dk).

Cost, Hours, Information: Castle entry costs 60 kr. It's open
daily April–Oct 10:00–17:00, Nov–March 11:00–15:00, tel. 48 26
04 39, www.frederiksborgmuseet.dk.

 Self-Guided Tour: From the entrance of the castle complex, it's an appropriately regal approach to the king's residence.
You can almost hear the clopping of royal hooves as you walk over
the moat and through the first island (which housed the stables
and small businesses needed to support a royal residence). Then
walk down the winding (and therefore easy-to-defend) lane to the
second island, which was home to the domestic and foreign ministries. Finally, cross over the last moat to the main palace, where
the king lived.

Main Courtyard: Survey the castle exterior from the Fountain
of Neptune in the main courtyard. Christian IV imported Dutch
architects to create this "Christian IV style," which you'll see all
over Copenhagen. The brickwork and sandstone are products of
the local clay and sandy soil. The building, with its horizontal
lines, triangles, and squares, is generally in Renaissance style, but
notice how this is interrupted by a few token Gothic elements
on the church's facade. Some say this homey touch was to let the
villagers know the king was "one of them."

Royal Chapel: Christian IV wanted to have the grandest royal chapel in Europe. For 200 years the coronation place
of Danish kings, this chapel is still used for royal weddings
(and extremely popular for commoner weddings—book long in
advance). The chapel is nearly all original, dating back to 1620.
As you walk around the upper level, notice the graffiti scratched
on the windows by the diamond rings of royal kids visiting for
the summer back in the 1600s. Most of the coats of arms show off

noble lineage (Eisenhower's, past the organ, is an exception). The organ is from 1620 with the original hand-powered bellows. (If you like music, listen for hymns on the old carillon at the top of each hour.) Leaving the chapel, you step into the king's oratory, with evocative romantic paintings (restored after a fire) from the mid-19th century.

Audience Room: Here, where formal meetings took place, a grand painting shows the king as a Roman emperor firmly in command (with his two sons prominent for extra political stability). Christian's military victories line the walls, and the four great continents—Europe, North America, Asia, and Africa—circle the false cupola.

Dutch Reformation: In Room 26, note the effort noble families put into legitimizing themselves with family trees and family seals. Over the door to the next room is the image of a monk invited by the king to preach the new thinking of the Reformation. In the case is the first Bible translated into Danish (from 1550—access to the word of God was a big part of the Reformation).

Time for Lunch: You can picnic in the castle's moat park or enjoy the elegant **Spisestedet Leonora** at the moat's edge (50–90-kr *smørrebrød* and sandwiches, 70-kr salads, 90–150-kr hot dishes, daily 10:00–17:00, slow service, tel. 48 26 75 16).

Louisiana

This is Scandinavia's most-raved-about modern-art museum. Located in the town of Humlebæk, beautifully situated on the coast 18 miles north of Copenhagen, Louisiana is a holistic place that masterfully mixes its art, architecture, and landscape. Wander from famous Chagalls and Picassos to more obscure art. Poets spend days here nourishing their creative souls with new angles, ideas, and perspectives.

Frequent special exhibitions offer visitors an extra treat (visit www .louisiana.dk for the latest). The views over the Øresund, one of the busiest passages in the nautical world, are nearly as inspiring as the art. The cafeteria, with indoor and outdoor seating, is reasonable and welcomes picnickers who buy a drink.

Cost and Hours: 80-kr museum admission, discount with Copenhagen Card, included in a special 140-kr round-trip tour ticket from Copenhagen—ask at any train station, daily 10:00–17:00, Wed until 22:00, tel. 49 19 07 91.

Getting There: Take the train from Copenhagen toward Helsingør, get off at Humlebæk (3/hr, 40 min), and follow the signs to Louisiana along a busy road about 15 minutes. Or walk 10 minutes through the woods: Exit the station and immediately go left onto Hejreskor Allé, a residential street, and then along a path through the trees. After you exit the trail, the museum is across the street. If you're coming from Frederiksborg Castle, catch the Lille Nord train at Hillerød station toward Helsingør. Change trains at Snekkersten or Helsingør, and go south to reach Humlebæk.

Karen Blixen Museum

Danish writer Karen Blixen, a.k.a. Isak Dinesen of *Out of Africa* fame, lived most of her life in Rungstedlund, her family house in Rungsted, on the Øresund coast. The house, one of the area's finest mansions, is now a museum about her life and writing. For fans of Blixen's works, the house is a ▲▲ sight, though Blixen's dramatic life story and the house's beautiful setting are enough to make a visit enjoyable even for anyone who's never heard of *Out of Africa*.

Unlike many houses-turned-museums that file you past roped-off doorways, you'll don slippers to pad through the house, mostly unchanged from the time of Blixen's life. Over headphones, listen to Blixen read selections from her own stories as you look out at the same views she enjoyed. She wrote her best-known books (including *Babette's Feast*) in this house, surrounded by mementos of her 17 years in Kenya. Her simple grave is a short walk away through the mansion's backyard gardens.

Cost and Hours: 40 kr, May–Sept Tue–Sun 10:00–17:00, closed Mon; Oct–April Wed–Fri 13:00–16:00, Sat–Sun 11:00–16:00, closed Mon–Tue; tel. 45 57 10 57, www.karen-blixen.dk.

Getting There: From Copenhagen, take the train 30 minutes to Rungsted Kyst (3/hr). From the station, take bus #388, or simply walk (15–20 min, follow signs to the house). Rungsted is a short hop away from Humlebæk (7 min by train) and Helsingør (18 min).

Kronborg Castle

Kronborg Castle is located in Helsingør, a small, pleasant little Danish town that's often confused with its Swedish sister, Helsingborg, just two miles across the channel. Helsingør has a TI (tel. 49 21 13 33), a medieval center, Kronborg Castle, and lots of Swedes who come over for the lower-priced alcohol.

Kronborg Castle (also called Elsinore) is a ▲▲ sight famous for its questionable (but profitable) ties to Shakespeare. Most of

Øresund Region

When the Øresund (UH-ra-soond) Bridge, which connects Denmark and Sweden, opened in July 2000, it created Europe's most dynamic new metropolitan area. The link forged an economic power with the 12th-largest gross domestic product in Europe, almost overnight. The Øresund region has surpassed Stockholm as the largest metro area in Scandinavia. Now 3.5 million Danes and Swedes—a highly trained and highly technical workforce—are within a quick commute of each other.

The bridge opens up new questions of borders. Historically, southern Sweden (the area across from Copenhagen, called Skåne) had Danish blood. It was Danish for a thousand years before Sweden took it in 1658. Notice how Copenhagen is the capital on the fringe of its realm—at one time it was in the center.

The 10-mile-long link, which has a motorway for cars (225-kr toll) and a two-track train line, ties together the main islands of Denmark with Europe and Sweden. The $4 billion project consists of a 2.5-mile-long tunnel, an artificial island called Peberholm, and a five-mile-long bridge. With speedy connecting trains, Malmö in Sweden is now an easy half-day side-trip from Copenhagen (72 kr each way, 3/hr, 35 min). The train drops you at the station right in the center of Malmö, and all the important sights are within a short walk. The *Malmö This Week* publication (free from Copenhagen TI) has everything you need for a well-organized visit.

the "Hamlet" castle you'll see today, darling of every big bus tour and travelogue, was built long after the historical Hamlet died (more than a thousand years ago), and Shakespeare never saw the place. But this Renaissance castle existed when a troupe of English actors performed here in Shakespeare's time (Shakespeare may have known them). To see or not to see? It's most impressive from the outside.

If you're heading to Sweden, Kalmar Castle (see the South Sweden chapter) is a better medieval castle. But you're here, and if you like castles, see Kronborg. Duck into the creepy casements under the castle, where the servants and guards lived.

The royal apartments include English explanations (75 kr; May–Sept daily 10:30–17:00; April and Oct Tue–Sun 11:00–16:00, closed Mon; Nov–March Tue–Sun 11:00–15:00, closed Mon; tel. 49 21 30 78 for recorded info, or tel. 49 21 80 88, www.kronborgcastle .com). Take a free tour of the casements (daily at 12:30 and 13:30), or use the helpful 2-kr guide. If you're particularly fascinated, go for the more extensive 40-kr guide available at the ticket counter.

In the basement, notice the statue of Holger Danske, a mythical Viking hero revered by Danish children. The story goes that if the nation is ever in danger, this Danish superman will awaken and restore peace and security to the land.

The free grounds between the walls and sea are great for picnics, with a pleasant view of the strait between Denmark and Sweden.

Getting There: Helsingør is a 50-minute train ride from Copenhagen (3/hr). Exit the station at track 3, then look for the sign for the TI, where you can pick up a free map or use the WC. The castle is a 10-minute walk around the harbor.

TRANSPORTATION CONNECTIONS

Route Tips for Drivers

Copenhagen to Hillerød (45 min) **to Helsingør** (30 min) **to Kalmar** (6 hrs): Just follow the town-name signs. Leave Copenhagen, following signs for E-4 and Helsingør. The freeway is great. *Hillerød* signs lead to the Frederiksborg Castle (not to be confused with the nearby Fredensborg Palace) in the pleasant town of Hillerød. Follow signs to *Hillerød C* (for "center"), then *slot* (for "castle"). Though the E-4 freeway is the fastest, the Strandvejen coastal road (152) is pleasant, passing some of Denmark's grandest mansions (including that of Karen Blixen—see page 101.)

The 10-mile Øresund Bridge linking Denmark with Sweden (235-kr toll) lets drivers and train travelers skip nonstop from one country to the next.

If you're nostalgic for the pre-bridge days, the Helsingør–Helsingborg ferry still putters across the Øresund Channel twice hourly (follow the signs to Helsingborg, Sweden—freeway leads to dock). Buy your ticket as you roll on board (235–255 kr one-way for car, driver, and up to nine passengers; round-trip gives you the return at less than half price). Reservations are free but not usually necessary, as ferries depart every 20 minutes (tel. 33 15 15 15, or book online at www.scandlines.dk; also see www.hhferries .se). If you arrive early, you can probably drive onto any ferry. The 20-minute Helsingør–Helsingborg ferry ride gives you just enough time to enjoy the view of the Kronborg "Hamlet" castle, be impressed by the narrowness of this very strategic channel, and exchange any leftover Danish kroner into Swedish kronor (the ferry exchange desk's rate is decent).

In Helsingborg, follow signs for E-4 and Stockholm. The road is good, traffic is light, and towns are all clearly signposted. At Ljungby, road 25 takes you to Växjö and Kalmar. Entering Växjö, skip the first Växjö exit and follow the freeway into *Centrum*, where it ends. It takes about four hours to drive from Copenhagen to Kalmar.

CENTRAL DENMARK

Ærø and Odense

The sleepy isle of Ærø is the cuddle after the climax. It's the perfect time-passed world in which to wind down, enjoy the seagulls, and take a day off. Get Ærø-dynamic and pedal a rented bike into the essence of Denmark. Have lunch in a traditional *kro* (country inn). Settle into a cobbled world of sailors, who, after the invention of steam-driven boat propellers, decided that building ships in bottles was more their style.

Between Ærø and Copenhagen, drop by bustling Odense, home of Hans Christian Andersen and a fine open-air folk museum.

Planning Your Time

Odense is a transportation hub, the center of the island of Funen. It's an easy stop, worth a few hours on the way to or from Ærø. More out of the way, Ærø is worth the journey. Once there, you will want two nights and a day to properly enjoy it.

Ærø

This small (22 by 6 miles) island on the south edge of Denmark is as salty and sleepy as can be. A typical tombstone reads: "Here lies Christian Hansen at anchor with his wife. He'll not weigh until he stands before God." It's the kind of island where baskets of strawberries sit in front of houses—for sale on the honor system.

Ærø statistics: 7,000 residents, 500,000 visitors, and 80,000 boaters annually, 350 deer, seven priests, no crosswalks, and three police officers. The three big industries are farming, shipping, and

Central Denmark

tourism—in that order. Twenty percent of the Danish fleet still resides on Ærø, in the town of Marstal. But jobs are scarce, the population is slowly dropping, and family farms are consolidating into larger units. Ærø, home to several windmills and one of the world's largest solar power plants, is going "green." Soon it's likely all local energy will be wind and solar, and all the produce will be organically grown.

Because Ærø is only nine miles across the water from Germany, you'll see plenty of Germans who return regularly to this peaceful retreat.

Ærøskøbing

Ærøskøbing is Ærø's town in a bottle. The government, recognizing the value of this amazingly preserved little town, prohibits modern building anywhere in the center. It's the only town in Denmark protected in this way. Drop into the 1680s, when Ærøskøbing was the wealthy home port of a hundred windjammers. The many Danes and Germans who come here for the tranquility—washing up the cobbled main drag in waves with the landing of each boat—call it the fairy-tale town. The Danish word for "cozy" *(hyggelig)* describes Ærøskøbing well.

Ærøskøbing is simply a pleasant place to wander. Stubby little porthole-type houses, with their birth dates displayed in proud decorative rebar, lean on each other like drunk, sleeping sailors. Wander under flickering old-time lamps. Snoop around town. It's OK. Peek into living rooms (if people want privacy, they shut their drapes). Notice the many "snooping mirrors" on the houses.  Antique locals are following your every move. The harbor now caters to holiday yachts, and on midnight low tides you can almost hear the crabs playing cards.

The town economy, once rich with the windjammer trade, hit the rocks in modern times. Kids 15 to 18 years old go to a boarding school in Svendborg; many don't return. It's an interesting discussion: Should the island folk pickle their culture in tourism or forget about the cuteness and get modern?

ORIENTATION

Ærøskøbing is tiny. Everything's just a few cobbles from the ferry landing.

Tourist Information: The TI faces the ferry landing (late-June–mid-Aug Mon–Sat 10:00–15:30, Sun 10:00–15:00; mid-Aug–mid-Sept Mon–Wed and Fri–Sat 10:00–15:30, Sun 10:00–15:00, closed Thu; mid-Sept–late-June Mon–Wed and Fri–Sat 10:00–13:00, closed Thu and Sun, tel. 62 52 13 00, fax 62 52 14 36, www.arre.tse.dk). They have Internet access, give out brochures about the various sights and activities in the area, and can help you find a room if the listings below are booked (25-kr fee).

Helpful Hints

Money: The town has two cash machines (at the top of Vestergade and on Torvet Square).

Internet Access: Try the TI or the library on Torvet Square.

Laundry: A self-service launderette is on Gyden, between Vestergade and Brogade (daily 7:30–21:00). Instructions are posted in English and soap is available. To pay, you'll need one 50-kr note, one 5-kr coin, and three 2-kr coins. Beware: You can get locked inside if you don't leave before the doors automatically lock at 21:00.

Ferries: Drivers should call well in advance—especially in summer—to reserve a spot on the Svendborg/Ærø ferry (free and easy, just give name and license-plate number, Mon–Fri 8:00–16:00, Sat–Sun 9:00–15:00, tel. 62 52 40 00, fax 62 52 20 88, booking also possible online at www.aeroe-ferry.dk, info@aeroe-ferry.dk). If you haven't booked ahead, try parking your car overnight in the "ticketless" lane; up to four spots are opened up on a first-come, first-served basis in the morning (if they aren't needed for ambulance service). For more on the ferry, see "Transportation Connections," page 116.

Bike Rental: Rent a bike from the **Energi Station** at the top of town on Pilebækken (45 kr for three-speed bikes, 25 kr for worthwhile *cykel* map; Mon–Fri 9:00–17:00, Sat 9:00–13:00, closed Sun except in July—when it's open 10:00–13:00; go through green door at Sondergade end of Torvet Square, past garden to next road, Pilebækken 7; tel. 62 52 11 10). **Hotel Ærøhus** rents seven-speed bikes (75 kr, daily from 8:00). The hostel and the campground also rent bikes (longer hours, see "Sleeping," page 113, for contact information). There are no deposits and few locks on Ærø.

Rainy-Day Activities: The cute little 30-seat theater near Torvet Square plays movies in their original language nightly (new titles begin every Mon). The best antiques shopping is at Vestergade 60 (its rejects fill the nearby alley and courtyard, both open June–Sept only). Or hit the bowling alley (hot dogs and cheese sandwiches, arcade games, usually open late).

SELF-GUIDED WALK

Welcome to Ærøskøbing

Ideally, take this ▲▲▲ stroll with the sun low, the shadows long, and the colors rich. From the harbor and TI, walk up the main street a block and go left on **Smedegade** (the poorest street in town, with the most architectural charm). Have a close look at the "street spies" on the houses—clever mirrors letting old women inside keep an eye on what's going on outside. The ship-in-a-bottle **Bottle Peter**

Museum is on the right. Notice the gutters—some protect only the doorway. Appreciate the finely carved old doors. Number 37, from the 18th century, is Ærøskøbing's cutest house. Its tiny dormer is from some old ship's poop deck.

Ærøskøbing

1 Hotel/Rest. Ærøhus
2 Pension Vestergade
3 Toldbodhus B&B
4 Det Lille Hotel/Rest.
5 Café Aroma
6 Ærøskøbing Røgeri Smoked Fish
7 Vaffelbageriet Ice Cream
8 Hos Grethe Restaurant
9 Restaurant Mumm
10 Landbogaarden Pub

11 Arrebo Pub
12 Bakery
13 Netto Supermarket
14 Spar Market
15 Ærø Museum
16 Bottle Peter Museum
17 Hammerich House Museum
18 Movie Theater
19 Bike Rental
20 Launderette

Smedegade ends at the Folkehøjskole (folks' high school). Inspired by the Danish philosopher, Nikolaj Gruntvig—who wanted people to be able to say "I am good at being me"—it offers people of any age the benefit of government-subsidized cultural education (music, art, theater, and so on).

Jog left and stroll along the peaceful harborside **Molestien Lane,** lined with gardens, a quiet beach, and a row of small-is-beautiful houses—beginning with humble and progressing to captain's class. Each garden is cleverly and lovingly designed.

Nicknamed "Virgin's Lane," this was where kids could court within view of their parents.

The dreamy-looking **island** immediately across the way is a nature preserve and a resting spot for birds making their long journey from the north to the Mediterranean. In the winter, when the water freezes, locals slip and slide over for a visit.

From the end of the lane, a trail leads farther along the water to a place the town provides for fishermen to pull out their boats and tidy up their nets.

Molestien Lane leads around to the right (past the modern firehouse) to **Østergade,** Ærøskøbing's east gate. In the days of German control, all island trade was legal only within the town. All who passed this point would pay various duties and taxes at a tollbooth that once stood here.

Look through windows to see the sea. Peek into living rooms. Catch snatches of Danish life. Ponder the beauty of a society with such a keen sense of civic responsibility that fishing permits commit you "to catch only what you need."

At the first square, stay left on Sondergade. Wrought-iron anchors were added to hold together bulging houses. Ærøskøbing's **oldest houses**—the only ones that survived a fire from a Swedish war—are #36 and #32. Notice the dates and the hatches upstairs where masts and sails were stored for the winter. The red on #32's door is the original paint job—ox blood, which, when combined with the tannin in the wood, really lasts. It never rots.

The **courtyard** behind #18 was a parking lot in pre-car days. Farmers, in town for their shopping chores, would leave their

horses here. Even today, the wide-open fields are just beyond.

Wander down to Torvet, Ærøskøbing's **main square.** Notice the two pumps. Until 1951, townspeople came here for their water. The linden tree is the town symbol. The rocks around it celebrate the reunion of a big chunk of southern Denmark, which was ruled by Germany from 1864 to 1920. See the town seal featuring a linden tree, over the door of the old City Hall (now the library). Read the Danish on the wall: "With law shall man a country build."

SIGHTS AND ACTIVITIES

▲**Ærø Museum**—This museum presents the island's local history, from seafaring to farming. Explore the collection, featuring 19th-century outfits, household objects, and an actual old-time pharmacy. A fun diorama shows an aerial view of Ærøskøbing in 1862—notice the big gardens behind nearly every house. This museum carries on the tradition with its own garden out back. Pick up an English-language flier near the entrance (25 kr, 50-kr combo-ticket with Bottle Peter Museum and Hammerich House, guided tours in July—inquire for details; mid-April–Oct Mon–Fri 10:00–16:00, Sat–Sun 11:00–15:00; Nov–mid-April Mon–Fri 10:00–13:00, closed Sat–Sun, tel. 62 52 29 50).

▲**Bottle Peter Museum**—This fascinating house has 750 different bottled ships. Old Peter Jacobsen, who made his first bottle at 16 and his last at 85, bragged that he drank the contents of each bottle, except those containing milk. He died in 1960 (and is most likely buried in a glass bottle), leaving a lifetime of tedious little creations for visitors to squint and marvel at (25 kr, 50-kr combo-ticket with Ærø Museum and Hammerich House, guided tours in July—inquire at Ærø Museum; mid-June–mid-Aug daily 10:00–17:00; April–mid-June and mid-Aug–mid-Oct daily 10:00–16:00; mid-Oct–March Tue–Fri 13:00–15:00, Sat–Sun 10:00–12:00, closed Mon; Smedegade 22, tel. 62 52 29 51).

▲**Hammerich House**—These 12 funky rooms in three houses are filled with 200- to 300-year-old junk (25 kr, 50-kr combo-ticket with Ærø Museum and Bottle Peter Museum, mid-June–mid-Sept daily 12:00–16:00, closed off-season, just east of Torvet Square, on Brogade, tel. 62 52 29 50).

▲▲**Beach Bungalow Sunset Stroll**—At sunset, stroll to Ærøskøbing's sand beach. Facing the ferry dock, go left, following the harbor. Upon leaving the town you'll pass a children's playground and see a row of tiny, Monopoly-like huts past the wavy wheat field. This is Vestre Strandvejen, facing the sunset. And these tiny huts are beach escapes. Each is different, but all are stained with merry memories of locals enjoying themselves Danish-style. It's a fine walk out to the end of Urehoved, as this spit of land is called.

Ærø Island Bike Ride (or Car Tour)

This 18-mile trip shows you the best of this windmill-covered island's charms. The highest point on the island is only 180 feet above sea level, but the wind can be strong and the hills seem long. This ride is good exercise. Rent a bike in town (see "Helpful Hints," page 107). Be sure to pick up a detailed map of this and other cycling routes when renting your bike (or at the TI).

Leave Ærøskøbing to the west on the road to Vrå (Vråvejen,

Ærø Island Bike Ride

signed *Bike Route 90*). You'll see the first of many **U-shaped farms,** typical of Denmark. The three sides block the wind and store cows, hay, and people. *Gaard* (farm) shows up on many local surnames. At Osemarksvej, bike along the coast in the protection of the dike built in 1856 to make the once-salty swampland to your left farmable. Today, the soil is good for hay and little else. At the T-junction, go right toward Borgnæs. Keep to the right (passing two Vindeballe turnoffs), following signs to Bregninge. After a secluded beach, head inland (to O. Bregninge). Pass the island's only water mill, and climb uphill over the island's 2,700-inch-high summit to Bregninge. The tallest point on Ærø is called Synnes Hoej ("seems high"). Turn right and roll through Denmark's "second-longest village" to the church.

The interior of the 12th-century **Bregninge church** is still painted as a Gothic church would have been. Tradition says that if the painter (his self-portrait is behind the pulpit, right of front pew) wasn't happy with his pay, he'd paint a fool's head in the church. Note the hole for a bell-ringing rope (left above first pew).

The **altarpiece**—gold leaf on carved oak—is from 1528, six years before the Reformation came to Denmark. The cranium carved into the bottom indicates it's a genuine masterpiece by Claus Berg (from Lübeck, Germany). This Crucifixion scene is such a commotion it seems to cause Christ's robe to billow up. Strangely, the three wise men, each a Danish king, made it to this Crucifixion. Notice the escaping souls of the two thieves—the one who converted on the cross being carried happily to heaven, and the other, with its grim-winged escort, heading straight to hell. Since this is a Catholic altarpiece, a roll call of saints lines the wings. During the restoration, the identity of the two women on the lower right was unknown, so the lettering—even in Latin—is clearly gibberish. (Public WC in churchyard.)

Roll back through Bregninge past many more U-shaped *gaards*. About a mile down the main road, in Vindeballe, take the Vodrup Klint turnoff to the right. (The Vindeballe Kro is a traditional inn serving decent food and cold draft beer.)

A road leads downhill (with a jog to the right) to a rugged bluff called **Vodrup Klint.** If I were a pagan, I'd worship here—the sea, the wind, and the chilling view. Notice how the land steps in sloppy slabs down to the sea. When saturated with water, the slabs of clay that make up the land here get slick and entire chunks can slide.

Hike down to the foamy beach (where you can pick up some flint, chalk, and wild thyme). While the wind at the top could drag a kite-flier, the beach below can be ideal for sunbathing. Because Ærø is warmer and drier than the rest of Denmark, this island is home to plants and animals found nowhere else in the country.

Backtrack 200 yards and follow the sign to Tranderup. You'll pass a lovely pond famous for its bell frogs, happy little duck houses, and the Sami-style tepee (a nature camp). Still following signs for Tranderup, stay parallel to the big road through town. You'll pass a lovely farm and a potato stand. At the main road, turn right. At the Ærøskøbing turnoff, just before the tiny little white house, turn left to the big stone (commemorating the return of the island to Denmark from Germany in 1750) and a grand **island panorama.** Seattleites might find Claus Clausen's rock interesting (in the picnic area, next to WC). It's a memorial to an extremely obscure pioneer from the state of Washington.

Return to the big road, pass the little white house, pass through Olde, and head toward Store Rise (REE-zuh), the next church spire in the distance. (Think of medieval travelers using spires as navigational aids.) Thirty yards after the Stokkeby turnoff, follow the rough, tree-lined path on the right to the Langdysse (Long Dolmen) Tingstedet, just behind the church spire. This is a 6,000-year-old dolmen, an **early Neolithic burial place.** Though Ærø once had more than 200 of these prehistoric tombs, only

13 survive. *Ting* means assembly spot. Imagine a thousand years ago: Viking chiefs representing the island's various communities gathering here around their ancestors' tombs. For 6,000 years, this has been a holy spot. (A possible reason: Two underground streams cross here.) The stones were considered fertility stones. For centuries, locals in need of virility ground up bits and took the powder home (the hollows in the rock near the information post are mine).

Bundle up your powder and carry on down the lane to the **Store Rise church.** Inside you'll find little ships hanging in the nave, a fine 12th-century altarpiece, and Martin Luther keeping his Protestant hand on the rudder in the stern. The list in the church allows today's pastor to trace his pastoral lineage back to Doctor Luther himself. The churchyard is circular—echoing the shape of the Viking holy spot, which stood here long before the church. Can you find anyone buried in the graveyard whose name doesn't end in "sen"?

Continue down the main road (direction: Dunkær) with the three, 330-foot-high modern **windmills** on your right. These windmills are communally owned and, as they are a nonpolluting source of energy, state-subsidized. From Dunkær, take the small road, signed *Lille Rise,* past the topless windmill. Except for the Lille Rise, it's all downhill from here, as you coast past great sea views and the hostel back home to Ærøskøbing.

Still rolling? Bike past the campground along the **Urehoved beach** (*strand* in Danish) for a look at the coziest little beach houses you'll never see back in the "big is beautiful" US. This is Europe, where the concept of sustainability is neither new nor subversive.

SLEEPING

In Ærøskøbing

$$$ Hotel Ærøhus is big and sprawling with 33 rooms. Although it is less personal and cozy than some of the other listings here, it's the closest thing to a grand hotel in this capital of quaint (S-450 kr, Sb-770–890 kr, D-650 kr, Db-1,090–1,190 kr, higher prices for rooms with more comforts and/or terrace, extra charge to pay with credit card or for one-night stays, two blocks up from ferry on Vestergade, tel. 62 52 10 03, fax 62 52 21 23, www.aeroehus-hotel .dk, mail@aeroehus.dk). They also rent holiday apartments with kitchenettes at the nearby Hotel Ærø Marina; these can be a good value for families.

$$ Pension Vestergade is your best home away from home in Ærøskøbing. It's lovingly run by Susanna Greve and her daughters, Henrietta and Celia. Susanna is a wealth of knowledge about the town's history and takes good care of her guests. Built in 1784 for

---

Sleep Code

(6 kr = about $1, country code: 45)
S = Single, **D** = Double/Twin, **T** = Triple, **Q** = Quad, **b** = bathroom,
s = shower. You can assume credit cards are accepted and breakfast is included unless otherwise noted.

To help you sort easily through these listings, I've divided the rooms into three categories, based on the price for a standard double room with bath during high season:

$$$ **Higher Priced**—Most rooms 800 kr or more.
$$ **Moderately Priced**—Most rooms between
          400–800 kr.
$ **Lower Priced**—Most rooms 400 kr or less.

---

a sea captain's daughter, this eight-room place—with each room named for its particular color scheme—is on the main street in the town center. Reserve well in advance (S-450 kr, D-730 kr, two-night minimum, cash only, non-smoking, cuddly hot-water bottles, shared bathrooms, Vestergade 44, tel. & fax 62 52 22 98, www.pension-vestergade44.dk, pensionvestergade44@post.tele .dk). Picnic in the back garden and get to know clever dog Hector.

$$ Toldbodhus B&B, once a toll house, now rents four delightful rooms to travelers. Three rooms share two bathrooms in the main house, and a small garden house has a double room with a detached bathroom (includes bathrobes). Karin and John Steenberg named each room after cities they've lived in: Amsterdam, København (Copenhagen), London, and Hong Kong (D-750 kr, cash only, near harbor on corner of Smedegade at Brogade 8, tel. 62 52 18 11, fax 62 52 18 02, www.toldbodhus.com, toldbodhus@mail.dk).

$$ Det Lille Hotel, a former 19th-century captain's home with six tidy rooms, is warm, modern, and shipshape (S-590 kr, D-690 kr, extra bed-265 kr, Smedegade 33, 5970 Ærøskøbing, tel. & fax 62 52 23 00).

Just Outside of Town

Drivers may opt for this countryside B&B, a 10-minute drive or bus ride from Ærøskøbing: **$$ Graasten B&B** is a non-smoking, family-friendly cattle farm 300 yards from the sea run by a British/ Danish couple, Julie and Aksel Hansen (D-480 kr, extra bed-230 kr, under age 7-220 kr, discount for longer stays, kitchenette available, bike rentals arranged for guests, cash only, Østermarksvej 20, short ride on bus #990—direction Marstal, or drive from Ærøskøbing toward Marstal, tel. 62 52 24 25, fax 62 52 13 49, www .graastenfarmb-b.com, greyfarm@adr.dk).

$ **Ærøskøbing Youth Hostel** comes equipped with a fine living room, members' kitchen, and family rooms with two or four beds (dorm bed-122 kr, S-300 kr, D-300 kr, T-360 kr, non-members pay extra 35 kr/night or 160 kr for a 1-year membership, breakfast-50 kr, sheets-50 kr, towels-10 kr, 500 yards out of town at Smedevejen 15, tel. 62 52 10 44, fax 62 52 16 44, www.hihostels .com). The place is packed in July.

The three-star $ **campground,** on a fine beach, offers a lodge with a fireplace, campsites, and cabins (camping-65 kr per person, cabins-125–200 kr plus per-person fee, May–Sept, a short walk from "downtown"—facing the water, follow waterfront to the left, tel. 62 52 18 54, www.aeroecamp.dk).

EATING

Ærøskøbing has a handful of eateries, and each summer a few other burger-joint-type places seem to pop up for a couple of months. Starting at the ferry dock (with your back to the harbor), you'll find a *pølse* stand to the right. Note: Because water is expensive in Denmark, you may be charged for tap water if it's your only beverage. Some restaurants also charge a service fee if you pay with a credit card.

Café Aroma, an inexpensive Danish café, has good, reasonably priced entrées, sandwiches, and burgers for 60–175 kr. Order at the bar (May–Aug daily 12:00–22:00, closed off-season, on Vestergade).

Ærøskøbing Røgeri, facing the harbor, is great for a light meal of smoked fish served with potato salad and bread for about 60 kr. They have picnic tables outside, or take it to go. Find a pleasant picnic site at the beach or at the park located on the street behind the fish house (May–Sept daily 10:00–18:00, later in July, Havnen 15, tel. 62 52 40 07). A smoked fish dinner and a couple of cold Carlsbergs are a well-earned reward after a long bike ride.

The town's two fine-dining options are **Restaurant Mumm** (near Torvet Square, tel. 62 52 12 12) and **Hos Grethe** (across the street from Pension Vestergade). Both have 150–250-kr entrées and reservations are recommended.

Det Lille Hotel serves meals in an inviting dining room or garden (see hotel listing, above; 60–100-kr lunches, 120–250-kr dinners, daily 12:00–21:00, Smedegade 33, tel. 62 52 23 00).

Hotel Ærøhus offers a traditional Danish menu in addition to a summertime grill menu, with seating indoors or on the patio (see listing above; open daily, on Vestergade, tel. 62 52 10 03).

Heading up Vestergade, past the pink and popular **Vaffel-bageriet** (ice-cream–filled homemade waffle cones—try the Ærø Special), you'll find a few summer cafés cooking up burgers or light meals.

For a sweet treat, try the **bakery,** which sells homemade bread, cheese, yogurt, and tasty pastries (Mon and Wed–Fri 7:00–17:00, Sat–Sun 7:00–14:00, closed Tue, top of Vestergade).

Ærøskøbing's two bars are at the top and bottom of Vestergade: **Arrebo Pub** (near the ferry landing, young crowd) and **Landbogaarden** (top of Vestergade, older crowd, sometimes serves food).

Grocery: For picnic fixings plus wine and beer, try the **Spar Market** (Mon–Fri 9:00–18:00, Sat 10:00–13:00, closed Sun, on Torvet Square) or **Netto** (Mon–Fri 9:00–19:00, Sat 8:00–19:00, closed Sun, across street from ferry dock).

TRANSPORTATION CONNECTIONS

Ærøskøbing is accessible by ferry from **Svendborg.** It's a relaxing 75-minute crossing (149 kr round-trip per person, 332 kr round-trip per car—not including driver/passengers, crew collects fares on ferry after departure, you'll save a little money with round-trip tickets, you can leave the island via any of the three different Ærø ferry routes).

Svendborg–Ærø Ferry: Departures from Svendborg are Monday through Saturday at 7:30, 10:30, 13:30, 16:30, 19:30, and 22:30—but no 7:30 departure on Saturday. Departures from Ærøskøbing are daily at 5:55, 8:55, 11:55, 14:55, 17:55, and 20:55—no 5:55 departure on weekend mornings. While walk-ons always get on, cars need reservations (tel. 62 52 40 00 or reserve online at www.aeroe-ferry.dk, info@aeroe-ferry.dk). A ferry/bus combo-ticket gives you the whole island with stopovers (178 kr round-trip, must return within 24 hrs, bus runs throughout island, same contact info as above). If you won't use your car in Ærø, park it in Svendborg (big, safe lot two blocks in from ferry landing). On Ærø, parking is free.

Trains Connecting with Ærø–Svendborg Ferry: Svendborg train arrivals and departures are coordinated with the Ærø ferry schedule. If you're arriving by train in Svendborg (to continue by ferry to Ærø), a ferry will leave five minutes after your train arrives. From Svendborg's train station, it's a short walk to the ferry dock. Head downhill to the harbor and look right for the Ærø sign. When you depart Ærø by ferry and dock at Svendborg, a train will leave for Copenhagen (via Odense) within 15 minutes of your arrival. The Copenhagen–Svendborg trip takes about 2.75 hours.

Buses Connecting with Ærø–Svendborg Ferry: If you're going from Ærø to Copenhagen, a ferry/bus/train combo shaves about 30 minutes off the ferry/train journey covered above. Bus #910, which coordinates with the ferry, runs from Svendborg to the town of Nyborg, which is linked by direct train to Copenhagen. The twice-hourly bus trip takes 45 minutes, arriving and departing Nyborg within 15–20 minutes of the Copenhagen train (2/hr, 1.25 hours). Note that if you have a railpass, or if you're going to Odense or to points west, taking the train from the ferry is a better option.

Bus and Train Schedules: For a complete schedule of buses and trains in Denmark, visit www.rejseplanen.dk.

Odense

Founded in A.D. 988 and named after Odin (the Nordic Zeus), Odense is the birthplace of storyteller Hans Christian Andersen (whom the Danes call simply H. C., pronounced "hoe see"). He is Odense's favorite son—you'll find his name and image all over town, including on some crosswalk signals. He once said, "Perhaps Odense will one day become famous because of me." Today, Odense (OH-then-za) is one of Denmark's most popular tourist destinations. As Denmark's third-largest city, with 186,000 people, it is big and industrial. But its old center retains some of the fairy-tale charm it had in the days of H. C. A.

Tourist Information
The TI is in the Town Hall (Rådhuset), right in the middle of Odense. They can book you a room for a 35-kr fee (mid-June–Aug Mon–Fri 9:30–18:00, Sat–Sun 10:00–15:00; Sept–mid-June Mon–Fri 9:30–16:30, Sat 10:00–13:00, closed Sun; tel. 66 12 75 20, fax 66 12 75 86, www.visitodense.com). From the train station, cross through the Kongens Have (King's Garden) park and head south (away from train station) down Jernabanegade. When you come to Vestergade, take a left and follow this fine pedestrian street 100 yards to the TI (10 min total).

Arrival in Odense
For a quick visit, check your luggage at the train station, pick up a free map inside the ticket office, jot down the time your train departs, and hit the town.

SIGHTS

▲▲**Hans Christian Andersen Hus**—This museum is packed with mementos from the writer's life and hordes of children and tourists. Exhibits in the modern section of the museum include a display on the era in which Andersen lived (1805–1875), a short introductory film about his life (about 10 min, plays continuously), a library of

Andersen's books from around the world (his tales were translated into nearly 150 languages), and headsets and benches throughout for you to listen to a selection of fairy tales. It's fun if you like the man and his tales (55 kr, 20 kr for kids; daily mid-June–mid-Aug 9:00–18:00; off-season Tue–Sun 10:00–16:00, closed Mon; Bangs Boder 29, tel. 65 51 46 01). Because the museum includes good descriptions in English, the guidebook is unnecessary (but pick up the free map/city guide next to entrance turnstiles if you aren't stopping by the TI). For more on the author, see the sidebar on page 57.

The garden fairy-tale parade—with pleasing vignettes—thrills kids daily in July in the museum garden at 11:00, 13:00, and 15:00. The museum gift shop is full of mobiles, cut-paper models, and English versions of Andersen's fairy tales. An attached café offers seating indoors and out with sandwiches, soups, and salads (50–100 kr).

▲**Møntergården Urban History Museum**—This humble little museum, very close to the Hans Christian Andersen Hus, offers Odense history and early town photos (free, Tue–Sun 10:00–16:00, closed Mon, Overgade 48, tel. 65 51 46 01).

▲**Funen Art Museum**—This small, pleasant museum collects Danish art from 1750 to the present, paying particular attention to artists of the island of Funen, or *Fyn* in Danish (30 kr, Tue–Sun 10:00–16:00, closed Mon, Jernbanegade 13, tel. 65 51 46 01).

▲**Den Fynske Landsby Open-Air Museum**—The sleepy gathering of 26 old buildings preserves the 18th-century culture of this region. There are no explanations in the buildings, because the many school groups who visit play guessing games. Pick up the 15-kr guidebook (55 kr, free on Sun late-Oct–late-March; June–Aug daily 10:00–19:00, late March–May and Sept–late Oct Tue–Sun 10:00–17:00, closed Mon; late Oct–late March Sun only 11:00–15:00; tel. 65 51 46 01). From mid-July to early August, H. C. Andersen musicals (in Danish) run in the theater daily at 16:00. The 80-kr musical ticket includes museum admission 90 minutes earlier (not before 14:30).

SLEEPING

(6 kr = about $1, country code: 45)

$$$ Radisson H. C. A. Hotel is big, comfortable, impersonal, and a block from the Hans Christian Andersen Hus (Sb-1,265 kr, Db-1,465 kr, special summer deal mid-June–Aug: Sb or Db-850 kr with breakfast, Claus Bergs Gade 7, tel. 66 14 78 00, fax 66 14 78 90, hcandersen@radissonsas.com).

$$ Hotel Domir, located on a quiet side street just a few minutes from the train station, offers 35 tidy, simple, little rooms amidst its tiny halls. Many of the rooms are clustered around a courtyard (Sb-495 kr, twin Db-595 kr, Db-695 kr, Tb-795 kr, includes breakfast, extra charge if you pay by credit card, Hans Tausensgade 19, tel. 66 12 14 27, fax 66 12 14 13, www.domir.dk).

$$ Ydes Hotel, down the street and run by the same reception as Hotel Domir, offers 25 slightly larger rooms with similar comforts (Sb-450 kr, twin Db-550 kr, Db-650 kr, Tb-745 kr, includes breakfast, extra charge if you pay with credit card, Hans Tausensgade 11, tel. 66 12 11 31, www.ydes.dk).

$ Jytte (U-ter) Gamdrup rents two well-appointed rooms in her 17th-century home a few doors down from the Hans Christian Andersen Hus. This is probably your best Odense home, located on a fairy-tale street (D-350 kr, breakfast-40 kr, Ramsherred 17, tel. & fax 66 13 89 36, mobile 21 45 49 72, www.jyttes-bb.dk).

EATING

If you are in town for a just short stopover to visit the Hans Christian Andersen Hus, consider the café at the museum for lunch (see details under "Sights," above). Otherwise, Odense's main pedestrian shopping streets, Vestergade and Kongensgade, offer the best atmosphere and most options for lunch and dinner. (Note: In Denmark, you may be charged an extra fee if your only beverage is tap water or if you pay by credit card.)

Vintapperstræde is an alleyway full of restaurants just off Vestergade, one street before Kongensgade if you're walking from the TI. Choose from Danish, Mexican, Italian, and more. Study the menus posted outside each restaurant to decide, then grab a table inside or join the locals at an outdoor table.

Eydes Pub and Restaurant is a woodsy old pub serving mostly grilled meat, chicken, potatoes, and other kinds of pub grub. They also offer a global beer menu, but you're better off sticking with the local Albani brand brew. Pick a table, note the number, and place your order at the bar. Servings are huge, but thankfully they offer small-portion alternatives at dinner (lunches and small portions for 60–100 kr, large portions for 85–180 kr, daily 11:00–22:00, bar open much later, Kongensgade 31A, tel. 66 19 19 50).

TRANSPORTATION CONNECTIONS

From Odense by Train to: Copenhagen (2/hr, 1.5–2 hrs), **Århus** (2/hr, 1.5 hrs), **Billund/Legoland** (2/hr, 50-min train to Vejle, transfer to bus #244, allow 2 hrs total), **Svendborg/Ærø ferry** (2/hr, 40 min, to Ærø ferry), **Roskilde** (2/hr, 70 min).

Route Tips for Drivers

Århus or Billund to Ærø: Figure about two hours to drive from Billund (or 2.5 hours from Århus) to Svendborg. The freeway takes you over a suspension bridge to the island of Fyn; from Odense, take the highway south to Svendborg.

Leave your car in Svendborg (at the convenient long-term parking lot two blocks from the ferry dock) and sail for Ærø. It's an easy 75-minute crossing; note there are only five or six boats a day (see "Transportation Connections" for Ærøskøbing, page 116). Cars need reservations but walk-on passengers don't. A ferry/bus combo-ticket gives you the whole island with stopovers.

Ærø to Copenhagen via Odense: From Svendborg, drive north following signs to Fëborg, past Egeskov Castle, and on to Odense. For the open-air folk museum (Den Fynske Landsby), leave Route 9 just south of town at Højby, turning left toward Dalum and the Odense campground (on Odensevej). Look for *Den Fynske Landsby* signs (near the train tracks, south edge of town). If you're going directly to the Hans Christian Andersen Hus, follow the signs.

Continuing toward Copenhagen, you'll take the world's second-longest suspension bridge (200-kr toll, 12.5 miles long, free exhibition center on bridge in Halsskov, July–Aug Wed–Sun 11:00–16:00, closed Tue and off-season, take exit 43 off E-20). Follow signs marked *København* (Copenhagen). At Ringsted, signs point you to Roskilde. Aim toward the twin church spires and follow signs for *Vikingskibene* (Viking ships).

Copenhagen is 30 minutes from Roskilde. If you're heading to the airport, stay on the freeway to the end, following signs to *København C*, then to *Dragør/Kastrup Airport.*

JUTLAND

Legoland and Århus

Jutland, the part of Denmark that juts up from Germany, is a land of sand dunes, Lego toys, moated manor houses, and fortified old towns. Make a pilgrimage to the most famous land in all of Jutland: the pint-sized kids' paradise, Legoland. In Århus, the lively capital of Jutland (Jylland in Danish), wander the pedestrian street of this busy port, tour its boggy prehistory, and visit centuries-old Danish town life in its open-air folk museum.

Planning Your Time

Jutland (YEWT-land) is worth a day (more if you have kids) on a three-week trip through Scandinavia. If you arrive in Århus by early afternoon (after catching the 9:00 boat from Kristiansand, Norway, and driving about 2.5 hours), spend the rest of the afternoon at Den Gamle By (the Old Town open-air museum) and the next morning in downtown Århus. Stop by the ARoS art museum and have lunch at a canalside café before moving on. If you have kids, visit Legoland on the way to or from Århus. Speedy travelers can make Århus an afternoon stop and drive to Legoland that evening (which is free if you enter late).

Legoland

Legoland is Scandinavia's top kids' sight. If you have a child (or think you might be one), it's a fun stop. This huge park is a happy combination of rides, restaurants, trees, smiles, and 33 million Lego bricks creatively arranged into such wonders as Mount Rushmore, the Parthenon, "Mad" King Ludwig's castle, and the

Jutland

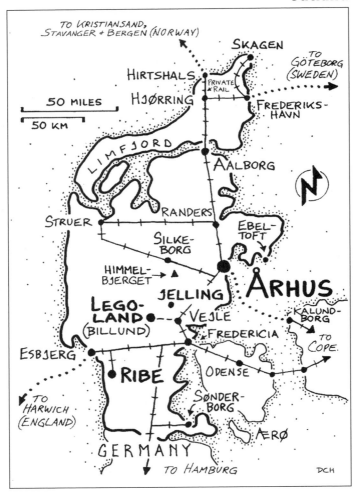

Statue of Liberty. It's a Lego world here, as everything is cleverly related to this popular toy. Surprisingly, the restaurants don't serve Legolamb.

The indoor museum features the company history, high-tech Lego creations, a great doll collection, and a toy museum full of mechanical wonders from the early 1900s, many ready to jump into action with the push of a button. There's a Lego playroom for hands-on fun—and a campground across the street if your kids refuse to move on.

Cost and Hours: 199-kr entry, 185 kr for kids ages 3–13, 185 kr for kids over 60 (gets you on all the rides). Generally open April–Oct daily 10:00–18:00, until 20:00 Sat–Sun and most of Aug, until 21:00 daily in July, closed Nov–March and Wed–Thu in Sept–mid-Oct (tel. 75 33 13 33, see "Legoland Billund" at www .legoland.dk). Legoland doesn't charge in the evening (free after 19:30 in July and late Aug, otherwise after 17:30). Activities close an hour before the park, but it's basically the same place after dinner as during the day—with fewer tour groups.

SIGHTS

Near Legoland

Jelling—If you've always wanted to see the hometown of the ancient Danish kings Gorm the Old and Harald Bluetooth, this is your chance. The village of Jelling (12 miles from Legoland, just off the highway near Vejle) has a church with Denmark's oldest frescoes and two ancient runic stones in its courtyard—often called "Denmark's birth certificate."

▲**Ribe**—A Viking port 1,000 years ago, Ribe is the oldest, and possibly loveliest, town in Denmark. It's an entertaining mix of cobbled lanes and leaning medieval houses, with a fine cathedral (12 kr, modern paintings under Romanesque arches). The **TI** can find accommodations for a 25-kr booking fee (Torvet 3, tel. 75 42 15 00). Take the free Night Watchman tour (daily May–mid-Sept at 22:00, extra tour at 20:00 June–Aug). The **Weis' Stue,** a smoky, low-ceilinged, atmospheric inn, rents primitive rooms and serves good meals (S-425 kr, D-625 kr, includes breakfast, across from the church, tel. 75 42 07 00).

SLEEPING

Legoland or Nearby, in Billund

$$$ Legoland Hotel adjoins Legoland (Sb-1,445 kr, Db-1,845 kr, special family deals: 2,545 kr for room big enough for 2 adults and 2 kids, room prices include 2-day admission to park, prices slightly lower Sept–May or for 2 or more nights, tel. 75 33 12 44, fax 75 35 38 10, www.hotellegoland.dk, hotel@legoland.dk).

$$$ Hotel Svanen is close by in Billund (Sb-895–995 kr, Db-995–1,095 kr, extra bed-100 kr, Nordmarksvej 8, tel. 75 33 28 33, fax 75 35 35 15, www.hotelsvanen.dk, info@hotelsvanen.dk).

$$ Legoland Village is a family youth hostel offering inexpensive rooms that sleep one to five people (Ds-660–830 kr, sheets and towels-55 kr, includes breakfast, Ellehammers Alle 2, tel. 75 33 27 77, fax 75 33 28 77, www.legolandvillage.dk, info @legolandvillage.dk).

Sleep Code

(6 kr = about $1, country code: 45)
S = Single, **D** = Double/Twin, **T** = Triple, **Q** = Quad, **b** = bathroom,
s = shower. You can assume credit cards are accepted unless otherwise noted.

To help you sort easily through these listings, I've divided the rooms into three categories based on the price for a standard double room with bath during high season:

$$$ **Higher Priced**—Most rooms 1,000 kr or more.
$$ **Moderately Priced**—Most rooms between
450–1,000 kr.
$ **Lower Priced**—Most rooms 450 kr or less.

$ Private rooms are the key to a budget visit here. In a forest just outside of town, **Erik and Mary Sort** have a great setup: a cottage sleeping up to six people and two double rooms. Their guests enjoy a huge living room, a kitchen, lots of Lego toys, and a kid-friendly yard (150–170 kr per person in the doubles, 400 kr for the cottage, breakfast-35 kr, cash only, leave Billund on Grindsted Road, turn right on Stilbjergvej, go a half mile to Stilbjergvej 4B, tel. 75 33 23 27, www.visitbillund.dk—click "Accommodation," then "Bed & Breakfast," and then find "Gregersminde").

TRANSPORTATION CONNECTIONS

Legoland is easiest to visit by car, but doable by public transportation (at Vejle, the nearest train station to Billund, transfer to the #244 bus to travel the remaining 25 miles to Billund). For details on transportation, see www.legoland.dk or www.rejseplanen.dk.

To Billund from: Copenhagen (hourly trains, 2.25 hrs to Vejle, then take bus #244 to Billund, allow 3.5 hrs total), **Odense** (2/hr, 50 min to Vejle, transfer to bus #244, figure on 2 hrs total), **Århus** (2/hr, 45 min to Vejle, switch to bus #244, allow 2 hrs total).

Århus

Århus (OAR-hoos), Denmark's second-largest city, has a population of 300,000 and calls itself the "World's Smallest Big City." Århus is Jutland's capital and cultural hub. Its Viking founders, ever conscious of aesthetics, chose a lovely wooded setting where the river hits the sea. Today, Århus bustles with a lively port, an

Århus

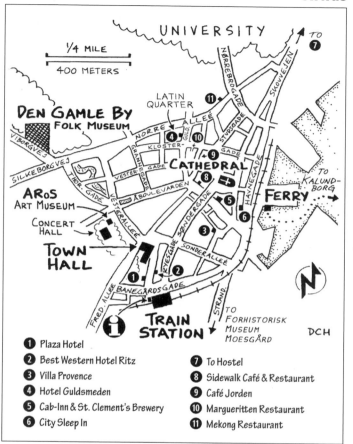

¼ MILE
400 METERS

UNIVERSITY

DEN GAMLE BY
FOLK MUSEUM

LATIN QUARTER

AROS
ART MUSEUM

CONCERT
HALL

TOWN
HALL

CATHEDRAL

FERRY

TO
KALUND-
BORG

TRAIN
STATION

TO
FORHISTORISK
MUSEUM
MOESGÅRD

DCH

1 Plaza Hotel
2 Best Western Hotel Ritz
3 Villa Provence
4 Hotel Guldsmeden
5 Cab-Inn & St. Clement's Brewery
6 City Sleep In
7 To Hostel
8 Sidewalk Café & Restaurant
9 Café Jorden
10 Margueritten Restaurant
11 Mekong Restaurant

important university, and an adorable "Latin Quarter" filled with people living very, very well. The town has a great pedestrian street that lasts at least two ice-cream cones from the cathedral to the train station (Søndergade/Clements Torv). Århus is well worth a stop.

Tourist Information: The TI is next to the train station (May–mid-June Mon–Fri 9:30–17:00, Sat 10:00–13:00, closed Sun; mid-June–early Sept Mon–Fri 9:30–18:00, Sat 9:30–17:00, Sun 10:00–13:00; early Sept–April Mon–Fri 9:30–16:00, Sat 10:00–13:00, closed Sun; tel. 87 31 50 10, fax 86 12 95 90). Consider the **Århus Passet,** which covers all sights, a 2.5-hour introductory bus tour, and public transportation (119 kr/day, 149 kr/2 days).

Getting Around Århus: City buses (17-kr tickets) easily

connect the downtown and train station with the Den Gamle By open-air folk museum and the Forhistorisk Museum Moesgård prehistory museum.

TOURS

▲▲**City Bus Tour**—The TI's great 2.5-hour bus tour winds all over the city. You'll tour the cathedral, have 40 minutes to blitz Den Gamle By, drive through the university (30,000 students, Denmark's first outside Copenhagen), and see Denmark's biggest container port (55 kr, tours daily mid-June–early Sept at 10:00, departs from TI, includes 24 hours unlimited bus travel in city).

SIGHTS

▲▲▲**ARoS**—The Århus Art Museum is a must-see sight, if only for the building's architecture. Square and unassuming from the outside, the bright white interior, with its spiral staircase winding up the museum's three floors, is surprising. The building has two sections, one for the exhibits and one for administration. The halves are divided by a passageway, which has free entry if you just want to peek at the building itself. You'll also see the squatting sculpture of *Boy* (by Australian artist Ron Mueck), realistic yet 15 feet high.

The permanent collection features paintings from the Danish Golden Age (1800–1850) to modern art, including many multimedia installations and works by Bill Viola, James Turrell, and others such as Danish artist Per Kirkeby. Be sure to visit the basement, where (amid the black walls) artists from around the world exhibit their works of light and sound in each of the nine rooms *(De 9 Rum)*.

Pick up a museum floor plan at the ticket counter. Don't miss the rooftop terrace and its super view of the city (76 kr, Tue–Sun 10:00–17:00, until 22:00 on Wed, closed Mon, lunch café on ground floor, exclusive restaurant on top floor, ARoS Allé 2, tel. 87 30 66 00, www.aros.dk).

▲**Århus Cathedral**—Denmark's biggest church, more than 330 feet long and tall, began as Romanesque in 1201 and finished as Flamboyant Gothic in the 15th century (free, daily May–Sept 9:30–16:00, Oct–April 10:00–15:00). The altarpiece, dating from 1479, features the 12 apostles surrounding John the Baptist and St. Clement, the patron saint of Århus and sailors (his symbol is the anchor). On top, Jesus is crowning Mary in heaven. This is a polyptych (a many-paneled altarpiece). The model in the apse behind demonstrates how it flips to different scenes through the church year. The fresco on the aisle (right of altar) shows a three-part universe: heaven, Earth (at Mass), and—under the thick black line—hell (with the tortuous bagpipe band). The kid on the gallows illustrated medieval disciplinary sermons for children. Notice the angels trying desperately to save the damned. Just a little more money to the Church...and...I...think we can...pull...grandpa...OUT.

▲**Latin Quarter**—The small, trendy, pedestrian-friendly streets just beyond the cathedral will make you fall in love with Århus.

▲▲▲**Den Gamle By**—The Old Town open-air folk museum puts Århus on the touristic map. Seventy half-timbered houses and crafts shops come with old furnishings. Highlights include Torvet (the main square), the Mayor's House (from 1597), and the toy museum (Legetoj). Unlike other Scandinavian open-air museums that focus on rural folk life, Den Gamle By re-creates old Danish town life (80 kr, daily July–Aug 9:00–18:00, April–June and Sept–Nov 10:00–17:00, shorter hours off-season, the 10-kr mini-guide adds little to the brief English building descriptions and maps throughout the park; from train station catch bus #3, #14, #55, or #25, or walk 15 min to Viborgvej 2; tel. 86 12 31 88). For lunch, consider eating at the cheery indoor/outdoor Simonsens Have tea garden. After hours, the buildings of the open-air museum are locked, but the peaceful park is open. A fine botanical garden is next door.

▲ **Forhistorisk Museum Moesgård**—This prehistory museum at Moesgård, just south of Århus, is famous for its incredibly well-preserved Grauballe Man. The 2,000-year-old "bog man" looks like a fellow half his age. You'll see his skin, nails, hair, and even the slit in his throat he got at the sacrificial banquet. The museum has fine Stone Age exhibits (45 kr, April–Sept daily 10:00–17:00; Oct–March Tue–Sun 10:00–16:00, closed Mon, museum cafeteria sells picnics to go; take bus #6, 20 min, 2/hr, from Århus train station to last stop, Moesgård Allé 20; tel. 89 42 11 00).

Behind the museum, a trail with a few model Viking buildings, including a 12th-century stave church (included in Forhistorisk Museum admission, same hours, good 15-kr guide booklet), stretches two miles down to a fine beach (but you'll need to walk back—there's no bus).

Other Attractions—There's lots more to see in Århus, such as the small Viking museum (free, Mon–Fri 10:00–16:00, Thu until 17:30, closed Sat–Sun, in a bank basement across from cathedral), and the "Tivoli" amusement park offering great fun for the family (50 kr, daily 12:00–22:00, less off-season; bus #1, #4, #6, #8, or #18 to edge of town; tel. 86 14 73 00).

SLEEPING

(6 kr = about $1, country code: 45)

All accommodations come with a breakfast buffet and are centrally located near the train station and TI. The TI can set you up in a 300-kr double (with shared bath) in a private home for a 30-kr fee. They also have summer deals on ritzy hotels (Db-about 750 kr).

$$$ Plaza Hotel rents 162 well-furnished, business-class rooms 100 yards from the station. The lower range of prices listed apply to summer, from late June through early August (Sb-875/1,455 kr, Db-980/1,665 kr, bedroom suite-2,160 kr, extra bed-200 kr, kids under age 14 free, includes breakfast, sauna/gym/hot tub, smoke-free rooms, Banegårdspladsen 14, tel. 87 32 01 00, fax 87 32 01 99, www.scandic-hotels.com, plaza.aarhus@scandic -hotels.com).

$$$ Best Western Hotel Ritz, across the street from Plaza Hotel, has similar-quality rooms but less enthusiasm for its clients (Sb-1,030 kr, Db-1,495 kr; Fri, Sat, Sun, or July–Aug: Sb-675 kr, Db-795–995 kr; extra bed-300 kr, extra bed for child under age 14-150 kr, Banegårdapladsen 12, tel. 86 13 44 44, fax 86 13 45 87, www.hotelritz.dk, mail@hotelritz.dk).

$$$ Villa Provence, named for the owners' favorite vacation destination, is a *petit* taste of France in the center of Århus. Its 39 rooms, impeccably and uniquely decorated, surround a quiet courtyard. Prices vary depending on the size and elegance of the room, and the most expensive have large bathtubs and a sitting area (Sb-895–1,470 kr, Db-995–1,590 kr, includes breakfast, suites available, parking-85 kr/day, 10-min walk from station, near Åboulevarden at Fredens Torv 12, tel. 86 18 24 00, fax 86 18 24 03, www.villaprovence.dk, hotel@villaprovence.dk).

$$$ Hotel Guldsmeden is a small, welcoming, and sparkling-clean hotel with 20 rooms, fluffy comforters, and a young, disarmingly friendly staff. A steep staircase takes you to the best rooms, while the cheaper rooms (without private facilities) are in a ground-floor annex behind the stay-awhile garden (S-795kr, Sb-895 kr, D-995 kr, Db-1,195 kr, extra bed-200 kr, 20 percent off rooms with private bath with this book in 2007 based on availability, suites available, penthouse apartment available for longer stays, includes breakfast, 15-min walk or 70-kr taxi from the station, in Århus' quiet Latin Quarter at Guldsmedgade 40, tel. 86 13 45 50, fax 86 13 76 76, www.hotelguldsmeden.dk, aarhus@guldsmeden.dk).

$$ Cab-Inn, overlooking the atmospheric Åboulevarden canal, has small but comfortable rooms with a single bed that expands into a twin and one or two fold-down bunks on the walls. The service, like the rooms, is no-nonsense (Sb-525 kr, Db-645 kr, Tb-765 kr, Qb-885 kr, breakfast-50 kr, easy parking-60 kr, rooms overlook canal or quieter courtyard, Kannikegade 14, tel. 86 75 70 00, fax 86 75 71 00, www.cabinn.dk, cabinn@cabinn.dk).

$ The creative **City Sleep In,** an independent hostel open 24 hours a day year-round, has a kitchen, fun living and games room, laundry service, lockers, and bikes for rent. It's on a busy road facing the harbor, a 10-minute hike from the station (dorm beds-120 kr, D-380 kr, Db-420 kr, sheets-48 kr, breakfast-48 kr, Havnegade 20, tel. 86 19 20 55, fax 86 19 18 11, www.citysleep-in.dk, sleep-in @citysleep-in.dk).

$ **Danhostel Århus,** an official HI hostel with 120-kr beds and plenty of two- and four-bed rooms, is near the water two miles out of town (dorm bed-120 kr, S/D-440 kr, Sb/Db-488 kr, sheets-45 kr, towels-10 kr, breakfast-50 kr, bus #1 to the end, follow signs, Marienlundsvej 10, tel. 86 16 72 98, fax 86 21 21 20, www.aarhus -danhostel.dk info@aarhus-danhostel.dk).

EATING

Don't be surprised if your bill includes a charge for using your credit card or ordering tap water as your only beverage—this is becoming increasingly common in pricey Denmark.

The Åboulevarden canal (two blocks southwest of cathedral in old center) is lined with trendy eateries, such as the **Sidewalk Café and Restaurant,** a fine place for a canalside drink or meal. Big salads, pasta dishes, burgers, and tipsy, toppling sandwiches run 60–100 kr (daily 9:00–24:00, later Fri–Sat, indoor seating available, Åboulevarden 56, tel. 86 18 18 66).

The Latin Quarter, north of the cathedral, is a *hyggelig* neighborhood of small lanes and charming little cafés. **Café Jorden,** with tasty sandwiches, salads, and burgers, is a good bet for lunch or a light dinner (50–80-kr dishes, Mon–Sat 9:30–24:00, later on Fri–Sat, Sun 10:00–23:00, Badstuegade 3, tel. 86 19 72 22). They serve a fun and fruity "brunch" indoors or on the quiet but people-filled square (80 kr, daily 10:00–15:00, carnivorous or vegetarian).

St. Clement's Brewery is the only pub in town that has a built-in brewery. Choose from a hearty menu and eat amid shiny copper vats. Lunch and light meals are 60–100 kr; hearty dinners are 120–200 kr (Mon–Sat 11:30–24:00, closed Sun, Bryggeriet Sct. Clemens, Kannikegade 10–12, tel. 86 13 80 00).

Margueritten, tucked into a small alley between Badestuegade and Guldsmedgade, has both a casual, candlelit indoor setting and a cozy courtyard. Choose from a variety of meat and fish dishes, stylishly presented and served with lots of vegetables and delectable sauces (lunches-50–80 kr, dinners-190–250 kr, Mon–Sat 11:30–21:30, Fri–Sat until 22:30, Sun 17:00–21:30, Guldsmedgade 20, tel. 86 19 60 33).

For cheap and good Vietnamese or Thai food, try the homey little **Mekong Restaurant** (Tue–Sat 17:00–22:30, Sun 17:00–21:30, closed Mon, Nørregade 10, tel. 86 18 49 55).

TRANSPORTATION CONNECTIONS

From Århus by Train to: Odense (2/hr, 1.5 hrs), **Copenhagen** (1–2/hr, 3 hrs), **Hamburg, Germany** (5/day, 2 direct trains, 5 hrs), **Hirtshals/Ferry to Kristiansand, Norway** (hourly, 2.5–3 hrs; to meet the Color Line ferry, transfer at Hjørring and continue to Hirtshals Havn; note that Eurail and Scanrail passes don't cover the Hjørring-Hirtshals train, but do give a 50 percent discount; buy your ticket in Hjørring or on board—12 kr with railpass, 23 kr without; for the latest ferry schedule, see www.colorline.com).

Route Tips for Drivers
From the Ferry Dock at Hirtshals to Århus to Billund: From the dock in Hirtshals, drive south (signs to Hjørring, Ålborg). It's about 2.5 hours to Århus. (To skip Århus, skirt the center and follow E-45 south.) To get to downtown Århus, follow signs to the center, then Domkirke. Park in the pay lot across from the cathedral. Signs all over town direct you to Den Gamle By open-air folk museum. From Århus, it's 60 miles to Billund/Legoland (go south on Skanderborg Road; follow signs to Vejle, Kolding). For Legoland, take the Vejle S (after Vejle N) exit for Billund.

NORWAY

NORWAY

(Norge)

 Norway is stacked with superlatives—it's the most mountainous, most scenic, and most prosperous of all the Scandinavian countries. Ice ages have carved out and shaped the steep mountains and deep fjords the country is famous for.

Norway is a land of rich harvests—timber, oil, and fish. In fact, its wealth of resources is a major reason why Norwegians have voted *"nei"* to membership in the European Union. They don't want to be forced to share fishing rights with EU countries.

The country's relatively recent independence (in 1905, from Sweden) makes Norwegians notably patriotic and proud of their traditions and history.

Norway's Viking past (c. A.D. 800–1050) can still be seen today in the country's 28 remaining stave churches—a decorative nod to Viking ship prows—and the Viking artifacts housed in Oslo's Viking Ship Museum.

The Vikings, who also lived in present-day Denmark and Sweden, were great traders, ship builders, and explorers. However, they are probably best known for their infamous invasions that terrorized much of Europe. The sight of their dragon-prowed ships on the horizon struck fear into the hearts of people from Ireland to the Black Sea.

Named for the Norse word "vik," which means inlet, the Vikings sailed their sleek sea-worthy ships on extensive voyages, laden with amber and furs for trading—and weapons for fighting. They traveled up the Seine deep into Russia, through the Mediterranean east to Constantinople, and across the Atlantic to Greenland and even "Vinland" (Canada). In fact, they touched the soil of the Americas centuries before Columbus, causing proud "ya sure ya betcha" Scandinavian immigrants in the US to display bumper stickers that boast, "Columbus Used a Viking Map!"

Both history and Hollywood have painted a picture of the Vikings as fierce barbarians, an image reinforced by the colorful names of leaders like Sven Forkbeard, Erik Bloodaxe, and Harald Bluetooth. Unless you're handy with an axe, these don't sound like

Norway

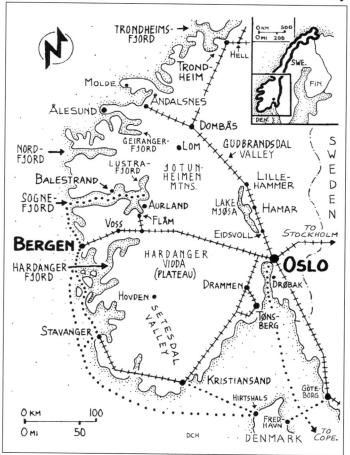

the kind of men you want to hoist a tankard of mead with. They kept slaves and were cruel (though there is no evidence that they forced their subjects to eat lutefisk). But the Vikings also had a gentle side. Many were farmers, fishermen, and craftsmen who created delicate works with wood and metal. Faced with a growing population constrained by a lack of arable land, they traveled south not just to rape, pillage, and plunder, but in search of greener pastures. Sometimes they stayed and colonized, as in northeast England, which was called the "Danelaw," or in northwest France, which became known as Normandy ("Land of the North-men").

The Vikings worshipped many gods and had a rich tradition of mythology. Epic sagas were verbally passed down through

Norway Almanac

Official Name: Kongeriket Norge—the Kingdom of Norway—or simply Norway.

Population: Norway's 4.6 million people (about 30 per square mile) are mainly of Nordic and Germanic heritage, with a small population of indigenous Sami people in the north. The rapidly growing number of immigrants are primarily from Pakistan, Sweden, Denmark, Iraq, Vietnam, and Somalia. Most speak one of two official forms of Norwegian: Bokmål and Nynorsk, and the majority speak English as a second language. About 86 percent belong to the state Church of Norway; 3 percent are Pentecostal, Roman Catholic, or other Christian religions; 2 percent are Muslim; and 9 percent are unchurched.

Latitude and Longitude: 62°N and 10°E, similar latitude to Canada's Northwest Territories.

Area: 148,900 square miles, slightly larger than New Mexico.

Geography: Sharing the Scandinavian Peninsula with Sweden, Norway has short northern borders with Finland and Russia. Its 51,575-mile coastline extends from the Barents Sea in the Arctic Ocean to the Norwegian Sea and North Sea in the North Atlantic. Shaped by glaciers, Norway has a rugged landscape of mountains, plateaus, and deep fjords. Part of Norway extends north of the Arctic Circle and is known for summer nights when the sun never sets, and winter days when the sun never comes up.

generations or written in angular runic writing. The sagas told the heroic tales of the gods, who lived in Valhalla, the Viking heaven, presided over by Odin, the god of both wisdom and war (and how in the world did those two things go together?). Like the Egyptians, the Vikings believed in life after death, and chieftains were often buried in their ships within burial mounds, along with prized possessions such as jewelry, cooking pots, food, and Hagar the Horrible cartoons. Many of our own names for the days of the week come from Viking gods. Thursday is named after Thor, Odin's son, the god of physical strength.

Like the Greeks and Etruscans before them, the Vikings never became organized on a large national scale, and eventually faded away due to bigger, better-organized enemies and the powerful influence of Christianity. By 1150, the Vikings had become Christianized and assimilated into European society. But their memory lives on in Norway.

Beginning in the 14th century, Norway came under Danish rule for more than 400 years, until the Danes took the wrong side

Biggest Cities: Norway's capital city, Oslo, has a population of 542,000; more than 825,000 live in the metropolitan area.

Economy: The Norwegian economy grew at a 3.7 percent rate in 2005, contributing to a healthy $194 billion Gross Domestic Product and a per capita GDP of $42,300. Its primary export is oil, ranking behind only Saudia Arabia and Russia in the amount of oil exported, and making Norway one of the world's richest countries.

Currency: 6.5 Norwegian kroner (kr) = about $1.

Government: As the leader of Norway's constitutional monarchy, King Harald V has largely ceremonial powers. The head of state since October 2005 has been Prime Minister Jens Stoltenberg. The legislative body is the Stortinget, with 169 members elected for four-year terms. The Labor Party currently holds 61 seats, followed the Progress Party with 38, the Conservative Party with 23, the Socialist Left Party with 15. The remaining seats are divided among smaller political parties.

Flag: The Norwegian flag is red with a blue cross outlined in white.

The Average Norwegian: The average Norwegian is 38 years old, has 1.78 children, and will live to be 79. One in three Norwegians is employed in the service sector, one in four in industry, and only 4 percent in agriculture.

in the Napoleonic Wars. The Treaty of Kiel forced Denmark to cede Norway to Sweden in 1814. Sweden's rule of Norway lasted until 1905, when Norway voted to dissolve the union. Like many European countries, Norway temporarily lost its independence during World War II. April 1940 marked the start of five years of Nazi occupation, during which a strong resistance movement developed and hindered some of the Nazi war efforts.

Each year on May 17, Norwegians celebrate their new constitution with fervor and plenty of flag-waving. Men and women wear folk costumes *(bunads)*, each specific to a region of Norway. Parades are held throughout the country. The parade in Oslo marches past the Royal Palace, where the royal family waves to the populace from their balcony. While Norway is ruled by a parliament and prime minister, the royal family is still highly revered and respected.

Four holidays in early summer disrupt transportation schedules: Constitution Day (May 17, mentioned above), Ascension Day (May 17 in 2007), and Whitsunday and Whitmonday (a.k.a.

Pentecost and the following day, May 27–28 in 2007).

High taxes contribute to Norway's high standard of living. Norwegians receive cradle-to-grave social care: university education, health care, nearly yearlong maternity leave, and an annual six weeks of vacation. Norwegians feel there is no better place than home and have voted Norway the most livable country in the world (UN Human Development Index, 2002).

Despite being looked down upon as less sophisticated by their Scandinavian neighbors, Norwegians are proud of their rich folk traditions—from handmade sweaters and folk costumes to the small farms that produce sweet goat cheese, called *geitost.* Less than seven percent of the country's land is arable, resulting in numerous small farms. The government recognizes the value of farming, especially in the remote reaches of the country, and provides rich subsidies to keep this tradition alive. These subsidies would not be allowed if Norway joined the European Union—yet another reason the country is an EU holdout.

While the majority of the population under 70 years of age speaks English, a few words in Norwegian will serve you well. If you visit a Norwegian home, be sure to leave your shoes at the door; indoors is usually meant for stocking feet only. At the end of a meal, it's polite to say "Thanks for the food"—*"Takk for maten"* (tahk for MAH-ten). Norwegians rarely feel their guests have eaten enough food, so be prepared to say *"Nei, takk"* (nigh tahk; "No, thanks"). You can always try *"Jeg er met"* (yigh air met; "I am full"), but be careful not to say *"Jeg er full"*—"I am drunk."

OSLO

While Oslo is the smallest and least earth-shaking of the Scandinavian capitals, this brisk little city offers more sightseeing thrills than you might expect. Sights of the Viking spirit—past and present—tell an exciting story. Prowl through the remains of ancient Viking ships, and marvel at more peaceful but equally gutsy modern boats (the *Kon-Tiki*, *Ra*, and *Fram*). Dive into the traditional folk culture at the Norwegian open-air folk museum, and get stirred up by the country's heroic spirit at the Norwegian Resistance Museum.

For a look at modern Oslo, browse through the yuppie-style harbor shopping complex, tour the striking City Hall, take a peek at sculptor Gustav Vigeland's people pillars, climb the towering Holmenkollen ski jump (closes as early as 16:00 in winter), and then celebrate the world's greatest peacemakers at the Nobel Peace Center.

Situated at the head of a 60-mile-long fjord, surrounded by forests, and populated by more than 500,000 people, Oslo is Norway's cultural hub and an all-you-can-see *smörgåsbord* of historic sights, trees, art, and Nordic fun.

Planning Your Time

Oslo offers an exciting two-day slate of sightseeing thrills. Ideally, spend two days, and leave on the night boat to Copenhagen or on the scenic train to Bergen the third morning. Spend the two days like this:

Day 1: Take my self-guided walk, and say hello to Oslo (see page 143). Tour the Akershus Fortress and the Norwegian Resistance Museum. Catch the City Hall tour. Spend the afternoon at Frogner Park (Vigeland statues) and at the Holmenkollen ski jump and museum (closes at 16:00 in winter). For dinner, consider hiking to the classy Frognerseteren Hovedrestaurant near the ski jump, or taking a picnic or fast-food meal on the harbor mini-cruise (summer only; best in July–Aug, when boats run until 19:00).

Day 2: Ferry across the harbor to Bygdøy and tour the *Fram, Kon-Tiki,* and Viking Ship museums. Spend the afternoon at the Norwegian Folk Museum. Back downtown, browse the National Gallery and stroll the harborfront Aker Brygge mall/restaurant complex.

ORIENTATION

Oslo is easy to manage. Its sights cluster around the main boulevard, Karl Johans Gate (with the Royal Palace at one end and the train station at the other), and in the Bygdøy district, a 10-minute ferry ride across the harbor.

The monumental, homogenous city center contains most of the sights, but head out of the core to see the more colorful neighborhoods. Choose from Majorstuen (chic boutiques, trendy restaurants), Grünerløkka (bohemian cafés, hippies), and Grønland (multi-ethnic immigrants' zone).

Tourist Information

Oslo has two TIs: one across from City Hall and one in front of the train station.

The **Oslo Information Center** faces City Hall at Fridtjof Nansens Plass 5 (June–Aug daily 9:00–19:00, shorter hours and closed Sat–Sun off-season, tel. 24 14 77 00, www.visitoslo.com, info@visitoslo.com). The TI in front of the **train station,** though simpler, has much longer hours, and handles your needs just as well (daily 7:00–20:00 all year). A late-night visit avoids the lines; otherwise, grab a number as you enter and wait.

At either TI, pick up the Oslo map (with a transit map on the reverse side), the annual *Oslo Guide* (with plenty of details on sightseeing, shopping, and eating), the *What's On in Oslo* monthly (for the most accurate listing of museum hours and special events), and *Streetwise* magazine (an insightful, worthwhile student guide that's fun to read and full of offbeat ideas—see below). The free *Oslo Fjord Islands* flier covers affordable ways to get out and afloat. If you're traveling on, pick up the *Bergen Guide* and information for the rest of Norway. It's all free. Consider buying the Oslo Pass (described below), unless you get the Oslo Package, which includes your hotel accommodation and an Oslo Pass (see "Sleeping," page 174). If you're interested in renting a bike, ask the TI for info (see "Helpful Hints," below).

Use It, a hardworking information center, is geared for students but is happy to offer anyone its solid, money-saving, experience-enhancing advice (mid-June–Aug Mon–Fri 9:00–18:00, closed Sat–Sun; Sept–mid-June Mon–Fri 11:00–17:00, closed Sat–Sun; Møllergata 3, tel. 24 14 98 20, www.unginfo.oslo .no). They can find you the cheapest beds in town (no booking fee), and offer free Internet access (30-min limit, may have to wait for a computer). Their free *Streetwise* magazine—packed with articles on Norwegian culture, ideas on eating and sleeping cheap, good nightspots, the best beaches, and so on—is a must for young travelers and worthwhile for anyone curious to probe the Oslo scene.

Oslo Pass: This pass covers the city's public transit and boats, entry to all sights, and parking, plus lots of discounts—all described in a useful handbook (210 kr/24 hrs, 300 kr/48 hrs, 390 kr/72 hrs; kids ages 4–15 save 60 percent on individual passes). Do the arithmetic carefully before buying; add up the individual costs of the sights you want to see to find out whether an Oslo Pass will save you money (sample charges: 24-hr transit pass-60 kr, ski jump-70 kr, City Hall-40 kr, 3 boat museums at Bygdøy-135 kr, National Gallery-free). Students with an ISIC card may be better off without the Oslo Pass. The TI's Oslo Package (see "Sleeping," page 174) includes this card with your discounted hotel room.

Entertainment Listings: The periodical *What's On in Oslo* has an extensive listing of happenings every day. Pick it up free at the TI, and review the busy line-up of special events, tours, and concerts. *Streetwise* magazine is also good.

Arrival in Oslo

By Train

The central train station (Oslo Sentralstasjon, or "Oslo S" for short) is slick and helpful. You'll find Internet cafés, ATMs, and a Forex exchange desk. The station is plugged into a lively modern shopping mall called Byporten (Mon–Fri 10:00–21:00, Sat 10:00–18:00, closed Sun). You'll also find a Bit sandwich shop with seating for a cheap meal (Mon–Fri 7:00–21:00, Sat 9:00–18:00, Sun 11:00–17:00), an ICA supermarket (daily 7:00–22:00), and a Vinmonopolet liquor store (see "Shopping," page 174). The TI is across the square in front of the station.

For tickets and train info, go to the station's ticket office (Mon–Fri 6:30–19:00, Sat–Sun 10:00–19:00) or to the helpful train office at the National Theater railway and T-bane station, which can have shorter lines (Mon–Fri 7:00–21:00, Sat–Sun 10:00–19:00, Ruseløkkveien, southwest of National Theater). There's also an after-hours full-service ticket desk at the train station, located between tracks 8 and 9 (open until 23:15). At each office, you can buy domestic, international, and Norway in a Nutshell tickets (for the most scenic way to connect Oslo and Bergen by train, boat, and bus, see the Norway in a Nutshell chapter). Pick up leaflets on the Flåm and Bergen Railway.

By Plane

Oslo Airport (Lufthavn) is about 30 miles north of the city center. Call tel. 81 55 02 50 for a great automated departure-confirming system for all flights (www.osl.no). For SAS, dial tel. 05400.

The speedy **Flytoget** train zips travelers between the airport and the central train station in 20–25 minutes (160 kr, less for students and seniors, 8/hr, runs roughly 5:00–24:00, not covered by railpasses, buy and validate ticket before boarding, keep it to exit, www.flytoget.no). Note that every other Flytoget train goes only to the central train station, and alternating trains continue on through Oslo, stopping at the National Theater station (which is much closer to many recommended hotels and uses the same ticket).

Local trains cost half as much as Flytoget and take only a little longer (80 kr, hourly, 40 min, covered by railpasses, also serve National Theater station). To reach the Flytoget and local train counters at the airport, exit right after you leave customs, and walk all the way to the corner; you'll see two separate ticket counters (one for Flytoget, NSB for the cheaper local trains) and separate TV screens showing the timetables for Flytoget and the "lokal–InterCity–fjerntog" trains.

Flybus airport buses make several downtown stops, including the central train station (130 kr one-way, 4/hr, 40 min).

Taxis run to and from the airport (600-kr fixed rate, confirm price before you commit, some companies have cheaper special deals). I prefer the slick and faster Flytoget train (listed above), but the taxi can be a good value for families and those with lots of luggage.

Helpful Hints

Pickpocket Alert: They're a problem in Oslo, particularly in crowds on the street and in subways and buses. Always wear your money belt. To call the police, dial 112.

US Embassy: It's the big place behind all the fortifications (Henrik Ibsens Gate 18, tel. 22 44 85 50).

Currency Exchange: Banks don't change money. Use ATMs or Forex (outlets near City Hall at Fridtjof Nansens Plass 6, at train station, and at Egertorget at the crest of Karl Johans Gate, Mon–Fri 9:00–17:00, Sat 9:00–16:00, closed Sun).

Internet Access at Train Station: Sidewalk Express, on the mezzanine level under the escalators, is the budget choice (19 kr/hr, open 24/7, coin-op). **@rtic Internet Café,** which is in the station's main hall and above track 13, is good but pricey (daily 8:00–24:00, sells international phone cards).

Post Office: The central P.O. is near the train station at Dronningens Gate 15 (tel. 23 14 78 20).

Pharmacy: Jernbanetorgets Apotek is open 24/7 (across from train station on Jernbanetorget, tel. 23 35 81 00).

Laundry: Selva Laundromat is on the corner of Wesselsgate and Ullevålsveien at Ullevålsveien 15, a half-mile north of the train station (daily 8:00–21:00, walk or catch bus #37 from station, tel. 41 64 08 33).

Bike Rental: Bikes are tough to rent in Oslo. A public system lets you grab simple city bikes out of a locked hanger at various points around town for a small fee. A more expensive conventional bike rental company delivers bikes to your hotel (details at TI).

Getting Around Oslo

By Public Transit: Commit yourself to taking advantage of Oslo's excellent transit system: It's made up of buses, trams, ferries, and a subway (*Tunnelbane,* or T-bane for short). The TI's free little Oslo city map has a fine transit map on the flip side, which makes things clear if you study it. The system runs like clockwork, with schedules clearly posted and followed. **Trafikanten,** the public-transit information center, faces the train station under the glass tower (Mon–Fri 7:00–20:00, Sat–Sun 8:00–20:00, tel. 177 or 81 50 01 76, www.trafikanten.no).

Individual **tickets** work on buses, trams, ferries, and T-bane for one hour (20 kr if bought at a Narvensen kiosk/convenience store, or 30 kr if bought on board). Other options include the **Flexicard** (160 kr for 8 rides, shareable, can buy from driver), the 24-hour **Dagskort Tourist Ticket** (60 kr, pays for itself in three rides), and the **Oslo Pass** (free run of entire system—see page 139).

By Taxi: Taxis come with an expensive minimum fare of 80 kr. To get a taxi, wave one down, find a taxi stand, or call 02323.

TOURS

By Boat, Bus, and Foot

Boat Tours—Several tour boats leave regularly from pier 3 in front of City Hall. **Båtservice** has a relaxing and scenic 50-minute mini-cruise, with a boring multi-language commentary, that departs on the hour (115 kr, 15 percent discount with Oslo Pass, daily late May–June 10:00–16:00, July–Aug until 19:00, no boats Sept–late May, tel. 23 35 68 90, www.boatsightseeing .com). They won't scream if you bring something to Munch. They also offer two-hour fjord tours (205 kr, 3–4/day May–Aug) and a Summer Evening on the Fjord dinner cruise (345 kr, joyride without narration that includes a shrimp buffet—just shrimp, bread, and butter, daily late June–Aug 19:00–22:00).

The cheapest way to enjoy the scenic Oslofjord is simply to ride the ferries that regularly connect the nearby islands with downtown (free with Oslo Pass or transit pass).

Bus Tours—**Båtservice,** which runs the harbor cruises (above), also offers three-hour bus tours of Oslo, with stops at the ski jump, Bygdøy museums, and Frogner Park (310 kr, 2/day late May–Aug, departs from ticket office on pier 3, longer tours also available, tel. 23 35 68 90, www.boatsightseeing.com). **HMK** also does daily city bus tours (200 kr/2 hrs, 280 kr/3 hrs, departs from TI across from City Hall, tel. 22 78 94 00, www.hmk.no). While there is a hop-on, hop-off bus service for Oslo, the city doesn't really work well with this kind of tour bus. Again, commit yourself to public transit to save lots of time, and try the tram tour listed below.

Guided Walking Tour—The local guides' union offers 90-minute historic walks from 80 kr (Mon, Wed, Fri at 17:30 in summer, from the inland side of City Hall, confirm departures at TI, tel. 22 42 70 20).

Local Guide—To hire a private guide, call the guides' association at tel. 22 42 70 20 (1,400 kr/3-hr tour, www.guideservice.no). Another local guide bureau is at tel. 22 42 28 18.

Self-Guided Hop-On, Hop-Off Tram Tour

Tram #12, which becomes tram #11 at Majorstuen, halfway through its loop, circles the city from the train station, lacing together many of Oslo's main sights. Apart from the practical value of being able to hop on and off as you sightsee your way around town (trams come by at least every 10 minutes), this 40-minute trip gives you a fine look at parts of the city you wouldn't otherwise see.

The route starts at the station, from the traffic-island tram stop located immediately in front of the transit tower. It finishes at the Stortorvet (the cathedral square), making 90 percent of a circle, and dropping you a three-minute walk from where you began the tour. If you're planning on making the entire loop, confirm with your driver that the tram #12 you're boarding becomes tram #11, and finishes at Stortorvet. Here's what you'll see, and ideas on where you might want to hop out:

From the station, you'll go through the old grid streets of 16th-century Christiana, King Christian IV's planned Renaissance town. Turning a corner at the fortress (get out here if you want to see the fortress and Norwegian Resistance Museum), you'll head for City Hall (hop off here for City Hall and harbor) and Aker Brygge (jump off for the harbor and restaurant row). Passing the harbor, you'll see on the left a few old shipyard buildings that still survive. The tram goes uphill, into a district of ugly 1960s buildings (when elegance was replaced by "functionality"), and heads onto the street known until recently as Drammensveien. It was renamed Henrik Ibsens Gate in 2006 to celebrate the centenary of the death of the man Norwegians claim is the greatest playwright since Shakespeare.

After Henrik Ibsens Gate, look for the besieged US Embassy. Bygdøyalle leads through the chic Frogner neighborhood, filled with fine 19th-century apartments from Oslo's Industrial Age. Turning the corner, you roll along the edge of Frogner Park, stopping at its grand gate (hop out here for Frogner Park and Vigeland statues). Turning onto Bogstadveien, the tram becomes #11 at a major stop. Bogstadveien is lined with trendy shops, restaurants, and cafés—it's a fun place to stroll. (You could get out here and walk along this street all the way to the Royal Palace park and the top of Karl Johans Gate.) The tram veers left before the palace, stopping at the National Historical Museum and National Gallery. Jump out at Stortorvet (a big square filled with flower stalls and fronted by the cathedral and the big GlasMagasinet department store). From here you're a three-minute walk from where you began.

SELF-GUIDED WALK

Welcome to Oslo

This stroll, worth ▲▲, covers the heart of Oslo—the zone most tourists find themselves walking—from the train station, up the main drag, and past City Hall to the harborfront. It takes a brisk 30 minutes if done nonstop.

Train Station: Start at the main entrance of Oslo's central train station (Oslo Sentralstasjon)—still marked *Østbanehallen,* or "East Train Station," from when Oslo had two stations. The statue of the tiger commemorates the 1,000th birthday of the town nicknamed Tigerstad (literally, "Tiger Town"). Back in the 1800s, Oslo was considered an urban tiger, leaving its mark on the soul of simple country folk who ventured into the wild and crazy New York City of Norway.

With your back to the train station, look for the glass Trafikanten tower that marks the **public transit office** (and TI); from here, trams zip to City Hall (harbor, boat to Bygdøy), and the underground subway (T-bane, or *Tunnelbane*) goes to Frogner Park (Vigeland statues) and the Holmenkollen ski jump. Tram #12— featured in the self-guided tram tour described above—leaves from directly across the street.

The green building behind the Trafikanten tower is a shopping

Welcome to Oslo Walk

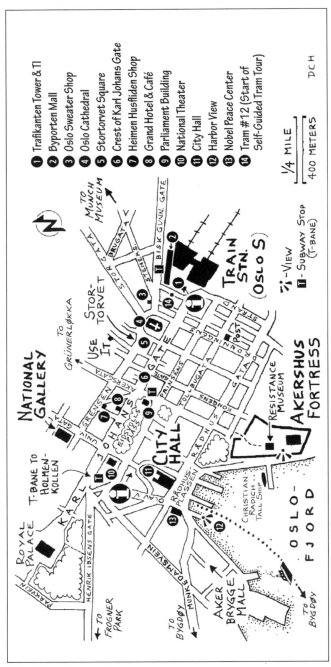

1 Trafikanten Tower & TI
2 Byporten Mall
3 Oslo Sweater Shop
4 Oslo Cathedral
5 Stortorvet Square
6 Crest of Karl Johans Gate
7 Heimen Husfliden Shop
8 Grand Hotel & Café
9 Parliament Building
10 National Theater
11 City Hall
12 Harbor View
13 Nobel Peace Center
14 Tram #12 (Start of Self-Guided Tram Tour)

DCH

¼ MILE
400 METERS

mall called **Byporten** (literally, "City Gate," see big sign on rooftop), built to greet those arriving from the airport on the shuttle train. Oslo's 37-floor pointed-glass **skyscraper,** the Radisson/SAS Hotel, looms behind that. Its 34th-floor pub welcomes the public with air-conditioned views and pricey drinks (daily 16:00–24:00). The tower was built with reflective glass so that, from a distance, it almost disappears. The area behind the Radisson—the lively and colorful "Little Karachi," centered along a street called Grønland—is where most of Oslo's immigrant population settled. It's become a vibrant nightspot, offering a fun contrast to the predictable homogeneity of Norwegian cuisine and culture (see sidebar).

Oslo allows hard-drug addicts and prostitutes to mix and mingle in the station area. Troubled young people come here from small towns in the countryside for anonymity and community. The two cameras near the top of the Trafikanten tower monitor drug deals. Signs warn that this is a "monitored area," but victimless crimes proceed while violence is minimized.

• *Turn your attention to Norway's main drag...*

Karl Johans Gate: This grand boulevard leads directly from the train station to the Royal Palace. The street is named for the French prince Jean Baptiste Bernadotte, who was given a Swedish name, established the current Swedish dynasty, and ruled as a popular king (1818–1844) during the period after Sweden took Norway from Denmark.

Walk three blocks up Karl Johans Gate. This stretch is referred to as **"Desolation Row"** by locals because it has no soul. (Shoppers can detour to the Oslo Sweater Shop, a block to the right down Skippergata—see "Shopping," page 174.)

• *Hook around the curved old brick structure and to the...*

Oslo Cathedral (Domkirke): This Lutheran church is where Norway celebrates and mourns its royal marriages and deaths. The most recent royal wedding was of Crown Prince Haakon Magnus and commoner Mette-Marit Tjessem Høiby—an unwed mom—in August 2001. Her father is a pensioner, poor enough to be a cheap source of gossip for the tabloids. It's a win-win situation, since locals enjoy all the latest...and he has new teeth and a free mobile phone paid for by Oslo's tabloid.

The cathedral's cornerstone (right of entrance), a thousand-year-old carving from Oslo's first and long-gone cathedral, shows how the forces of good and evil tug at each of us. Step inside beneath the red, blue, and gold seal of Oslo and under an equally colorful ceiling (closed through 2009 for restoration). The box above on the right is for the royal family.

Back outside, notice the tiny square windows midway up the copper cupola—once the lookout quarters of the fire watchman.

Walk behind the church. The **courtyard** is lined by a circa 1850 circular row of stalls from an old market. Rusty meat hooks now decorate the lamps of a peaceful café, which has quaint tables around a fountain. The atmospheric **Café Bacchus,** at the far left end of the arcade, serves food outside and in a classy café downstairs (light 120-kr meals, daily 11:00–23:00, salads, good cakes, coffee, tel. 22 33 34 30).

• *The big square that faces the cathedral is called...*

Stortorvet: Once a cattle market, it's now a flower market (Mon–Fri). The statue depicts Christian IV, the Danish king who ruled Norway around 1600. In 1624, he moved higgledy-piggledy old Oslo from here to the shelter of the fortress, built a fortified new town in a fine Renaissance grid plan, and named it (immodestly) Christiania. Oslo took back its old name only in 1925. Christian was serious about Norway. During his 60-year reign, he visited it 30 times (more than all other royal visits during 300 years of Danish rule combined). The big GlasMagasinet department store is a landmark on this square.

• *Return to Karl Johans Gate, and continue up the boulevard past street musicians, cafés, shops, and hordes of people. Kongens Gate leads left, past that first grid-plan town to the fortress. Continue hiking straight up to the crest of the hill, pausing to enjoy some of the street musicians along the way.*

The Crest of Karl Johans Gate: Look back at the train station. A thousand years ago, the original (pre-1624) Oslo was located near the wooded hill behind the station. Now look ahead to the Royal Palace in the distance, which was built in the 1830s "with nature and God behind it and the people at its feet." If the flag flies atop the palace, the king is in the country. Karl Johans Gate is a parade ground from here to the palace—the axis of modern Oslo. Each May 17th, Norway's Independence Day, this street turns into a sea of marching bands and costumed flag-wavers, while the royal family watches from the palace balcony. King Harald V and Queen Sonja moved back into the palace in 2001, after extensive (and costly) renovations. To quell the controversy caused by this expense, the public is now allowed inside to visit each summer.

On this square, the *T* sign marks a stop of the T-bane (Oslo's subway). Let W.B. Samson's bakery tempt you with its pastries (and short cafeteria line, WC in back). Next to that, David Andersen's jewelry store displays traditional silver art and fine enamel work. Inside, halfway down the wall on the right (next to the free water dispenser), is a display of Bunad jewelry—worn on big family occasions and church holidays. From here, the street called Akersgata kicks off a worthwhile stroll past the national cemetery and through a park-like river gorge to the trendy Grünerløkka quarter (a hour-long side-trip, described on page 170).

Immigration in Norway

Oslo has a big and growing immigrant community. While 18 percent of today's Norwegians are not ethnic Norwegians, Oslo's immigrant population is over 20 percent. The border was closed to immigration in 1975, but because immigrants already in Norway have been allowed to sponsor relatives—and because Norway still allows refugees to enter for humanitarian reasons—its immigrant population continues to grow.

These new "ethnic Norwegians" have provided a much-needed and generally appreciated labor force, filling jobs that wealthy Norwegians would rather not do. Immigrants are critical in the booming construction industry. Cab companies, restaurants, and hotels employ large numbers of immigrant workers. And entrepreneurial immigrants have opened wonderful ethnic restaurants, literally adding spice to the otherwise pretty drab local cuisine.

Near the train station, in particular, you'll see some of the downside of a country that is disinclined to be a melting pot. There have been scuffles between gangs and immigrant groups. Locals complain that the Norwegian government gives refuge to various ethnic groups who are historic enemies, and then houses them side-by-side. Another source of friction among blond locals is the tough love Norwegians get from their government compared to the easy ride needy immigrants get: "They even get pocket money in jail!"

While Norway is a leader among rich nations in per-capita giving to the developing world, the issue of "ethnic Norwegians" is an awkward one for locals to discuss. While many aren't eager to have their country become the next melting pot, they're also careful not to object too strenuously, wary of being labeled racist.

Hike two blocks down Karl Johans Gate, past the big brick Parliament building (on the left). On the right, a statue of the painter Christian Krohg marks a square nicknamed "the toilet lid" because it covers a public WC. A block down Arbeidergata is a **Heimen Husfliden** shop for Norsk souvenirs (see "Shopping," page 174); just beyond it is the cheap, cheery Kaffistova cafeteria (see "Eating," page 182). Farther down Karl Johans Gate, just past the Freia shop (Norway's oldest and best chocolate), the venerable **Grand Hotel** (Oslo's celebrity hotel—Nobel Peace Prize winners sleep here) overlooks the boulevard.

• *Ask the waiter at the Grand Café if you can pop inside for a little sightseeing (he'll generally let you).*

Grand Café: This historic café was for many years the meeting place of Oslo's intellectual and creative elite. Just inside the

Oslo at a Glance

▲▲▲**Frogner Park** Sprawling park with works by Norway's greatest sculptor, Gustav Vigeland, and the studio where he created them (now a museum). **Hours:** Garden—always open; Museum—June–Aug Tue–Sun 11:00–17:00, closed Mon; Sept–May Tue–Sun 12:00–16:00, closed Mon.

▲▲▲**Norwegian Folk Museum** Norway condensed into 150 historic buildings in a large open-air park. **Hours:** Daily mid-May–mid-Sept 10:00–18:00, off-season 11:00–15:00.

▲▲**City Hall** Oslo's artsy 20th-century government building, lined with huge, vibrant, municipal-themed murals, best visited with included tour. **Hours:** Daily May–Aug 8:30–17:00, until 16:00 off-season, tours Mon–Sat at 10:00, 12:00, and 14:00.

▲▲**Nobel Peace Center** New exhibit celebrating the ideals of the Nobel Peace Prize and the lives of those who have won it. **Hours:** May–Aug daily 10:00–19:00; Sept–April Tue–Sun 10:00–18:00, closed Mon.

▲▲**Norwegian Resistance Museum** Gripping look at Norway's tumultuous WWII experience. **Hours:** June–Aug Mon–Sat 10:00–17:00, Sun 11:00–17:00; Sept–May Mon–Fri 10:00–16:00, Sat–Sun 11:00–16:00.

▲▲**National Gallery** Norway's cultural and natural essence, captured on canvas. **Hours:** Tue–Fri 10:00–18:00, Thu until 20:00, Sat–Sun 10:00–17:00, closed Mon.

▲▲**Viking Ship Museum** An impressive trio of ninth-century Viking ships, with exhibits on the men who built them. **Hours:**

door by the window is the little round table the playwright Henrik Ibsen called home. Notice the photos and knickknacks on the wall. At the back of the café, a mural shows Norway's literary and artistic clientele—from a century ago—enjoying this fine hangout. On the far left, find Ibsen, coming in as he did every day at 13:00. Edvard Munch is on the right, leaning against the window, looking pretty drugged. Names are beneath the mural.

• *Cross the street to the little park facing Norway's Swedish-designed...*

Parliament Building (Stortinget): Norway's Parliament meets here. Built in 1866, the building seems to counter the Royal Palace at the other end of Karl Johans Gate. If the flag's flying, Parliament's in session. Today the king is a figurehead, and

Daily May–Sept 9:00–18:00, Oct–April 11:00–16:00.

▲▲*Fram* **Museum** Captivating exhibit on the Arctic exploration ship. **Hours:** Daily mid-June–Aug 9:00–18:45, Sept 9:00–17:45, Oct–April 10:00–15:45, May–mid-June 10:00–17:45.

▲▲**Holmenkollen Ski Jump and Ski Museum** Dizzying vista and schuss through skiing history. **Hours:** Daily June–Aug 9:00–20:00, May and Sept 10:00–17:00, Oct–April 10:00–16:00.

▲*Kon-Tiki* **Museum** Adventures of primitive *Kon-Tiki* and *Ra II* ships built by Thor Heyerdahl. **Hours:** Daily June–Aug 9:30–17:30, April–May and Sept 10:00–17:00, Oct–March 10:30–16:00.

▲**Akershus Fortress Complex and Tours** Historic military base and fortified old center, with guided tours, a ho-hum castle interior, and a couple of museums (including the excellent Norwegian Resistance Museum, listed above). **Hours:** Park open daily 6:00–21:00; 45-minute tours generally offered mid-June–mid-Aug Mon–Fri at 10:00, 12:00, 14:00, and 16:00, Sat–Sun at 12:00, 14:00, and 16:00, no tours off-season.

▲**Norwegian Maritime Museum** A cruise through Norway's rich seafaring heritage. **Hours:** Mid-May–Aug daily 10:00–18:00; Sept–mid-May daily 10:30–16:00, Thu until 18:00.

▲**Edvard Munch Museum** Works of Norway's famous Expressionistic painter. **Hours:** June–Aug daily 10:00–18:00; Sept–May Tue–Fri 10:00–16:00, Sat–Sun 11:00–17:00, closed Mon.

Norway is run by a Parliament and prime minister. Guided tours of Stortinget are offered for those interested in Norwegian government (free; mid-June–Aug daily at 10:00, 11:30, and 13:00; arrive 10 min early to get a spot, enter on Karl Johans Gate side).

• *Continue walking toward the palace through the park, past the fountain, to the...*

Statue of Wergeland: The poet Henrik Wergeland helped inspire the movement for Norwegian autonomy. In the winter, the pool here is frozen and covered with children happily ice-skating. Across the street behind Wergeland stands the **National Theater** and statues of Norway's favorite playwrights: Ibsen and Bjørnstjerne Bjørnson. Across Karl Johans Gate, the pale yellow building is the first university building in Norway, dating from 1854. A block to the right is the National Gallery, with Norway's best collection of paintings (free entry; see self-guided tour on page 154).

• *Follow Roald Amundsens Gate left, to the towering brick...*

City Hall (Rådhuset): Built in the 1930s with contributions from Norway's leading artists, City Hall is worth touring (see page 151). For the best exterior art, circle the courtyard clockwise, studying the colorful woodcuts in the arcade. Each shows a scene from Norwegian mythology, well-explained in English: Thor with his billy-goat chariot, Ask and Embla (a kind of Norse Adam and Eve), Odin on his eight-legged horse guided by ravens, the swan maidens shedding their

swan disguises, and so on. Circle around City Hall on the right to the front. The statues (especially the six laborers on the other side of the building, facing the harbor, who seem to guard the facade) celebrate the nobility of the working class. The 1930s were a period of labor rule in Norway—and the art wanted to imply a classless society, showing everyone working together.

• *Walk to the...*

Harbor: A few years ago, you would have dodged several lanes of busy traffic to get to the harborfront. But Oslo has made its town center relatively quiet and pedestrian-friendly by levying a traffic-discouraging 20-kr toll for every car entering town. (This system, like a similar one in London, subsidizes public transit.)

At the water's edge, find the shiny metal plaque (just left of center) listing the contents of a time capsule planted in the harbor for 1,000 years. You can see the little lighthouse in the harbor ahead. Go to the end of the stubby pier (on the right). This is the ceremonial "enter the city" point for momentous occasions, such as that exciting day in 1905 when Norway gained its independence from Sweden, and its Danish prince sailed in from Copenhagen to become the first modern king of Norway.

• *Stand at the harbor and give it a sweeping counterclockwise look.*

Harborfront Spin-Tour: Oslofjord is a playground, with 40 city-owned, parklike islands. Big, white cruise ships—a large part of the local tourist economy—dock just under the Akershus Fortress on the left. The historic *Christian Radich* tall ship calls this harbor home. Just past the fort's impressive 13th-century ramparts, a statue of FDR grabs the shade. He's here in gratitude for the safe refuge the US gave the king's royal family during World War II—while the king and his government-in-exile waged Norway's

---

Browsing

Oslo's pulse is best felt strolling. Three good areas are along and near the central Karl Johans Gate, which runs from the train station to the palace (see my "Welcome to Oslo" self-guided walk on page 143); in the trendy harborside Aker Brygge mall, a glass-and-chrome collection of sharp cafés and polished produce stalls (really lively at night, trams #10 and #12 from train station); and along Bogstadveien, a lively shopping street with no-nonsense modern commerce, lots of locals, and no tourists (T-bane to Majorstuen and follow this street back toward the palace and tourist zone). While most tourists never get out of the harbor/Karl Johans Gate district, the real, down-to-earth Oslo is better seen elsewhere, such as Bogstadveien. The bohemian, artsy Grünerløkka district, described on page 170, is also good for a wander.

---

fight against the Nazis from London.

Enjoy the grand view of City Hall. The yellow building farther to the left was the old West Train Station; today it houses the Nobel Peace Center, which celebrates the work of Nobel Peace Prize winners (see page 152). The next pier is the launchpad for harbor boat tours and the shuttle boat to the Bygdøy museums. A fisherman is often moored here, selling shrimp from the back of his boat (30 kr/half-liter, 60 kr/liter, Tue–Sun from 8:00 until sold out, not here Mon). Shrimp doesn't get fresher: He catches them and, while making the four-hour sail back into Oslo, cooks them up. At the other end of the harbor, shipyard buildings (this was the heart of Norway's once important ship-building industry) have been transformed into Aker Brygge—Oslo's thriving restaurant/shopping/nightclub zone (see "Eating," page 180).

• From here, you can tour City Hall (see below, cheap lunches Mon–Fri 12:30–13:30 only), visit the Nobel Peace Center (see below), hike up to Akershus Fortress (see page 153), take a harbor cruise (see "Tours," above), or catch a boat across the harbor to the museums at Bygdøy (from pier 3; see "Oslo's Bygdøy Neighborhood," page 165).

SIGHTS AND ACTIVITIES

Near the Harborfront

▲▲**City Hall (Rådhuset)**—City halls, rather than churches, are the dominant buildings in this northern corner of Europe, where people pay high taxes and are satisfied with what their governments do with the money. The main hall of Oslo's City Hall actually feels like a temple to good government (the altar-like mural celebrates "work, play, and civic administration"). The Nobel Peace Prize is awarded in the central hall here each December (though the general Nobel Prize ceremony occurs in Stockholm's City Hall). You can see videos of the ceremony and acceptance speeches in the adjacent Nobel Peace Center.

In 1931, Oslo tore down a slum and began constructing its richly decorated City Hall. It was finished—after a WWII delay—in 1950 to celebrate the city's 900th birthday. Norway's leading artists all contributed to the building, an avant-garde thrill in its day. The interior's 20,000 square feet of bold and colorful Romantic Social Realism murals show town folk, country folk, and people from all classes and walks of life working harmoniously for a better society. The huge paintings take you on a voyage through the collective psyche of Norway, from its simple rural beginnings through the scar tissue of the Nazi occupation and beyond. They're filled with significance and symbolism—and are well-described in English—but become more meaningful only with the excellent, 50-minute guided tours (40 kr; included tours Mon–Sat at 10:00, 12:00, and 14:00; City Hall open daily May–Aug 8:30–17:00, until 16:00 off-season; enter on Karl Johans Gate side, tel. 23 46 16 00). You can view the main hall for free from the lobby. There's a free WC and a wonderful budget lunch cafeteria downstairs that offers a simple hot meal and salad bar at a no-profit price; it's primarily for the building's workers, but the public is also welcome (Mon–Fri 12:30–13:30 only).

Fans of the explorer Nansen might enjoy a coffee or beer across the street at Fridtjof, a bar filled with memorabilia from Nansen's Arctic explorations (daily, 12:00 until late, Nansens Plass 7, near Forex).

▲▲**Nobel Peace Center (Nobels Fredssenter)**—"What is the opposite of conflict?" This question is posed throughout this thoughtful and thought-provoking museum, housed in the old West Train Station (Vestbanen). Oslo's newest museum celebrates past and present Nobel Peace Prize winners with engaging audio and video exhibits and high-tech gadgetry (all with good English explanations). Allow time for reading about past prizewinners, listening to acceptance speeches by recipients from President Carter to Mother Theresa, and check out the interactive book detailing the life and work of Alfred Nobel (60 kr; May–Aug daily 10:00–19:00; Sept–April Tue–Sun 10:00–18:00, closed Mon; Brynjulfs Bulls Plass 1, tel. 48 30 10 00, www.nobelpeacecenter.org).

Akershus Fortress Complex

This parklike complex of sights scattered over Oslo's fortified old center—worth ▲ overall—is still a military base. But as you dodge patrol guards and vans filled with soldiers, you'll see the castle, a prison, war memorials, the Norwegian Resistance Museum, the Armed Forces Museum, and cannon-strewn ramparts affording fine harbor views and picnic perches. There's an unimpressive changing of the guard daily at 13:30 (at the parade ground, deep in the castle complex). The park is open daily 6:00–21:00. From the harbor, follow the stairs (which lead past the FDR statue) to the park.

Fortress Information Center: Located immediately inside the gate, the information center has an interesting exhibit tracing the story of Oslo's fortifications from medieval times through the struggles (environmental) of today. Stop here to pick up a castle overview booklet, quickly browse through the museum, watch the quick video, and consider catching a tour (see below; museum entry free, mid-June–mid-Aug Mon–Fri 9:00–17:00, Sat–Sun 11:00–17:00, shorter hours off-season, tel. 23 09 39 17).

▲**Fortress Tours**—The free 45-minute, English-language walking tours of the grounds help you make sense of the most historic piece of real estate in Oslo (mid-June–mid-Aug Mon–Fri usually at 10:00, 12:00, 14:00, and 16:00; Sat–Sun at 12:00, 14:00, and 16:00; no tours off-season, depart from Fortress Information Center, call center in advance to confirm times, phone number above).

Akershus Castle—Although it's one of Oslo's oldest buildings, the castle overlooking the harbor is mediocre by European standards; the big, empty rooms recall Norway's medieval poverty. As you stand in the courtyard, steps on the left go to a one-way circuit of rooms open to the public. After hiking through these rooms, head for the chapel (at the far end of the courtyard). Behind the chapel altar, steps lead down to some royal tombs and deeper into the dungeon (50 kr, sparse English descriptions throughout, May–mid-Sept Mon–Sat 10:00–16:00, Sun 12:30–16:00; closed mid-Sept–April). The castle is interesting only with the tour (included 50-min English tours summer only; Mon–Sat at 11:00, 13:00, and 15:00; Sun at 13:00 and 15:00; more on busy days, tel. 22 41 25 21). There are terrific harbor views from the rampart just outside.

▲▲**Norwegian Resistance Museum (Norges Hjemmefront-museum)**—This fascinating museum tells the story of Norway's WWII experience: appeasement, Nazi invasion, resistance, liberation, and, finally, the return of the king. (It's a one-way, chronological, can't-get-lost route—enter through 1940 door.) The museum is particularly poignant, because many patriots featured were executed by the Germans right outside the front door. With wonderful English descriptions, this is an inspirational look at how the national spirit can endure total occupation by a malevolent force (30 kr, 60-kr family ticket covers two adults plus one or two kids, June–Aug Mon–Sat 10:00–17:00, Sun 11:00–17:00; Sept–May Mon–Fri 10:00–16:00, Sat–Sun 11:00–16:00; next to castle, overlooking harbor, tel. 23 09 31 38).

Armed Forces Museum (Forsvarsmuseet)—Across the fortress parade ground, a too-spacious museum traces Norwegian military history from Viking days to post–World War II. The early stuff is sketchy, but the WWII story is compelling (free; June–Aug Mon–Fri 10:00–17:00, Sat–Sun 11:00–17:00; shorter hours off-season, tel. 23 09 35 82).

National Historical Museum (Historisk Museum)—Facing Karl Johans Gate just below the palace is a fine Art Nouveau building offering a free and easy (if underwhelming) peek at Norway's history. The ground floor offers a walk through the local history from prehistoric times. It includes the country's top collection of Viking artifacts, displayed in low-tech, old-school exhibits with barely a word of English to give it meaning. There's also some medieval church art. The museum's highlight is upstairs: an exhibit (well-described in English) about life in the Arctic for the Sami people (also previously known to outsiders as Laplanders). In this overview of the past, a few Egyptian mummies and Norwegian coins through the ages are tossed in for good measure. The museum offers 45-minute Viking tours daily at noon in the summer (free; mid-May–mid-Sept Tue–Sun 10:00–17:00, closed Mon; mid-Sept–mid-May Tue–Sun 11:00–16:00, closed Mon; Frederiks Gate 2, tel. 22 85 99 12, www.khm.uio.no).

National Gallery (Nasjonalgalleriet)

While there are many schools of painting and sculpture displayed in Norway's National Gallery—a ▲▲ sight—focus on what's uniquely Norwegian. Paintings come and go in this museum, but the rooms generally maintain their themes. A thoughtful visit here gives those heading into the mountains and fjord country a chance to pack along a little of Norway's cultural soul. Tuck these images carefully away with your goat cheese—they'll sweeten your explorations.

The gallery also has several Picassos, a noteworthy Impressionist collection, and some Vigeland statues. Its many raving examples of Munch's work, including one of his famous *Scream* paintings, make a trip to the Edvard Munch

National Gallery

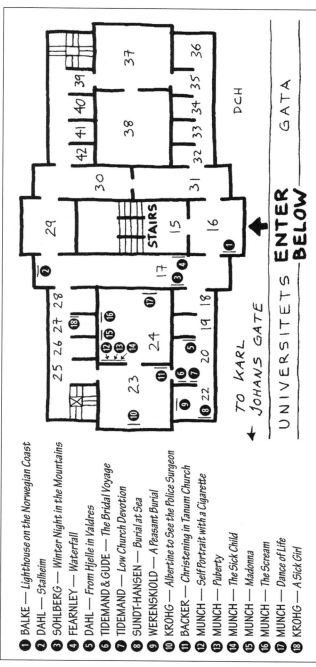

1 BALKE — *Lighthouse on the Norwegian Coast*
2 DAHL — *Stalheim*
3 SOHLBERG — *Winter Night in the Mountains*
4 FEARNLEY — *Waterfall*
5 DAHL — *From Hjelle in Valdres*
6 TIDEMAND & GUDE — *The Bridal Voyage*
7 TIDEMAND — *Low Church Devotion*
8 SUNDT-HANSEN — *Burial at Sea*
9 WERENSKIOLD — *A Peasant Burial*
10 KROHG — *Albertine to See the Police Surgeon*
11 BACKER — *Christening in Tanum Church*
12 MUNCH — *Self-Portrait with a Cigarette*
13 MUNCH — *Puberty*
14 MUNCH — *The Sick Child*
15 MUNCH — *Madonna*
16 MUNCH — *The Scream*
17 MUNCH — *Dance of Life*
18 KROHG — *A Sick Girl*

Museum unnecessary for most (see page 169).

Cost, Hours, Location: Free, Tue–Fri 10:00–18:00, Thu until 20:00, Sat–Sun 10:00–17:00, closed Mon, Universitets Gata 13, tel. 22 20 04 04, www.nationalmuseum.no.

Self-Guided Tour

This easy-to-handle museum gives an effortless tour back in time and through Norway's most beautiful valleys, mountains, and fjords, with the help of its Romantic painters (especially Johan Christian Dahl). The gallery is thoughtfully organized into themes with worthwhile general descriptions on the wall in each room. In every section, read the theme, and then enjoy the paintings in general while following this self-guided tour. Here are some of the highlights.

• *Begin in Room 16, near the top of the stairs.*

Landscape Paintings and Romanticism

Landscape painting has always played an important role in Norwegian art, perhaps because Norway provides such an awesome and varied landscape to inspire artists. Landscape painting here reached its peak during the Romantic period in the late 1800s, which stressed the beauty of unspoiled nature. (This passion for landscapes sets Norway apart from Denmark and Sweden.) Perhaps it was driven by Norway's need to find its national identity while it struggled for independence in the 19th century.

❶ **Peder Balke—*Lighthouse on the Norwegian Coast* (1855):** Peder Balke (1804–1887) traveled to the far north of Norway, and was inspired by the wild and desolate landscape. At the dawn of Norway's independence, the dark storm clouds loom in the distance. Will the storm wreck the tiny, wind-battered ship we glimpse out at sea, or will it see its way through the storm?

• *Continue into the next room, Room 17.*

❷ **Johan Christian Dahl—*Stalheim* (1842):** This painting epitomizes the Norwegian closeness to nature. It shows the same view 21st-century travelers enjoy on their Norway in a Nutshell excursion (see page 188): the mountains at the head of the Sognefjord as seen from the venerable Stalheim Hotel. Painted in 1842, it's textbook Romantic style. Nature rules—the background is as detailed as the foreground, and you are sucked in.

Johan Christian Dahl (1788–1857) is considered the father of Norwegian Romanticism. Romantics such as Dahl (and Turner, Beethoven, and Lord Byron) put emotion over rationality. They reveled in the power of nature—death and pessimism ripple through their work. The rainbow says it all: This is God's work. Nature is big. God is great. Man is small...and he's gonna die. The birch tree—standing boldly front and center—is a standard symbol for the politically downtrodden Norwegian people: hardy, cut down, but defiantly sprouting new branches. The tiny folks are in traditional dress. In the mid-19th century, Norwegians were awakening to their national identity. Throughout Europe, nationalism and Romanticism went hand-in-hand.

Find four typical Norse farms. They remind us that these are hardworking, independent, small landowners. There was no feudalism in medieval Norway. People were poor...but they owned their own land. You can almost taste the *geitost*.

• *Look at the other works in Room 17 (the biggest room in the gallery). Dahl's paintings and those by his Norwegian contemporaries, showing heavy clouds and glaciers, repeat these same themes—drama over rationalism, nature pounding humanity. Human figures are melancholy. Norwegians, so close to nature, are fascinated by those plush, magic hours of dawn and twilight. The dusk makes us wonder: What will the future bring? Focus on two paintings in particular....*

❸ **Harald Sohlberg—*Winter Night in the Mountains* (1914):** Harald Sohlberg was inspired by this image while skiing in the mountains in the winter of 1899. Over the years, he attempted to re-create the scene that inspired this remark: "The mountains in winter reduce one to silence. One is overwhelmed, as in a mighty, vaulted church, only a thousand times more so."

❹ **Thomas Fearnley—*Waterfall* (1817):** Man cannot control nature or his destiny. Lumberjacks are working. But the eagle says, "While you can cut these logs, they'll always be mine."

• *Continue through rooms 18 and 19 and into Room 20, past several busts and portraits of Norway's top artists, poets, and painters, including Dahl in a setting he typically painted.*

❺ **Dahl—*From Hjelle in Valdres* (1851):** Another typical Dahl setting: romantic nature and an idealized scene. The characters are wearing the *bunad* (national folk costume of Norway). This isn't everyday work wear, but it fits just fine in this nationalistic tableau.

❻ **Adolph Tidemand and Hans Gude—*The Bridal Voyage* (1848):** This famous painting shows the ultimate Norwegian

scene: a wedding party with everyone decked out in traditional garb, leaving the stave church and floating down the quintessential fjord (Hardanger). It's a studio work (not real) and a collaboration: Hans Gude painted the landscape, and Adolph Tidemand painted the people. Study their wedding finery. This work trumpets the greatness of both the landscape and Norwegian culture.

❼ **Tidemand—*Low Church Devotion* (1848):** This scene shows a dissenting Lutheran church group (of which there were many in the 19th century) worshipping in a smokehouse. The light of God powers through the chimney, illuminating salt-of-the-earth people with strong faiths. Rather than accept the Norwegian king's "High Church," they worshipped in their homes in a more ascetic style. Later, many of these people emigrated to America for greater religious freedom.

• *Enter Room 22.*

The Photographic Eye

At the end of the 19th century, Norwegian painters traded the emotions of Romanticism for more slice-of-life detail. This was the end of the Romantic period and the beginning of Realism. With the advent of photography, painters went beyond simple realism and into extreme realism.

❽ **Carl Sundt-Hansen—*Burial at Sea* (1890):** Carl Sundt-Hansen (1841–1907) was an early photo-realist. He finished only a few paintings, and is therefore not well-known. But study the faces of his *Burial at Sea,* and you'll wish there were more of his works.

❾ **Erik Werenskiold—*A Peasant Burial* (1885):** While Monet and the Impressionists were busy abandoning realism, Norwegian artists continued to embrace it. In this painting, you're invited to participate. Your presence completes the half-circle at the grave site. Rough Impressionistic brush strokes have replaced the tedious detail of earlier Romantic Age painters, but you still have earthy people immersed in nature. The hands speak volumes about the life of toil here. A common thread in Norwegian art is the cycle—the tough cycle—of life.

• *Backtrack through Room 21 to reach Room 23.*

Modern Life

In the 1880s, Europe's artistic community (which included a few Norwegians) turned to Paris. Impressionism took the art world by storm. French artists abandoned reality, using the physical object only as a rack upon which to hang light and color—their true subject matter. Inhibited Norwegians couldn't go quite that far. While their Naturalism (parallel to Impressionism) came with a new appreciation of light, their subjects remained real things.

❿ **Christian Krohg—*Albertine to See the Police Surgeon* (c. 1885–1887):** Christian Krohg (1852–1925) is known as Edvard Munch's inspiration, but to Norwegians, he is famous in his own right for his artistry and giant personality. Krohg had a sharp interest in social justice. In this painting, Albertine, a sweet girl from the countryside, has fallen into the world of prostitution in the big city. She's the new kid on the red-light block in the 1880s,

Edvard Munch
(1863–1944)

Edvard Munch is Norway's most famous and influential painter. His life was rich, complex, and sad. His father was a doctor who had a nervous breakdown. His mother and sister both died of tuberculosis. He knew suffering. And he gave us the enduring symbol of 20th-century pain, *The Scream*.

Munch's paintings have their own internal logic. Moonbeams at sea are phallic. Man plus woman equals need chained to exasperation. Hair becomes blood, which becomes sperm.

After a nervous breakdown in 1908, Munch emerged less troubled—but a less powerful painter. His late works were as a colorist—big, bright, less tormented...and less noticed.

as Oslo's prostitutes are pulled into the police clinic for their regular checkup. Note her traditional dress and the disdain she gets from the more experienced girls.

❶ Harriet Backer—*Christening in Tanum Church* (1892): Harriet Backer (1845–1932) was from an aristocratic family and therefore had the means to travel to Paris and hobnob with the Impressionists. Her paintings, while not as airy as Monet's, still have strong Impressionist influences. She plays with light well, allowing it to peek into her works.

• *Continue into Room 24.*

Turmoil

By the late 1800s, many prominent artists began to move away from the imitation of reality. Liberating their brushstrokes, they infused their work with emotion and expression at the expense of realism. Here we meet Norway's single most famous painter, Edvard Munch (see sidebar). Survey Room 24, viewing the paintings in clockwise order.

❷ Edvard Munch—*Self Portrait with a Cigarette* (1895): In this self-portrait, Munch is spooked, haunted—an artist working, immersed in an oppressive world. Indefinable shadows inhabit the background. His hand shakes as he considers his uncertain future. (Ironic, considering he created his masterpieces during this depressed period.) After a 1909 visit to a Danish clinic, he found peace—and lost his painting power. Afterward, Munch never again painted another strong example of what we love most about his art.

❸ Munch—*Puberty* (1895): Until this point, people were at the mercy of nature in Norwegian art. Now, people are at the mercy of their own psyche as well. This fragile young girl peers with wide and frightened eyes into the future.

⓮ Munch—*The Sick Child* (1896): The girl's face melts into the pillow. She's becoming two-dimensional, halfway between life and death. Everything else is peripheral, even her despairing mother saying goodbye. You can see how Munch scraped and repainted the face until he got it right.

⓯ Munch—*Madonna* (1894–1895): Munch had a tortured relationship with women. He never married. He dreaded and struggled with love, writing that he feared if he loved too much, he'd lose his painting talent. In his paintings, women are a threat—Medusas with wild and cascading vampire hair.

⓰ Munch—*The Scream* (1893): Munch's most famous work shows a man screaming, capturing the fright many feel as the human "race" does just that. The figure seems isolated from the people on the bridge—locked up in himself, unable to stifle his scream. Munch made four versions of this scene, which has become *the* textbook example of Expressionism. On one, he graffitied: "This painting is the work of a madman." He explained that the painting "shows today's society, reverberating within me... making me want to scream."

⓱ Munch—*Dance of Life* (1899–1900): In this scene of five dancing couples, we glimpse Munch's notion of femininity. To him, women were a complex mix of madonna and whore. We see Munch's take on the cycle of women's lives: she's a virgin (discarding the sweet flower of youth), a whore (a jaded temptress in red), and a widow (having destroyed the man, she is finally alone, aging, in black). With the phallic moon rising on the lake, Munch demonizes women as they turn men into green-faced, lusty monsters.

• *Go back through Room 23 to reach Room 25.*

Atmosphere

Landscape painters were often fascinated by the phenomena of nature, and the artwork in this room takes us back to this ideal from the Romantic Age. Painters were challenged by capturing atmospheric conditions at a specific moment, since it meant making quick sketches outdoors, before the weather changed yet again.

• *Continue into Room 27.*

Vulnerability

Death, disease, and suffering were themes seen again and again in art from the late 1800s. The most serious disease during this period was tuberculosis (which killed Munch's mother and sister).

⓭ Krohg—*A Sick Girl* (1880): This extremely realistic painting shows a child dying of tuberculosis, as so many did in Norway in the 19th century. The girl looks directly at you. You can almost feel the cloth, with its many shades of white.

• *On that cheery note, I'll leave you to enjoy the rest of the museum on your own.*

Frogner Park

▲▲▲**Vigeland Sculptures**—The 75-acre Frogner Park contains a lifetime of work by Norway's greatest sculptor, Gustav Vigeland (1869–1943). In 1921, he made a deal with the city. In return for a great studio and state support, he'd spend his creative life beautifying Oslo with this sculpture garden. From 1924 to 1943 he worked on-site, sculpting 192 bronze and granite statues—600

figures, each nude and unique. Vigeland even designed the landscaping. Today the park is loved and respected (no police, no fences, and no graffiti) by the people of Oslo. The garden is always open and free (bus #20, bus #45, tram #12, and tram #15 all stop immediately in front of the main entry; or T-bane: Majorstuen and a 5-min walk). The Frognerbadet swimming pool is also at Frogner Park (see page 170). The park is safe (cameras monitor for safety) and lit in the evening.

Vigeland's park is more than great art: It's a city at play. Appreciate its urban Norwegian ambience. The park is huge, but this visit is a snap. Here's a quick, four-stop, straight-line, gate-to-monolith tour:

1. Enter the Park from Kirkeveien: For an illustrated guide and fine souvenir, pick up the 70-kr book in the Visitors Center (Besøkssenter) on your right as you enter. The modern cafeteria has sandwiches (indoor/outdoor seating, daily 9:00–20:30, less Sun and off-season), plus books, gifts, and WCs. Look at the statue of Gustav Vigeland (hammer and chisel in hand, drenched in pigeon poop) and consider his messed-up life. He lived with his many models. His marriages failed. His children entangled his artistic agenda. He didn't age gracefully. He didn't name his statues, and refused to explain their meanings. While those who know his life story can read it clearly in the granite and bronze, I'd forget Gustav's troubles and see his art as observations on the bittersweet cycle of life in general—from a man who must have had a passion for living.

2. Bridge: The 300-foot-long bridge is bounded by four granite columns: Three show a man fighting a lizard, the fourth shows a woman submitting to the lizard's embrace. Hmmm. But enough lizard love; the 58 bronze statues along the bridge are a general study of the human body. Many deal with relationships between people. In the middle, on the right, find the circular statue of a man and woman going round and round—perhaps the eternal attraction and love between the sexes. But directly opposite, another circle feels like a prison—man against the world, with no refuge. From the man escaping, look down at the children's playground:

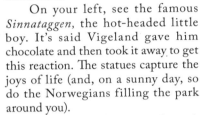

eight bronze infants circling a head-down fetus.

On your left, see the famous *Sinnataggen*, the hot-headed little boy. It's said Vigeland gave him chocolate and then took it away to get this reaction. The statues capture the joys of life (and, on a sunny day, so do the Norwegians filling the park around you).

3. Fountain: Continue through a rose garden to the earliest sculpture unit in the park. Six giants hold a fountain, symbolically toiling with the burden of life, as water—the source of life—cascades steadily around them. Twenty tree-of-life groups surround the fountain. Four clumps of trees (on each corner) show humanity's relationship to nature and the seasons of life: childhood, young love, adulthood, and winter.

Take a quick swing through life, starting on the right with youth. In the branches you'll see a swarm of children (Vigeland called them "geniuses"): a boy sits in a tree, boys actively climb while most girls stand by quietly, and a girl glides through the branches wide-eyed and ready for life...and love. Circle clockwise to the next stage: love scenes. In the third corner, life becomes more complicated: a sad woman in an animal-like tree, a lonely child, a couple plummeting downward (perhaps falling out of love), and finally an angry man driving away babies. The fourth corner completes the cycle, as death melts

into the branches of the tree of life and new geniuses bloom.

The 60 bronze reliefs circling the basin develop the theme further, showing man mixing with nature and geniuses giving the carousel of life yet another spin. Speaking of another spin, circle

Greater Oslo

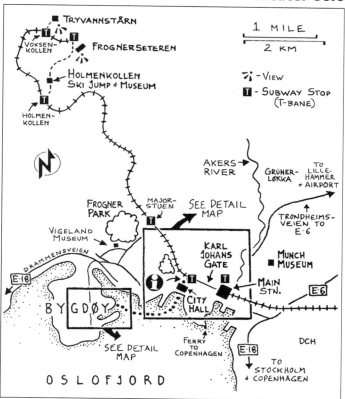

again and follow these reliefs.

The sidewalk surrounding the basin is a maze—life's long and winding road with twists, dead ends, frustrations, and, ultimately, a way out. If you have about an hour to spare, enter the labyrinth (on the side nearest the park's entrance gate, there's a single break in the black border) and follow the white granite path until (on the monolith side) you finally get out. (Tracing this path occupies older kids, affording parents a peaceful break in the park.) Or you can go straight to the monolith.

4. Monolith: The centerpiece of the park—a teeming monolith of life surrounded by 36 granite groups—continues Vigeland's cycle-of-life motif. The figures are hunched and clearly earthbound, while Vigeland explores a lifetime of human relationships. At the center, 121 figures carved out of a single block of stone rocket skyward. Three stone carvers worked daily for 14 years cutting Vigeland's full-size plaster model into the final 180-ton,

50-foot-tall erection.

Circle the plaza, once to trace the stages of life in the 36 statue groups, and a second time to enjoy how Norwegian kids relate to the art. The statues—both young and old—seem to speak to children.

Vigeland lived barely long enough to see his monolith raised. Covered with bodies, it seems inert at the base, and picks up speed as it ascends. Some people seem to naturally rise. Others struggle not to fall. Some help others. Although the granite groups around the monolith are easy to understand, Vigeland left the meaning of the monolith itself open. Like life, it can be interpreted many different ways.

From this summit of the park, look a hundred yards farther, where four children and three adults are intertwined and spinning in the Wheel of Life. Now, look back at the entrance. If the main gate is at 12 o'clock, the studio where Vigeland lived and worked—now the Vigeland Museum—is at 2 o'clock (see the green copper tower poking above the trees). His ashes sit in the top of the tower in clear view of the monolith. If you liked the park, visit the museum—it's a delightful five-minute walk—for an intimate look at the art and how it was made.

▲▲**Vigeland Museum**—Filled with original plaster casts and well-described exhibits on his work, this palatial city-provided studio was Vigeland's workplace. The high south-facing windows provided just the right light.

Vigeland, who had a deeply religious upbringing, was also inspired by visits to Rodin's studio in Paris in 1893. Vigeland said, "The road between feeling and execution should be as short as possible." Here, immersed in his work, Vigeland supervised his craftsmen like a father, from 1924 until his death in 1943 (45 kr; June–Aug Tue–Sun 11:00–17:00, closed Mon; Sept–May Tue–Sun 12:00–16:00, closed Mon; bus #20 or #45 or tram #12 or #15 to Frogner Plass, Nobelsgate 32, tel. 23 49 37 00).

Oslo City Museum (Oslo Bymuseum)—This hard-to-be-thrilled-about little museum tells the story of Oslo (50 kr, free on Sat, Tue 12:00–19:00, Wed–Sun 12:00–16:00, closed Mon, shorter hours off-season, borrow English description sheet, located in Frogner Park at Frogner Manor Farm across street from Vigeland Museum, tel. 23 28 41 70).

Oslo's Bygdøy Neighborhood

This exciting cluster of sights—worth ▲▲▲—is on a park-like peninsula just across the harbor from downtown. It provides a busy and rewarding half day (at a minimum) of sightseeing. Here, within a short walk, are five important sights:

• **Norwegian Folk Museum,** an open-air park with traditional log buildings from all corners of the country.

• **Viking Ship Museum,** showing off the best-preserved Viking longboats in existence.

• *Fram* **Museum,** showcasing the modern Viking spirit with the ship of arctic-exploration fame.

• *Kon-Tiki* **Museum,** starring the *Kon-Tiki* and the *Ra II,* in which Norwegian explorer Thor Heyerdahl proved that early civilizations—with their existing technologies—could have crossed the oceans.

• **Norwegian Maritime Museum,** which is most interesting to sailors, has a wonderfully scenic movie of Norway.

Getting There: Sailing from downtown to Bygdøy is half the fun, and it gets you in a seafaring mood. Ride the Bygdøy ferry—marked *Public Ferry Bygdøy Museums*—from pier 3 in front of City Hall (20 kr, uses same ticket as city transit, free with Oslo Pass, May–Sept daily 8:00–21:00, usually 3/hr; doesn't run Oct–April). Nearby, much more expensive tour boats depart. You want the public ferry. For a less memorable approach, you can take bus #30 (from train station or National Theater). Boats generally leave from downtown and from the museum dock at :05, :25, and :45.

Getting Around Bygdøy: The Norwegian Folk and Viking Ship museums are a 10-minute walk from the ferry's first stop (Dronningen). The other museums (*Fram, Kon-Tiki,* and

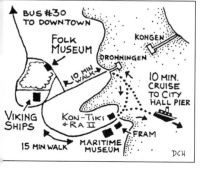

Maritime) are at the second ferry stop (Bygdøynes). All Bygdøy sights are within a pleasant (when sunny) 15-minute walk of each other. The walk gives you a picturesque taste of small-town Norway. A goofy and overpriced tourist train shuttles tired visitors from sight to sight (2/hr, daily 9:30–18:00, 25 kr per segment or 50 kr for all day). A city bus (#30) connects the sights four times hourly. If you take the bus within an hour of having taken the public ferry, your ticket is still good on the bus. Stops are immediately in front of the *Kon-Tiki* Museum, the Viking Ship Museum, and the Norwegian Folk Museum.

Eating at Bygdøy: Lunch options near the *Kon-Tiki* are a sandwich bar (relaxing picnic spots along the grassy shoreline), a cafeteria (with tables overlooking the harbor), or a stuffy indoor restaurant above the Maritime Museum (fancy 170-kr lunch buffet daily). The Norwegian Folk Museum has a decent cafeteria inside and a fun little farmers' market stall across the street from the entrance. For real food, your best bet is **Restaurant Lanternen** at the Dronningen dock, which serves *smørrebrød*, salads, and more (100–150 kr, daily 11:00–23:00, shorter hours on Sun, dressy interior or relaxing dockside tables, tel. 22 43 78 38).

▲▲▲**Norwegian Folk Museum (Norsk Folkemuseum)**— Brought from all corners of Norway, 150 buildings have been reassembled on these 35 acres. While Stockholm's Skansen was the first to open to the public (see page 286), this museum is a bit older, started in 1882 as the king's private collection (and the inspiration for Skansen).

Think of the visit in three parts: the park sprinkled with old buildings, the re-created old town, and the folk-art museum. In peak season, the park is lively, with craftspeople doing their traditional things (pick up the daily schedule of activities as you pay) and costumed guides all around. (They're paid to happily answer your questions—so ask many.) Don't miss the evocative old stave church (see page 231). The old town comes complete with apartments from various generations, offering an intimate look at lifestyles here in 1905, in 1930, and even from the 1970s.

The museum beautifully presents woody, colorfully painted folk art (ground floor), exquisite-in-a-peasant-kind-of-way folk costumes (upstairs), and especially interesting displays showing Norwegian traditions from birth to death. Everything is thoughtfully explained in English. Don't miss the best Sami culture exhibit I've seen in Scandinavia (across the courtyard in the green building).

Upon arrival, pick up the site map and review the list of activities on that day. The place is lively only June through mid-August, when buildings are open and staffed. Otherwise, the indoor museum is fine, but the park is just a walk past lots of locked-up log cabins. On summer Sundays, you can enjoy folk dancing at 14:00 (mid-May–mid Sept only). If you don't take a tour, glean information from the 10-kr guidebook and the informative attendants (90 kr, 70 kr off-season, daily mid-May–mid-Sept 10:00–18:00; off-season daily 11:00–15:00, free lockers, Museumsveien 10). Bus #30 stops immediately in front.

▲▲Viking Ship Museum (Vikingskiphuset)—Three great ninth-century Viking ships are surrounded by artifacts from their days of rape, pillage, and plunder. There are no museum tours, but everything is well described in English, and it's hard not to hear the English-speaking big-bus-tour guides. Climb to the viewpoints for a good look into the boats. There was a time when much of a  frightened Europe closed every prayer with, "And deliver us from the Vikings, Amen." Gazing up at the prow of one of these sleek, time-stained vessels, you can almost hear the screams and smell the armpits of those redheads on the rampage. The *Oseberg* ship is the big boat from A.D. 834, while the *Gokstad* dates from A.D. 950. (In 1892, a replica of this ship sailed from Norway to America in 44 days to counter the 400th anniversary of Columbus *not* discovering America.) The ships tend to steal the show, but don't miss the wing with artifacts, including a dark room with impressive Viking weaving and textiles (50 kr, daily May–Sept 9:00–18:00; Oct–April 11:00–16:00, tel. 22 13 52 80, www.khm.uio.no). The 5-kr booklet just repeats what you can read at each display.

▲▲*Fram* Museum (Frammuseet)—This great ship took modern-day Vikings Amundsen and Nansen deep into the Arctic and Antarctic, farther north and south than any ship had before. For three years, the *Fram* was part of an Arctic ice drift. The exhibit is engrossing. Read the ground-floor displays, then explore the boat. The building also tells the chilling tales of other Arctic and Antarctic adventures done under the Norwegian flag (40 kr, daily mid-June–Aug 9:00–18:45, Sept 9:00–17:45, Oct–April 10:00–15:45, May–mid-June 10:00–17:45, tel. 23 28 29 50, www.fram.museum.no).

▲▲*Kon-Tiki* Museum (*Kon-Tiki* Museet)—Next to the *Fram* is a museum housing the *Kon-Tiki* and the *Ra II*, the boats built by Thor Heyerdahl (1914–2002). Heyerdahl sailed the *Kon-Tiki* for 4,000 miles and the *Ra II* for 3,000 miles to prove that early South Americans could have sailed to Polynesia and Africans could have populated Barbados. Both boats are well displayed and described in English. Various 10-minute *Adventures of Thor Heyerdahl* movie clips play constantly in a small theater at the end of the exhibit (45 kr, daily June–Aug 9:30–17:30, April–May and Sept 10:00–17:00, Oct–March 10:30–16:00, tel. 23 08 67 67, www.kon-tiki.no).

▲Norwegian Maritime Museum (Norsk Sjøfartsmuseum)—If you like the sea, this museum is a salt lick, providing a look at

Norway's maritime heritage. Its collection includes the charred remains of Norway's oldest boat (2,200 years old), artifacts from the immigration days, and a case devoted to World War II (40 kr; mid-May–Aug daily 10:00–18:00; Sept–mid-May daily 10:30–16:00, Thu until 18:00; tel. 24 11 41 50, www.norsk-sjofartsmuseum .no). Don't miss the movie: *The Coast: A Way of Life,* included with your admission, is a breathtaking widescreen film swooping you scenically over Norway's dramatic sea and fishing townscapes from here all the way to North Cape in a comfy theater (20 min, shown at the top of the hour and often at the bottom—schedule at door, follow signs to *Supervideografen*).

The polar sloop *Gjøa* is dry-docked next to the ferry dock. This is the boat Amundsen and a crew of six used from 1903 to 1906 to "discover" the Northwest Passage.

Outer Oslo

▲▲**Holmenkollen Ski Jump and Ski Museum**—Overlooking Oslo is a tremendous ski jump with a unique museum of skiing. The T-bane gets you out of the city, through the hills, forests, and mansions that surround Oslo, and to the jump (take any westbound train—that's *tog mot vest*—to Majorstuen, then line #1 to Holmenkollen, and hike up the road 10 min). After touring the history of skiing in the museum, ride the elevator and climb the 100-step stairway to the top of the jump for the best possible view of Oslo—and a chance to look down the long and frightening ramp that has sent so many tumbling into the agony of defeat. In order to win the privilege of hosting the 2011 World Championship, Oslo agreed to rebuild the jump. Reconstruction will begin in 2008 (shutting it down to visitors for a while).

The **ski museum,** a must for skiers, traces the evolution of the sport, from 4,000-year-old rock paintings to crude 1,500-year-old wooden sticks to the slick and quickly evolving skis of modern times, including a fun exhibit showing the royal family on skis (70-kr ticket includes museum and jump, both open daily June–Aug 9:00–20:00, Sept and May 10:00–17:00, Oct–April 10:00–16:00, tel. 22 92 32 64, www.holmenkollen.com).

To cap your Holmenkollen experience, step into the **simulator** and fly down the Olympic slopes of Lillehammer in a virtual downhill ski race. My legs were exhausted after the five-minute terror. This stimulator, parked in front of the ski museum, costs 50 kr, or 40 kr with an Oslo Pass. (Japanese tourists, who wig out over this one, are usually given a free ride after paying for four.)

For an easy downhill jaunt through the Norwegian forest, with a woodsy coffee or meal break in the middle, stay on the T-bane past Holmenkollen to the end of the line (Frognerseteren) and walk 10 minutes downhill to the **Frognerseteren Hovedrestaurant** (described on page 185—fine traditional eatery with sod roof, reindeer meat on the griddle, and a city view). Continue on the same lane another 20 minutes downhill to the ski jump, and then to the Holmenkollen T-bane stop.

▲**Edvard Munch Museum (Munch Museet)**—The only Norwegian painter to have had a serious impact on European art, Munch (pronounced "monk") is a surprise to many who visit this fine museum. The emotional, disturbing, and powerfully Expressionistic work of this strange and perplexing man is arranged chronologically. You'll see paintings, drawings, lithographs, and photographs. The free National Gallery, which also displays many Munch works (see page 154), can be a good alternative if you find the Munch Museum, on the outskirts of the city, too expensive or time-consuming to reach (65 kr; June–Aug daily 10:00–18:00; Sept–May Tue–Fri 10:00–16:00, Sat–Sun 11:00–17:00, closed Mon; 25 kr audioguide, guided tours daily in the summer at 13:00; T-bane to Tøyen, Tøyengata 53, tel. 23 49 35 00, www.munch .museum.no).

The Munch Museum was in the news in August 2004, when two Munch paintings, including one version of his famous *Scream*, were brazenly stolen right off the walls in broad daylight. After several months of being closed, the museum reopened in June 2005 with extremely tight new security measures. Happily, in 2006, the paintings were recovered and returned to the museum. For more on Munch, see page 159.

Forests, Lakes, and Beaches—Oslo is surrounded by a vast forest dotted with idyllic little lakes, huts, joggers, bikers, and sun worshippers. Mountain-biking possibilities are endless (as you'll discover if you go exploring without a good map). Consider taking your bike on the T-bane (for the cost of a child's ticket) to the end of line #1 (Frognerseteren, 30 min from National Theater) to gain the most altitude possible. Then follow the gravelly roads (mostly downhill but with some climbing) past several dreamy lakes to Sognsvann at the end of T-bane line #3. Farther east, from Maridalsvannet, a bike path follows the Aker River all the way back into town. (The TI has details on bike rental options, which are few in Oslo.)

For plenty of trees and none of the exercise, ride the T-bane #3 to its last stop, Sognsvann (with a beach towel rather than a bike), and join in the lakeside scene. A pleasant trail leads around the lake.

Other popular beaches are located on islands in the harbor (such as Bygdøy Huk—direct boat from pier 3 in front of City Hall). The various island getaways are described in the TI's *Oslo Fjord Islands* flier and in Use It's *Streetwise* magazine.

Tusenfryd—This giant amusement complex just out of town offers a world of family fun. It's sort of a combination Norwegian Disneyland/Viking Knott's Berry Farm, with more than 50 rides, plenty of entertainment, and restaurants. Admission is based on your height: under 95 centimeters (3 feet)—free; under 1.2 meters (4 feet)—240 kr, over 1.2 meters (4 feet)—280 kr (daily June–mid-Aug 10:30–19:00, closed in winter, tel. 64 97 64 97, www .tusenfryd.no). A bus takes fun-seekers to the park from behind Oslo's train station (30 kr, 2/hr, 20-min ride, departs Oslo 10:00–16:00, departs Tusenfryd 14:30–17:30).

Wet Fun—Oslo offers a variety of water play. In Frogner Park, the **Frognerbadet** has a outdoor pools, a water slide, high dives, a cafeteria, and lots of young families (70 kr, students half-price, free with Oslo Pass, late May–mid-Aug Mon–Fri 7:00–19:30, Sat–Sun 10:00–18:00, last entry one hour before closing, closed mid-Aug–late May, Middelthunsgate 28, tel. 23 27 54 50).

Tøyenbadet is a modern indoor/outdoor pool complex with a 330-foot-long water slide, as well as a gym and sauna (65 kr, free with Oslo Pass, daily until 19:00, 10-min walk from Edvard Munch Museum, Helgengate 90, tel. 23 30 44 70). Oslo's free botanical gardens are nearby.

From Akers River to the Grünerløkka District

Connect the dots by following the self-guided "Walk up the Akers River to Grünerløkka" (below).

Akers River—This river, while only about five miles long, powered Oslo's early industry: flour mills in the 1300s, sawmills in the 1500s, and Norway's industrial revolution in the 1800s. A walk along the river not only spans Oslo's history, but also shows the contrast the city offers. The bottom of the river (where this walk doesn't go)—bordered by the high-rise Oslo Plaza Hotel and the "Little Pakistan" neighborhood of Grønland—has its share of drunks and drugs, reflecting a new urban reality in Oslo. Farther up, the river valley becomes a park as it winds past decent-size waterfalls and red-brick factories. The source of the river (and Oslo's drinking water) is the pristine Lake Maridal, situated at the edge of the Nordmarka wilderness. The idyllic recreation scenes along Lake Maridal are a world apart from the rougher reality downstream.

▲**Grünerløkka**—The Grünerløkka district is the largest planned urban area in Oslo. It was built in the latter half of the 1800s to house the legions of workers employed at the factories powered by the Akers River. The first buildings were modeled on similar places built in Berlin. (German visitors observe that there's now more turn-of-the-20th-century Berlin here than in present-day Berlin.) While slummy in the 1980s, today it's trendy. Locals sometimes

Grünerløkka/Grønland Area

Walk

1 Akersgata & Start of Walk
2 Vår Frelsers Cemetery
3 Gamle Aker Church
4 Telthusbakken Road
5 Åmot Bridge
6 Big Waterfall
7 Statue of Women Laborers
8 Thorvald Meyers Gate
9 Olaf Ryes Plass
10 Vaterlands Bridge & End of Walk

Eateries

11 Punjab Tandoori & Tandoori Curry Corner
12 Alibaba Restaurant
13 Asylet Restaurant
14 Olympen Brown Pub
15 Café Con Bar
16 Sudost Restaurant

refer to it as "Oslo's Greenwich Village." Although that's way over the mark, it is a bustling area with lots of cafés, good spots for a fun meal, and few tourists.

Grünerløkka can be reached from the center of town by a short ride on tram #11, #12, or #13, or by taking the short but interesting walk described below.

▲**Walk up the Akers River to Grünerløkka**—While every tourist explores the harborfront and main drag of Oslo, few venture into a neighborhood that evokes the Industrial Revolution. Once housing poor workers, it now attracts hip professionals. A 45-minute hike up the Akers River, finishing in the stylish Grünerløkka district, shines a truly different light on Oslo. Navigate with the TI's free city map, and the map on the previous page.

Begin the walk by leaving Karl Johans Gate at the top of the hill, and head right up Akersgata, which becomes Ullevålsveien. Akersgata is Oslo's "Fleet Street" (lined with major newspaper companies), and big government buildings. On the right notice the red-brick Supreme Court building and then the Department of Finance—an example of Jugendstil, or Art Nouveau, architecture. Then you'll pass the massive brick Trefoldighets Church, and St. Olav's Church before reaching the **Vår Frelsers (Our Savior's) Cemetery**. Enter the cemetery across from the baby shop.

Stop at the big metal map just inside the gate to chart your course through the Vår Frelsers Cemetery: Go through the green Æreslunden section—with the biggest plots and highest elevation—and out the opposite end (#13 on the metal map) onto Akersveien. En route, check out some of the tombstones of the illuminati and literati buried in the honorary Æreslunden section. They include Munch, Ibsen, Bjørnson, and many of the painters whose works you can see in the National Gallery (all marked on a map posted at the entrance). Exiting on the far side of the cemetery, walk left 100 yards up Akersveien to the church.

The Romanesque **Gamle Aker Church** (from the 1100s), the oldest building in Oslo, is worth a look inside (free, daily 12:00–14:00). The church, which fell into ruins and has been impressively rebuilt, is pretty bare except for a pulpit and baptismal font from the 1700s.

From the church, backtrack 20 yards, head left at the playground, and go downhill on **Telthusbakken Road** toward the huge, gray former grain silos (now student housing). The cute lane is lined with old wooden houses: The people who constructed these homes were too poor to meet the no-wood fire-safety building codes within the city limits, so they built in what used to be suburbs. At the bottom of Telthusbakken, cross the busy Maridalsveien and walk directly through the park to the Akers River. The lively Grünerløkka district is straight across the river from here, but if you have 20 minutes and a little energy, detour upstream first and hook back down. Don't cross the river yet.

Walk along the bike lane upstream through the river gorge park. Just above the first waterfall, cross **Åmatbrua,** the big white suspension footbridge from 1852, that was moved here in 1958. Keep hiking uphill along the river. At the base of the next big waterfall, cross over again to the large brick buildings, hiking up the stairs to the Beyer bridge (above the falls) with *Fabrikkjentene,* a statue of four women laborers. They're pondering the textile factory where they and 700 like them toiled long and hard. This gorge was once lined with the water mills that powered Oslo through its 19th-century Industrial Age boom. Cross over to the Ringnes Brewery and follow **Thorvald Meyers Gate** downhill directly into the heart of Grünerløkka. The main square, called **Olaf Ryes Plass,** is a happening place to grab a meal or drink. Trams take you from here back to the center.

To continue exploring, keep walking (always going straight) until you reach a T-intersection with a busy road. From there (passing the recommended Sudost Restaurant, see page 184), drop down to the riverside path, and follow it downstream to Vaterlands bridge in the Grønland district. From here the train station is a 5-minute walk down Stenersgata.

Near Oslo: Drøbak

This delightful fjord town is just an hour from Oslo by bus (68 kr one-way, 2/hr, bus #541 or #542 from behind the train station) or ferry (68 kr one-way, sporadic departures, check at pier 1 or ask at Oslo TI). Consider taking the 75-minute boat trip down, exploring the town, having dinner, and taking the bus back.

For holiday cheer year-round, stop into **Tregaarden's Julehuset** Christmas shop, right off Drøbak's main square (generally Mon–Fri 10:00–17:00, Sat 10:00–15:00, variable hours on Sun, closed Jan–Feb, tel. 64 93 41 78, www.julehus.no). Then wander out past the church and cemetery on the north side of town to a pleasant park. Looking out into the fjord, you can see the old **Oscarsborg Fortress,** where Norwegian troops fired their cannons to sink Hitler's battleship, *Blücher.* The attack bought enough time for Norway's king and Parliament to set up a government-in-exile in London during the Nazi occupation of Norway (1940–1945). Nearby, a monument is dedicated to the commander of the fortress, and the *Blücher's* anchor rests aground. (A 70-kr round-trip summer ferry shuttles visitors from the town harbor.)

If you want to spend the night, the **TI** can recommend accommodations (June–Aug Mon–Fri 8:00–18:00, Sat–Sun 10:00–16:00; Sept–May Mon–Fri 8:00–16:00, closed Sat–Sun; tel. 64 93 50 87). **Restaurant Skipperstuen** is a good option for dinner, with outdoor seating that overlooks the fjord and all the Oslo-bound boat traffic (entrées from 200 kr, Mon–Sat 11:00–21:00, closed Sun, tel. 64 93 07 03).

SHOPPING

Shops in Oslo are generally open 10:00–17:00. Many stay open until 20:00 on Thursday, and close early on Saturday and all day Sunday. Shopping centers are open Monday–Friday 10:00–20:00, Saturday 10:00–18:00, and are closed Sunday. Remember, when you make a purchase of 380 kr or more, you can get the 18 percent tax refunded when you leave the country if you hang on to the paperwork (see page 15).

Oslo's top department store is **GlasMagasinet** (near the cathedral on Stortorvet). Oslo's handiest big, splashy mall is **Byporten,** adjoining the central train station, with 70 shops (Mon–Fri 10:00–21:00, Sat 10:00–18:00, closed Sun). The trendiest boutiques and chic, high-quality shops lie along the street named **Bogstadveien** (running from behind the Royal Palace to Frogner Park). And on Saturday mornings you can browse the **flea market** under the bridge at Grønland.

Sweaters and colorful Norwegian folk crafts are on many visitors' shopping lists. The **Husfliden shop,** near City Hall and the harbor, is much appreciated for its traditional yarn and buyable Norsk folklore (Mon–Sat 10:00–18:00, closed Sun, Rosenkrantz Gate 19, tel. 22 42 10 75). For a superb selection of sweaters and other Norwegian crafts (top quality at high prices), visit **Heimen Husfliden** (Mon–Fri 10:00–17:00, Thu until 18:00, Sat 10:00–15:00, closed Sun, Rosenkrantz Gate 8, tel. 22 41 40 50). The **Oslo Sweater Shop** seems to have the best prices for sweaters (Mon–Sat 8:00–22:00, Sun 8:00–17:00, off Skippergata at Biskop Gunnerusgata 3, tel. 22 42 42 25). For flags (a long, skinny *vimple* dresses up a boat or cabin wonderfully), pop into **Oslo Flaggfabrikk** (near City Hall, across the street from Heimen Husfliden shop, at Rosenkrantz Gate 18).

Vinmonopolet stores are the only place where you can buy wine and spirits in Norway. The most convenient location is at the central station (Mon–Wed 10:00–17:00, Thu–Fri 10:00–18:00, Sat 9:00–15:00, closed Sun).

SLEEPING

In Oslo, the season and type of hotel dictate the best deals. The basic formula: In midsummer and on weekends, discounted business-class hotels offer the best value; otherwise, consider a cheap hotel, a room in a private home, or a hostel.

Like those in its sister Scandinavian capitals, Oslo's hotels are mostly designed for business travelers; they're expensive during the tourists' off-season (autumn through spring), full in May and June for conventions, and wide open otherwise. From July through

Sleep Code

(6.5 kr = about $1, country code: 47)
S = Single, **D** = Double/Twin, **T** = Triple, **Q** = Quad, **b** = bathroom,
s = shower. You can assume credit cards are accepted and
breakfast is included unless otherwise noted. Everyone speaks
English.

To help you sort through these listings easily, I've divided
the rooms into three categories, based on the price for a standard double room with bath:

$$$ Higher Priced—Most rooms 1,000 kr or more.
$$ Moderately Priced—Most rooms between
600–1,000 kr.
$ Lower Priced—Most rooms 600 kr or less.

mid-August, and weekends (Fri–Sat) year-round, fancy business-
class hotels deeply discount their rooms. Although these rooms
are still expensive—even at half-price (about 700–800 kr for a
double)—you get a huge breakfast and a lot of extra comfort for
little more than the cost of a cheap hotel.

During business days (Mon–Thu) outside of summer, business
hotels are going for their inflated "rack rates," and budget travelers
opt for Oslo's dumpy-for-Scandinavia (but still nice by European
standards) cheapie options: doubles for about 700 kr in central
"cheap" hotels, or 350 kr in private homes on the outskirts of the
city. For experience and economy—but not convenience—go for
a private home. For convenience and modern comfort, I like the
Thon Budget Hotels (for more on Thon Budget and Thon City
hotels, see below).

Only the TI can sort through all of the confusing hotel specials and get you the best deal going on fancy hotel rooms on the
push list. If it's late in the day, the TI's prices get even better.

The most predictable special is the TI's **Oslo Package,** which
offers business-class rooms plus an Oslo Pass for 460–760 kr per
person (based on double occupancy); prices vary depending on the
hotel you choose. The Oslo Package is offered between mid-June
and late August, weekends year-round (Fri–Sun, plus Thu if staying at least two nights), and, at certain hotels, daily year-round. It's
a good deal for couples and ideal for families with children under
16. Two kids under 16 sleep free, breakfast is included, and up to
four family members get free Oslo Passes, covering admission to
sights and all public transportation (see page 139). These passes
are valid for four days, even if you only stay one night at the hotel
(allowing you to squeeze two days of sightseeing out of a one-night

stay—for example, if you take an overnight train or boat out of town on your second evening). Buy the Oslo Package through your travel agent at home, ScanAm World Tours in the US (US tel. 800-545-2204), or—easiest—upon arrival in Oslo at the TI. For details on the Oslo Package, see www.visitoslo.com.

Near the Train Station and Karl Johans Gate

These accommodations are within a 15-minute walk of the station. While evidence of an earlier shady time survives, the hotels feel secure and comfortable. Parking in a central garage will run you about 170 kr per day.

Thon Hotels

This fast-growing chain of business-class hotels (in Oslo, Bergen—see page 233—and throughout Norway) knows which comforts are worth paying for. They offer little character, but provide maximum comfort per krone in big, modern, conveniently located buildings. There are umbrellas, televisions, telephones, and full modern bathrooms in each room. Each hotel has elevators, a cheery staff and lobby, tight but well-designed rooms, non-smoking floors, and a big buffet breakfast. And most Thon Hotels have the wonderful habit of leaving coffee in the lobby or the juice and milk bar in the breakfast room open all day.

There are two kinds of Thon hotels: Thon City Hotels are a cut above Thon Budget Hotels. While the City Hotels are much more expensive during business times (weekdays outside of summer), the Budget Hotels have the same rack rates all year. (They offer much smaller discounts based on the same two-tiered, demand-driven schedule.) In the Budget Hotels, rooms with double beds are a bit bigger than twins for the same price.

Their two-tiered price system is more expensive on Mon–Thu outside of summer, and cheaper on weekends all year, plus every day during the summer (late June–mid-Aug). "Weekend" means Fridays and Saturdays (and Sunday if you stayed at least Saturday, too). Extra beds cost 200 kr for adults and 100 kr for kids up to 16 (kids under 6 stow away for free).

The weekend and summer rates get even better with the purchase of a **Skanplus Hotel Pass** (90 kr per room, which pays for itself in one night—just reserve without it and buy it at the desk as you check in; www.skanplus.com). Those over 60 can buy a **60plus** pass that makes the entire year "one long weekend" (90 kr, giving you the deepest discounts throughout the year—assuming rooms are available even during the busy business season). The Thon chain has 14 hotels in Oslo (central booking tel. 23 08 02 00, www.thonhotels.no), but the following are the most convenient.

Oslo Hotels and Restaurants

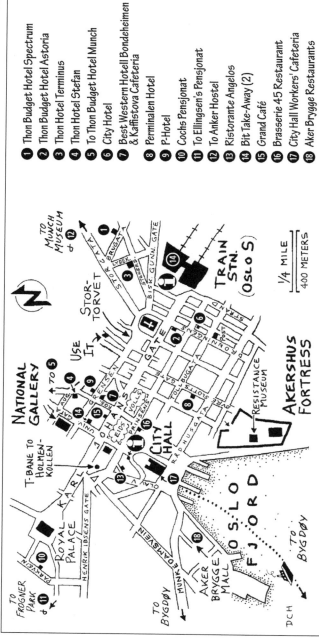

1. Thon Budget Hotel Spectrum
2. Thon Budget Hotel Astoria
3. Thon Hotel Terminus
4. Thon Hotel Stefan
5. To Thon Budget Hotel Munch
6. City Hotel
7. Best Western Hotell Bondeheimen & Kaffistova Cafeteria
8. Perminalen Hotel
9. P-Hotel
10. Cochs Pensjonat
11. To Ellingsen's Pensjonat
12. To Anker Hostel
13. Ristorante Angelos
14. Bit Take-Away (2)
15. Grand Café
16. Brasserie 45 Restaurant
17. City Hall Workers' Cafeteria
18. Aker Brygge Restaurants

$$$ Thon Hotel Stefan, in a classy and central location two blocks off Karl Johans Gate, is a cut above its sisters in comfort, charm, and price (rack rates: Sb-1,245 kr, Db-1,445 kr; Skanplus/ 60plus rates: Sb-730 kr, Db-940 kr; some tram noise, Rosenkrantz Gate 1, tel. 23 31 55 00, fax 23 31 55 55, www.thonhotels.no/stefan, stefan@thonhotels.no).

$$$ Thon Hotel Terminus is similar and closer to the station (rack rates: Sb-1,125 kr, Db-1,345 kr; Skanplus/60plus rates: Sb-670 kr, Db-890 kr; Stenersgate 10, tel. 22 05 60 00, fax 22 17 08 98, www.thonhotels.no/terminus, terminus@thonhotels.no).

$$ Thon Budget Hotel Spectrum has rack rates that are the same all year long; Skanplus discounts only apply on weekends and throughout the summer (rack rates: Sb-595 kr, Db-795 kr; Skanplus/60plus rates: Sb-550 kr, Db-750 kr; good-value break-fast-50 kr, 4 blocks from station, leave station out north entrance toward bus terminal, go across footbridge toward tall glass SAS Radisson Hotel, Brugata 7; tel. 23 36 27 00, fax 23 36 27 50, www .thonhotels.no/spectrum, spectrum@thonhotels.no). A quarter of its rooms are plagued by disco noise on weekends.

$$ Thon Budget Hotel Astoria has the least charm of my recommended Thon Hotels, but it's well located and perfectly service-able (rack rates: Sb-595 kr, Db-795 kr; Skanplus/60plus rates: Sb-550 kr, Db-750 kr; breakfast-50 kr, 3 blocks in front of station, 50 yards off Karl Johans Gate, Dronningens Gate 21, tel. 24 14 55 50, fax 22 42 57 65, www.thonhotels.no/astoria, astoria@thonhotels.no).

$$ Thon Budget Hotel Munch is like its sisters (tel. 23 21 96 00, Munchsgate 5, www.thonhotels.no/munch, munch @thonhotels.no).

More Hotels near the Train Station

$$$ Best Western Hotell Bondeheimen (literally, "Farmer's Home") is a historic hotel run by the farmers' youth league, *Bondeungdomslaget*. It once housed the children of rural farmers attending school in Oslo. Today its 127 rooms have all the comforts of a modern hotel (Mon–Thu: Sb-1,090–1,390 kr, Db-1,390–1,590 kr; Fri–Sun: Sb-840–1,040 kr, Db-1,090–1,290 kr; non-smoking rooms, elevator, Rosenkrantz Gate 8, tel. 23 21 41 00, fax 23 21 41 01, www.bondeheimen.com, booking@bondeheimen.com). If you book using their Web site, you'll always save money. This almost-100-year-old building is also home to the simple Kaffistova restaurant (see "Eating," page 182) and the Heimen Husfliden shop (see "Shopping," page 174).

$$ City Hotel has clean, basic, and well-worn but homey rooms, in a rather seedy location handy to the train station. The hotel originated 100 years ago as a cheap place for Norwegians to sleep while they waited to sail to their new homes in America. It now serves the opposite purpose. With prices the same throughout the year, this hotel is a good value on off-season weekdays (Mon–Thu), when other hotels are at their most expensive (S-450 kr, Sb-550 kr, D-575 kr, Db-650–750 kr, extra bed-180 kr, kids-100 kr, 10 percent discount with this book through 2007, non-smoking rooms, Prinsens Gate 6, tel. 22 41 36 10, fax 22 42 24 29, www .cityhotel.no, booking@cityhotel.no).

$$ Perminalen Hotel, a hotel for military personnel on leave, is perfectly central, spartan, inexpensive, and welcoming to civvies. Spliced invisibly into a giant office block on a quiet street, it has sleek woody furniture and a no-nonsense reception desk (Sb-495 kr, Db comes with full bathroom and twin beds-670 kr, some seventh-floor rooms come with balconies, entirely non-smoking, elevator, tram #12 from station to Øvre Slotts Gate 2, tel. 23 09 30 81, fax 23 41 18 58, www.perminalen.com, post@perminalen.iss.no). Single beds in shared quads segregated by sexes (with lockers and breakfast) rent for 300 kr each. Its cheap mess hall is open all day.

$$ P-Hotel, the latest thing in economic hotels in Oslo, rents 92 business-class, hardwood-slick rooms for the same great price every day of the year. You get a boxed breakfast in your room, as well as free Internet access and Wi-Fi. Avoid a little street noise by requesting a room high up or in the back (Sb-645 kr, Db-745 kr, bigger rooms add 100 kr per person up to five, some sixth-floor rooms come with balconies, Grensen 19, T-bane: Storting, tel. 23 31 80 00, www.p-hotels.com, oslo@p-hotels.no).

The West End

$$ Cochs Pensjonat has 88 plain rooms (20 remodeled doubles), many with kitchenettes. It's right behind the Royal Palace (S-420 kr, Sb-500–560 kr, D-580 kr, Db-660 kr, newly refurnished Db-740 kr, extra bed-155 kr, no breakfast, non-smoking rooms, elevator, T-bane to National Theater and walk through park or ride tram #11 to Parkveien 25, tel. 23 33 24 00, fax 23 33 24 10, www .cochspensjonat.no, booking@cochs.no).

$$ Ellingsen's Pensjonat rents 18 clean, bright rooms with fluffy down comforters. It's located in a residential neighborhood four blocks behind the Royal Palace (S-330 kr, Sb-460 kr, D-540 kr, Db-650 kr, extra bed-140 kr, no breakfast, cash only, non-smoking, back rooms come with less street noise, tram #19 from central station, near Uranienborg church at Holtegata 25, tel. 22 60 03 59, fax 22 60 99 21, www.ellingsenspensjonat.no, post @ellingsenspensjonat.no).

Private Homes

The TI can find you a 350-kr double for a 45-kr fee (minimum two-night stay, likely a tram ride out of the center).

Hostels

$ Anker Hostel, a huge student dorm open to travelers of any age, offers 250 of Oslo's best cheap doubles. Though it comes with the ambience of a bomb shelter, each of its rooms is spacious, simple, and clean. There are kitchens, free parking, and elevators (bed in 6-bed room-175 kr, bed in quad-195 kr, Db-500 kr, sheets-45 kr, towel-15 kr, breakfast-60 kr at adjacent Best Western hotel; self-serve laundry; tram #11, #12, or #13, or bus #30, #31 or #32 from central station; Storgata 55, tel. 22 99 72 00, fax 22 99 72 20, www.ankerhostel.no).

$ Haraldsheim Youth Hostel (IYHF), a huge, modern hostel open all year, comes with a grand view, laundry, self-service kitchen, 270 beds...and a long commute (2.5 miles out of town). Beds in the fancy quads with private showers and toilets are 250 kr per person (bed in simple quad with bathroom down the hall-220 kr). They also offer private rooms (S-350 kr, Sb-425 kr, bunk-bed D-485 kr, Db-575 kr; all include breakfast, sheets-50 kr, catch bus #31 or #32 or tram #17 from Oslo's central train station to Sinsenkrysset, then 5-min uphill hike to Haraldsheimveien 4, tel. 22 22 29 65, fax 22 22 10 25, www.haraldsheim.oslo.no, post @haraldsheim.oslo.no). Eurailers can train to the hostel with their railpass (2/hr, to Grefsen and walk 10 min).

Sleeping on the Train or Boat

Norway's trains and ferries offer ways to travel while sleeping. The eight-hour trip between Bergen and Oslo leaves at about 23:00 in each direction (nightly except Sat). Eurail hobos sleep cheap, if not well, for the cost of a train reservation (sleep on a train ride out, cross platform, and sleep back)—for example, Oslo–Vinstra (direction: Trondheim) 23:05–2:56, Vinstra–Oslo 3:15–7:10. There are trains almost every night in the summer to Stockholm. And, while there are no more overnight trains connecting Oslo with Copenhagen, the overnight cruise between these Nordic capitals is a clever way to avoid a night in a hotel and to travel while you sleep, which saves a day in your itinerary (see "Overnight Cruise to Copenhagen," page 187).

EATING

Eating Cheaply

How do the Norwegians afford their high-priced restaurants? They don't eat out much. This is one city in which you might just settle for simple or ethnic meals—you'll save a lot and miss little. Many menus list small and large plates. Because portions tend to be large, choosing a small plate or splitting a large one makes some otherwise pricey options reasonable. You'll notice many locals just

Oslo's One-Time Grills

Norwegians are experts at completely avoiding costly restaurants. "One-time grills," or *engangsgrill*, are the rage for locals on a budget. All that's required is a sunny evening, a grassy park, a one-time grill, and a group of friends. During balmy summer evenings, the air in Oslo's city parks is thick with the smell of disposable grills. It's fun to see how prices for this kind of "dining" aren't that bad in the supermarket: Norwegian beer-10 kr/bottle, potato salad-20 kr/tub,

cooked shrimp-75 kr/half kilo, "ready for grill" steak-two for 100 kr, *grill polse* hot-dogs-60 kr per dozen, *lomper* (Norwegian tortillas for wrapping hot dogs)-10 kr per stack, and the actual grill itself-20 kr.

Bars are also too expensive for the average Norwegian. Young night owls drink at home before *(forspiel)* and after *(nachspiel)* an evening on the town, with a couple of hours, generally around midnight, when they go out for a single drink in a public setting. A beer in a bar costs about $8 (compared to $4 in Ireland and $1 in the Czech Republic), while they can get an entire six-pack for that price in a grocery store.

drink tap water—even in fine restaurants. For a description of Oslo's classic (and expensive) restaurants, see the TI's *Oslo Guide* booklet.

Splurge for a hotel that includes breakfast, or pay for it if it's optional. At 75 kr, a Norwegian breakfast fit for a Viking is a good deal. Picnic for lunch or dinner. Basements of big department stores have huge, first-class supermarkets with lots of alternatives to sandwiches for picnic dinners. The little yogurt tubs with cereal come with collapsible spoons. Wasa crackers and meat, shrimp, or cheese spread in a tube are cheap and pack well. The central station has an ICA supermarket with long hours (Mon–Fri 7:00–22:00, Sat–Sun 9:00–22:00).

You'll save 12 percent by getting take-away food from a restaurant rather than eating inside. (The VAT on take-away food is 12 percent; restaurant food is 24 percent.) Fast-food restaurants ask if you want to take away or not before they ring up your order on the cash register. Even McDonald's has a two-tiered price list.

Oslo is awash with little budget eateries (modern, ethnic, fast food, pizza, department-store cafeterias, and so on). **Deli de Luca** is a cheery convenience store chain, notorious for having a store on every key corner in Oslo. Most are open 24/7, selling sandwiches, pastries, sushi, and to-go boxes of warm pasta or Asian noodle dishes. You can fill your belly here for about 50 kr. Some outlets (such as the one at the corner of Karl Johans Gate and Rosenkrantz Gate) have seating on the street or upstairs. Beware: Because this is still a *convenience* store, not everything is well-priced. Convenience stores—while convenient—charge double what supermarkets do.

Eating Cheaply on or near Karl Johans Gate

Consider the restaurants and eateries listed below. They're grouped by those that are from Karl Johans Gate and slightly to the north (between this main boulevard and the National Gallery) and to the south (between Karl Johans Gate and City Hall).

Strangely, **Karl Johans Gate** itself—the most Norwegian of boulevards—is lined with a strip of good-time American chain eateries where you can get ribs, burgers, and pizza, including TGI Fridays and the Hard Rock Café. Egon Pizza offers a daily 100-kr all-you-can-eat pizza deal (11:00–18:00). Each place comes with great sidewalk seating and essentially the same prices.

Near Karl Johans Gate and the National Gallery

Perhaps the most venerable place in town, the **Grand Café** serves elegant food any time, but it's most tempting for its summer buffet (available daily June–Aug 18:00–22:00). Graze through a bounty of traditional dishes, as well as shrimp, salads, fruit, and desserts, for one 300-kr price (free water available). À la carte plates go for around 200 kr each. Reserve a window and, if you hit a time when there's no tour group, you're suddenly a posh Norwegian (Karl Johans Gate 31, tel. 23 21 20 18).

Kaffistova is where my thrifty Norwegian grandparents always took me. It's changed little in 30 years. This alcohol-free cafeteria serves simple, hearty, and typically Norwegian (read: bland) meals for a great price. For about 100 kr, you get your choice of an entrée (meatballs and other Norse classics) with salad, cooked vegetables, and "flat bread" (Mon–Fri 9:30–21:00, Sat–Sun 10:30–19:00, Rosenkrantz Gate 8, tel. 23 21 42 10).

Brasserie 45, overlooking Stortingsgata and the National Theater from its second-floor perch, is a modern eatery offering fine and affordable continental cuisine with energetic service. While larger entrées go for about 160 kr, their "light plates" (about 100 kr) are plenty for me (Mon–Thu 15:00–23:00, Fri–Sat 14:00–24:00, always a veggie option, Stortingsgata 20, tel. 22 41 34 00).

It's worth calling ahead to reserve a window seat overlooking Karl Johans Gate.

Ristorante Angelos serves filling Italian food at reasonable prices in a classy setting where Italy meets Norwegian wood. Their 90-kr all-you-can-stomach pizza special is available daily from 15:00 to 20:00 (pizzas and pastas for 120–150 kr, fish and meat entrées from 200 kr, daily 11:00–23:00, Klingenberggate 4, tel. 22 82 86 50).

Near Karl Johans Gate and City Hall

Bit, a block from the National Gallery, is a favorite among locals for its freshly made take-away calzones and sandwiches. With a drink, you've got a 70-kr meal to munch in the nearest park, next to the National Theater (Mon–Fri 8:00–19:00, Sat 10:00–17:00, closed Sun, Universitets Gata 20). Another branch is in the central station's Byporten mall (with seating, Mon–Fri 7:00–21:00, Sat 9:00–18:00, Sun 11:00–17:00).

The **City Hall workers' cafeteria,** just steps off the harborfront, welcomes the public with the cheapest lunch I've found anywhere in Oslo. It has soup, an inexpensive salad bar measured by weight (35 kr for a meal-sized bowl), and a daily hot dish for 25–45 kr (12:30 to 13:30 Mon–Fri only). While City Hall workers get access to the place before 12:30 and the food can be pretty picked over, it's still a fine, handy value. From the grand harbor entrance, it's up one flight of stairs above the city info desk and WC. From the tour entrance on its inland courtyard, it's just downstairs.

Dining Harborside in Aker Brygge

The **Aker Brygge** harborfront mall isn't cheap, but it has some inviting cafés, classy delis, and restaurants with outdoor harborview tables. Before making your selection, you might want to walk the entire lane (including the back side), considering both the regular places (some with second-floor view seating) and the various floating options. Nearly all are open for lunch and dinner. If you're on a budget, get a take-out meal from the fast-food stands and grab a bench along the boardwalk. The ICA "Gourmet" grocery store, just a few steps behind all the fancy restaurants about midway down the boardwalk, has salads, warm take-away dishes, and more (Mon–Fri 9:00–22:00, Sat 9:00–20:00, closed Sun).

Druen, the first restaurant on the strip—while not a particularly good food value—is best for people-watching. I like the balcony seats upstairs, under outside heaters and with a harbor view. They serve international dishes—spicy Asian, French, and seafood—in small plates for 150 kr, and big meals for 220–260 kr (daily, Stranden 1, Aker Brygge, tel. 23 11 54 60).

Two restaurants are right on the water with a view of the harbor rather than the river of strolling people. **Lekter'n,** which has the best harbor view and offers live music nightly, serves hamburgers, pizza, and shrimp buckets. Budget eaters can split a 150-kr pizza (all outdoors, Stranden 3, tel. 22 83 76 46). Farther out, **Herbern Marina** is *the* place for shrimp on a balmy evening. In the midst of lots of pleasure boats, couples enjoy the fun, laid-back dockside ambience, and fill up by splitting a 190-kr liter bucket of shrimp with bread. Request a free peeling lesson; rinse in the finger bowl (pizzas, burgers, and salads from 100 kr; daily 11:00–22:00, Stranden 30, tel. 22 83 19 90).

Rorbua, the "Fisherman's Cabin," is a lively yet cozy eatery tucked into this mostly modern stretch of restaurants. It's extremely woody with a mod rustic charm and candle-lit picnic tables surrounded by harpoons and old B&W photos. Grab a stool at one of the wooden tables, and choose from a menu of meat-and-potato dishes (100–200 kr) and seafood offerings (150–200 kr). There's a hearty daily special for 100 kr with coffee until it sells out (daily 12:00–23:00, Stranden 71, tel. 22 83 53 86).

Lofoten Fiskerestaurant serves perhaps Oslo's best fish amid a classy yacht-club atmosphere at the end of the strip. While it's beyond the people-watching action, it's a delight even in cold and blustery weather because of its heated atrium, which makes a meal here practically outdoor dining (lunch-150–200 kr, dinner from 250 kr, open daily, reservations smart—especially if you want a harborside window table, Stranden 75, tel. 22 83 08 08).

Trendy Dining at the Bottom of Grünerløkka

Sudost Restaurant, once a big bank, now fills its vault with wine (which makes sense given Norwegian alcohol prices). Today it's popular with trendy Norwegian professionals as a place to see and be seen. It's a fine mix of Norwegian chic woody ambience, a big riverside terrace, an open fire grill, smart service, and modern continental cuisine (200–250-kr plates, at bottom of Grünerløkka, tram #17 to Trondheimsveien 5, tel. 23 35 30 70).

Dining near Frogner Park

Lofotstua Restaurant feels transplanted from the far northern island it's named for. Kjell Jenssen proudly serves up fish Lofoten-style: just big portions of simple, unadulterated fish. If you want meat, they've got it—whale or seal (180 kr-250 kr dinner plates, Mon–Fri 15:00–22:00, a short walk from gate of Vigeland statue garden, tram #12 in Majorstuen at Kirkeveien 40, tel. 22 46 93 96).

Curry and Ketchup Indian Restaurant is filled with in-the-know locals enjoying tasty and hearty meals for 90 kr. This mellow place requires no reservations and feels like an Indian market (daily 14:00–23:00, near gate of Vigeland statue garden in Frogner Park, tram #12, in Majorstuen at Kirkeveien 51, tel. 22 69 05 22). If you want a reasonable Indian meal in Oslo, this is hard to beat.

Eating Cheap and Spicy in Grønland

Grønland is the New York City of Oslo, a grungy melting pot, and the heart of a colorful slice of otherwise pretty bland and blonde Oslo. Here backpackers and immigrants munch street food for dinner. Cheap and tasty *börek* (feta, spinach, mushroom) is sold hot and greasy to go for 15 kr. Try any of the places located within a block of Grønland's main square (T-bane: Grønland).

Punjab Tandoori (at Grønlandsleiret 24) and **Tandoori Curry Corner** (next door at Grønlandsleiret 22) are both open daily (11:00–23:00) and serve hearty meals (lamb and chicken curry, tandoori specials) for under 70 kr.

Alibaba Restaurant is clean, inviting, filled with smart locals, and cheap for Turkish food. They have good indoor or outdoor seating (daily 99-kr fixed-price meal, daily 12:30–22:30, corner of Grønland and Tøyengata at Tøyengata 2, tel. 22 17 22 22).

Asylet is more expensive and feels like it was here long before Norway ever saw a Pakistani. This big, traditional eatery—like a Norwegian beer garden—has a rustic, cozy interior and a gravelly backyard filled with picnic tables (150–170 kr plates, daily 11:00–22:00, Grønland 28, tel. 22 17 09 39).

Olympen Brown Pub, one of the oldest pubs in Oslo, has a clientele that seems to have been here since day one. Still smoky from a century of action, this quirky time warp smells of beer and tobacco and serves the cheapest beer (29 kr)—with live schmaltzy music often tossed in for no extra (daily, Grønland 19).

Cafe Con Bar is a trendy yuppie eatery on the downtown edge of Grønland. Locals consider it to have the best burgers in town (110 kr). While the interior seating is very noisy, the sidewalk tables are great for people-watching (daily, where Grønland hits Brugata).

Roasted Rudolph Under a Thatched Roof High on the Mountain

Frognerseteren Hovedrestaurant, nestled high above Oslo (and 1,400 feet above sea level), is a classy, sod-roofed old restaurant. Its terrace, offering a commanding view of the city, is a popular stop for famous apple cake and coffee. The café is casual and less expensive, with indoor and outdoor seating (sandwiches and cold dishes-70–75 kr, hot dishes-125 kr, daily 11:00–22:00, reservations unnecessary). The elegant view restaurant is pricier (230–300-kr plates, 500-kr three-course meals, Mon–Sat 12:00–22:00, Sun 13:00–21:00, reindeer specials, reserve for evening dining, tel. 22 92 40 40).

You can combine a trip into the forested hills surrounding the city with lunch or dinner and get a chance to see the famous ski jump up close. Ride T-bane line #1 to the last stop (Frognerseteren), walk about 10 minutes down a traffic-free dirt lane, stop for your meal, and walk another 20 minutes (1.25 miles) downhill on the same lane to the ski jump (and the Holmenkollen T-bane station).

TRANSPORTATION CONNECTIONS

For train information, call 81 50 08 88 and press 4 for English. For international trains, dial 81 56 81 00. Even if you have a rail-pass, reservations are required for long rides (e.g., a reservation to Stockholm in first class costs 140 kr, second class for 60 kr). First class often comes with a hot meal, fruit bowl, and unlimited juice and coffee.

Be warned that international connections from Oslo are often in flux. Schedules can vary depending on the day of the week, so carefully confirm the specific train you need and purchase any required reservations in advance. Aside from the occasional direct train to Stockholm, most trips from Oslo to Copenhagen or Stockholm require a change in Göteborg, Sweden. There are direct night trains from Oslo to Stockholm and in the spring and summer to Malmö, Sweden (which is very close to Copenhagen).

From Oslo by Train to Bergen: Oslo and Bergen are linked by a spectacularly scenic train ride (4–6/day, 7 hrs). Many travelers take it as part of the **Norway in a Nutshell** route, which combines train, ferry, and bus travel in an unforgettably beautiful trip. For information on times and prices, see the next chapter.

By Train to: Lillehammer (9/day, 2.5 hrs), **Kristiansand** (4/day, 4.5 hrs), **Copenhagen** (2/day, 8.5 hrs, transfer at Göteborg; for night train—which may not run in winter—sleep on the direct train to Malmö, Sweden, arrive Malmö around 6:00, transfer to Copenhagen), **Stockholm** (some days there's a 6.5-hour direct InterCity train, otherwise 2/day, 8–9 hrs, with a change in Göteborg and likely also Halden; plus a direct 8.75-hour night train that doesn't run every night).

By Bus to Stockholm: Busing to Stockholm is cheaper and can be slightly faster than taking the train (7/day, 7–12 hrs, www.swebusexpress.se).

Overnight Cruise to Copenhagen

Since there's no night train between Oslo and Copenhagen, consider connecting them by cruise ship. The boat leaves daily from Oslo at 17:00 (arrives in Copenhagen at 9:30 the following morning; going the other way, it departs Copenhagen at 17:00 and arrives in Oslo around 9:30; about 16 hours sailing each way). The boat leaves Oslo from the far (non-City Hall) side of the Akershus Fortress peninsula (get there via bus #60 from in front of train station). From Oslo, you'll sail through the Oslofjord—not as dramatic as Norway's western fjords, but impressive if you're not going to Bergen. On board are three gourmet restaurants, a sauna, hot tub, and swimming pool. This is fun and convenient, but more expensive and not as nice as the Stockholm–Helsinki cruise (see page 330).

You can take this cruise one-way or do a round-trip from either city. To make a reservation, call DFDS Seaways' Norwegian office at tel. 22 41 90 90 (Mon–Fri 8:00–17:00, closed Sat–Sun, www.dfdsseaways.com), or, in the US, tel. 800-533-3755 (www.seaeurope.com). For specifics and sample prices, see "Overnight Cruise to Oslo" on page 94.

NORWAY IN A NUTSHELL

A Scenic Journey

While Oslo and Bergen are the big draws for tourists, Norway is essentially a place of natural beauty. There's a certain mystique about the "land of the midnight sun," but you'll get the most scenic travel thrills per mile, minute, and dollar by going west from Oslo rather than north.

Norway's greatest claims to scenic fame are her deep, lush fjords. A series of well-organized and spectacular bus, train, and ferry connections, appropriately called Norway in a Nutshell, lays Norway's beautiful fjord country spread-eagled on a scenic platter. You can do it as a day trip from Oslo or from Bergen, or en route between Oslo and Bergen.

You'll see the seductive Sognefjord, with tiny but tough ferries, towering canyons, and isolated farms and villages marinated in the mist of countless waterfalls. You're an eager Lilliputian to the Gulliver of Norwegian nature.

Today, the region enjoys mild weather for its latitude, thanks to the warm Gulf Stream. But three million years ago, an ice age made this land as inhabitable as the center of Greenland. As the glaciers of that ice age advanced and cut their way to the sea, they gouged out long grooves—today's fjords. Since the ice was thicker inland, with only a relatively thin lip at the coast, the gouging was deeper inland. The average fjord is 4,000 feet deep far inland and only about 600 feet deep where it reaches the open sea.

The entire west coast is slashed by stunning fjords, but the Sognefjord, Norway's longest (120 miles) and deepest (1 mile), is tops. Anything but the Sognefjord is, at best, foreplay. This is it—the ultimate natural thrill Norway has to offer.

Aurland, a good home base for your exploration, is on Aurlandsfjord, a remote, scenic, and accessible arm of the Sognefjord. The local weather is actually decent, with about 24 inches of rain per year, compared to 80 inches annually in nearby Bergen. (For more fjords in your life, consider extending your trip northwest of Aurland to the town of Balestrand for fewer crowds, more hikes, and lots of day-trip possibilities—see the next chapter.)

Planning Your Time

Even the blitz tourist needs a day for the Norway in a Nutshell trip. This is easily done as a long day trip from Oslo or Bergen. (All connections are designed for tourists, explained in English, convenient, and easy—see below.) Ideally, if you have more time, break the trip with an overnight in Aurland, Flåm, or even Balestrand

(see next chapter) and carry on into Bergen, to enjoy some time there. Fly home from Bergen, or return to Oslo—maybe via night train (sleeping through all the scenery you saw westbound).

Those with a car and only one day should leave the car in Oslo and take the train. With more time, drivers can improve on the Nutshell by taking a northern route: from Oslo, drive through the Gudbrandsdal Valley, go over the Jotunheimen Mountains, then along Lustrafjord, stopping in Balestrand en route to Bergen. These sights are covered in the next two chapters.

ORIENTATION

The most exciting single-day trip you could make from Oslo or Bergen is this circular train/boat/bus/train jaunt through fjord country. It's famous, everybody does it...and if you're looking for the scenic grandeur of Norway, so should you.

Tourist offices and train stations have souvenir-worthy brochures with photos, descriptions, and exact times (for sample schedules, see page 193).

Route Overview: The route works in a variety of ways: round-trip from Oslo or Bergen, or on the way between Oslo and Bergen (going in either direction). The basic idea is this: Take a train halfway across the mountainous spine of Norway, make your way down to the Aurlandsfjord (a branch of the Sognefjord) for a boat cruise, then climb back up out of the fjord and get back on the main train line.

Leaving from Oslo, you'll ride the Oslo–Bergen train to Myrdal (MEER-doll), hop on the cogwheel train waiting at the

Norway in a Nutshell

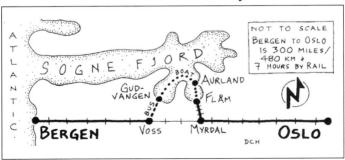

Myrdal train station, take it down to the small town of Flåm, and catch the fjord cruise to Gudvangen. From Gudvangen, a bus climbs up to the scenic town of Voss, which is on the same Oslo–Bergen line where you started (take this train back to Oslo or on to Bergen). Leaving from Bergen, it's the same thing in reverse: Train to Voss, bus down to Gudvangen, boat to Flåm, cogwheel train up to Myrdal, back to the main train line. The Nutshell trip is possible all year. Some say it's most beautiful in winter (though it's not possible then to do as a day trip from Oslo).

Eating: Options along the route aren't great. The fjord cruises and Oslo-Bergen trains sell open-face sandwiches and some hot dishes for 50–100 kr. Flåm is your best lunch-stop option, although you won't have a lot of time there if making the journey all in one day from Oslo to Bergen. Your best bet is to pack a picnic lunch. Most large hotels will allow you to pack a lunch from the breakfast buffet for about 85 kr (a good deal if hard-boiled eggs and fruit are available). Or you can plan ahead and buy picnic fixings to bring along.

On Your Own vs. Package Deal

If you have a railpass, or if you're a student or a senior (and therefore eligible for discounts), do the trip on your own. Otherwise, the Fjord Tours packages (described below) will save you time and a bit of money.

On Your Own

If you want to do the Nutshell but don't have a railpass, allow 1,115 kr for a one-way trip between Oslo and Bergen, 790 kr for a round-trip from Bergen, or 1,825 kr for a round-trip from Oslo.

If you have a Scanrail, Eurailpass, or Eurail Selectpass, the Oslo–Bergen train is covered (except a 50-kr reservation fee, free for first-class passholders) and the Myrdal–Flåm train is discounted (to 120 kr). You still have to pay full fare for the fjord cruise (205 kr, student discounts available) and the Gudvangen–Voss bus (80

Nutshell Route and Beyond

kr). Your total cost between Bergen and Oslo: about 405 kr with a first-class pass, or 455 kr with a second-class pass.

Get train tickets for the journey, including the Myrdal–Flåm segment, at the train station in Oslo or Bergen; purchase your fjord-cruise ticket on the boat or from the TI in Flåm; and buy the tickets for the Gudvangen bus on board from the driver. Always ask about senior and student discounts.

Reservations: If you're traveling during peak season (July–mid-Aug), it's wise to make reservations several weeks in advance for the Oslo–Bergen train segment of your trip (for specifics, see Oslo–Bergen train listing under "Sights," page 192).

Package Deal

Fjord Tours sells the Nutshell package and other package trips at all Norwegian State Railways stations, including Oslo and Bergen, or through their customer-service line in Norway (tel. 81 56 82 22, www.fjordtours.no). The costs of the Nutshell package are as follows: one-way from Bergen or Oslo-1,115 kr; round-trip from Oslo via Voss-1,585 kr (same-day trip possible only mid-June–mid-Sept); round-trip from Oslo via Bergen-1,825 kr (available year-round); round-trip from Bergen-790 kr.

SELF-GUIDED TOUR

Norway in a Nutshell

If you only have one day for this region, it'll be a thrilling day. The following segments of the Nutshell route are narrated from Oslo to Bergen. If you're going the other way, hold the book upside-down.

Oslo–Bergen Train

This is simply the most spectacular train ride in northern Europe. The scenery crescendos as you climb over Norway's mountainous spine. After a mild three hours of deep woods and lakes, you're into the barren, windswept heaths and glaciers. These tracks were begun in 1894 to link Stockholm and Bergen, but Norway won its independence from Sweden in 1905, so the line served to link the two main cities in the new country—Oslo and Bergen.

Note that the Nutshell route includes only part of this train ride (as a day trip from Oslo, for instance, you take the Oslo–Myrdal and Voss–Oslo segments).

The entire railway, an amazing engineering feat completed in 1909, is 300 miles long; peaks at 4,266 feet, which, at this Alaskan latitude, is far above the tree line; goes under 18 miles of snow sheds; trundles over 300 bridges; and passes through 200 tunnels in just under seven hours.

Reservations: This train can get booked up in peak season (July–mid-Aug), so it's smart to reserve a seat several weeks ahead if you're traveling during this time and your itinerary is set: Dial 81 50 08 88, press 4 for English, and book with a credit card. If you have a second-class railpass and just want to book a seat reservation, you can use a credit card to pay the 50-kr fee (free with first-class pass) when you call.

If you prefer to book through a US agent, go to www.nsb.no/internet/en/booking/agents.

Nutshell Route from Oslo to Myrdal: Leaving Oslo, you pass through a six-mile-long tunnel and stop in Drammen, Norway's fifth-largest town. The scenery stays mild and woodsy up Hallingdal Valley until you reach Geilo, a popular ski resort.

Sample Norway in a Nutshell Schedules

Connections along the Nutshell route are carefully coordinated, so you'll probably make your connection even if trains, boats, or buses are running late. But off-season, limited schedules can cause frustrations. The following are the optimum times for one-way and round-trips made within a day's time in peak season (late June–mid-Sept). If you'll be overnighting on the fjord in Flåm or Aurland, you can easily start your trip later in the day. While I've made every effort to provide the most accurate and up-to-date information possible, always confirm schedules, connections, and prices locally or online (latest info posted each May on www .ruteinfo.net).

Oslo–Bergen: Train departs Oslo-8:11, arrives Myrdal-12:53; cogwheel train departs Myrdal-13:27, arrives Flåm-14:25; boat departs from Flåm-15:00, arrives Gudvangen-16:50; bus departs Gudvangen-17:45 (or upon arrival), arrives Voss-19:05; train departs Voss-19:20, arrives Bergen-20:35.

Day Trip from Oslo: Train departs Oslo-6:33, arrives Myrdal-11:41; cogwheel train departs Myrdal-12:11, arrives Flåm-13:05; boat departs from Flåm-13:20, arrives Gudvangen-15:20; bus departs Gudvangen-15:30, arrives Voss-16:50; train departs Voss-17:11, arrives Oslo-22:32.

A similar day trip can be done from Bergen to Oslo, or as a day trip from Bergen. There is also a fast-boat option for the Flåm–Bergen trip (see page 196).

Then you enter a land of big views and tough little cabins. Finse, at about 4,000 feet, is the highest stop on the line. From here, you enter the longest high-mountain stretch of railway in Europe. Much of the line is protected by snow tunnels. The scenery gets more dramatic as you approach Myrdal. Just before Myrdal, look to the right and down into the Flåm Valley (Flåmsdalen), where the branch line winds its way down to the fjord. Nutshell travelers get off at Myrdal.

Myrdal–Flåm Train

The little 12-mile spur line leaves the Oslo–Bergen line at Myrdal (2,800 feet), which is nothing but a scenic high-altitude train junction with a decent cafeteria. From Myrdal, the train winds down to Flåm (sea level) in 55 thrilling minutes (175-kr ticket,

275-kr round-trip or 120-kr supplement for railpass-holders, departures nearly hourly). It's party time on board, and the engineer even stops the train for photos at the best waterfall. According to a Norwegian legend, a temptress lives behind these falls and tries to lure men to the rocks with her singing...look out for her. This line has 20 tunnels (more than three miles' worth) and is so steep that the train has five separate braking systems (stations have a

cool souvenir pamphlet with lots of info on the trip; also see www .flaamsbana.no).

Flåm

On the Nutshell route, this scenic, touristy "town" at the head of the Aurlandsfjord feels more like a transit junction with a train

station and ferry landing. Services include a baggage check (25 kr, daily 8:15–19:50, next to train tracks, on your right as you depart the train, ring bell if nobody's there), a grocery store (Mon–Fri 9:00–18:00, Sat 9:00–15:00, closed Sun),

a post office, public WC, Internet access (in same building as TI, listed below), souvenir shops (overpriced reindeer pelts—cheaper in Bergen), rowboat/canoe rental (Flåm Marina and Apartments), kayak tours (Njord Tours), and a cluster of hotels and hostels.

At the **TI,** you can purchase your boat tickets and load up on handy brochures (daily June–Aug 8:30–16:00 & 16:30–20:00, May and Sept 8:45–17:00, closed Oct–April, tel. 57 63 21 06). Answers to most of your questions can be found on the walls and at the counter here. Bus schedules, boat and train timetables, maps, and more are photocopied and available for your convenience (and the staff's).

Most Nutshellers just take the next ferry to Gudvangen, but if you want to linger in this scenic area, you can overnight in Flåm (see "Sleeping," below) or better yet, stay in nearby Aurland, which is more of a town (easily accessible from Flåm by boat or bus, and described below). For a longer stay, consider Balestrand (connected by express boat from Flåm, see next chapter). Nightlife in Flåm is sparse.

Flåm–Gudvangen Fjord Cruise

At Flåm, if you're doing the Nutshell route nonstop, follow the crowds and hop on the sightseeing boat (listen for the train conductor to announce which pier number to go to). Boats leave Flåm daily at 9:00, 11:00, 13:20, and 15:00 (fewer off-season), dock briefly at the town of Aurland, then continue to Gudvangen (205 kr one-way, 98 kr for students with ISIC cards, 280 kr round-trip, no railpass discounts). With minimal English narration, the boat takes you close to the goats, sheep, waterfalls, and awesome cliffs.

You'll cruise up the lovely Aurlandsfjord and hang a left at the stunning Nærøyfjord. The trip is breathtaking in any weather.

For two glorious hours, camera-clicking tourists scurry around the drool-stained deck like nervous roosters, scratching fitfully for a photo that will catch the magic. Waterfalls turn the black cliffs into bridal veils, and you can nearly reach out and touch the cliffs of the Nærøyfjord. It's the world's narrowest fjord: six miles long and as little as 820 feet wide. On a sunny day, the ride is one of those fine times—like when you're high on the tip of an Alp—when a warm camaraderie spontaneously combusts between the strangers who came together for the experience.

Most people stay on the boat, but you can request to be dropped off in Undredal (see below) or Styvi (which has a farm museum, 20 kr). There's an idyllic 2.5-mile shoreline along the 17th-century postal road from Styvi to Bleikindli and back (you'll likely have to walk back to Styvi for a ferry pickup to Gudvangen or Flåm; if you're at the pier, the boat is supposed to stop).

Gudvangen–Voss Bus

Gudvangen is little more than a boat dock and giant tourist kiosk. Norway Nutshellers get off the boat at Gudvangen and take the bus up the Nærøydalen (literally, "Narrow Valley") to Voss. Try to catch a bus taking the extra-scenic route via Stalheim. At the end of Nærøydalen, the bus climbs a corkscrew series of switchbacks before stopping at the Stalheim Hotel for a last grand view back into fjord country (80 kr, pay on board, about a 1-hr ride; buses meet each ferry—but confirm this if you want to take the last boat of the day, which arrives in Gudvangen at about 17:00).

Voss

A plain town in a lovely lake-and-mountain setting, Voss has a **TI** (June–Aug Mon–Sat 9:00–19:00, Sun 12:00–19:00; Sept–May

Mon–Fri 8:00–15:30, closed Sat–Sun; tel. 56 52 08 00), an interesting folk museum (40 kr, daily June–Aug 10:00–17:00, shorter hours and closed Sun off-season), a 13th-century church, and a few other historic sights, but it's basically a home base for summer or winter sports. **Nordic Ventures** offers kayak trips on the Sognefjord (575 kr/half-day, 895 kr/day, 1,895 kr/2-day excursion, includes meals, depart from their office—100 yards from Voss train station, tel. 56 51 00 17, mobile 95 20 80 36, www.nordicventures.com).

The Nutshell bus from Gudvangen drops you at the Voss train station, which is on the Oslo–Bergen train line. Drivers should zip right through. You can spend the night (consider the luxurious **Voss Youth Hostel,** tel. 56 51 20 17), though I wouldn't.

SIGHTS AND ACTIVITIES

On the Aurlandsfjord, on or near the Nutshell Route

If you can afford more than just one day, the branch of the Sognefjord called Aurlandsfjord has more to offer. Here are some satisfying tangents to consider tying in to your Norwegian explorations.

▲▲**Sognefjord Scenic Express Boat**—Boats speed between Flåm and Bergen through the Sognefjord, making stops along the way, including Balestrand (see next chapter). In peak season (May–Sept), boats depart Bergen daily at 8:00, stop in Balestrand at 11:50, and arrive in Flåm at 13:25; depart Flåm at 15:30, stop in Balestrand at 16:55, and arrive in Bergen at 20:40 (Bergen to Flåm: 585 kr one-way, 755 kr round-trip, discounted with ISIC card—ask; all boats stop in Aurland, tel. 55 90 70 70). Ask if they'll pull up close to one of the scenic waterfalls.

Fjord Tours sells a round-trip package from Bergen: express boat to the Sognefjord, then return to Bergen via the second half of the Nutshell trip described above (bus, then train; 790 kr total, tel. 81 56 82 22, www.fjordtours.no).

▲▲**Flåm Valley Bike Ride or Hike**—For the best single-day activity from Flåm, take the train to Myrdal, then hike or mountain bike the gravel road back down to Flåm (2–3 hrs, great mountain scenery but no fjord views). The Flåm TI rents bikes (30 kr/hr, 175 kr/day for mountain bikes; it costs 60 kr to take a bike to Myrdal on the train). You could just hike the best two hours from Myrdal to Berekvam, where you can catch the train into the valley. Pick up the helpful map with this and other hiking options (easy to strenuous) at the Flåm TI.

▲**Rowboat or Kayak Rental**—Consider renting a rowboat or kayak to take you out on the usually calm, peaceful waters of the fjord. You can paddle near the walls of the fjord and really get a sense of the immensity of these mountains. **Flåm Marina and Apartments** rents rowboats, canoes, and more (check for the latest availability and prices, roughly 50 kr/hr; see "Sleeping" section for Flåm, page 198). **Njord Tours** offers two-hour and four-hour kayak tours (2-hr tour: 350 kr, at 8:30, 11:00, and 14:00; 4-hr tour: 490 kr, at 10:00; longer tours available on request, tel. 91 32 66 28, http://njord.as).

▲▲**Aurland**—A few miles north of Flåm, Aurland is more of a town and less of a tourist depot. Nothing exciting, but it's a good, easygoing fjordside home base (see "Sleeping," below). The harborside public library is a pleasant refuge (free Internet access, Mon 14:00–19:00, Tue–Thu 11:00–14:00, closed Fri–Sun), and the 800-year-old church is worth a peek.

The **TI** stocks English-language brochures about hikes and day trips from the area, as well as the *Bergen Guide* (mid-June–Aug Mon–Fri 9:00–19:00, Sat–Sun 10:00–17:00; shorter hours and closed Sat–Sun off-season, tel. 57 63 33 13, fax 57 63 11 48, www.alr.no).

If you want to stay overnight in Aurland, note that every train (except for the late-night one) arriving in Flåm connects with a bus or boat to Aurland. Eleven buses and at least four ferries link the towns daily in summer (bus-26 kr, 10 min; boat-66 kr, 20 min). The Flåm–Gudvangen boat stops at Aurland en route, so it's theoretically easy to continue the Nutshell route from Aurland without backtracking to Flåm. However, in July and August, when the boat from Flåm can be packed (and unable to take on more passengers in Aurland), it may make sense to double back to Flåm by bus (only 10 min) to ensure a spot on the boat.

▲**Undredal**—This almost impossibly remote community of about 100 people (and 500 goats) was accessible only by boat until 1988,

when the road from Flåm was opened. There's not much in the town, which is famous for its church and its goat cheese, but I'll never forget the picnic I had on the ferry wharf. For more information on the town, see www.undredal.no.

Undredal has Norway's smallest still-used **church,** seating only 40 people for services every fourth Sunday. The original church was built in 1147 (look for the four original stave pillars inside). It was later expanded, pews were added, and the interior was painted in the Norwegian *rosemaling* style (30 kr, mid-June–mid-Aug daily 11:00–17:30; mid-Aug–mid-June only open Sat 11:00–17:30).

The local **cheese** is beloved. The brown version is unaged and slightly sweet, while the white cheese has been aged, and is mild and a bit salty. For samples, visit the grocery store (up the hill to the right from the boat dock, Mon–Fri 9:30–17:30, Sat 9:30–16:00, Sun 12:00–16:00).

The 15-minute drive from Flåm is mostly through a new tunnel. By sea, you'll sail past Undredal on the Flåm–Gudvangen boat (you can request a stop). To get the ferry to pick you up in Undredal, turn on the blinking light (though some express boats will not stop).

Sleeping in Undredal: **$$ Undredal Overnatting** rents four modern, woody, comfortable rooms on a back street with little character (Db-600 kr, apartments for 2–6 people with bathroom and kitchenette-950 kr, tel. 57 63 30 80 or 57 63 31 00, underdalsbui @c2i.net, or just ask at the grocery).

SLEEPING

In Flåm

Note that the season is boom or bust here. It can be dead in June and packed in July and August.

$$ Heimly Pensjonat is doing its best to go big-time in a small-time town. With 23 rooms, it's clean, efficient, and the best small hotel in town. Sit on the porch with new friends and watch the clouds roll down the fjord (Sb-775 kr, Db-980 kr, extra bed-195 kr, includes breakfast, cheaper mid-Sept–May, try to reserve a room with a view, attached restaurant; bike, boat, and car rental; tel. 57 63 23 00, fax 57 63 23 40, www.heimly.no, post@heimly.no). The basement annex has additional rooms and a shared bath (D-450 kr, sheets and towels-85 kr, breakfast 95-kr). Located along the harbor a quarter-mile from the station, they will pick up and drop off at the station/dock for 10 kr round-trip. To walk, follow the wooden dock along the guest harbor or the main road.

$$ Flåm Marina and Apartments sits right on the fjord and is ideal for families and longer stays. They offer 10 self-catering apartments (i.e., clean it yourself, or pay extra for cleaning service) that sleep 2–5 people each. All units offer views of the fjord with a balcony, kitchenette, and small eating area (from 900 kr June–late Sept, from 700 kr off-season, price depends on the number of people, check online or ask about specials for longer stays, no breakfast, sheets and towels-75 kr, cleaning supplies provided, boat rental, laundry facilities, next to the guest harbor just below Heimly Pensjonat—see above, tel. 57 63 35 55, fax 57 63 35 44, www.flammarina.no, booking@flammarina.no).

$ Flåm Youth Hostel and Camping Bungalows, recently voted Scandinavia's most beautiful campground, has the cheapest beds in the area. On the river just behind the Flåm train station,

Sleep Code

(6.5 kr = about $1, country code: 47)
S = Single, **D** = Double/Twin, **T** = Triple, **Q** = Quad, **b** = bathroom, **s** = shower. All of these places accept credit cards.

To help you sort easily through these listings, I've divided the rooms into three categories, based on the price for a standard double room with bath:

$$$ **Higher Priced**—Most rooms 1,000 kr or more.
$$ **Moderately Priced**—Most rooms 500–1,000 kr.
$ **Lower Priced**—Most rooms 500 kr or less.

the place, run by the Håland family, offers dorm bunks in four-bed hostel rooms (165 kr per bed with kitchenette). They also have some private rooms with shared facilities (S-260 kr, D-420–470 kr, Q-660 kr, four-bed cabins ranging from 500–550 kr to a deluxe cabin for 800–850 kr, sheets-65 kr, towels-20 kr, showers-10 kr, tel. 57 63 21 21, fax 57 63 23 80, camping@flaam-camping.no). The folks at the check-in cabin can recommend some good hikes nearby.

In Aurland

$$$ Aurland Fjordhotell is big, modern, and centrally located, with amenities such as a sauna and steam bath. Some of its 30 rooms come with fjord-view balconies (Sb-845 kr, Db-1,190 kr, includes breakfast, attached restaurant, tel. 57 63 35 05, fax 57 63 36 22, www.aurland-fjordhotel.com, post@aurland-fjordhotel.com).

$$ The **Aabelheim Pension/Vangen Motel** complex, dominating the old center of Aurland, is run from one reception desk (tel. 57 63 35 80, fax 57 63 35 95, vangsgas@online.no, Astrid). **Vangen Motel,** nestled between Aabelheim and the fjord, is a simple, old hotel offering basic rooms, a large self-serve kitchen, and a dining and living area (S-400 kr, Ds-600 kr, Db-825 kr, breakfast-75 kr, open all year). **Aabelheim Pension** is far and away Aurland's best cozy-like-a-farmhouse place. "Cozy" is *koselig*, a good Norwegian word (S-400 kr, D-600 kr, Db-825 kr; 2–6-person cabins including kitchen, bathroom, and 2 bedrooms-1,025 kr; sheets-55 kr, extra bed-55 kr, 75-kr breakfasts are served in a wonderfully traditional dining room, fine old-time living room).

$$ At the **Skahjem Gård** farmhouse, Aurland's former deputy mayor, Nils Tore, rents out family apartments (590–690 kr with private bathroom and kitchenette, 450 kr for a cozy fishing cabin with separate bathroom, sheets and towels-70 kr, two miles up the valley on the road toward Oslo, tel. 57 63 33 29, mobile 95 17 25 67, www.skahjem.com, nskahjem@online.no). It's a 20-minute walk from town, but Nils will pick up and drop off travelers at the ferry. This is best for families who are driving.

$ Lunde Camping offers 14 cabins overlooking the river one mile out of Aurland (at the Aurland exit off the big road). Each cabin has four beds in two bunks, a kitchenette, and a river view (350–450 kr with no bathroom, deluxe cabins for up to 4 people-650–800 kr, sheets or towels-50 kr, open May–Sept, generally full June 20–Aug 20, tel. 57 63 34 12, fax 57 63 31 65, lunde.camping @alb.no, Jens Lunde).

EATING

In Aurland

The Vangen Motel runs the **Duehuset Pub** (75–250-kr dinners, daily 15:00–23:00, shorter hours in winter). For cheap eats on dockside benches, gather a picnic at the **grocery store** (Mon–Fri 9:00–20:00, Sat 9:00–18:00, closed Sun, next to Vangen Motel).

MORE ON THE SOGNEFJORD

Balestrand and Lustrafjord

Norway's world of fjords is decorated with medieval stave churches, fishing boats, and brightly painted shiplap villages. If you want to linger in fjord country, this chapter is for you.

Snuggle into the village of Balestrand on the Sognefjord, a handy jumping-off spot for adventures great and small, plus it has a variety of walking and biking options and a fun local arts scene. Farther east is the Lustrafjord, a branch of the Sognefjord, offering drivers a scenic string of towns, churches, waterfalls, ferry rides, and rugged passes.

Planning Your Time

A day and a night in Balestrand is doable, but to take advantage of the various day-trip options, consider staying two days and a night (leaving by boat in the late afternoon of the second day).

Located on the express-boat route between Bergen and Flåm, Balestrand is easy to visit using public transportation. To add the town to the popular Norway in a Nutshell route, you can take the express boat from Flåm to Balestrand, then return by express boat (transferring at Midtfjord—literally from boat to boat, in the middle of the fjord—to the Kaupanger–Gudvangen ferry; possible only June–Aug) to continue the Nutshell route down the Nærøyfjord to Gudvangen.

Or, if beginning your Nutshell journey in Bergen, take the four-hour express boat to Balestrand, spend a night or two, and then continue along the Nutshell route. For all the Nutshell nuts and bolts, see the previous chapter.

The Lustrafjord, better by car, is a logical extension of the driver's route from Oslo to Bergen—through the Gudbrandsdal Valley, the Jotunheimen Mountains, and then the Lustrafjord (with a possible stop in Balestrand). This trip can be done just as easily and scenically in reverse (rent a car in Bergen, drive to Oslo, drop off car). For more on the Gudbrandsdal Valley and the Jotunheimen Mountains, and a suggested driving itinerary, see the next chapter.

Balestrand

This pleasant fjordside village (pop. 1,850) is away from the Norway in a Nutshell crowd. From here you can side-trip to nearby Fjærland (a.k.a. "Mundal") and the awesome Jostedal glacier. Consider this worthwhile detour to the typical fjord visit—so you can dig deeper into the Sognefjord, just like the glaciers did during the last ice age.

ORIENTATION

Most travelers arrive in Balestrand on the express boat from Bergen or Flåm. The tidy harbor area has a TI, two small grocery

stores (Co-op and Spar), a couple of galleries, a town history museum, and a small aquarium devoted to sea life found in the fjord. The historic wooden Kvikne's Hotel and its modern annex dominate Balestrand's waterfront. Balestrand is tiny—from the harbor to the Balestrand

Hotel is a five-minute stroll, and you can walk from the aquarium to Kvikne's Hotel in less than that.

The town has outdoor activities for everyone, from easy to strenuous mountain hikes and mostly flat bike rides. Note that Balestrand pretty much shuts down from September through May. While rooms and dinner are available at Kvikne's Hotel during this period, the rest of the activities, sights, hotels, and restaurants listed below are likely closed.

Balestrand

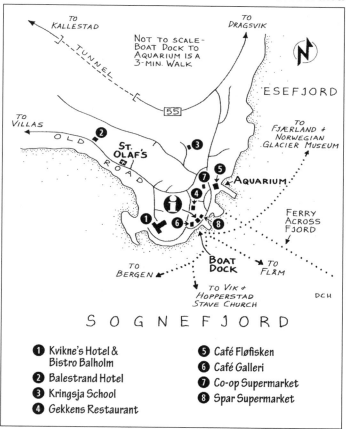

TO KALLESTAD

TO DRAGSVIK

NOT TO SCALE— BOAT DOCK TO AQUARIUM IS A 3-MIN. WALK

TUNNEL

ESEFJORD

N

55

TO VILLAS

OLD

ST. OLAF'S

ROAD

TO FJÆRLAND & NORWEGIAN GLACIER MUSEUM

AQUARIUM

FERRY ACROSS FJORD

BOAT DOCK

TO BERGEN

TO FLÅM

TO VIK & HOPPERSTAD STAVE CHURCH

DCH

S O G N E F J O R D

❶ Kvikne's Hotel & Bistro Balholm
❷ Balestrand Hotel
❸ Kringsja School
❹ Gekkens Restaurant
❺ Café Fløfisken
❻ Café Galleri
❼ Co-op Supermarket
❽ Spar Supermarket

Tourist Information

At the TI, located next to the Spar grocery at the harbor, pick up the free, helpful *Balestrand Map*. The TI has numerous brochures about the Sognefjord area and detailed information on the more challenging hikes. It offers Internet access, rents bikes (35 kr/hr, 60 kr/half-day, 90 kr/day), sells day-trip excursions to the glacier, and more (late-June–Aug Mon–Sat 7:30–19:00, Sun 10:00–15:00, shorter hours in spring and fall, closed mid-Sept–April, tel. 57 69 12 55).

SIGHTS AND ACTIVITIES

In Balestrand

Town Walking Tour—Following the route on the *Balestrand Map* (free at the TI or your hotel), take the self-guided walking tour of town (20 min to an hour one-way, depending on your pace and how many stops you make along the way). You'll stroll along a lightly traveled paved road punctuated with benches (some with great fjord views)—perfect for a break or picnic. Most sights are signposted in English.

You'll stroll the "old road"—once the main road from the harbor—along the fjord's edge, passing numerous "villas" from the late 1800s. These were built in the popular Swiss style of the period by

locals attempting to introduce a dose of Romanticism into Norwegian architecture. Look for the dragons' heads (copied from Viking-age stave churches) decorating the gables. Along the walk, you'll see two burial mounds from the Viking age, marked by a ponderous statue of a Viking king. Check out the wooden shelters for the postboxes; some give the elevation (*m.o.h.* stands for "meters over *havet*"—the sea—not too high, are they?). If you'd prefer a guided walk, contact Bjørg Bjøberg (see "Galleries," below).

St. Olaf's Church—This distinctive wooden church was built in 1897 by the wife of Knut Kvikne (of the Kvikne's Hotel family; see "Sleeping," below). This devout Englishwoman wanted a church in Balestrand where English services were held...and indeed they still are, by British clergy in summer (free, open daily, services in English every Sun late May–Aug).

Aquarium—The tiny aquarium gives you a good look at sea life in the Sognefjord.

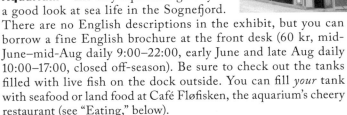

There are no English descriptions in the exhibit, but you can borrow a fine English brochure at the front desk (60 kr, mid-June–mid-Aug daily 9:00–22:00, early June and late Aug daily 10:00–17:00, closed off-season). Be sure to check out the tanks filled with live fish on the dock outside. You can fill *your* tank with seafood or land food at Café Fløfisken, the aquarium's cheery restaurant (see "Eating," below).

Galleries—Of the galleries on the harbor, *Det Gylne Hus* (The Golden House) is the best. It combines a town history museum (upstairs) with the art of Bjørg Bjøberg and Arthur Adamson. A local watercolorist and historian, Bjørg sells cards, prints, and calendars of her watercolors (free, daily 10:00–22:00, less Sept–May, tel. 91 56 28 42). Ask Bjørg about her walking tours of Balestrand or any questions about the history exhibit.

Biking—The roads here are relatively flat, and you can cycle around town or farther by circling the Esefjord. Bike rentals are available from the TI and, for guests, at some hotels.

Kayaking—**Moreld** offers three-hour tours for 390 kr, departing Balestrand daily at 13:00 and 15:00 (tel. 97 19 57 40, info@moreld .net).

Near Balestrand

Hopperstad Stave Church—The most accessible stave church in the area is located just 15 minutes away by ferry in nearby Vik. Stave churches (28 remain in Norway—see page 231) are named for their unique architectural style, with vertical wooden "staves" that form the framework of the church (45 kr, mid-June–mid-Aug daily 9:00–19:00, mid-May–mid-June and mid-Aug–mid-Sept daily 10:00–17:00, tel. 57 69 66 93). Pick up the 29-kr color booklet about the church.

The church is located a mostly flat 20-minute walk from the harbor. From the boat landing in Vik, walk up the main street from the harbor about 200 yards (past the TI, a grocery store, and hotel). Take a right at the sign for *Hopperstad Stavkyrkje*, walk 10 minutes, and you'll see the church perched on a small hill in the distance.

Boats run daily between Balestrand and Vik (62 kr one-way, 15 min, departs Balestrand at 7:55 year-round, plus 11:30 May–early-June and late-Aug–late-Sept; departs Vik at 11:30 year-round, plus 16:05 in early and late summer).

Glacier Excursions—You can see a glacier and the Norwegian Glacier Museum on a half-day or full-day excursion sold by the TI or on board the boat. This is the full-day version:

Depart Balestrand by boat and take a 90-minute fjord cruise along Fjærland's fjord. You'll see the Jostedal glacier in the distance, perched atop the mountains. Once you reach the town of Fjærland (a.k.a. "Mundal"), a bus meets the boat and takes you to the informative **Norwegian Glacier Museum** (Norsk Bremuseum), where you'll have about two hours of free time. You'll learn how glaciers were formed, experiment with your own hunk of glacier, and weigh evidence of the woolly mammoth's existence in Norway (80 kr, daily June–Aug 9:00–19:00, April–May and Sept–Oct 10:00–16:00, Nov–March on request, tel. 57 69 32 88, www.bre .museum.no).

After the museum, a bus takes you to a nearby arm of the glacier for a closer look.

Full-day excursions depart Balestrand at 8:30 (475 kr, May–Sept, two hours at museum, visit two glaciers). Half-day excursions

Near Balestrand: Glacier Excursions

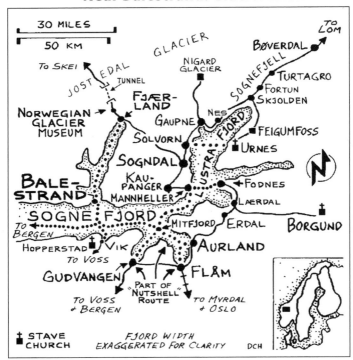

depart Balestrand at 12:00 (440 kr, one hour at museum, visit only one glacier). Both excursions return at 16:55—in time to allow you to catch the last express boat from Balestrand to Bergen.

SLEEPING

$$$ Kvikne's Hotel, a big, old, wooden hotel with a modern annex, is the place for a splurge. It's the classy grande dame of Balestrand, dominating the town and packed with tour groups (Sb-1,045–1,545 kr, Db-1,590–2,590 kr, higher prices for rooms in the historic wooden hotel section and demi-suites, cheaper off-season, includes breakfast, family rooms available; deals for stays of 2 or more nights, including half-pension with *store koldt bord* buffet dinner; tel. 57 69 42 00, fax 57 69 42 01, www.kviknes.no).

Sleep Code

(6.5 kr = about $1, country code: 47)
S = Single, **D** = Double/Twin, **T** = Triple, **Q** = Quad, **b** = bathroom,
s = shower. Unless otherwise noted, these accommodations
accept credit cards.

To help you sort easily through these listings, I've divided
the rooms into three categories, based on the price for a standard double room with bath:

$$$ **Higher Priced**—Most rooms 1,000 kr or more.
 $$ **Moderately Priced**—Most rooms between
500–1,000 kr.
  $ **Lower Priced**—Most rooms 500 kr or less.

$$ **Balestrand Hotel,** family-run by Unni-Marie Kvikne, her
California-born husband Eric Palmer, and their three children, is
your best fjordside home. Open late May through early September,
this cozy, welcoming place has 30 well-appointed, comfortable,
quiet rooms; a large, modern common area with lots of English
paperbacks; balconies (in some rooms) and outdoor benches for
soaking in the scenery; and Internet and laundry service available
for extra. When reserving, let them know your arrival time, and
they'll pick you up at the ferry (Sb-590–670 kr, Db-840–990 kr,
150 kr less without a view or balcony, includes breakfast, 5-min
walk from dock, past St. Olaf's church—or free pick-up, tel. 57 69
11 38, www.balestrand.com).

$$ **Kringsja School,** a camp school for sixth-graders, rents
beds and rooms to budget travelers mid-June to mid-August (bunk
in 4-bed dorm-210 kr, Sb-510 kr, Db-720 kr, includes breakfast,
sheets/towels-50 kr, cash only, tel. 57 69 13 03, www.kringsja.no).

EATING

Gekkens is an informal summer restaurant serving grilled meat,
fish, and vegetarian dishes, along with burgers, fish and chips, and
other fried fare (most meals 70–170 kr, June–Aug daily 12:00–22:00,
closed Sept–May, at the harbor, next to TI, tel. 97 51 29 26).

Bistro Balholm, in the lobby of Kvikne's Hotel, is essentially a pub, but has a pleasant atmosphere and reasonable prices
(lunch—sandwiches, soup, salads, and hot dishes for 60–175 kr;
dinner—pasta, meat, or fish dishes for 180–300 kr; daily 12:00–
22:00, closed off-season).

Kvikne's Hotel offers a splendid, spendy *store koldt bord* buffet dinner. Take your time. Get a new plate with each course and

save room for dessert. Consider taking a preview tour before you dive in so you can budget your stomach space (395 kr per person, four-course dinner for 500–600 kr, May–Sept daily 19:00–21:00, closed Oct–April). After dinner, head into the grand lounges to pick up your (included) cup of coffee or tea, which you'll sip sitting on classy old-fashioned furniture and basking in fjord views.

Café Fløfisken, the informal café at the aquarium, serves sandwiches for lunch (50–80 kr) and seafood and land food dinners (100–150 kr) at indoor or outdoor tables (mid-June–mid-Aug daily 9:00–22:00; in early June and late Aug only light meals available and closes at 21:00; closed off-season).

Café Galleri, adjacent to Bjørg Bjøberg's art gallery at the harbor, serves sandwiches, cakes, and beverages throughout the day, and grilled meats and fish after 15:00 (mid-April–mid-Sept daily 11:00–21:00, indoor and outdoor seating).

The Co-op and Spar **supermarkets** at the harbor have basic grocery supplies, including bread, meats, cheeses, and drinks—perfect for a picnic lunch. Co-op is bigger and has more selection (both open Mon–Fri 9:00–18:00, Sat 9:00–15:00, closed Sun). The **bakery** sells bread, pastries, and on weekends, open-face sandwiches (Sun and Tue–Fri 10:00–17:00, Sat 9:00–14:00, closed Mon, between Co-op and Spar markets).

TRANSPORTATION CONNECTIONS

Balestrand is connected to the rest of Norway via the **Fylkesbaatane express boat** (buy tickets on boat or at TI, discounts for students and seniors, tel. 55 90 70 70, www.fjord1.no)

The boat trip between **Bergen and Balestrand** takes four hours (425 kr, departs Bergen May–Sept daily at 8:00, also Mon–Fri at 16:30, Sat at 14:15, some Sun at 16:30—but not mid-June–late Aug; Oct–April Mon–Fri at 8:00, Sun–Fri at 16:30, Sat at 14:15; departs Balestrand May–Sept daily at 16:30, Mon–Sat at 7:55, some Sun at 11:30—but not mid-June–late Aug; Oct–April Mon–Sat at 7:55, Sun at 16:25). In summer, the 8:00 boat continues to **Flåm.**

Going by boat between **Flåm and Balestrand** takes about 1.5 hours (205 kr, departs Flåm May–Sept daily at 15:30, stops at Aurland, arrives in Balestrand at 16:55; second boat sometimes runs from Flåm Mon–Fri at 6:00, arrives Balestrand at 8:00; departs Balestrand daily at 11:50, Mon–Fri at 8:30; no express boats between Flåm–Balestrand Oct–April).

From **Oslo,** you can take an early train to Flåm (no later than the 8:11 train as part of the Norway in a Nutshell route—see previous chapter), then catch the 15:30 express boat to Balestrand. After your visit, you can continue on the express boat to Bergen, or return to the Nutshell route by taking the express boat to *Midtfjord*, and transferring to the next boat to Gudvangen.

For more on connecting Flåm and Bergen with this express boat (via Balestrand), see "Sognefjord Scenic Express Boat," page 196 of previous chapter.

Lustrafjord

This arm of the famous Sognefjord is rugged country—only 2 percent of the land is fit to build or farm on. Lustrafjord is ringed with tiny villages where farmers sell cherries and giant raspberries. Drivers can pick and choose among the sights below.

SIGHTS

The towns and sights are listed from north to south.

Skjolden—This village, at the north tip of Lustrafjord, has a good **TI** (tel. 97 60 04 43) with advice on fjord ferries and glacier hikes, and a cozy youth hostel on the river (dorm bed-160 kr, S-235 kr, D-520 kr, non-members pay 50 kr extra, open mid-May–mid-Aug, tel. 57 62 75 75).

Nes and Waterfall View—From the little town of Nes on the west bank of the Lustrafjord, look across the fjord at the impressive Feigumfoss waterfall. Drops and dribbles come from miles around for this 650-foot tumble. **Viki Fjord Camping,** located directly across from the waterfall, has great fjordside huts (tel. 57 68 64 20, http://home.c2i.net/sanaess).

Dale—This village on the west bank of the Lustrafjord boasts a 13th-century stone Gothic church with 14th-century frescoes; it's unique and worth a peek.

▲▲**Urnes' Stave Church**—The town of Urnes, perched on the east bank of the Lustrafjord, has Norway's oldest stave church (1130), one of 28 remaining stave churches in the country—see page 231 (45 kr, May–Aug Mon–Fri 10:30–17:30, Sat–Sun 11:30–17:30, call for an English tour, steep but pleasant 20-min walk from town, tel. 57 68 39 45).

Ferries running between Solvorn and Urnes depart Solvorn at the top of most hours and Urnes at the bottom of most hours (28-kr one-way passenger fare, 15-min ride).

Solvorn—On the west bank of the Lustrafjord, 10 miles east of Sogndal, Solvorn is a sleepy little Victorian town. Its tiny ferry crosses the fjord regularly to Urnes and its famous little stave church (see above).

Sleeping in Solvorn: $$$ **Walaker Hotel,** a former inn and coach station, has been run by the Walaker family since 1690 (that's a lot of pressure on the ninth generation). In the main house, tradition drips like butter through the halls and living rooms. A warm family feeling pervades the building and there are only patriotic hymns on the piano. Most of the rooms are simple but good, and four rooms are fancy, done in 18th-century style. The hotel, set right on the Lustrafjord (with the perfect garden to relax and recover from stress), is open May through September. Oda and Hermod Walaker and their son, Ole Henrik, are a wealth of information, and they serve fine food (Sb-1,280–1,990 kr, Db-1,420–1,990 kr, some rooms with fjord views, higher prices are for rooms in historic building, includes breakfast, four-course dinner-445 kr includes tour of attached gallery, tel. 57 68 20 80, fax 57 68 20 81, www.walaker.com, hotel@walaker.com). The cheery Linahagen Café, next door, has Internet access and a fun window full of live fish.

Sogndal—About 10 minutes (by car) from the Mannheller–Fodnes ferry, Sogndal is the only sizable town in this region. It's big enough to have a busy shopping street and a helpful **TI.**

Sleeping in Sogndal: $$ **Loftenes Pensjonat** houses travelers mid-June through mid-August, and mostly students—but a few travelers—during the school year (S-400 kr, Sb-475 kr, D-650–700 kr, Db-700–750 kr, includes breakfast, near the water, tel. & fax 57 67 15 77). Sogndal also has a fine $ **youth hostel** (bunk in 3- to 4-bed room-100 kr, S-175 kr, D-250 kr, Db-400 kr, breakfast-60 kr, sheets-50 kr, towel-25 kr, members' kitchen—B.Y.O. pots, closed 10:00–17:00, at fork in the road as you enter town, tel. 57 62 75 75, mobile 90 93 51 71, fax 57 62 75 70, www.vandrerhjem.no, sogndal .hostel@vandrerhjem.no).

Scenic Drives from Lustrafjord

Note that car ferries cost roughly $5 per hour for walk-ons and $15 per hour for a car, driver, and passenger. Reservations are generally not necessary (and sometimes not possible), but in summer—especially on Friday and Sunday, I'd get one to be safe (free and easy, tel. 55 90 70 70 or 57 75 70 70).

▲▲**From Sogndal to Aurland**—This drive to Aurland (via Mannheller, Fodnes, Lærdal, and Hornadalen—see map on page 191—takes you over an incredible mountain pass, offers classic aerial fjord views, and winds into the pleasant fjordside town of Aurland (see previous chapter).

Near Sogndal, catch the Mannheller–Fodnes ferry (2/hr at :00 and :30 past the hour, 15 min, no reservations possible) and drive through the tunnel to Lærdal. Though the 15-mile-long tunnel (the world's longest—paid for by North Sea oil profits) from Lærdal under Hornadalen to Aurland is the fastest way to go, the scenic route over the pass is worth the messy pants.

From the ferry, take the first road to the right (to Erdal). Leave E68 at Erdal (just west of Lærdal) for the breathtaking 60-minute, 30-mile drive to Aurland over 4,000-foot-high Hornadalen. This road, open only in summer, passes remote mountain huts and terrifying mountain views before its 12-hairpin zigzag descent into the Aurlandsfjord.

Stop at the first fjord viewpoint (look for the *Utsiktspunkt* sign) as you begin your descent; it's the best. (Better yet, climb the rock 30 feet above the road.)

▲**From Kaupanger to Bergen**—Car ferries take tourists between Kaupanger (on the southern end of the Lustrafjord) and Gudvangen (on the Norway in a Nutshell route) through an arm and elbow of the Sognefjord, including the staggering Nærøyfjord. While this ferry ride is great and saves substantial time, this shortcut over the full Aurland/Flåm–Gudvangen cruise does cost you some of the scenery. Boats leave Kaupanger daily at 9:20, 12:05, 16:00, and 18:50 for the two-hour trip (car and driver-467 kr, adult passenger-191 kr, reserve one day in advance, tel. 55 90 70 60, updated schedules posted each May, www.ruteinfo.net). While Kaupanger is little more than a ferry landing set on the scenic Sognefjord, the small stave-type church at the edge of town merits a look.

From Gudvangen, it's a 90-mile drive to Bergen. Get off the ferry in Gudvangen and drive up the Nærøydalen (literally, "Narrow Valley") past a river bubbling excitedly about the plunge it just took. You'll see the two giant falls just before the road marked *Stalheimskleiva*. Follow the sign (exiting left) to the little Stalheimskleiva road. This incredible road doggedly worms its way up into the ozone. My car overheated in a few minutes. Take it easy. (The main road gets you there more easily—through a tunnel and 0.8 miles back up a smaller road.) As you wind up, you can view the falls from several turnouts. At the top, stop for a break at the touristy Stalheim Hotel. Though this hotel dates from 1885, there's been an inn here since about 1700, where the royal mailmen would change horses. The hotel is geared for tour groups (genuine trolls sew the pewter buttons on the sweaters), but the priceless view from the backyard is free.

The road continues into a mellower beauty, past lakes and farms, toward Voss. Tvindefossen, a waterfall with a handy campground/WC/kiosk picnic area right under it, is worth a stop. Unless you judge waterfalls by megatonnage, the 500-foot-long fall has nuclear charms. The grassy meadow and flat rocks at its base were made especially for your picnic lunch.

The highway takes you through Voss and into Bergen. If you plan to visit Edvard Grieg's home and the nearby Fantoft Stave Church, now is the ideal time, since you'll be driving right by and they're a headache to reach from downtown. Both are overrated but almost obligatory, and open until 18:00 in summer (see page 230).

GUDBRANDSDAL VALLEY and JOTUNHEIMEN MOUNTAINS

Norway in a Nutshell is a great day trip, but with more time and a car, consider a scenic meander from Oslo to Bergen. You'll arc up the Gudbrandsdal Valley and over the Jotunheimen Mountains, then travel along the Lustrafjord (see previous chapter).

After an introductory stop in Lillehammer, with its fine folk museum, you might spend the night in a log-and-sod farmstead-turned-hotel, tucked in a quiet valley under Norway's highest peaks. Next, Norway's highest pass takes you on an exhilarating roller-coaster ride through the heart of the myth-inspiring Jotunheimen (literally, "Giants' Home"), bristling with Norway's biggest mountains. The road then hairpins down into fjord country (see previous chapter).

Planning Your Time

While you could spend five or six days in this area on a three-week Scandinavian rampage, this slice of the region is worth three days. By car, I'd spend them like this:

Day 1: Leave Oslo early, and spend midday at the Maihaugen Open-Air Folk Museum for a tour and picnic. Drive up the Gudbrandsdal Valley, stopping at the Lom church. Stay overnight in Jotunheimen.

Day 2: Drive out of the mountains, along the Lustrafjord (see previous chapter), over Hornadalen Pass, and into Aurlandsfjord. Sleep in Aurland.

Day 3: Cruise the Aurland and Nærøy fjords (round-trip or have the poor driver meet the rest at Gudvangen) before carrying on to Bergen.

Gudbrandsdal Valley and Jotunheimen Mountains

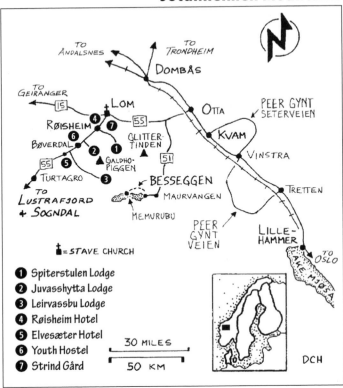

= STAVE CHURCH

1. Spiterstulen Lodge
2. Juvasshytta Lodge
3. Leirvassbu Lodge
4. Røisheim Hotel
5. Elvesæter Hotel
6. Youth Hostel
7. Strind Gård

30 MILES

50 KM

DCH

The last two days can be condensed into a single day if rushed. (For specifics on Aurland accommodations and the fjord cruise, see the Norway in a Nutshell chapter.)

Gudbrandsdal Valley

The Gudbrandsdal Valley is the tradition-steeped country of Peer Gynt, the Norwegian Huck Finn. This romantic valley of time-worn hills, log cabins, and velvet farms has connected northern and southern Norway since ancient times. Throughout this region, the government subsidizes small farms to keep the countryside populated and healthy. (These subsidies would not be permitted if Norway were a member of the European Union.)

Lillehammer

Lillehammer, a pleasant winter and summer resort town of 25,000, was briefly world-famous in 1994 when it hosted the Winter Olympics. Lillehammer has a happy, old, woody pedestrian zone and several interesting museums, including the Maihaugen Open-Air Folk Museum.

Tourist Information: The TI is right in the colorful pedestrian shopping zone (mid-June–mid-Aug Mon–Sat 9:00–18:00, Sun 12:00–17:00; mid-Aug–mid-June Mon–Fri 9:00–16:00, Sat 10:00–14:00, closed Sun; Jernbanetorget 2, tel. 61 28 98 00, www.lillehammerturist.no).

SIGHTS

In Lillehammer

Norwegian Olympics Museum (Norges Olympiske Museum)— This museum, housed in the Olympic ice-hockey arena, gives you the highlights of the town's 1994 glory days. Try the bobsled simulator at the ski jump (60 kr, mid-May–Aug daily 10:00–18:00; Sept–mid-May Tue–Sun 11:00–16:00, closed Mon; Håkon Hall, 15-min walk from train station toward Maihaugen, tel. 61 25 21 00, www.ol.museum.no). In the summer, ski jumpers practice on the smaller of the two ski jumps, which is sprayed with water. Drive up to take a peek.

▲▲**Maihaugen Open-Air Folk Museum (Friluftsmuseet)**—This idyllic park, full of old farmhouses and pickled slices of folk culture, provides a good introduction to the Gudbrandsdal Valley. Anders Sandvig, a "visionary dentist," started the collection in 1887. The outdoor section has 180 old buildings from the Gudbrandsdal region and a town re-created from the 1920s. While July is busy with crafts in action and people living here from ages ago (à la Williamsburg), other months are pretty dead, with no live crafts and most of the buildings locked up.

The museum's three indoor exhibits (near the turnstile) are excellent. The "We Won the Land" exhibit sweeps you through Norwegian history from the Ice Age to the Space Age. The Gudbrandsdal art section shows village art at its best. And you can walk through Dr. Sandvig's old dental office and the original shops of 40 crafts- and tradespeople such as a hatter, cooper (barrelmaker), and bookbinder.

Upon arrival, ask about special events, crafts, or music. Because English descriptions are scant, you'll need the 95-kr English guidebook or a guided tour to learn much. Free 45-minute guided tours in English go daily (tours cost extra off-season; call ahead for tour schedule—tel. 61 28 89 00; museum entry-100 kr; mid-May–Sept daily 10:00–17:00; spring and fall Tue–Sun 11:00–16:00, closed Mon; in winter, the park is open but the houses are closed; www.maihaugen.no). Maihaugen is a steep 15-minute walk or short bus ride (hourly) from the Lillehammer train station. While the museum welcomes picnickers and has a simple cafeteria, the town itself (a 10-min walk below the museum), with lots of fun eateries, is better for lunch.

In the Gudbrandsdal Valley

▲**Eidsvoll Manor**—During the Napoleonic period, control of Norway went from Denmark to Sweden. This ruffled the patriotic feathers of Norway's Thomas Jeffersons and Ben Franklins, and on May 17, 1814, Norway's constitution was written and signed in this stately mansion (in the town of Eidsvoll Verk, north of Oslo). While Sweden still ruled, Norway had more autonomy than ever. The mansion is full of elegant furnishings and stirring history (50 kr, May–Aug daily 10:00–17:00, shorter hours and closed Mon off-season, tel. 63 92 22 10, www.eidsvoll1814.no).

Scenic Drives—Two side-trips give visitors a good dose of this land's wild beauty. Peer Gynt Veien (a 60-kr toll road) leaves E6 at Tretten, loops west for 25 miles, and rejoins E6 at Vinstra. This trip sounds romantic, but it's basically a windy, curvy dirt road over a high, desolate heath and scrub-brush plateau with fine mountain views: it's scenic, but so is E6. The second scenic side-trip, Peer Gynt Seterveien, is not much better.

SLEEPING

In and near Lillehammer

$$ Gjestehuset Ersgaard, with 30 rooms in a peacefully rural setting a mile east of and above Lillehammer, offers those with a car a fine value with a view of the valley (S-390 kr, Sb-490 kr, D-590 kr, Db-690 kr, Db with a view-790 kr, includes breakfast, these prices valid through 2007 with this book, Nordseterveien 201, tel. 61 25 06 84, fax 61 25 31 09, www.ersgaard.no, oeilande@online.no).

$ The **GjesteBu** private hostel is another option for cheap beds (bunk in 8-bed dorm-120 kr, S-250 kr, D-350 kr and up; apartment with kitchen and bath-550 kr plus 100 kr per person, up to 5 people; sheets-50 kr, no breakfast, cash only, 3 blocks from TI, Gamleveien 110, tel. & fax 61 25 43 21, gjestebu@lillehammer.no).

In Kvam, in the Gudbrandsdal Valley

This is a popular vacation valley for Norwegians, and you'll find loads of reasonable small hotels and campgrounds with huts for those who aren't quite campers (*hytter* means "bungalows," *rom* is

Sleep Code

(6.5 kr = about $1, country code: 47)
S = Single, **D** = Double/Twin, **T** = Triple, **Q** = Quad, **b** = bathroom,
s = shower. You can assume credit cards are accepted unless otherwise noted.

To help you sort easily through these listings, I've divided the rooms into three categories, based on the price for a standard double room with bath:

$$$ **Higher Priced**—Most rooms 1,000 kr or more.
$$ **Moderately Priced**—Most rooms between 500–1,000 kr.
$ **Lower Priced**—Most rooms 500 kr or less.

"private room," and *ledig* means "vacancy"). These huts normally cost about 400–600 kr, depending on size and amenities, and can hold from four to six people. Although they are simple, you'll have a kitchenette and access to a good WC and shower. When available, sheets rent for an extra 60 kr per person. Local TIs can find you rooms. Reservations are generally only necessary in July. Here are a couple of listings in the town of Kvam, located midway between Lillehammer and Lom.

$$ Sinclair Vertshuset Motel has an inexpensive cafeteria and pub but no personality (Sb-690 kr, Db-890 kr, includes breakfast, tel. 61 29 54 50, fax 61 29 54 51, www.vertshuset-sinclair.no, post @vertshuset-sinclair.no). The motel was named after a Scotsman who led a band of adventurers into this valley, attempting to set up their own Scottish kingdom. They failed. All were kilt.

$ Kirketeigen Ungdomssenter ("Church Youth Center"), 100 yards away from the Sinclair Vertshuset, welcomes travelers year-round (camping spots-110 kr per tent or van; cabins with kitchen and bath-590 kr, up to 6 people; simple four-bed rooms-320 kr for 2–4 people with sheets; sheets and blankets-65 kr, breakfast-70 kr, Visa is only credit card accepted, behind town church, tel. 61 21 60 90, www.kirketeigen.no).

Jotunheimen Mountains

You can play roller coaster with mountain passes, take rugged hikes, wind up scenic toll roads, and get up close—nice and icy—to a huge glacier. The gateway to the mountains is the unassuming town of Lom.

SIGHTS AND ACTIVITIES

Lom

While Lom isn't much of a town, its great stave church causes the closest thing to a tour-bus traffic jam this neck of the Norwegian woods will ever see. Park by the church; you'll see its dark spire just over the bridge.

Tourist Information: The TI is across the street from the church (mid-June–mid-Aug Mon–Fri 9:00–19:00, Sat–Sun 10:00–19:00, shorter hours and closed Sat–Sun off-season, tel. 61 21 29 90, www.visitlom.com).

▲▲**Lom Stave Church**—In spite of its extensive renovations, Lom's church (from 1170) is a textbook example of a stave church

(for more on stave churches, see sidebar on page 231). Inside, look high for the parts from 1170, such as the circle of X-shaped St. Andrew crosses and the Norman arches above them. The apse (behind the altar) is from 1240. Lepers came to the grilled window in the apse for a blessing. When the Reformation hit in 1536, the old paintings were whitewashed over. The transepts, pews, and windows were added in the 17th century. Men sat on the right, women on the left, and prisoners sat with the sheriff in the caged area in the rear (40 kr, daily mid-June–mid-Aug 9:00–20:00, mid-May–mid-June and mid-Aug–mid-Sept 10:00–16:00, closed in winter and during funerals, fine 5-kr leaflet, small groups can arrange for a tour, even after hours, by calling 97 07 53 97). Check out the little footbridge over the waterfall, and peek at the only surviving stave-church dragon-head "steeple" in the museum adjacent to the shop in the church parking lot.

In the Jotunheimen Mountains

Sognefjell

Norway's highest pass (4,600 feet), rated ▲▲, is a thrilling drive through a cancan line of northern Europe's tallest mountains. The highest is Galdhøpiggen (8,100 feet). In previous centuries, the farmers of Gudbrandsdal took their horse caravans over this difficult mountain pass on their necessary treks to Bergen. Today, the road (Route 55) is still narrow, windy, and otherworldly (and usually closed mid-Oct–May). The 10 hairpin turns between Turtagrø and Fortun are white-knuckle exciting. Be sure to stop, get out, look around, and enjoy the lavish views. Treat each turn as if it were your last.

Scenic Drives and Hikes

From the main road near Bøverdal and Røisheim, you have several options springing from three toll roads. The Lom TI has a mountain museum and plenty of maps and good information on hikes in the region.

Spiterstulen: From Røisheim, this 11-mile toll road (60 kr) takes you to the Spiterstulen mountain hotel/lodge (3,600 feet). This is the best destination for serious all-day hikes to Norway's two mightiest mountains, Glittertinden (8,100 feet) and Galdhøpiggen (a 4-hr hike up and a 3-hr hike down, doable without a guide).

Juvasshytta: This toll road, starting from Bøverdal, takes you the highest you can drive and the closest you can get to Galdhøpiggen by car (6,050 feet). At the end of the 80-kr toll road, there are daily guided six-hour hikes across the glacier to the summit and back (150 kr, at 10:00 and 11:30 in the summer, 4 miles each way, hiking shoes a good idea, easy ascent but very dangerous without a guide). You can sleep in the **$$ Juvasshytta lodge** (Db-660 kr with sheets, D without sheets-450 kr, sheets-50 kr, breakfast-90 kr, dinner-250 kr, tel. 61 21 15 50, www.juvasshytta.no).

Leirvassbu: This 11-mile, 50-kr toll road is most scenic for car hikers. It takes you to a lodge at 4,600 feet with great views and easy walks. A serious (4-hr round-trip) hike goes to the lone peak, Kyrkja (6,660 feet).

Besseggen: This ridge offers an incredible opportunity to hike between two lakes separated by less than five feet of land and a 1,000-foot cliff. To get to the trailhead, drivers detour down road 51 after Otta south to Maurvangen. Turn right to Gjendesheim to park your car. From Gjendesheim, catch the boat to Memurubu, where the path starts at the boat dock. Hike along the ridge—with a blue lake on one side and a green lake on the other—and keep your balance. The six-hour trail leads back to Gjendesheim. (This is a thrilling but potentially hazardous hike, and it's a major detour: Gjendesheim is about an hour, or 55 miles, from Røisheim.)

Jostedal's Nigardsbreen Glacier Hike

Jostedal is the most accessible branch of mainland Europe's largest glacier (185 square miles), and the Nigardsbreen Glacier hike offers a good opportunity, rated ▲, for a hands-on glacier experience. It's an easy drive up Jostedal from Lustrafjord.

From Gaupne, road 604 dead-ends after 23 miles at a glacier

museum. From there, a 25-kr toll road continues two miles to a lake facing the actual tongue of the glacier.

Breheimsenteret, the glacier information center for the national park, stands at the entrance to the Nigardsbreen Glacier valley (before the toll road, 1.5 miles past Gjerde). The center boldly charges 50 kr for a relaxing 20-minute slide presentation showing ice climbing and glacier scenery with no words and a small gallery of glacier-related exhibits (daily mid-June–mid-Aug 9:00–19:00, May–mid-June and mid-Aug–Sept 10:00–17:00, closed Oct–April, free Internet access, shop, cafeteria, tel. 57 68 32 50).

From the end of the toll road, you can hike or take a special boat (30 kr round-trip, 2/hr, 15 min, mid-June–mid-Sept 10:00–18:00) to a spot just 20 minutes from the glacier. The walk is steep and slippery. Follow the red marks. There are guided family-friendly walks on the glacier (160 kr, 80 kr for kids, minimum age 5, I'd rate the walks PG-13 myself, 90-min, daily departures 11:30–13:00 depending on demand, you get clamp-on crampons). Tougher glacier hikes are also offered (starting at 350 kr, includes boots and real crampons, June–Aug daily at 11:45 and 12:45, additional departure in July and Aug at 14:30, 3.5–4.5 hrs, book by phone the day before—tel. 57 68 32 50, arrive at the glacier center 30 min early to buy tickets and pick up your gear). For information on the glacier, go to www.jostedal.com.

Respect the glacier. It's a powerful river of ice, and fatal accidents are not uncommon. The guided walk is the safest option and plenty exciting. Use the Gaupne TI to confirm your plans (tel. 57 68 15 88). If this is your first glacier, it's worth the time and hike even without the tour; but if glaciers don't give you tingles and you're feeling pressed, it's not worth the time.

Sleeping near the Glacier: **$$ Jostedal Hotel** rents 19 cozy rooms—with hardwood floors and fluffy comforters—split between two buildings on a farm, three miles from the Nigardsbreen Visitors Center (Sb-650 kr, Db-850 kr, attached restaurant with outdoor terrace, tel. 57 68 31 19, fax 57 68 31 57, www.jostedalhotel.no, post@jostedalhotel.no, Laila Gjerde).

SLEEPING

Near Lom
(6.5 kr = about $1, country code: 47)
The first three listings are a 15-minute drive up the road from Lom. Røisheim and Elvesæter are hotel road stops in the wild. The youth hostel is in the tiny village of Bøverdal.

$$$ Røisheim, in a marvelously remote mountain setting, is a storybook hotel composed of a cluster of centuries-old, sod-roofed log farmhouses. It's filled with antiques, Norwegian travelers, and the hard work of its owners, Ingrid and Haavard Lunde. Røisheim is a cultural end in itself. Each room is rustic but elegant. Some rooms are in old, wooden farm buildings—*stabburs*—with low ceilings and heavy beams. The deluxe rooms have king beds and some have fireplaces. Call ahead so they'll be prepared (open mid-May–Sept; standard Sb-2,100 kr, Sb with king bed-2,500 kr, Sb plus fireplace-2,800 kr, standard Db-2,700 kr, Db with king bed-3,000 kr, Db plus fireplace-3,400 kr; includes breakfast, packed lunch, and an over-the-top 3-course traditional dinner served at 19:30; 10 miles south of Lom on Sognefjell Road 55 in the Bøver Valley, tel. 61 21 20 31, fax 61 21 21 51, www.roisheim.no, booking @roisheim.dvgl.no).

$$ Elvesæter Hotel is as Old World romantic as Røisheim, but bigger, cheaper, and less impressed with itself (open late May–mid-Sept, Sb-800 kr, Db-995 kr, Tb-1,200 kr, Qb-1,350 kr, includes breakfast, wonderful 225-kr buffet dinners, strictly non-smoking, swimming pool, a few minutes farther up Road 55, just past Bøverdalen, tel. 61 21 99 00, fax 61 21 21 01, www.elveseter .no, post@elveseter.no). They also offer apartments with kitchens and all bedding (3–6 people, minimum 2 nights, 2,000–2,900 kr for 2 nights without breakfast). The Elvesæter family has done a great job of retaining the historic character of their medieval farm, even though the place is big enough to handle large tour groups. Even if you're not staying here, stop to wander through the public spaces and pick up a flier explaining the towering Sagasøyla column celebrating Norwegian independence. It was built to stand in front of Oslo's parliament building but, because of changing political winds after World War II, was eventually erected here in 1992.

$ Bøverdalen Youth Hostel offers cheap but comfortable beds and a far more rugged clientele—real hikers rather than car hikers (open late May–Sept, 150 kr per bunk in 4- to 6-bed rooms, D-350 kr; 4-person cabins-550 kr with shower and toilet, 400 kr without; sheets-60 kr, breakfast-65 kr, hot and self-serve meals, in Bøverdal, tel. & fax 61 21 20 64, boeverdalen.hostel@vandrerhjem .no). It's in the center of a little community (store, campground, and toll road up to Galdhopiggen area).

$ Strind Gård, a rustic 150-year-old farmhouse and a last resort, rents dingy rooms in sod-roofed huts and in the main house (hut D-200 kr, house D-300 kr, apartment for 4–6 with private bath-700 kr, sheets-50 kr, no breakfast, valley views, 2 miles outside Lom on Route 55 toward Sogndal, tel. 61 21 12 37, www .strind-gard.no).

TRANSPORTATION CONNECTIONS

Cars are better, but if you're without wheels: **Oslo to Lillehammer** (9 trains/day, 2.5 hrs), **Lillehammer to Otta** (6 trains/day, 1.5 hrs); a bus meets some trains (confirm schedule at the train station in Oslo) for travelers heading on to **Lom** (2 buses/day, 1 hr) and from **Lom to Sogndal** (2 buses/day, 4 hrs).

Route Tips for Drivers

Use low gears and lots of patience both up (to keep the engine cool) and down (to save your brakes). Uphill traffic gets the right-of-way, but drivers, up or down, dive for the nearest fat part of the road whenever they meet. Ask backseat drivers not to scream until you've actually been hit or have left the road.

From Oslo to Jotunheimen: It's 2.5 hours from Oslo to Lillehammer and three hours after that to Lom. Wind out of Oslo following signs for *E6* (not to *Drammen*, but for *Stockholm* and then to *Trondheim*). In a few minutes, you're in the wide-open pastoral countryside of eastern Norway. Norway's Constitution Hall is a five-minute detour off E6, several miles south of Eidsvoll in Eidsvoll Verk (follow the signs to *Eidsvoll Bygningen*). Then E6 takes you along Norway's largest lake (Mjøsa), through the town of Hamar, and past more lake scenery into Lillehammer. Signs direct you uphill from downtown Lillehammer to the Maihaugen Open-Air Folk Museum. There's free parking near the pay lot above the entrance. From Lillehammer, signs to *E6/Trondheim* take you up the valley of Gudbrandsdal. At Otta, exit for Lom.

BERGEN

Bergen is permanently salted with robust cobbles and a rich sea-trading heritage. Norway's capital in the 12th and 13th centuries, Bergen's wealth and importance came thanks to its membership in the heavyweight medieval trading club of merchant cities called the Hanseatic League. Bergen still wears her rich maritime heritage proudly.

Famous for lousy weather, Bergen gets an average of 80 inches of rain annually (compared to 30 inches in Oslo). A good year has 60 days of sunshine. With 230,000 people, Bergen has its big-city tension, parking problems, and high prices, but visitors sticking to the old center find it charming.

Enjoy Bergen's salty market, then stroll the easy-on-foot old quarter. From downtown Bergen, a funicular zips you up a little mountain for a bird's-eye view of this sailors' town.

Planning Your Time

Bergen can be enjoyed even on the tail end of a day's scenic train ride from Oslo before returning on the overnight train. But that teasing taste will make you wish you had more time. On a three-week tour of Scandinavia, Bergen is worth a whole day. Start that day at the harborfront fish market and spend the rest of the morning in the Bryggen quarter (tours at 11:00 and 13:00, June–Aug only).

Bergen, a geographic dead-end for most travelers, is an efficient place to begin or end your Scandinavian tour. Consider flying "open jaw"—for example, into Bergen and out of Helsinki (or vice-versa).

ORIENTATION

The action is on the waterfront. Nearly everything listed in this chapter is within a few minutes' walk of the fish market (Fisketorvet). The busy Torget (market square and fish market) is at the head of the bay. Facing the sea from here, Bergen's TI is behind you on your left. Its historic Hanseatic quarter (Bryggen) lines the harbor on the right. Hydrofoils from Flåm and Stavanger dock at the harbor on the left. Two blocks from the market square (behind Bryggen), a

funicular stands ready to whisk you to the top of Mount Fløyen.

Tourist Information

The TI, filling the historic old Bergen Exchange building, is frescoed with old murals showing local and traditional life. It covers Bergen and western Norway, has information and tickets for tours and concerts, and maintains a daily events board (June–Aug daily 8:30–22:00; May and Sept daily 9:00–20:00; Oct–April Mon–Sat 9:00–16:00, closed Sun; on the harborfront, 10-min walk from train station, across from fish market at Vågsallmenningen 1, tel. 55 55 20 00, fax 55 55 20 01, www.visitbergen.com). The free *Bergen Guide* lists all sights, hours, and special events, and has a fine map. For a 30-kr booking fee, they can help you find a hotel room.

Bergen Card: The Bergen Card gives you free use of the city buses and the Mount Fløyen funicular, free admission to most museums, and discounts on some tours, events, and sights—including a 60 percent discount on Edvard Grieg's Home (170 kr/24 hrs, 250 kr/48 hrs, sold at TI, train station, and most hotels). While the card doesn't cover the Hanseatic Museum in summer (June–Aug), it may save you money if you'll be using the bus a lot.

Arrival in Bergen

By Train or Bus: Bergen's train and bus stations are on Strømgaten, facing a park-rimmed lake. The train station has an office open long hours for booking all your travel in Norway (Mon–Fri 6:45–21:30, Sat 7:30–16:15, Sun 7:30–21:30). There are 24-hour luggage lockers, pay toilets, a Narvesen newsstand, a Bon Appetit sandwich shop, and a coffee shop. (To get to the bus station, follow the covered walkway behind the Narvesen via the Storcenter shopping mall.) Taxis are waiting beyond the exit on your right, behind the luggage lockers.

From the train station, it's a 10-minute walk to the TI: Walk around the lake to the square called Ole Bulls Plass; from here,

Bergen

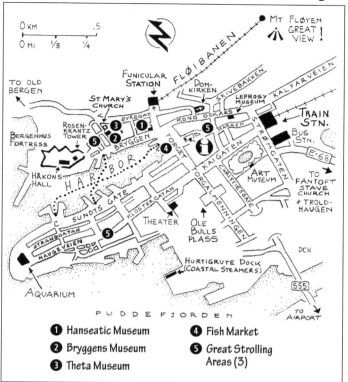

- **1** Hanseatic Museum
- **2** Bryggens Museum
- **3** Theta Museum
- **4** Fish Market
- **5** Great Strolling Areas (3)

the wide street called Torgalmenningen leads down to Torget, where you'll find Bergen's famous and fragrant fish market, the waterfront, and the TI. Alternatively, for a longer (15 min), more scenic approach to town from the train station, cross the street (Strømgaten) in front of the station and take Marken, a cobbled street, down to the TI and fish market.

By Plane: The airport bus runs between Bergen's Flesland Airport and downtown Bergen, stopping at the SAS hotel in Bryggen, Hotel Norge, and the bus station at platform 17 (72 kr, 4/hr, 40 min, tel. 177). Taxis take up to four people and cost about 400 kr for the 30-minute ride. SAS info: tel. 81 52 04 00.

Helpful Hints

Laundry: Jarlens Vaskoteque is at Lille Øvregate 17, near Korskirken (2-hr drop-off service for 100 kr, self-service for less, Mon–Fri 10:00–18:00, Wed–Thu until 20:00, Sat 10:00–15:00, closed Sun, tel. 55 32 55 04).

Getting Around Bergen

By Foot and Bus: Most sights can be seen on foot. Buses cost 24 kr per ride or 100 kr for a 48-hour Tourist Ticket (buy from driver). Buses are also covered by the Bergen Card (described above). The best buses for a city joyride are #20 and #21 (along the coast) and #11 (into the hills).

By Ferry: The *Beffen*, a little orange ferry, chugs across the harbor every half hour (15 kr, Mon–Fri 7:10–16:15, no weekend runs). This three-minute "poor man's cruise" has great harbor views. The Vågen ferry departs from in front of the fish market for the aquarium, and gives you a 25 percent discount on the aquarium admission (30 kr one-way, 50 kr round-trip, 2–3/hr, daily mid-May–Aug 10:00–18:00, doesn't run Sept–mid-May).

By Taxi: For a taxi, call 07000.

TOURS

▲▲▲**Bryggen Walking Tour**—This tour, described on page 227, is one of Bergen's best activities (80 kr, discount with Bergen Card, June–Aug daily at 11:00 and 13:00, 90 min).

Bus Tours—The TI sells tickets for bus tours (270 kr, 3 hrs, depart daily at 10:00 and 14:00). These trips venture out to Edvard Grieg's home, Troldhaugen; the 10:00 departure also includes Gamle Bergen (mid-May–Sept), while the 14:00 departure visits the Fantoft Stave Church (May–Aug). There are also full-day tour options from Bergen, including bus/boat tours to nearby Hardanger and Sogne fjords. The TI is packed with brochures describing all the excursions.

Harbor Tours—The *White Lady* leaves from the fish market daily in summer at 14:30 for a 60-minute cruise (100 kr, June–late Aug). A four-hour option is also available (380 kr, May–late Sept daily at 10:00, July–late Aug also daily at 15:30, tel. 55 25 90 00).

Tourist Train—The tacky little Bergens-Expressen train departs from in front of the Hanseatic Museum for a 55-minute loop around town (100 kr, late May daily 10:00–16:00, June–late Aug daily 10:00–19:00, late Aug–Sept daily 11:00–15:00, 2/hr on the half hour, with English-language headphone narration).

Local Guides—To hire your own private guide, call tel. 55 30 10 60.

SIGHTS AND ACTIVITIES

Bergen's Hanseatic Quarter (Bryggen)

Bergen's old German trading center was called "the German wharf" until World War II, and is now just called "the wharf," or "Bryggen" (BREW-gun). From 1370 to 1754, German merchants controlled Bergen's trade. In 1550, it was a German city of

2,000 workaholic merchants—walled and surrounded by 8,000 Norwegians. Bryggen, which has burned down several times, is now touristy and boutiquey, but still lots of fun. Explore. You'll find plenty of sweater shops, restaurants, planky alleys, leaning old wooden warehouses, atmospheric eating, and two worthwhile museums within a five-minute walk of each other.

Bryggen Walking Tour: Local guides take visitors on an excellent 90-minute walk through 900 years of Bergen history

via the old Hanseatic town (30 min in Bryggens Museum, 30-min walk through old quarter, and 30 min in Hanseatic Museum). Tours cost 80 kr (10 percent discount with Bergen Card) and leave from the Bryggens Museum (next to the big, modern SAS Hotel). When you consider that the tour price includes entry tickets to the Hanseatic and Bryggens museums and the Hanseatic Assembly Rooms (called Schøtstuene, worthwhile only with a guide), the tour is practically free (June–Aug daily at 11:00 and 13:00, you can re-enter museums with tour ticket for the rest of the day, tel. 55 58 80 10).

▲▲**Hanseatic Museum (Hanseatiske Museum)**—This won-

derful little museum is in an atmospheric old merchant house furnished with dried fish, antique ropes, an old oxtail (used for wringing spilled cod-liver oil back into the bucket), sagging steps, and cupboard beds from the early 1700s—one with a medieval pinup girl (45 kr, not covered by Bergen Card in summer, daily June–Aug 9:00–17:00, Sept–May 11:00–14:00, good 45-min guided tours, tel. 55 54 46 90, www .hanseatisk.museum.no). Admission includes entry to the medieval Hanseatic Assembly Rooms (Schøtstuene, separate entrance behind St. Mary's Church).

▲▲**Bryggens Museum**—This modern museum on the archaeo-logical site of the earliest Bergen (1050–1500), with interesting temporary exhibits upstairs, offers adequate English-language information. To understand the exhibits better, borrow the museum guidebook, follow the included 30-minute audioguide tour, or take the walking tour described above (40 kr, May–Aug daily 10:00–17:00; Sept–April Mon–Fri 11:00–15:00, Sat 12:00–15:00, Sun 12:00–16:00; tel. 55 58 80 10, www.bymuseet.no). The museum has an inexpensive cafeteria with soup-and-bread specials.

▲▲**Fish Market (Fisketorvet)**—This famous, bustling market has become touristy but still offers lots of smelly photo fun.

Many stands sell pre-made smoked-salmon *(laks)* sandwiches, fish soup, and other snacks ideal for a light lunch (ask the price first). If you want to try Norwegian jerky, pick up a bag of dried cod snacks *(torsk)*. The red meat for sale is minke whale, caught off the coast of northern Norway. Many stands also sell local fruit in season and hand-knit sweaters for decent prices (June–Aug daily 7:00–19:00; Sept–May Mon–Sat 7:00–16:00, closed Sun).

St. Mary's Church (Mariakirken)—Dating from the 12th century, this is Bergen's oldest building and one of Norway's finest churches (10 kr, late June–mid-Aug Mon–Fri 9:30–11:30 & 13:00–16:00, closed Sat–Sun; mid-Aug–late June Tue–Fri 11:30–12:30, closed Sat–Mon; tel. 55 31 59 60). Ask about evening concerts, usually held every Tuesday at 19:30 from late June through August.

Theta Museum—This small museum highlights Norway's resistance movement during the Nazi occupation in World War II (20 kr, mid-May–mid-Sept Tue and Sat–Sun 14:00–16:00, closed off-season, Enhjørningsgården).

Elsewhere in Bergen

▲**Håkon's Hall/Rosenkrantz Tower**—These reminders of Bergen's medieval importance sit barren and boldly out of place on the harbor just beyond Bryggen. Håkon's Hall, which is the largest secular medieval building in Norway, was a royal residence 700 years ago when Bergen was the political center of Norway. The Rosenkrantz Tower—the keep of a 13th-century castle—is pretty empty but offers a fine harbor view from the rooftop.

Tours, which cover both sights and provide a serious introduction to Bergen's history, start in Håkon's Hall and leave on the hour (50 kr covers hall and tower entries and the tour, daily mid-May–Aug 10:00–16:00, Sept–mid-May 12:00–15:00, tours last 45 min, final tour 1 hour before closing, tel. 55 31 60 67). To visit only the tower, it's 30 kr.

▲▲**Fløibanen**—Bergen's popular funicular climbs 1,000 feet in seven minutes to the top of "Mount" Fløyen for the best view of the town, surrounding islands, and fjords all the way to the west coast. The top is a popular picnic or pizza-to-go dinner spot (a Peppe's Pizza is a block away from the base of the lift) and the starting point for many peaceful hikes. There are often concerts at the top in the summer; check with the TI. Sunsets are great here. And if you need a goofy giant troll to pose with, look no further. It's a pleasant walk back down into Bergen—but to save your knees, get off at the Promsgate stop halfway down, and then wander through the delightful cobbled and shiplap lanes. For more hikes around Mt. Fløyen, ask for the "Fløyen Hiking Map" at the Fløibanen ticket window at the base (70 kr round-trip, Mon–Fri 7:30–23:00, Sat from 8:00, Sun from 9:00, May–Aug until 24:00, departures each way on the half hour and often on the quarter hour, tel. 55 33 68 00, www.floibanen.no). This funicular is regularly used by locals commuting into and out of downtown.

Leprosy Museum (Lepramuseet)—This unique museum is in St. Jørgens Hospital, a leprosarium that goes back to about 1700. Up until the 19th century, as much as three percent of Norway's population had leprosy. This hospital—once called "a graveyard for the living"—has a meager exhibit in a thought-provoking shell attached to a 300-year-old church (30 kr, daily mid-June–Aug 11:00–15:00, closed Sept–mid-June, pick up English pamphlet, Kong Oscars Gate 59, tel. 55 96 11 55, www.lepra.no).

▲▲**Wandering**—Bergen is a great strolling town. The harborfront is a fine place to kick back and watch the pigeons mate. Other good areas to explore are over the hill past Klostergate, Marken, Knosesmanet, Ytre Markevei, and the area behind Bryggen. The modern town—especially around Ole Bulls Plass—also has a pleasant ambience. To get away from the crowds, stroll around the artificial lake, Lille Lungegaardsvann.

▲▲**Aquarium (Akvariet)**—Small, but great fun if you like fish, this aquarium claims to be the second-most-visited sight in Bergen. A pleasant 20-minute walk from the center, it's wonderfully laid out and explained in English. Check out the informative exhibit downstairs on Norway's fish-farming industry (100 kr, kids-50 kr, May–Sept discount with Bergen Card, Oct–April fully covered by Bergen Card, daily June–Aug 9:00–19:00, Sept–May 10:00–18:00; feeding times at 12:00, 15:00, and 18:00 in season; cheery cafeteria with light sandwiches, Nordnesbakken 4, bus #11, tel. 55 55 71 71, www.akvariet.com). The handy little Vågen ferry (see "Getting Around Bergen," above) sails from the fish market to near the aquarium (50 kr, 2–3/hr, show your boat ticket at aquarium to receive a 25 percent discount). The lovely park behind the aquarium has views of the sea. The totem pole erected here was a gift from Bergen's sister city in the US—Seattle.

Swimming—Nordnes Sjøbad, near the aquarium, offers swimmers an outdoor heated pool and a protected area of the sea (25 kr, kids-10 kr, free with Bergen Card, mid-May–Aug Mon–Fri 9:00–19:00, shorter hours Sat–Sun, closed off-season, Nordnesparken 30).

▲**Old Bergen (Gamle Bergen)**—This is a Disney-cute gathering of forty 18th- and 19th-century shops and houses offering a cobbled look at "the old life." It's free to wander through the town and duck into the art galleries and gift shops housed in historic buildings. English tours (60 kr) departing on the hour get you into the 20 or so museum buildings (mid-May–Aug daily 9:30–17:30, closed Sept–mid-May, tel. 55 39 43 04, www.gamlebergen.museum.no). Take any bus heading west from Bryggen (such as #20, direction: Lonborg) to Gamle Bergen (first stop after the first tunnel). Or hop the M/F Dokken harbor ferry from the fish market (50 kr, July–mid-Aug 10:00–17:00, hourly, no boats off-season).

▲**Bergen Art Museum (Bergen Kunstmuseum)**—If you need to get out of the rain (and you enjoyed the National Gallery in Oslo), check out the Rasmus Meyer Collection. This tidy little museum has a good collection by Norwegian painters—Harriet Backer, J. C. Dahl, Christian Krohg, Edvard Munch, and others. Small description sheets in English can be found in each room. The Stenersen Collection next door has some interesting modern art, including Munch and Picasso (50 kr for both galleries, free with Bergen Card, daily 11:00–17:00, closed Mon mid-Sept–mid-May, Rasmus Meyers Allé 3, tel. 55 56 80 00, www.bergenartmuseum.no).

Near Bergen

▲**Fantoft Stave Church**—This huge, preserved-in-tar stave church burned down in 1992. It was rebuilt and reopened in 1997, but it will never be the same (for more on stave churches, see sidebar). Situated in a quiet forest next to a mysterious stone cross, this replica of a 12th-century wooden church is bigger, though no better, than others covered in this book. But it's worth a look if you're in the neighborhood, even after-hours, for its evocative setting (30 kr, mid-May–mid-Sept daily 10:30–14:00 & 14:30–18:00, interior closed mid-Sept–mid-May, no English information, 3 miles south of Bergen on E39 in Paradis; for public transportation, see next listing).

▲**Edvard Grieg's Home, Troldhaugen**—Norway's greatest composer spent his last 22 years here (1885–1907), soaking up inspirational fjord beauty and composing many of his greatest works. In a romantic Victorian setting, this place is pleasant for anyone and

Stave Churches

These churches are the finest architecture to come out of medieval Norway. Wood was plentiful and cheap, and locals had an expertise with woodworking (from all that boat-building). In 1300, there were 800 stave churches in Norway. After a 14th-century plague, Norway's population dropped and many churches fell into disuse. By the 19th century, with only several dozen stave churches surviving, they became recognized as part of the national heritage, and were protected. Today 28 stave churches remain. A distinguishing feature of the "stave" design is its vertical planks (as opposed to the "laft" horizontal structure of typical log cabins). The sill along the bottom and a thick coat of tar kept the planks from decaying over the centuries. Stave churches were dark, with almost no windows. Even after the Vikings stopped raiding, they ornamented their churches with warlike, evil spirit–fighting dragons reminiscent of their ships.

essential for Grieg fans. The house and adjacent museum are full of memories, and his little studio hut near the water makes you want to sit down and modulate (60 kr, 65 percent discount with Bergen Card, May–Sept daily 9:00–18:00; Oct–Nov and mid-Jan–March Mon–Fri 10:00–14:00, closed Sat–Sun; April Mon–Fri 10:00–14:00, Sat–Sun 12:00–16:00; closed Dec–mid-Jan; tel. 55 92 29 93, www.troldhaugen.com).

Ask the TI about concerts in the on-site concert hall (220 kr, 160 kr on Sat and any day with Bergen Card, free shuttle bus from TI if you show concert ticket; concerts scheduled roughly mid-June–late-Aug Sun at 19:30; through early Aug also Wed at 19:30, Sat at 14:00, Sept–Oct Sun at 14:00).

Getting to Fantoft and Troldhaugen: The daily three-hour bus tour promoted by the TI is worthwhile for the informative guide, easy transportation, and doorstep service (260 kr, 10:00 departure goes to Troldhaugen and Gamle Bergen, 14:00 departure goes to Troldhaugen and Fantoft). For public transportation, see the detailed instructions in the *Bergen Guide*. Allow roughly 10–15 minutes by bus, then 10 minutes on foot to Fantoft or 20 minutes on foot to Troldhaugen.

SHOPPING

Most shops are open Mon–Fri 9:00–17:00, Thu until 19:00, Saturday 9:00–15:00, and closed Sunday. Many of the tourist shops at the harborfront strip along Bryggen are open daily—even during holidays—until 20:00 or 21:00.

Bryggen is bursting with sweaters, pewter, and trolls. The Husfliden Shop is popular for its handmade Norwegian sweaters and goodies (good variety and quality but expensive, just off the market square at Vågsalmenning 3).

The Galleriet shopping center on Torgalmenningen has six floors of shops, cafés, and restaurants. You'll find a pharmacy, photo shops, clothing, sporting goods, bookstores, and a basement grocery store (Mon–Fri 9:00–20:00, Sat 9:00–18:00, closed Sun).

NIGHTLIFE

Folk Evenings—The **Fana Folklore show** is Bergen's most-advertised folk evening. An old farm hosts this touristy collection of cultural clichés, with food, music, dancing, and colorful costumes. While some think it's too gimmicky and others think it's lots of fun, nobody likes the meager dinner (350 kr includes short bus trip and meal, June–Aug Thu and Fri 19:00–22:30, additional evenings in May and Sept and other days during the season, reservations required, tel. 55 91 52 40 or book at TI or through your hotel, www.fanafolklore.no).

The **Bergen Folklore show** offers a smaller, homier program, featuring a good music-and-dance look at rural and traditional Norway (100-kr tickets sold by TI and at the door, 1 hr; early June and mid-late Aug Tue at 21:00 at Hanseatic Assembly Rooms; tel. 55 31 20 06).

Concerts—From mid-June through August, you'll find concerts at the restaurant on top of Mount Fløyen, at Domkirken (cathedral), at St. Mary's Church, and other places. Ask the TI for details (tel. 55 55 20 00).

SLEEPING

There are two kinds of demands on the hotel scene in Bergen: Business travelers fill up the fancy hotels outside of summer and weekends, and tourists take the budget places from June through mid-August.

If you want cheap accommodations in summer, reserve ahead. But if you just show up at the TI in summer, unless you're unlucky and hit some convention, you'll get a great deal on a business-class hotel.

Sleep Code

(6.5 kr = about $1, country code: 47)
S = Single, **D** = Double/Twin, **T** = Triple, **Q** = Quad, **b** = bathroom,
s = shower. You can assume credit cards are accepted unless
otherwise noted.

To help you sort easily through these listings, I've divided
the rooms into three categories, based on the price for a standard double room with bath:

$$$ **Higher Priced**—Most rooms 1,000 kr or more.
 $$ **Moderately Priced**—Most rooms between
                                    650–1,000 kr.
  $ **Lower Priced**—Most rooms 650 kr or less.

The private homes and hostel-style accommodations listed are
inexpensive, central, and well run. If you can handle showers down
the hall and cooking your own breakfast in a communal kitchen,
several pensions offer rooms with a homey atmosphere and fine
locations for half the cost of a hotel room.

Thon Hotels

For a description of this popular chain of business-class hotels,
see page 176 in the Oslo chapter. They offer three kinds of rooms:
singles (plenty of these for businesspeople), "combi" twins (slightly
smaller rooms with twin beds or "combi" beds—a twin and a sofa
bed, only available at Bergen Brygge), and full double rooms. Twin
rooms are preferable to combi rooms at the same price. A big buffet breakfast is included.

The Thon hotels offer steep discounts if you purchase a 90-
kr **Skanplus Hotel Pass** from them (www.thonhotels.no or www
.skanplus.com). You'll save nearly 400 kroner per night every day
in summer (mid-June–mid-Aug) and weekends (Fri–Sat) the rest
of the year. If you're over 60, the 90-kr **60plus** card extends those
same discounts daily year-round. Both cards also give you every
sixth night free. These cards are a great deal. Unless you're truly
desperate, don't pay the rack rate (their highest rate).

$$$ Thon Hotel Rosenkrantz is one block behind Bryggen,
between the Bryggens Museum and the Fløibanen funicular sta-
tion (rack rates: Sb-1,295 kr, Db-1,495 kr; Skanplus/60plus rates:
Sb-770 kr, Db-970 kr; extra bed-200 kr, 100 kr for children under
12, Rosenkrantzgate 7, tel. 55 30 14 00, fax 55 31 14 76, www
.thonhotels.no/rosenkrantz, rosenkrantz@thonhotels.no).

$$$ Thon Hotel Bristol is a block off Ole Bulls Plass (rack
rates: Sb-1,345 kr, Db-1,545 kr; Skanplus/60plus rates: Sb-770 kr,

Db-970 kr; extra bed-215 kr, 115 kr for children under 12, Torgalmenningen 11, tel. 55 55 10 00, fax 55 55 10 01, www.thonhotels.com/bristolbergen, bristol.bergen@thonhotels.no).

$$ Thon Hotel Bergen Brygge is beyond Bryggen near Håkon's Hall (rack rates: Sb-625 kr, Db-825 kr; Skanplus/60plus rates: Sb-570 kr, Db-775 kr; extra bed-175 kr, breakfast-85 kr, Bradbenken 3, tel. 55 30 87 00, fax 55 32 94 14, bergenbrygge @thonhotels.no).

More Hotels and Pensions

$$$ Hotel Hordaheimen, old, prestigious, and central, is just off the harbor. It has sleek and comfy rooms, and is a good value if you can score a discount: Ask about their frequent customer card, which offers 20 percent savings on rooms from late June to mid-August (Sb-1,290 kr, Db-1,600 kr, includes breakfast, non-smoking, Sundts Gate 18, tel. 55 33 50 00, fax 55 23 49 50, www.hordaheimen.no, info@hordaheimen.no).

$$$ Hotel Park Pension is classy, comfortable, and in a fine central-but-residential neighborhood. It's tinseled in Old World, lived-in charm (34 rooms, 22 in classy old hotel, 12 in annex across the street; Sb-940 kr, Db-1,140 kr, extra bed-325 kr, includes breakfast, winter weekend discounts, Harald Hårfagres Gate 35, tel. 55 54 44 00, fax 55 54 44 44, www.parkhotel.no).

$ Skansen Pensjonat, situated a steep but scenic four-minute climb above the entrance to the Fløibanen funicular and overlooking the fish market, rents eight rooms and three spacious apartments in an elegant old house (S-450 kr, D-600 kr, fancy D on corner with view and balcony-700 kr, these prices promised in 2007 with this book, includes breakfast, 2 showers on ground floor, sinks in rooms, family room with TV, Db apartments with no breakfast but kitchen-750 kr, 1 parking place, non-smoking). To get there, follow the switchback road behind the Fløibanen station halfway up the hillside (about 3 switchbacks) to Vetrlidsalmenning 29 (tel. 55 31 90 80, fax 55 31 15 27, www.skansen-pensjonat.no, mail@skansen-pensjonat.no, Alvær/Skjøtskift family).

Private Homes

These private homes are inexpensive, quite private, and lack a lot of chatty interaction with your hosts. The Heskja and Dahl rooms—far more quiet, homey, and convenient than hostel beds, and for less money when you consider sheet rental—are the best values in town.

$ Alf and Elizabeth Heskja rent four non-smoking doubles that share a shower, two WCs, and a kitchen in their home. It's beautifully situated on a steep, cobbled lane called "the most painted street in Bergen" (D-400 kr, reserve in advance and

Bergen Hotels and Restaurants

1. Thon Hotel Rosenkrantz
2. Thon Hotel Bristol
3. Thon Hotel Bergen Brygge
4. Hotel Hordaheimen
5. Hotel Park Pension
6. Skansen Pensjonat
7. Heskja Rooms
8. Olsne Rooms
9. Dahl Rooms
10. Marken Gjestehus
11. Citybox
12. Bergen YMCA Hostel
13. To Montana Family & Youth Hostel
14. Bryggeloftet & Stuene, Enhjørningen & Rest. To Kokker
15. Restaurant New Castle
16. Vagsbunnen Restaurant & Kong Oscar's Pølse Stand
17. Kjøttbasaren Food Hall & Egon Restaurant
18. Fløien Folkerestaurant
19. Fish Market (Fisketorvet)
20. Lido Cafeteria
21. Zachariasbryggen Eateries
22. Dickens Restaurant
23. Café Opera

mention this book, 4 blocks from station at Skivebakken 17, tel. 55 31 30 30, mobile 90 05 30 30, rs@skiven.no). From the station, go down Kong Oscars Gate, uphill on D. Krohns Gate, and up the many stairs at the end of the block on the left.

$ The **Olsne family,** across the street from the Heskja home, keeps backpackers happy with its cheap, basic rooms and a shared kitchen (Sb-350 kr, D-350 kr, Db-400 kr, extra bed-100 kr, cash only, Skivebakken 24, tel. 55 31 20 44, svolsne@online.no).

$ **Marit and Hugo Dahl** devote two floors of their fine, old house to guests. One floor of the Dahl house has four simple and clean twins and doubles (which share a shower and two WCs). The lower floor is a comfy living room and kitchen. Though a 15-minute hike from the station, it's in the middle of fairy-tale old Bergen in a tranquil, cobbled, residential neighborhood a 10-minute walk from the fish market (D-390 kr, cash only, just more than halfway between train station and aquarium at Trangesmauet 14, tel. 55 23 16 69, mobile 93 68 37 93, maritd2@online.no).

Dorms and Hostels

$ **Marken Gjestehus** is quiet, tidy, well run, and conveniently positioned between the station and the harborfront. Its rooms are spartan but modern and cheery (dorm bed in 8-bed room-155 kr, in 6-bed room-175 kr, in 4-bed room-195 kr, S-380 kr, Sb-495 kr, D-480 kr, Db-610 kr, Tb-795 kr, extra bed-125 kr, sheets-60 kr, towels-15 kr, breakfast-75 kr, elevator, kitchen, laundry, open all year, fourth floor at Kong Oscars Gate 45, tel. 55 31 44 04, fax 55 31 60 22, www.marken-gjestehus.com, post@marken-gjestehus .com).

$ **Citybox** is a unique, no-nonsense hotel concept. This well-located hotel is plain, clean, and practical. It rents rooms online and provides you with a confirmation number for an automated check-in upon arrival—kind of like an e-ticket for hotels (S-400 kr, Sb-500 kr, D-500 kr, Db-600 kr, extra bed-150 kr, breakfast-75 kr, elevator, Nygårdsgate 31, tel. 55 31 25 00, fax 55 31 60 22, www .citybox.no, post@citybox.no).

$ **Bergen YMCA Hostel (IYHF),** just off Vågsallmenningen square in front of the TI and across from the fish market, is the best location for the price (bunk in 12- to 40-bed dorm with shared shower and kitchen-155 kr, bunk in 6-bed family room with private bathroom and kitchen-195 kr, Db with kitchen-600 kr, sheets-45 kr, breakfast-55 kr, fully open May–Aug, fewer beds off-season, Nedre Korskirkeallmenningen 4, tel. 55 60 60 55, www .bergenhostel.com, ymca@online.no).

Away from the Center: $$ **Montana Family & Youth Hostel (IYHF),** while one of Europe's best, is high-priced for a hostel and way out of town. Still, the bus connections (#31, 15 min from the center) and the facilities—modern rooms, classy living room, no curfew, huge parking lot, and members' kitchen—are excellent (dorm bed-185 kr mid-May–Aug only, bed in Q-235 kr, bed in Qb-250 kr, Sb-465 kr, Db-710 kr, sheets-65 kr, includes breakfast, singles not available mid-June–mid-Aug, 30 Johan Blydts Vei, tel. 55 20 80 70, fax 55 20 80 75, www.montana.no, booking @montana.no).

EATING

Bergen has numerous choices:
- Restaurants with rustic, woody atmosphere, candlelight, and steep prices (200–350-kr entrées).
- Inexpensive cafeterias, restaurants, and ethnic eateries where you can get quality food at lower prices (75–200 kr) with less atmosphere (except for the ethnic restaurants).
- Chain restaurants that serve pizza, burgers, ribs, and chicken (150–250-kr entrées and pizzas).
- Take-away sandwich shops, bakeries, and cafés for a light bite (50–80 kr). Remember, if you get your food to go, you'll save 12 percent.

In the Tourist Zone, or near Bryggen

The old Hanseatic quarter is lined with restaurants that serve traditional Norse food by candlelight. If you're in the mood for a little Donner or Blitzen, you're in luck.

Splurges

You'll pay a premium to eat at these three restaurants, but you'll have a memorable meal in a pleasant setting. To ensure getting a table, call in a reservation.

Bryggeloftet & Stuene Restaurant is on two levels, and serves seafood and traditional meals (80–150-kr lunches, 200–300-kr dinners). Upstairs feels less stuffy and less touristy (Mon–Sat 11:00–23:30, Sun 13:00–23:30, #11 on Bryggen harborfront, consider reserving a view window upstairs, tel. 55 31 06 30). If there's a line downstairs, climb the stairs.

Enhjørningen Restaurant (literally, "The Unicorn") is *the* place in Bergen for seafood. They offer fine seafood dinners from about 275 kr (nightly from 16:00, #29 on Bryggen harborfront—look for anatomically correct unicorn on the old wharf facade, try to reserve a window table, tel. 55 32 79 19).

Restaurant To Kokker, down the alley from Enhjørningen, serves seafood, along with plenty of meat dishes, in an elegant, old, wooden building (300 kr and up, Mon–Sat 17:00–23:00, closed Sun, tel. 55 32 28 16).

Mid-Range Options

Restaurant New Castle, an inexpensive eatery at the far end of Bryggen near the Rosenkrantz Tower, serves up 170–200-kr entrées in a clean, homey atmosphere. This is probably your best opportunity to try whale without harpooning your wallet. You can get light meals, soups, and salads for 70–100 kr and sandwiches for 20–50 kr (Mon–Fri 11:00–22:00, Sat 12:00–22:00, Sun 13:00–23:00, Slottsgate 3, tel. 55 32 07 11).

Vagsbunnen Restaurant is hardworking, unpretentious, and family-run. They serve tasty, traditional, candlelit Norwegian meals for 125–220 kr (daily 14:30–22:30, 2 blocks in from fish market at Kong Oscars Gate 5, tel. 55 90 03 94).

Fløien Folkerestaurant, atop Mount Fløyen, offers meals with a panoramic view. The cheaper cafeteria section has coffee, cake, and sandwiches from 50 kr (June–Aug daily 10:00–22:00, Sept–May only Sat–Sun 12:00–17:00). The restaurant section has decent dinners for about 150 kr (daily 17:00–24:00, tel. 55 32 18 75). From mid-June through late August, have a bite and take in a concert (tickets-160 kr, 120 kr with Bergen Card, 195 kr with salad and bread).

Lido, overlooking the fish market, serves basic food in its upstairs self-service cafeteria (50–100-kr lunches, 100–150-kr dinners, Mon–Sat 10:00–22:00, Sun 13:00–22:00, closes earlier off-season, second floor, Torgalmenningen 1, tel. 55 32 59 12).

Good Chain Restaurants: You'll find two tasty chain restaurants in Bergen, and throughout Norway. **Egon** is a ribs-chicken-and-burgers kind of place where you can get a substantial meal for 150–200 kr (below the Kjøttbasaren food hall—listed below). **Peppe's Pizza** has cold beer and great pizzas (medium size for 1–2 people from 175 kr, large for 2–3 people from 275 kr, take-out possible; consider the *Moby Dick*, with curried shrimp, leeks, and bell peppers). There are four Peppe's in Bergen, including one across the street from Egon, behind the Hanseatic Museum.

Budget Bets

For a tasty, memorable, and inexpensive meal in Bergen, assemble a seafood picnic at the **fish market (Fisketorvet)**. The stalls are bursting with salmon sandwiches, fresh shrimp, fish and chips, and fish cakes (ask prices first; June–Aug daily 7:00–19:00; Sept–May Mon–Sat 7:00–16:00, closed Sun).

Kong Oscar's Pølse Stand, near Kong Oscar Gate, is a sausage stand selling artery-clogging guilty pleasures (open daily until late). Sausages range in size, price, and flavor—they even have reindeer!

Kjøttbasaren, the restored meat market of 1887, is a food hall with stalls selling picnic supplies or pre-made food to go (Mon–Fri 10:00–17:00, Thu until 18:00, Sat 9:00–16:00, closed Sun).

Zachariasbryggen, a modern restaurant complex, lines a pier at the head of the harbor (on Torget). Ignore the overpriced Italian and Tex-Mex restaurants. Look instead for **Baker Brun,** which makes sandwiches, including wonderful shrimp baguettes, and pastries such as *skillingsbolle*—cinnamon rolls—warm out of the oven (open from 9:00, seating inside or take-away). **Bon Appetit** also sells baguette sandwiches (about 60 kr), plus wraps (50 kr) and ice cream. You'll see Baker Brun and Bon Appetit shops in Bryggen, too.

From Ole Bulls Plass up to the Theater

Bergen's "in" cafés are stylish, cozy, small, and open very late—a great opportunity to experience the local yuppie scene. Around the cinema on Neumannsgate, there are numerous ethnic restaurants, including Italian, Middle Eastern, and Chinese.

The lively **Dickens** serves beautifully presented entrées of fish, chicken, and steak (150–250 kr). The window tables in the atrium are great for people-watching (Mon–Sat 11:00–24:30, later on Fri and Sat nights, Sun 13:00–24:30, reservations smart, Kong Olav V's Plass 4, tel. 55 36 31 30).

The trendy **Café Opera** is good for pasta, vegetarian dishes, and sandwiches (120–140-kr dinners, 60–80-kr lunches, daily 11:00–24:00, often live music Fri–Sat, live locals nightly, English newspapers, chess, across from theater, Engen 18, tel. 55 23 03 15).

TRANSPORTATION CONNECTIONS

Bergen is conveniently connected to **Oslo** by plane and train (trains depart Bergen daily at 7:58, 10:28, 15:58, and 22:58, arrive at Oslo 7 scenic hours later, additional departures in summer and fall, confirm times at station, 50-kr seat reservation required—but free with first-class railpass, book several weeks in advance if traveling mid-July–Aug). From Bergen, you can take the Norway in a Nutshell train/bus/ferry route; for information, see the Norway in a Nutshell chapter. Train info: tel. 55 96 69 00 or 81 50 08 88.

To get to **Stockholm or Copenhagen,** you'll go via Oslo (see Oslo's "Transportation Connections" on page 186)...unless you fly. Before buying a ticket for a long train trip from Bergen, look into cheap flights.

By Express Boat to Balestrand and Flåm (on Sognefjord): The handy Fylkesbaatane express boat links Bergen with Balestrand

(4 hrs) and Flåm (5.5 hrs). For details, see the "Transportation Connections" for Balestrand (page 208).

By Bus to Kristiansand: If you're heading to Denmark on the ferry from Kristiansand, catch the Haukeli express bus (departing Bergen daily at 7:30). After a nearly two-hour layover in Haukeli, take the bus at 14:40, arriving at 18:50 in Kristiansand in time for the overnight ferry to Denmark (for boat details, see page 256 in the South Norway chapter).

By Boat to Stavanger: Flaggruten catamarans sail to Stavanger (2–4/day, 4 hrs, 575 kr one-way, 690 kr round-trip; nearly half-price for students, railpass-holders, or for 1 partner when a couple travels together; tel. 55 23 87 80, www.hsd.no). From Stavanger, trains run to Kristiansand and Oslo, and a boat floats to Denmark (for Stavanger's transportation connections, see South Norway chapter, page 243).

By Boat to Denmark: The Color Line runs a boat service from Bergen to Hirtshals, Denmark (Norwegian tel. 81 00 08 11, Danish tel. 99 56 19 77, www.colorline.com). However, because this is such a long journey (more than 20 hours at sea), it's far more interesting to simply take the train to Stavanger or Kristiansand, then take the boat from there to Denmark.

By Boat to Newcastle, England: Fjordline sails from Bergen to Newcastle, England (mid-May–mid-Sept Tue–Sun, no runs Mon, less off-season, tel. 81 53 35 00, www.fjordline.com). The cheapest summer crossing for the 22-hour trip is 900 kr for a berth in a three- or four-berth in a cabin below the car deck. From late June to early August, those same berths are 1,200 kr. Bunks in a two-berth window cabin are about 375 kr extra per person. Drivers with one or two passengers pay 1,850–2,900 kr, or with three to five passengers pay 2,900–4,300 kr (price includes an inside cabin).

By Boat to the Arctic: Hurtigruten/Norwegian Coastal Voyage coastal steamers depart daily (mid-April–mid-Sept at 20:00, mid-Sept–mid-April at 22:30) for the seven-day trip north up the scenic west coast to Kirkenes on the Russian border.

This route was started in 1893 as a postal and cargo delivery service along the west coast of Norway. Although no longer delivering mail, their ships still fly the Norwegian postal flag by special permission, and deliver people, cars, and cargo from Bergen to Kirkenes. A lifeline for remote areas, the ships call at 34 fishing villages and cities.

For the seven-day trip to Kirkenes, allow from $1,399 on up per person based on double occupancy (includes three meals per day, taxes, and port charges). Prices vary greatly depending on the season (highest June–July), cabin, and type of ship. Their fleet includes those with a bit of brass built in the 1960s, but the majority of the ships were built in the mid-1990s and later. Shorter voyages are possible (including even just a day trip to one of the villages along the route). Cabins should be booked well in advance. Ship services include a 24-hour cafeteria, a launderette on newer ships, and optional port excursions ($28–158). Check online for senior and off-season (Oct–March) specials at www .hurtigruten.com.

Call Norwegian Coastal Voyage in New York (US tel. 800-323-7436) or in Norway (tel. 81 03 00 00). For most travelers, the ride makes a great one-way trip, but a flight back south is a logical last leg (rather than returning to Bergen by boat—a 12-day round-trip).

SOUTH NORWAY

Stavanger, Setesdal Valley, Hovden, and Kristiansand

South Norway is not about must-see sights or jaw-dropping scenery—it's simply pleasant and pretty. Spend a day in the harborside town of Stavanger. Delve into your Scandinavian roots at the Norwegian Emigration Center or into the oil industry at the surprisingly interesting Petroleum Museum. Window-shop in the old town, cruise the harbor, or hoof it up Pulpit Rock for a fine view.

A series of time-forgotten towns stretch across the Setesdal Valley, with sod-roofed cottages and locals who practice fiddles and harmonicas, rose painting, whittling, and gold- and silverwork. The famous Setesdal filigree echoes the rhythmical designs of the Viking era and Middle Ages. Each town has a weekly rotating series of hikes and activities for the regular, stay-put-for-a-week visitor. The upper valley is dead in the summer but enjoys a bustling winter.

In Kristiansand, Norway's answer to a seaside resort, promenade along the strand, sample a Scandinavian zoo, or set sail to Denmark.

Planning Your Time

Even on a busy itinerary, Stavanger warrants a day. If you are an avid genealogist, consider two. The port town is connected by boat to Bergen (and Hirtshals, Denmark) and by train to Kristiansand.

Frankly, without a car, the Setesdal Valley is not worth the trouble. There are no trains in the valley, bus schedules are as sparse as the population, and the sights are best for joyriding. If you're in Bergen with a car, and want to get to Denmark, this route is more interesting than repeating Oslo. On a three-week Scandinavian trip, I'd do it in one long day, as follows: 7:00-Leave

Bergen; 9:00-Catch Kvanndal ferry to Utne; 10:00-Say goodbye to the last fjord at Odda; 13:00-Lunch in Hovden at the top of Setesdal Valley; 14:00-Frolic south with a few short stops in the valley; 16:30-Arrive in Kristiansand for dinner. Spend the night and catch the 9:00 boat to Denmark the next morning.

Kristiansand is not a destination town, but rather a place to pass through, conveniently connecting Norway to Denmark by ferry.

Stavanger

This burg of about 115,000 feels more cosmopolitan than most Norwegian cities. This is thanks in part to the oil industry, with its multinational workers and the money they bring into the city. Known as Norway's festival city, Stavanger hosts several lively events, including jazz (May 9–13 in 2007), chamber music (Aug 6–12), and wooden boats (May 13–15). With all of this culture, it's no surprise that Stavanger has been selected a European Capital of Culture for 2008.

ORIENTATION

The most scenic and interesting parts of Stavanger surround its harbor. Here you'll find the Norwegian Emigration Center, lots of shops and restaurants, the indoor fish market, a produce market (Mon–Sat 9:00–16:00, closed Sun), and the TI. The artificial Lake Breiavatnet—bordered by Kongsgaten on the east and Olav V's Gate on the west—separates the train and bus stations from the harbor.

Tourist Information
The helpful staff at the TI can help you plan your time in Stavanger, and can also give you hiking tips and day-trip information. Pick up a free city guide and map (June–Aug daily 9:00–20:00; Sept–May Mon–Fri 9:00–16:00, Sat 9:00–14:00, closed Sun; Domkirkeplassen 3, tel. 51 85 92 00, www.visitstavanger.com).

Arrival in Stavanger
By Boat: Express boats from Bergen dock at Fiskepiren. From here, you can take a public bus to the center of town or to the train station. A taxi to a hotel downtown costs 75–85 kr.

By Train and Bus: Stavanger's train and bus stations are a five-minute walk around Lake Breiavatnet to the harbor (train ticket and reservation office Mon–Fri 6:30–20:00, Sat 8:30–15:45, Sun 12:00–20:00). Luggage lockers and Norway-wide train timetables

Stavanger

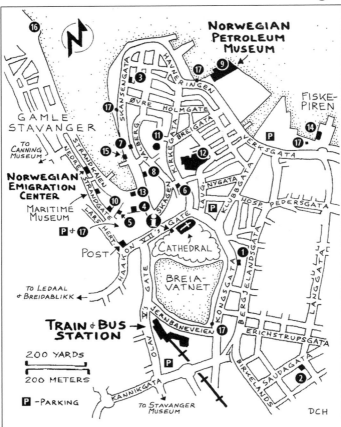

200 YARDS

200 METERS

P – Parking

1. Thon Hotel Maritim
2. Stavanger B&B
3. Skansen Hotell & Gjestehus
4. Ekofisk Café
5. Nye La Piazza Restaurant
6. Verthuset Mat & Vin Rest.
7. N. B. Sorensen's Dampskibsexpedition Pub & Rest.
8. Sjøhuset Skagen Restaurant
9. Bølgen og Moi Restaurant
10. Meny Supermarket
11. Valberg Tower
12. Culture Center
13. Fish Market
14. Boats to Bergen
15. Boats to Lysefjord & Pulpit Rock
16. International Ferries to Hirtshals (Denmark)
17. Flybussen (Airport Bus) stops

are available at the train station.

By Plane: Stavanger's Sola Airport, about nine miles outside the city, is connected to downtown by the Flybussen (70 kr, buy ticket on bus, Mon–Fri 7:45–24:15, 3–4/hr, less Sat–Sun, 30 min). This airport bus shuttles travelers to the bus station (Byterminalen) and train station (next to each other), the city center, and the boat terminal (Fiskepiren). To get to the airport from the city center, catch the shuttle at any of these stops.

SIGHTS

▲▲**Norwegian Petroleum Museum (Norskolje Museum)**—This entertaining, informative museum—dedicated to the discovery of

 oil in Norway's North Sea in 1969 and the industry built up around it—offers something for everyone. It describes how oil was formed, how it's found and produced, and what it's used for. There are interactive exhibits covering everything from the "History of the Earth" (4.5 billion years displayed on a large overhead globe, showing how our planet has changed—stay for the blast that killed the dinosaurs!), to day-to-day life on an offshore platform, to petroleum products in our lives. Kids love the model drilling platform that they can climb on. The museum's architecture was designed to echo the foundations of the oil industry—bedrock (the stone building), slate and chalk deposits in the sea (slate floor of the main hall), and the rigs (cylindrical platforms). While the museum has its fair share of propaganda, it also has several good exhibits on the environmental toll of drilling and consuming oil (80 kr; June–Aug daily 10:00–19:00; Sept–May Mon–Sat 10:00–16:00, Sun 10:00–18:00; tel. 51 93 93 00, www.norskolje.museum.no). The small museum shop sells various petroleum-based products.

Eating at the Museum: The **Bølgen og Moi** restaurant has an inviting terrace over the water for thirsty museumgoers. They also serve lunch (from 150 kr) and dinner (from 250 kr), with a fantastic view over the harbor (daily 11:00–22:00, reservations recommended for dinner, tel. 51 93 93 51).

▲**Norwegian Emigration Center (Det Norske Utvandrersenteret Ble)**—This fine museum, in an old warehouse near the wharf where the first boats sailed with emigrants to "Amerika" in 1825, is worth ▲▲▲ for anyone seeking their Norwegian roots. On the second floor, you'll find a study center and library. There are computers (Internet and microfilm) free for use to look up your relatives. The library is lined with shelves of *bygdebøker*—books from farm districts all over Norway, documenting the history of landowners and local families. For 200 kr per hour, the staff will give you a step-by-step consultation. Otherwise, they'll help answer questions and steer you in the right direction for free. The third floor has a small exhibit everyone will enjoy: It tells the story of the first emigrants who left for America—why they left, the journey, and what life was like in the New World (library free, 20 kr for the museum, Mon–Fri 9:00–15:00, closed Sat–Sun, tel. 51 53 88 60, www.emigrationcenter.com). If you want to look up relatives, do some homework ahead of time and have at least two or three of the following: family surname, farm name, birth year, and emigration year.

Stavanger Museum—This "museum" is actually five different buildings/museums covered by one 50-kr ticket: the **Stavanger Museum,** featuring the history of the city and a zoological exhibit (Muségate 16); Stavanger **Sjøfartsmuseum,** the maritime museum (Nedre Strandgate 17–19); **Norsk Hermetikkmuseum,** the Norwegian canning museum (*brisling*—herring—is smoked mid-June–mid-Aug Tue and Thu, Øvre Strandgate 88A); **Ledaal,** a royal residence and manor house (Eiganesveien 45); and **Breidablikk,** a wooden villa from the late 1800s (Eiganesveien 40A). Pick up the handy brochure and buy your ticket from the TI (mid-May–mid-June Mon–Fri 11:00–15:00, Sun 11:00–16:00, closed Sat; mid-June–mid-Aug daily 11:00–16:00; mid-Aug–mid-Sept Mon–Thu 11:00–15:00, closed Fri–Sun; mid-Sept–Nov and Jan–mid-May Sun 11:00–16:00, closed Mon–Sat; closed Dec; www.stavanger.museum.no).

Gamle Stavanger—Stavanger's "old town" centers on Øvre Strandgate, on the west side of the harbor. Wander the narrow, winding back lanes and peek into a workshop or gallery to find ceramics, glass, jewelry, and more (free, shops and galleries open roughly daily 10:00–16:00, coinciding with the arrival of cruise ships).

Stavanger Cathedral (Domkirke)—The cathedral was originally built in 1125 in a Norman style, with basket-handle Romanesque arches. After a fire badly damaged the church in the 13th century, a new chancel was added in the pointy-arched Gothic style. Have a look inside and see where the architecture changes about three-quarters of the way up the aisle (free; June–Aug daily 11:00–19:00; Sept–May Tue–Thu 11:00–16:00, Sat–Sun 11:00–16:00, closed Mon and Fri).

Day Trips to Lysefjord and Pulpit Rock

The nearby Lysefjord is an easy day trip. Those with more time (and strong legs) can hike up to the top of the 1,800-foot-high Pulpit

Rock (Preikestolen). The dramatic 270-square-foot plateau atop the rock gives you a fantastic view of the fjord and surrounding mountains. The TI has brochures for several boat tour companies and sells tickets.

Boat Tour of Lysefjord—Rodne Clipper Fjord Sightseeing offers four-hour round-trip excursions from Stavanger to Lysefjord (including a view of Pulpit Rock). Boats depart from the east side of the harbor, in front of Skansegaten, along Skagenkaien. Buy your ticket on board or at the TI (300 kr, July–mid-Aug daily at 10:30 and 14:30; June and mid-Aug–mid-Sept daily at 12:00; May Wed–Sun at 12:00; tel. 51 89 52 70, www.rodne.no).

Ferry and Bus to Pulpit Rock—Public transportation to the trail's starting point is a snap. Then comes the hard part: the two-hour hike to the top. The total distance is 4.5 miles and the elevation gain is roughly 1,000 feet. Pack a lunch and plenty of water and wear good shoes. Here are some approximate schedules for a day trip, but reconfirm all times at the TI before you go: Ferries depart from Fiskepiren to Tau (35 kr, 25–40 min; late June–Sept Mon–Fri at 8:00; mid-May–mid-Sept Sat at 8:00, 9:00, and 12:25 and Sun at 8:25, 9:45, and 12:25; no boats Oct–mid-May). In Tau, buses meet the incoming ferries and head to Pulpit Rock cabin—Preikestolhytta (55 kr, 35–40 min). Return buses from Preikestolhytta depart for Tau and meet with a corresponding ferry (Mon–Fri at 15:40—plus late June–mid-Aug at 14:00; Sat at 13:50, 15:35, and 19:45; Sun at 13:45, 15:35, and 20:00). Pick up the helpful leaflet and confirm details at the TI. They can also give you details about more strenuous hikes.

SLEEPING

$$$ Thon Hotel Maritim, about two blocks from the train station, near the artificial Lake Breiavatnet, can be a good deal for a big-business class hotel. If you buy the 90-kr Skanplus Hotel Pass or 60plus Hotel Pass (both described on page 176), you'll get big discounts daily in summer (mid-June–mid-Aug) and weekends the rest of the year (rack rates: Sb-1,195 kr, Db-1,395 kr; weekends Sb-775 kr, Db-975 kr; Skanplus/60plus rates: Sb-682 kr, Db-882 kr; includes breakfast, elevator, Kongsgaten 32, tel. 51 85 05 00, fax 51 85 05 01, www.thonhotels.no/maritim, maritim@thonhotels.no).

$$$ Skansen Hotell & Gjestehus splits 28 rooms between its hotel (newer, more expensive rooms) and guest house (less expensive for essentially the same quality). Most of the rooms are on the street and can be noisy, but you're just off the harbor in a great location (hotel: Sb-1,030 kr, Db-1,190 kr; guest house: Sb-930 kr, Db-1,090 kr; about 300 kr cheaper on Fri, Sat, and Sun nights; includes breakfast, non-smoking floors, elevator to most floors,

Sleep Code

(6.5 kr = about $1, country code: 47)
S = Single, **D** = Double/Twin, **T** = Triple, **Q** = Quad, **b** = bathroom,
s = shower. All of these places accept credit cards.

To help you sort easily through these listings, I've divided the rooms into three categories, based on the price for a standard double room with bath:

$$$ Higher Priced—Most rooms 1,000 kr or more.
$$ Moderately Priced—Most rooms between
600–1,000 kr.
$ Lower Priced—Most rooms 600 kr or less.

Skansengate 7, tel. 51 93 85 00, fax 51 93 85 01, www.skansenhotel
.no, post@skansenhotel.no).

$$ Stavanger B&B is your best home away from home in Stavanger. This large, red house among a sea of white houses has 14 tidy rooms, each with its own shower (but the toilet's down the hall). Waffles, coffee, and friendly chatter are served up every evening at 21:00 (Ss-540 kr, Ds-640 kr, Ts-790 kr, Qs-890 kr, includes breakfast, 10-min walk behind train station in residential neighborhood, Vikedalsgate 1A, tel. 51 56 25 00, fax 51 56 25 01, www.stavangerbedandbreakfast.no, peck@online.no). If you let them know in advance, they can pick you up or drop you off at the boat dock or station.

EATING

Casual Dining

Ekofisk, named after Norway's first oil-drilling platform, is a small fish market and café with a few indoor and outdoor tables. You can try fish cakes (a tasty cake made from white fish, cream, herbs, and spices—ask for a sample), fish soup, or *bacalao* (dried, salted cod cooked in a tomato sauce) with salad and bread for 60–80 kr. You'll pay less for take-away, so do like the locals do: Picnic on the floating docks in the guest harbor across the street (Mon–Fri 9:00–16:30, Sat 9:00–14:00, closed Sun, at the end of the harbor at Nedre Strandgate 13, tel. 51 52 54 09).

Nye La Piazza, just off the harbor, has an assortment of pasta and other Italian dishes, including pizza, for 125–200 kr (Mon–Sat 12:00–24:00, Sun 12:00–22:00, Rosenkildettorget, tel. 51 52 02 52).

Verthuset Mat & Vin, in an elegant setting, serves up big portions of traditional Norwegian food and pricier contemporary fare (200–270 kr, light meals-90–150 kr, 100–150-kr specials

Sailing to Denmark

The Color Line runs direct boats to Hirtshals, Denmark, from Stavanger (at night), Kristiansand (during the day), and Bergen (not advised because of length of journey—more than 20 hours). Prices are higher on weekends and in summer (especially mid-June–mid-Aug), and lower on weekdays and off-season (especially Oct–April). You'll pay the same for deck passage whether you sail from Stavanger or Kristiansand (200 kr for off-season weekdays, up to 500 kr for peak-season weekends). Taking a car costs 275–630 kr (depending on the day). If you're traveling with a small group, consider the "car package" (up to five passengers plus the car for 800–1,925 kr). Ask about specials: Students and seniors save about 50 percent, and round-trip fares can be lower than one-way fares. Ferries have all the usual amenities: decent *store koldt bord* buffets, music, duty-free shopping, a desk to process your Norwegian duty-free tax rebates, and a bank. Confirm schedules at www.colorline.com.

Night Boat from Stavanger: Consider taking this night boat to save the cost of a hotel. Enjoy an evening in Stavanger, then sleep (or vomit) as you sail to Denmark. The boat generally sails three times a week (usually Mon, Wed, and Fri, departing Stavanger at 20:15 and arriving in Hirtshals at 8:30 the next day; days of the week and departure/arrival times can vary, so confirm specific schedules). The deck passage rates listed above include a reclining chair (except in peak season, when the chair costs 50 kr extra). But if you're efficient enough to spend this night traveling, you owe yourself the comfort of a private room. In peak season, cabins start as low as 60 kr per person for a two-berth cabin with shared bathroom below the car deck, up to 1,045 kr per person for a luxury suite with a balcony.

Day Boat from Kristiansand: There are two boats: The *Christian IV* is slow and steady (4.5 hrs, same rates as listed above), while the *Silvia Ana* is speedier (2.5 hrs), more expensive, and includes a meal (135 kr extra at breakfast time, 235 kr extra during lunch/dinner). In summer (April–Aug), boats sail daily at 8:15 (slow boat, Tue–Sun only except in mid-June–mid-Aug, when it's daily), 9:00 (fast boat), 17:00 (fast boat), and 19:15 (slow boat). Mysteriously, the schedule is slightly different late April–mid-May: slow boats at 8:15 and 19:15, with a fast boat at 12:00. Off-season, only the slower *Christian IV* runs (daily at 19:15, Tue–Sun also at 8:15).

Reservations: When you can commit to a firm date, call Color Line to make a reservation (pay when you get to the dock, Norwegian tel. 81 00 08 11, Danish tel. 99 56 19 77, phones answered long hours daily, www.colorline.com).

served Mon–Fri 11:00–18:00 and Sun 12:30–22:00, open daily 11:00–22:00, a block behind main drag along harbor at Skagen 10 ved Prostbakken, tel. 51 89 51 12).

Meny is a large supermarket with a good selection and a fine deli for super-picnic shopping (Mon–Fri 10:00–20:00, Sat 10:00–18:00, closed Sun, Nedre Strandgate).

Dining Along the Harbor with a View

The harborside street of Skansegata is lined with lively restaurants and pubs, and most serve food. Here are a couple options:

N. B. Sorensen's Dampskibsexpedition consists of a lively pub on the first floor (150–200 kr for pasta, fish, meat, and vegetarian dishes, Mon–Sat 11:00–23:00, Sun 13:00–24:00) and a fine-dining restaurant on the second floor, with tablecloths, view tables overlooking the harbor, and entrées from 300 kr (Mon–Thu 11:00–23:00, Fri–Sat 11:00–24:00, Sun 18:00–24:00, Skagenkaien 26, tel. 51 84 38 22). The restaurant is named after an 1800s company that shipped from this building, among other things, Norwegians heading to the US. Passengers and cargo waited on the first floor, and the manager's office was upstairs. The place is filled with emigrant-era memorabilia.

Sjøhuset Skagen, with a woodsy interior, invites diners to its historic building for lunch or dinner. The building, from the late 1700s, housed a trading company. Today, you can choose from local seafood specialties with an ethnic flair, as well as plenty of meat options (lunch-100–150 kr, dinner-200–250 kr, Mon–Sat 11:00–23:00, Sun 14:00–23:00, Skagenkaien 16, tel. 51 89 51 80).

TRANSPORTATION CONNECTIONS

From Stavanger by Train to: Kristiansand (4–6/day, 3 hrs), **Oslo** (3/day, 8 hrs, overnight possible).

By Boat to Bergen: Flaggruten catamarans sail between Bergen and Stavanger (2–4/day, 4 hrs, 575 kr one-way, 690 kr round-trip; nearly half-price for students, railpass-holders, or for one partner when a couple travels together; tel. 55 23 87 80, www.flaggruten.no).

By Boat to Hirtshals, Denmark: For details on this boat, see the "Sailing to Denmark" sidebar on page 249.

The Setesdal Valley

Welcome to the remote, and therefore very traditional, Setesdal Valley. Probably Norway's most authentic cranny, the valley is a mellow montage of sod-roofed water mills, ancient churches,

The Setesdal Valley

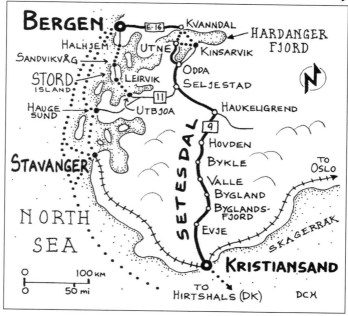

derelict farmhouses, yellowed recipes, and gentle scenery.

The Setesdal Valley joined the modern age with the construction of the valley highway in the 1950s. All along the valley you'll see the unique two-story storage sheds called *stabburs* (the top floor was used for storing clothes; the bottom, food) and many sod roofs. Even the bus stops have rooftops the local goats love to munch.

In the high country, just over the Sessvatn summit (3,000 feet), you'll see herds of goats and summer farms. If you see an *Ekte Geitost* sign, that means genuine, homemade goat cheese is for sale. (It's sold cheaper and in more manageable sizes in grocery stores.) To some, it looks like a decade's accumulation of earwax. I think it's delicious. Remember, *ekte* means all-goat—really strong. The more popular and easier-to-eat regular goat cheese is mixed with cow's-milk cheese.

For more information on the Setesdal Valley, see www.setesdal .com.

From Odda to Hovden

These attractions from here to Kristiansand are listed roughly from north to south.

Odda—At the end of the Hardanger Fjord, just past the huge zinc and copper industrial plant, you'll hit the industrial town of Odda (well-stocked **TI** for whole region and beyond; in summer Mon–Fri 7:30–20:00, Sat 10:00–17:00, Sun 11:00–18:00; off-season Mon–Fri 7:30–16:00, closed Sat–Sun; tel. 53 65 40 05). Odda brags that Kaiser Wilhelm came here a lot, but he's dead and I'd drive right through. If you want to visit the tongue of a glacier, drive to Buar and hike an hour to Buarbreen. From Odda, drive into the land of boulders. The many mighty waterfalls that line the road seem to have hurled huge rocks (with rooted trees) into the rivers and fields. Stop at the giant double waterfall (on the left, pullout on the right, drive slowly through it if you need a car wash).

Røldal—Continue over Røldalsfjellet and into the valley below, where the old town of Røldal is trying to develop some tourism. Drive on by. Its old church isn't worth the time or money. Lakes are like frosted mirrors, making desolate huts come in pairs. Haukeliseter, a group of sod-roofed buildings filled with cultural clichés and tour groups, offers pastries, sandwiches, and reasonable hot meals (from 100 kr) in a lakeside setting. Try the traditional *rømmegrøt* porridge.

Haukeligrend—Haukeligrend is a bus/traffic junction, with daily bus service to/from Bergen and to/from Kristiansand (TI inside the café, open daily all year 10:00–19:00, brochures available all the time, TI staff available periodically, Internet access, tel. 35 07 03 67).

Hovden

Hovden is a ski resort at the top of the Setesdal Valley (2,500 feet). It's barren in the summer and painfully in need of charm. Still, it makes a good home base if you want to explore the area for a couple of days. Locals come here to walk and relax for a week.

Tourist Information: The TI is open all year (Mon–Fri 9:00–16:00, summer Sat 10:00–14:00, July also Sun 12:00–16:00, otherwise closed Sat–Sun, tel. 37 93 93 70, www.hovden.com, post@hovden.com).

SIGHTS AND ACTIVITIES

Canoe Rental—Hegni Center, on the lake at the south edge of town, rents canoes (290 kr/day, 150 kr/half-day, hourly rentals also possible, cash only, mid-June–Aug daily 11:00–18:00, early Sept daily 11:00–16:00, mid-Sept–mid-Oct Sat–Sun 12:00–16:00, closed mid-Oct–mid-June, tel. 37 93 97 00).

Hikes near Hovden—Good walks offer you a chance to see reindeer, moose, arctic fox, and wabbits—so they say. The TI and most hotels stock brochures, maps, and other information about moderate to strenuous hikes in the area. Berry picking is popular in late August, when small, sweet blueberries are in season. A chairlift sometimes takes sightseers to the top of a nearby peak, with great views in clear weather (look to see if the chairs are moving, or ask at the TI). Hunting season starts in late August for reindeer (only in higher elevations), and later in the fall for grouse and moose.

Moose Safari—Hovden Aktiv offers a three-hour *Elg Safari* (that's Norwegian for "moose"). Learn more about this "king of the forest" during a late-night drive through Setesdal's back roads with a stop for moose-meat soup (335 kr, June–Aug only; generally Tue, Fri, and Sun at 22:00—more often based upon demand; money-back guarantee if you don't see a moose, tel. 37 93 97 00, www.hovdenaktiv.no).

Museum of Iron Production (Jernvinnemuseum)—Learn about iron production from the late Iron Age (about 1,000 years ago) with the aid of drawings, exhibits, and recorded narration from a "Viking" (available in English; free, mid-June–mid-Aug daily 11:00–17:00, otherwise ask for the key at the TI or Hegni Center). The museum is about 100 yards behind the Hegni Center (look for the sign from the road to *Jernvinnemuseum*).

Swimming Pool—A super indoor spa/pool complex, the Hovden Badeland, provides a much-needed way to spend an otherwise dreary and drizzly early evening here (145 kr for 3 hours or more, cheaper for shorter visits, daily 11:00–19:00 in summer, shorter hours off-season, tel. 37 93 93 93).

SLEEPING AND EATING

$$ Hovden Fjellstoge is a big, old ski chalet renting Hovden's only cheap beds. Even if you're just passing through, their café is a good choice for lunch or an early dinner. Check out the mural in the balcony overlooking the lobby—an artistic rendition of this area's history. Behind the mural is a frightening taxidermy collection (hotel: Sb-490 kr, bunk-bed Db-790 kr, includes breakfast; cabins: starting at 590 kr for 2–4 people with bathroom and kitchen; dorms: dorm bed-190 kr, D-490 kr, 25 kr extra if you're not a hostel member, breakfast-70 kr, sheets-70 kr, towel-20 kr; tel. 37 93 95 43, www.hovdenfjellstoge.no, post@hovdenfjellstoge.no).

From Hovden to Kristiansand

▲**Dammar Vatnedalsvatn**—Nine miles south of Hovden is a two-mile side-trip to a 400-foot-high rock-pile dam (look for the *Dammar* signs). Enjoy the great view and impressive rockery. This is one of the highest dams in northern Europe. Read the chart. Sit out of the wind a few rows down the rock pile and ponder the vastness of Norwegian wood.

▲**Bykle**—The most interesting folk museum and church in Setesdal are in the teeny town of Bykle. The 17th-century church has two balconies—one for men and one for women (free, mid-June–mid-Aug daily 11:00–17:00, tel. 37 93 85 00).

Grasbrokke—On the east side of the main road (at the *Grasbrokke* sign), you'll see an old water mill (1630). A few minutes farther south, at the sign for *Sanden Såre Camping*, exit onto the little road to stretch your legs at another old water mill with a fragile rotten-log sluice.

Flateland—The **Setesdal Museum** (Rygnestadtunet) offers more of what you saw at Bykle (30 kr, two buildings; late June and Aug daily 10:00–17:00; July daily 10:00–18:00; off-season Mon–Fri 12:00–15:00, closed Sat–Sun; 1 mile east of the road, tel. 37 93 63 03). Unless you're a glutton for culture, I wouldn't do both.

Honneevje—Past Flateland is a nice picnic and WC stop, with a dock along the water for swimming...for hot-weather days or polar bears.

▲**Valle**—This is Setesdal's prettiest village (but don't tell Bykle). In the center, you'll find fine silver- and gold-work, traditional dinners in the cozy Bergtun Hotel (150–200 kr, summer only), homemade crafts next to the TI, and old-fashioned *lefse* cooking demonstrations (in the small log house by the Valle Motell). The fine suspension bridge attracts kids of any age (b-b-b-b-bounce) and anyone interested in a great view over the river to the strange mountains that look like polished, petrified mudslides. European rock climbers, tired of the over-climbed Alps, often entertain spectators with their sport. Is anyone climbing? (TI open early June–late Aug Mon–Fri 11:00–17:00, Sat 10:00–14:00, closed Sun; off-season Mon–Fri 8:00–15:00, closed Sat–Sun; tel. 37 93 75 29, valle@setesdal.com.)

Sleeping in Valle: **$$ Bergtun Hotel,** run by Halvor Kjelleberg, has a folksy, sit-a-spell Setesdal lodge full of traditional furniture, paintings, and carvings in each charming room (S-590 kr, D-750 kr, some rooms have bunks, extra bed-125 kr, includes breakfast, open June–mid-Aug, tel. 37 93 77 20, fax 37 93 77 15). Off-season, **$$ Valle Motell** answers Bergtun's phone and rents rooms (Sb-590 kr, Db-750 kr, includes breakfast, cabins with kitchen and bath but no breakfast-600–850 kr, tel. 37 93 77 00, www.valle-motell.no, motell@online.no).

Nomeland—The Sylvartun silversmith shop sells Setesdal silver in a 17th-century log cabin (May–Sept Mon–Sat 10:00–18:00, Sun 11:00–18:00, closed Oct–April, tel. 37 93 63 06).

Grendi—The Ardal Church (1827) has a rune stone in its yard. Three hundred yards south of the church is a 900-year-old oak tree.

Evje—A huge town by Setesdal standards (3,500 people), Evje is famous for its gems and mines. Fancy stones fill the shops here. Rock hounds find the nearby mines fun; for a small fee, you can hunt for gems. The TI is by Highway 9 in the center of Evje (mid-June–Aug Mon–Fri 9:30–17:00, Sat–Sun 10:00–15:00, closed Sept–mid-June, tel. 37 93 14 00). The **Setesdal Mineral Park** is on the main road, two miles south of town (75 kr, June–Aug daily 10:00–18:00).

Kristiansand

This "capital of the south" has 75,000 inhabitants, a pleasant Renaissance grid-plan layout (Posebyen), a famous zoo with Norway's biggest amusement park (6 miles toward Oslo on the main road), a daily bus to Bergen, and lots of big boats going to England and Denmark. It's the closest thing to a beach resort in Norway. Markensgate is the bustling pedestrian market street—a pleasant place for good browsing, shopping, eating, and people-watching. Stroll along the Strand Promenaden (marina) to Christiansholm Fortress.

The **TI** is at Vester Strandgate 32, across the street from the boat, bus, and train station (mid-June–mid-Aug Mon–Fri 8:30–18:00, Sat 10:00–18:00, Sun 12:00–18:00; mid-Aug–mid-June Mon–Fri 8:30–15:30, closed Sat–Sun; tel. 38 12 13 14). The bank at the Color Line terminal opens for each arrival and departure (even the midnight ones). The Fønex Kino cinema complex is within two blocks of the ferry and TI (70–85 kr, seven screens, movies shown in English, schedules at the entrance).

SLEEPING

(6.5 kr = about $1, country code: 47)
Kristiansand hotels are expensive and nondescript.

$$$ Rica Hotel Norge is a modern option (rack rates: Sb-1,195 kr, Db-1,295 kr; June–mid-Aug: Sb-890 kr, Db-1,090 kr;

weekend rates year-round: Sb-725 kr, Db-925 kr; Dronningensgate 5, tel. 38 17 40 00, fax 38 17 40 01, www.hotel-norge.no, firmapost @hotel-norge.no).

$$$ Thon Hotel Wergeland is inviting for a large chain hotel. It's within earshot of the church bells and busy Kirkegate, but quieter rooms away from the street are available (Sb-995, Db-1,195, about 300 kr less on weekends if you buy 90-kr Skanplus Hotel Pass or anytime with a 90-kr 60plus Hotel Pass—see page 176, includes breakfast, non-smoking rooms, no elevator, Internet access, Kirkegate 15, tel. 38 17 20 40, fax 38 02 73 21, www .thonhotels.no/wergeland, wergeland@thonhotels.no).

$$ At Frobusdalen Rom, Arild and Inger Nilssen rent seven clean, bright rooms and two apartments in a beautiful guest house. You'll have access to the garden, a full kitchen, and a large sitting room filled with lovely antiques and wooden wainscoting (Sb-400–450 kr, Db-550–700 kr, Db with balcony-800 kr, higher prices are for slightly larger room, no breakfast, laundry service available, free parking; 5-min walk from the boat, bus, and train terminals at Frobusdalen 2; tel. 91 12 99 06, www.gjestehus.no, imsan@start.no).

EATING

The otherwise uninteresting harbor area has a cluster of wooden buildings called **Fiskebasaren** (Fish Bazaar). While the indoor fish market is only open during the day, numerous restaurants (serving fish, among other dishes) provide a nice atmosphere for dinner. Follow Vester Strandgate past the Fønix movie theater to Østre Strandgate, take a right, and follow the signs to Fiskebrygga.

TRANSPORTATION CONNECTIONS

From Kristiansand by Train to: Stavanger (4–6/day, 3 hrs), **Oslo** (4/day, 4.5 hrs).

By Boat to Hirtshals, Denmark: For details on this boat, see the "Sailing to Denmark" sidebar on page 249.

Route Tips for Drivers

Bergen to Kristiansand via the Setesdal Valley (10 hrs): Your first key connection is the Kvanndal–Utne ferry (a two-hour drive from Bergen, departures hourly 6:00–23:00, reservations not possible or even necessary if you get there 20 min early, breakfast in cafeteria). If you make the 9:00, your day will be more relaxed. Driving comfortably, with no mistakes or traffic, it's two hours from your Bergen hotel to the ferry dock. Leaving Bergen is a bit confusing. Pretend you're going to Oslo on the road to Voss (signs for *Nestune, Landås, Nattland*). About a half hour out of town, after a long tunnel, leave the Voss road and head for Norheimsund. This road, treacherous for the famed beauty of the Hardanger Fjord it hugs as well as for its skinniness, is faster and safer if you beat the traffic (which you will with this plan).

The ferry drops you in Utne, where a lovely road takes you to Odda and up into the mountains. From Haukeligrend, turn south and wind up to Sessvatn at 3,000 feet. Enter the Setesdal Valley. Follow the Otra River downhill for 140 miles south to the major port town of Kristiansand. Skip the secondary routes. South of Valle, you'll have to pass a 25-kr tollbooth. The most scenic stretch is between Hovden and Valle. There is a lot more logging (and therefore less scenic). As you enter Kristiansand, pay a 10-kr toll and follow signs for Denmark.

SWEDEN

SWEDEN

(Sverige)

Scandinavia's heartland, Sweden is far bigger than Denmark and far flatter than Norway. This family-friendly land is home to Ikea, Volvo, ABBA, and long summer vacations at red-painted, white-trimmed summer cottages. Its capital, Stockholm, is Scandinavia's grandest city.

Once the capital of blond, Sweden is now home to a huge immigrant population. Sweden is committed to its peoples' safety and security, and proud of its success in creating a society with the lowest poverty rate in the world. Yet Sweden has thrown in its lot with the European Union, and locals debate whether to open their economy even further.

Swedes are often stereotyped as sex-crazed, which could not be further from the truth. Several steamy films and film stars from the 1950s and 1960s stuck Sweden with the sexpot stereotype, which still reverberates among male tourists. Italians continue to travel up to Sweden looking for those bra-less, loose, and lascivious blondes...but the real story is just that Sweden relaxed film censorship earlier than other European countries. Like other Scandinavians, Swedes are frank and open about sexuality. Sex education in schools is routine, living together before marriage is the norm (and has been common for centuries), and teenagers have easy access to condoms. But Swedes choose their partners carefully.

While Sweden is 85 percent Lutheran, less than 5 percent of the population goes to church regularly. Swedes are more likely to find religion in nature, hiking in the vast forests or fishing in one of the thousands of lakes or rivers. Sweden is almost 80 percent wilderness, and modern legislation incorporates an ancient common law called *allemans rätt*, which guarantees people the right to move freely through Sweden's natural scenery without asking the landowner for permission, as long as they behave responsibly. In summer Swedes take advantage of the long days and warm evenings for festivals such as Midsummer (in late June) and crayfish parties in August. Many Swedes have a summer cottage—or know someone who has one—where they spend countless hours

Sweden

swimming, soaking up the sun, and devouring boxes of juicy strawberries.

While Denmark and Norway look westward to Britain and the Atlantic, Sweden has always faced east across the Baltic Sea. Swedes traveled to Russia in the early Middle Ages, founding Novgorod and Kiev and even serving as royal guards in Constantinople (modern-day Istanbul). During the later Middle Ages, German settlers and traders strongly influenced Sweden's culture and language. By the 17th century, Sweden was a major European power, with one of the largest naval fleets in Europe and an empire extending around the Baltic, including Finland, Estonia, Latvia, and parts of Poland, Russia, and Germany. But by the early 19th century, Sweden's war-weary empire had shrunk. The country's current borders date from 1809.

During a massive wave of emigration from the 1860s to World War II, about a quarter of Sweden's people left for the Promised Land—America. Many emigrants were farmers from the southern region of Småland. The museum in Växjö tells their story (see page

Sweden Almanac

Official Name: Konungariket Sverige—the Kingdom of Sweden—or simply Sweden.

Population: Sweden's 9 million people (about 50 per square mile) are mostly ethnically Swedish. Foreign-born and first-generation immigrants account for about 10 percent of the population, and are primarily from Finland, the former Yugoslavia, and the Middle East. Sweden is also home to about 17,000 indigenous Sami people. Swedish is the dominant language, with most speaking English as well. About 85 percent of Swedes are Lutheran. Other represented religions include Roman Catholic, Orthodox, Baptist, Muslim, Jewish, and Buddhist.

Latitude and Longitude: 62°N and 15°E, similar latitude to Canada's Northwest Territories.

Area: 173,700 square miles (a little bigger than California).

Geography: A chain of mountains divides Sweden from Norway on the Scandinavian Peninsula. Sweden's mostly forested landscape is flanked to the east by the Baltic Sea, which contributes to the temperate climate. Sweden also includes several islands, of which Gotland and Öland are the largest.

Biggest City: Sweden's capital city, Stockholm, has a population of 776,000; more than 1.8 million live in the metropolitan area.

Economy: Sweden has a $268 billion Gross Domestic Product and a per capita GDP of $29,898—similar to the United Kingdom. Manufacturing, telecommunications, automobiles, and pharmaceuticals rank among its top industries, along with timber, hydropower, and iron ore. Eighty-five percent of Swedish workers belong to a labor union.

Currency: 7 Swedish kronor (kr) = about $1.

Government: King Carl XVI Gustav is the ceremonial head of Sweden's constitutional monarchy. Elected every four years, the 349-member Swedish Parliament (Riksdag) is currently led by Prime Minister Goran Persson (re-elected in September 2002).

Flag: The Swedish flag is blue with a golden cross.

The Average Swede: The average Swede is 41 years old, has 1.66 children, and will live to be 80.

312), as does the movie *The Immigrants,* based on the book trilogy by Vilhelm Moberg.

The 20th century was good to Sweden. While other European countries were embroiled in the two World Wars, neutral Sweden grew stronger, finding a balance between the extremes of communism and the free market. After a recession hit in the early 1990s, and the collapse of Soviet communism reshaped the European political scene, some started to criticize Sweden's "middle way" as extreme and unworkable. But during the last decade, Sweden's economy improved, buoyed by a strong line-up of successful multinational companies. Saab, Volvo, Scania (trucks and machinery), Ikea, and Ericsson (the telecommunications giant) are leading the way in manufacturing, design, and technology.

Since the 1960s, Sweden (like Denmark and Norway) has accepted many immigrants and refugees from southeastern Europe, the Middle East, and elsewhere. This praiseworthy humanitarian policy has dramatically (and sometimes painfully) diversified a formerly homogenous country. The suburbs of Rinkeby, Tensta, and Botkyrka are Stockholm's ethnic neighborhoods, and are worth visiting. Many of the service-industry workers you will meet have come to Sweden from elsewhere.

For great electronic fact sheets on everything in Swedish society from health care to its Sami people, see www.sweden.se.

Most Swedes speak English, but a few Swedish words are helpful. "Hello" is *"Hej"* (hay) and "Goodbye" is *"Hej då"* (hay doh). "Thank you" is *"Tack"* (tahk), which can also double for "Please."

STOCKHOLM

If I had to call one European city home, it could be Stockholm. One-third water, one-third parks, one-third city, on the sea, surrounded by woods, bubbling with energy and history, Sweden's stunning capital is green, clean, and underrated.

Crawl through Europe's best-preserved old warship and relax on a scenic harbor boat tour. Browse the cobbles and antique shops of the lantern-lit Old Town. Take a trip back in time at Skansen, Europe's first and best open-air folk museum. Marvel at Stockholm's glittering City Hall, slick shopping malls, and art museums.

While progressive and sleek, Stockholm respects its heritage. In summer, mounted bands parade daily through the heart of town to the Royal Palace, announcing the Changing of the Guard and turning even the most dignified tourist into a scampering kid.

Planning Your Time

On a two- to three-week trip through Scandinavia, Stockholm is worth two days. For the busiest and best two-day plan, I'd suggest this:

Day 1: 9:00-See *Vasa* warship (starting with video and tour); 11:00-Visit Nordic Museum; 13:00-Tour Skansen open-air museum and grab lunch there (or at Nordic Museum); 16:00-Ride boat to Nybroplan, then shop near Sergels Torg and drop by the Sweden House TI (pick up map, check for special events, and confirm sightseeing plans); 18:00-Take Royal Canal tour (last boat departs earlier Sept–April); 20:00-Enjoy a *smörgåsbord* feast at the Grand Hotel or wander Gamla Stan in search of dinner.

Day 2: 10:00-Catch 90-minute bus tour from the Royal

Opera House or take the City Hall tour and climb City Hall tower for a fine view; 12:15-Catch the Changing of the Guard at the palace (13:15 on Sun); 13:00-Lunch on Stortorget; 14:00-Tour Royal Palace Museums and Armory and follow my Old Town self-guided walk; 18:30-Free evening (could take a harbor dinner cruise).

Day 3: With an extra day, add a cruise through the scenic island archipelago (easy to do from Stockholm); tour the Queen's palace at Drottningholm; and/or explore the city's fine shopping streets, markets, and impressive stores.

ORIENTATION

(area code: 08)

Greater Stockholm's 1.8 million residents live on 14 islands that are woven together by 54 bridges. Visitors need only concern themselves with four islands:

Stockholm: City of Islands

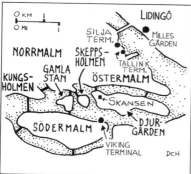

Norrmalm is downtown, with most of the hotels and shopping areas, and the train-and-bus station. **Gamla Stan** is the Old Town of winding, lantern-lit streets, antiques shops, and classy cafés clustered around the Royal Palace. **Skeppsholmen** is the small, central, traffic-free park/island with the Museum of Modern Art and two fine youth hostels. The park island of **Djurgården** is Stockholm's wonderful green playground, with many of the city's top sights (bike rentals just over bridge as you enter island).

Södermalm, aptly called "Stockholm's Brooklyn," is residential (apart from its fine views, it's of less interest to those on a quick visit).

Tourist Information

Sweden House (Sverige Huset), Stockholm's official tourist office, is a six-block walk from the central train and bus station. They've got free city maps, pamphlets on everything, Stockholm Cards (see below), transportation passes, a huge souvenir shop, day-trip and bus-tour information and tickets, and a room-booking

service (60-kr fee on generally great discounted rates for business-class hotels). Also check out their helpful "today's events" board (Mon–Fri 9:00–19:00, Sat 10:00–17:00, Sun 10:00–16:00, in the basement of Hamngatan 27, T-bana: Kungsträdgården, tel. 08/5082-8508, www.stockholmtown.com). *What's on Stockholm* is a free monthly listing with the opening times and directions to sights, special events, and much more.

Those arriving by train or bus can get limited tourist information at **Hotellcentralen** (Hotel Center), a branch of the TI—located in the central train station's main hall—whose primary purpose is helping visitors with hotel bookings (May–Aug daily 8:00–20:00; Sept–April Mon–Sat 9:00–18:00, Sun 12:00–16:00). While Hotellcentralen is often crowded, the Sweden House (six blocks away) has more space, more staff, and more information. Though excellent free maps are all over town, Hotellcentralen stocks only a 25-kr map. However, they're good at finding discounted business-class hotel rooms (60-kr booking fee).

The Stockholm Card, a 24-hour pass for 270 kr, includes all public transit, almost every sight (70 places), some free or discounted tours, free parking, and a handy sightseeing handbook. An added bonus is the substantial pleasure of doing everything without considering the cost (many of Stockholm's sights are worth the time but not the money). As more and more sights are now free, this card has become a lesser value, but it pays for itself if you use public transportation and see Skansen, the *Vasa* Museum, and Millesgården. You can stretch it by entering Skansen on your 24th hour. A child's pass (age 7–17) costs 100 kr. The Stockholm Card also comes in 48-hour (420 kr) and 72-hour (540 kr) versions. Cards are sold at the two TIs listed above, hotels, hostels, larger subway stations, and at www.stockholmtown.com.

Arrival in Stockholm

By Train or Bus

Stockholm's combined train and bus station is a hive of services, shops, exchange desks, and people on the move. The bus section (called Cityterminalen) is up the escalators from the train station's main hall. The station has a subway (T-bana) stop and taxi stands, and is six blocks away from the Sweden House TI (see above). Those sailing to Finland will find the Viking Line office in the bus terminal.

By Plane

Stockholm's Arlanda Airport is 28 miles north of town (airport info: tel. 08/797-6000, SAS toll-free tel. 0770-727-727). The airport info desk has no lines, and—while not an official TI—it answers questions, sells Stockholm Cards, and gives out maps and

Greater Stockholm

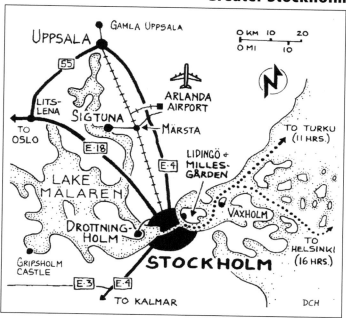

What's On Stockholm booklets (daily, long hours).

The **airport shuttle train,** the Arlanda Express, is the best way to zip between the airport and the central train station (200 kr, covered by railpass; 4/hr—usually departing at :05, :20, :35, and :50 in each direction; 20 min, has its own dedicated platform in train station—follow signs to Arlanda, toll-free tel. 020-222-224, www.arlandaexpress.com). Buy your ticket either at the window near the track or from a machine (or pay a 50-kr fee on board). The summer special (available mid-June–mid-Aug) lets two people travel for nearly half-price (two for 220 kr).

Airport shuttle buses (Flygbussarna) run between the airport and the train and bus station (95 kr, 6/hr, 40 min, may take longer at rush hour, buy tickets from ticket windows or driver, www .flygbussarna.se).

Taxis from the airport take about 30–40 minutes (at a fixed rate of about 400 kr, depends on company). You'll see most cabs advertising their fixed rate painted onto their doors.

The **cheapest airport connection** is to take bus #583 from the airport to Märsta, then switch to the *pendeltåg* (suburban train, 2/hr), which goes to Stockholm's central station (total journey time 60 min, covered by Stockholm Card).

By Boat

For information on Stockholm's cruise-ship terminals, see page 367 for boats to Tallinn, or page 330 for boats to Helsinki.

By Car

Only a Swedish meatball would drive his car in Stockholm. Park it and use the public transit. The TI has a *Parking in Stockholm* brochure. Those with the Stockholm Card can park free at parking meters for the duration of the ticket (ask for parking card and specifics when buying your Stockholm Card). Those sailing to Finland or Estonia should ask about long-term parking at the terminal when reserving their ticket; to minimize the risk of theft and vandalism, pay extra for the most secure parking garage.

Helpful Hints

Museum Prices: As long as the current left-wing government has its way, Stockholm's national museums will remain free. If the right retakes the Parliament, fees will be reinstated. For now, I'm assuming the trend toward free admission will continue.

Emergency Assistance: In case of an emergency, dial 112.

Medical Help: For around-the-clock medical advice, call 08/320-100, then press 2 to get into the queue. A 24-hour pharmacy is near the train station at Klarabergsgatan 64 (tel. 08/454-8130).

Telephone Calls: For operator assistance, call 118-118. Numbers starting with 020 are toll-free. Numbers beginning with 070 and 073 are mobile phones—about triple the cost of a regular call. Kiosks sell cheap international phone cards (1 kr/min calls to the US).

Internet Access: 7-Eleven stores and **Pressbyran** newsstands all over town host "Sidewalk Express" Internet terminals. These are the best deal going. Just buy a card (30 kr/90 min), remember your password, and you can pop into participating branches anywhere in town to log on. The card is sharable (but only one person at a time can use it) and valid for seven days (branches open daily until late). There's a Sidewalk Express nook at the airport departure lounge (good if you have time to kill and an unexpired card).

Bookstore: The **Sweden Bookshop** has English versions of books by local writers, with a great selection of books by Astrid Lindgren (including her classic, *Pippi Longstocking*), local guidebooks, and tiny booklets on various aspects of Swedish life (Mon–Fri 10:00–18:00, Sat 11:00–16:00, closed Sun, at the bottom of the Palace Hill at Slottsbacken 10, tel. 08/453-7800, www.swedenbookshop.com).

Laundry: Tvättomaten is a rare find in central Stockholm (self-serve-80 kr, same-day full service-175 kr, next-day full service-120 kr; Mon–Fri 8:30–18:30, Sat 9:30–15:00, closed Sun year-round and Sat July–Aug; across from Gustav Vasa church, Västmannagatan 61 on Odenplan, T-bana: Odenplan, tel. 08/346-480).

Bike Rental: Rent bikes, in-line skates, and boats at **Djurgårdsbrons Sjöcafe,** next to Djurgårdsbron Bridge near the *Vasa* Museum (rowboats and canoes—75 kr/hr, skates and bikes—65 kr/hr or 250 kr/day, handy city cycle maps, May–Oct daily 9:00–21:00, tel. 08/660-5757). It's ideally situated as a springboard for a pleasant bike ride around the park-like Djurgården island. **John's Bikes** rents bikes in the city center at the boat office on Strömkajen by the Grand Hotel (100 kr/2 hrs, 40 kr/hr after that, daily 9:00–18:00 in summer, closed off-season).

Getting Around Stockholm

By Subway and Bus: Stockholm has a fine subway (called "T-bana") and bus system, and special passes that take the bite out

of the cost. It's a spread-out city, so most visitors will need public transport at some point (transit info tel. 08/600-1000 and press * for English, www .sl.se/english). The subway is easy to figure out, but many sights are better served by bus. The main lines are listed on the map in *What's On Stockholm.* A more detailed system map is posted around town and available free from subway ticket windows and SL (Stockholm Transport) info desks in main stations. Check out the modern public art in the subway (e.g., at Kungsträdgården station).

A simple ticket takes you anywhere in town on either the subway or buses. For tickets you have three options: a single ticket (20 kr, good for an hour), a book of 10 tickets (180 kr, saving a stingy 10 percent), or a 24-hour ticket (60 kr, buy at Pressbyran convenience stores).

By Harbor Shuttle Ferry: In summer, ferries let you make a fun, practical, and scenic shortcut across the harbor to Djurgården island. Boats leave from Slussen (at the south end of Gamla Stan) every 10–20 minutes, docking near the Gröna Lund amusement park on Djurgården (May–mid-Sept only, 10-min trip, 30 kr). Another company makes the five-minute journey from Nybroplan to Djurgården, landing next to the *Vasa* Museum. While less

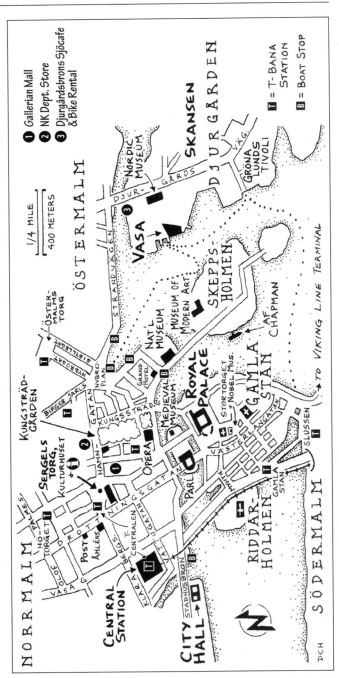

Stockholm

1 Gallerian Mall
2 NK Dept. Store
3 Djurgårdsbrons Sjöcafe
   & Bike Rental

T = T-BANA
    STATION
B = BOAT STOP

1/4 MILE
400 METERS

NORRMALM
ÖSTERMALM
SÖDERMALM
DJURGÅRDEN
SKANSEN
GAMLA STAN
RIDDAR-HOLMEN
SKEPPS-HOLMEN

NORDIC MUSEUM
VASA
GRÖNA LUNDS TIVOLI
NAT'L MUSEUM
MUSEUM OF MODERN ART
AF CHAPMAN
ROYAL PALACE
MEDIEVAL MUSEUM
GRAND HOTEL
STORTORGET & NOBEL MUS.
CITY HALL
CENTRAL STATION
SERGELS TORG
KULTURHUSET
KUNGSTRÄD-GÅRDEN
ÖSTER-MALMS TORG
OPERA
PARL

TO VIKING LINE TERMINAL

STRANDVÄGEN
DJUR-GÅRDS
SIBYLLEGATAN
NYBROGATAN
NYBRO-PLAN
BIRGER JARLS GATAN
KUNGSTRÄD GATAN
HAMN-GATAN
REGERINGSGATAN
VÄSTER LÅNGGATAN
GAMLA STAN
SLUSSEN
STADSHUSBRON
KLARA BERGSGATAN
VASA G.
OLOF PALMES G.
HÖTORGET
POST ÅHLÉNS
T-CENTRALEN
DROTTNINGGATAN

N

PCH

practical than buses and trams (which run between the same points for about half the price—see page 286), this does get you out onto the water (3/hr, June–late Aug daily 10:00–20:00, 35 kr).

By Taxi: Taxis are very expensive (minimum ride about 40 kr). To get a taxi quickly, flag one down or call Taxi Stockholm (tel. 08/150-000) or Taxi Kurir (tel. 08/300-000).

TOURS

By Bus
Hop-on, Hop-off Bus Tour—Like hop-on, hop-off buses throughout Europe, Open Top Tour's topless double-decker bus makes a 90-minute circuit of the city, stopping at the 14 essential places. You can hop off, tour a sight, and catch a later bus. The recorded commentary is good (190-kr ticket good for 24 hours, buses run roughly April–Oct, every 20 min in July–Aug, otherwise every 30 min, first departure at 10:00 from Kulturhuset on Sergels Torg, last departure 16:00, tel. 08/442-9483). The bus provides a convenient connection to sights from Skansen to City Hall.

Quickie Orientation Bus Tour—Several different city bus tours leave from the Royal Opera House on Gustav Adolfs Torg. City Sightseeing's Stockholm Panorama tour provides a good overview (210 kr, 90 min; late March–Dec daily at 10:00, 12:00, and 14:00; more frequent midsummer, tel. 08/587-14020, www.citysightseeing .com). This trip can be done in combination with their 60-minute Old Town walk (290 kr for both, saves 10 kr, allow 2.5 hours).

By Boat
▲**City Boat Tour**—For a good floating look at Stockholm and a pleasant break, consider a sightseeing cruise. The handiest are the

Stockholm Sightseeing boats, which leave from Strömkajen in front of the Grand Hotel (tel. 08/5871-4020). You have two choices: short and scenic or long and informative. Both come with a tape-recorded spiel. The short, scenic 50-minute Royal Canal tour is a joyride through lots of greenery (120 kr, early and late departures covered by Stockholm Card, departing at :30 past each hour, generally daily May–Aug 10:30–19:30, April and Sept 10:30–15:30, Oct–Dec 10:30–13:30, none Jan–March). The nearly two-hour Under the Bridges tour goes through two locks and under 15 bridges (170 kr, not covered by Stockholm Card, early June–mid-Sept daily 10:00–20:00, departures on the hour). They also do a 2.5-hour archipelago tour (190 kr, departs daily at 9:30

Stockholm at a Glance

▲▲▲**Skansen** Europe's first and best open-air folk museum, with more than 150 old homes, churches, shops, and schools. **Hours:** Daily May 10:00–20:00, June–Aug 10:00–22:00, Sept 10:00–17:00, Oct–April 10:00–16:00.

▲▲▲**Vasa Museum** Ill-fated 17th-century warship dredged from the sea floor, now the showpiece of an interesting museum. **Hours:** Daily mid-June–mid-Aug 8:30–18:00, off-season 10:00–17:00, winter Wed until 20:00.

▲▲▲**Nordic Museum** Danish Renaissance palace design and five fascinating centuries of traditional Swedish lifestyles. **Hours:** Late June–Aug daily 10:00–17:00, Sept–late June Mon–Fri 10:00–16:00, Sat–Sun 11:00–17:00.

▲▲▲**Royal Armory** Europe's most spectacular collection of medieval royal armor, in the Royal Palace. **Hours:** June–Aug daily 10:00–17:00; Sept–May Tue–Sun 11:00–17:00, Thu until 20:00, closed Mon.

▲▲**Military Parade and Changing of the Guard** Punchy daily pomp starting at Nybroplan and finishing at Royal Palace outer courtyard. **Hours:** Mid-May–Sept starts Mon–Sat at 11:45 (at palace at 12:15), Sunday at 12:45 (at palace at 13:15).

▲▲**City Hall** Gilt mosaic architectural jewel of Stockholm and site of Nobel Prize banquet, with tower offering the city's best views. **Hours:** Tours daily at 10:00 and 12:00, more in summer; tower open May–Sept daily 10:00–16:15, closed Oct–April.

▲▲**Millesgården** Dramatic cliffside museum and grounds featuring works of Sweden's greatest sculptor, Carl Milles. **Hours:** Mid-May–Sept daily 11:00–17:00; Oct–mid-May Tue–Sun 12:00–17:00, Thu until 20:00, closed Mon.

▲▲**Drottningholm Palace** Resplendent 17th-century royal residence with a Baroque theater. **Hours:** May–Aug daily 10:00–16:30,

and 13:30 in season).

Hop-on, Hop-off Boat Tour—Stockholm is a city surrounded by water, making this boat option enjoyable and practical. The boat makes a small loop, stopping at key spots such as Djurgården (Skansen and *Vasa* Museum), Gamla Stan (near Slussen and again near Royal Palace), and Nybroplan. Use the boat strictly as transport from Point A to Point B, or make the whole 50-minute, five-

Sept daily 12:00–15:30, Oct–April Sat–Sun only 12:00–15:30.

▲▲**Archipelago** Mostly half-day cruises to Vaxholm and many other small island destinations. **Hours:** Several options per day in summer, some including a meal onboard.

▲**Nobel Museum** Star-studded tribute to some of the world's most accomplished scientists, artists, economists, and politicians. **Hours:** Mid-May–mid-Sept daily 10:00–17:00, Tue until 20:00; off-season Tue–Sun 11:00–17:00, Tue until 20:00, closed Mon.

▲**Royal Palace Museums** Complex of Swedish royal museums, the two best of which are the State Apartments and Royal Treasury. **Hours:** Mid-May–Aug daily 10:00–17:00; Sept–mid-May Tue–Sun 10:00–16:00, closed Mon and for one month in winter (usually Jan).

▲**Royal Coin Cabinet and Swedish Economy Museum** Europe's best look at the history of money, with a sweep through the evolution of the Swedish economy to boot. **Hours:** Daily July–Sept 9:00-17:00, Oct–June 10:00-16:00.

▲**Kungsträdgården** Stockholm's lively central square, with life-size chess games, concerts, and perpetual action. **Hours:** Always open.

▲**Sergels Torg** Modern square with underground mall. **Hours:** Always open.

▲**National Museum of Fine Arts** Convenient, crowd-free gallery with work of locals Larsson and Zorn, along with Rembrandt, Rubens, and Impressionists. **Hours:** Tue–Sun 11:00–17:00, Tue until 20:00, closed Mon.

▲**Thielska Galleriet** Enchanting waterside mansion with works of local artists Larsson, Zorn, and Munch. **Hours:** Mon–Sat 12:00–16:00, Sun 13:00–16:00.

stop loop and enjoy the tape-recorded commentary (100-kr ticket good 24 hours, runs June–Aug 10:00–16:00, first departure from near Royal Palace, tel. 08/5871-4020, www.citysightseeing.com).

By Foot

Old Town Walk—City Sightseeing offers a 60-minute Old Town walk (90 kr, daily July–Aug at 11:30 and 13:30, leaves from Gustav

Adolfs Torg, near the Royal Opera House, tel. 08/5871-4020, www.citysightseeing.com).

Local Guides—To hire a private guide, call 08/789-2496 (Mon-Fri 9:00–17:00, closed Sat–Sun) or visit www.guidestockholm .com. The standard rate is about 1,100 kr for a half-day tour.

Marita Bergman is a schoolteacher and a licensed guide who enjoys taking around visitors during her breaks (1,200 kr/half-day tour, tel. 08/5909-3931, mobile 073-511-9154, maritabergman @bredband.net).

SELF-GUIDED WALK

Welcome to Stockholm's Old Town

Stockholm's historic island core (Gamla Stan) is charming, photogenic, and full of antiques shops, street lanterns, painted ceilings, and surprises. Until the 1600s, all of Stockholm fit on Gamla Stan. Stockholm traded with other northern ports such as Amsterdam, Lübeck, and Tallinn. German culture influenced art, building styles, and even the language, turning Old Norse into modern Swedish. With its narrow alleys and stairways, Gamla Stan mixes poorly with cars and modern economies. Today, it's been given over to the Royal Palace and to the tourists—sometimes seemingly unaware that most of Stockholm's best attractions are elsewhere—who throng Gamla Stan's main drag, Västerlånggatan.

While you could just happily wander, give this quick ▲▲ walk a try first:

• *Start at the base of Slottsbacken (the palace hill esplanade) leading up to the...*

Royal Palace: Check out the ❶ **statue of King Gustav III** gazing at the palace (bottom of Slottsbacken, palace described on page 280), which was built on the site of Stockholm's first castle. Gustav loved the arts, and founded the Royal Dramatic Theater and the Opera in Stockholm. Ironically, he was assassinated at a masquerade ball at the Royal Opera House in 1792, inspiring Verdi's opera *Un Ballo in Maschera.*

Walk up the broad, cobbled boulevard. (The fine Sweden Bookshop is on the left near the bottom—see "Helpful Hints," page 268.) Partway up the hill, stop and scan the harbor. The grand building (across the water) is the National Museum, which is often mistaken by illiterate tourists for the palace. In the distance beyond that is a fine row of buildings—Strandvägen. Until the 1850s, this area was home to peasant shacks, but as Stockholm was entering its grand stage, it was cleaned up and replaced by fine apartments, including some of the city's smartest addresses. Live here, and you call Tiger Woods (who married a Swede) your neighbor. The TV tower—a major attraction back in the 1970s—stands tall in

Self-Guided Walk: Stockholm's Old Town

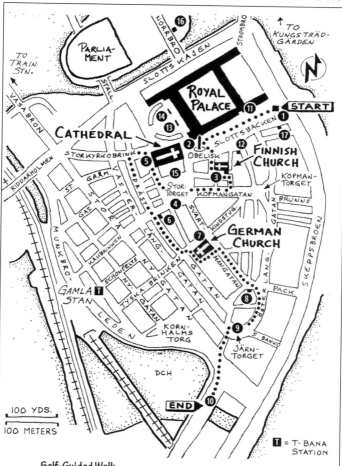

100 YDS.

100 METERS

T = T-BANA STATION

Self-Guided Walk

❶ King Gustav III Statue
❷ Obelisk
❸ Iron Boy Statue
❹ Stortorget
❺ Cathedral
❻ Rune Stone
❼ German Church
❽ Viewpoint
❾ Järntorget
❿ Bridge & Lock

Additional Sights

⓫ Royal Armory
⓬ Royal Coin Cabinet & Swedish Economy Museum
⓭ Palace Info Booth
⓮ Changing of the Guard
⓯ Nobel Museum
⓰ Museum of Medieval Stockholm
⓱ Sweden Bookshop

the distance. The Viking ship moored closest to you is friendly (it's now a tour boat and restaurant). Turn to the palace facade on your left (finished in 1754, replacing one that burned in 1697). The niches are filled with Swedish bigwigs (literally) from the mid-18th century.

The ❷ **obelisk** honors Stockholm's merchant class for its support in a war against Russia (1788). In front of the obelisk are tour buses (their drivers worried about parking cops) and a sand pit used for *boules*. The royal family took a liking to the French game during a Mediterranean vacation, and it's quite popular around town today. Behind the obelisk stands Storkyrkan, Stockholm's cathedral (which we'll visit later in this walk). Opposite the palace (orange building on left) is the Finnish church (Finska Kyrkan), which originated as the royal tennis hall.

Stroll behind the Finnish church into the shady churchyard where you'll find the fist-size ❸ *Iron Boy,* the tiniest public statue (of about 600) in Stockholm. Swedish grannies knit caps for him in the winter when it's cold. Local legend says the statue honors the orphans who had to transfer cargo from sea ships to lake ships before Stockholm's locks were built. Some people rub his head for good luck (which the orphans didn't have). Others, likely needy when it comes to this gift, rub his head for wisdom.

• *Continue through the yard, cross Trädgårdsgatan, go down the tiny lane to Kopmangatan (the medieval merchants' street, now popular with antiques dealers), turn right, and head for Stortorget, the old square.*

❹ **Stortorget, Stockholm's Oldest Square:** The grand building on the right is the Stock Exchange. This building now houses the noble Nobel Museum (described on page 279). Upstairs is the Swedish Academy, which awards the Nobel Prize for literature each year. On the immediate left is the Stockholm Stadsmission (offering the cheapest and best lunch around, at Grillska Huset—see "Eating," page 299), and at #5 is their secondhand shop, affording those who peek in a fine look at the richly decorated ceilings characteristic of the Gamla Stan in the 17th century. The exotic flowers and animals implied that the people who lived or worked here were worldly. The town well is still a popular meeting point.

Scan the fine old facades. The site of Stockholm's bloodbath of 1520, this square has a notorious history. During a Danish power grab, many of Stockholm's movers and shakers—Swedish aristocracy, leading merchants, and priests—who had challenged Danish rule were beheaded. Each of the 80 or so white stones in the fine red facade across the square symbolizes one of the victims. Rivers of blood were said to have flowed through the streets. (Three years later, the Swedes elected their first king, Gustav Vasa, who ushered in a great period in Swedish history—the Swedish Renaissance.) Later, this square held the town's pillory.

• *At the far end of the square (under the finest gables), turn right and follow Trangsund toward the cathedral.*

❺ Cathedral (Storkyrkan): Just before the church, you'll see my personal phone booth (Rikstelefon) and the gate to the churchyard being guarded by statues of Caution and Hope. Enter the cathedral (30 kr, daily mid-May–mid-Sept 9:00–18:00, until 16:00 off-season; the free and worthwhile English-language flier describes the interior).

The interior is cobbled with centuries-old tombstones; more than 2,000 people are buried under the church. The tombstone of the Swedish reformer Olaus Petri sits appropriately simple and appropriately located—under the pulpit. The royal pews date from 1684. In front (on the left), *Saint George and the Dragon* (1489) is carved of oak and elk horn. To some, this symbolizes the Swedes' overcoming the evil Danes. In a broader sense, it's an inspiration to take up the struggle against even non-Danish evil. Regardless, it must be the gnarliest dragon's head in all of Europe. Near the exit, a painting depicts Stockholm in the early 1500s, showing a walled city filling only today's Gamla Stan. It's a 1630 copy of the 1535 original. The strange sun and sky predicted big changes in Sweden—and as a matter of fact, that's what happened. Gustav Vasa brought on huge reforms in religion and beyond.

The fancy door on the left (and the plain one on the right) lead to free WCs. The exit door next to the painting takes you into the kid-friendly churchyard (which was once the cemetery).

• *With your back to the church, turn right and continue down Trangsund. At the next corner, go downhill on Storkyrkobrinken and take the first left on...*

Prästgatan Lane: Enjoy a quiet wander down this peaceful "Priests' Lane." (Västerlånggatan, the touristy drag, parallels this lane one block to the right—you can walk back up on it later.) As you stroll this 15th-century lane, look for sewage drain spouts (a foot or so off the cobbles—an improvement over the toss-it-out-the-window days, but raw nevertheless), tie bolts (iron bars necessary to bind the timber beams of tall buildings

together), flaming gold phoenixes under red-crown medallions (telling firefighters this house paid its insurance and could be saved in case of fire), and small coal or wood hatches for fuel delivery back in the good old days.

After two blocks (at Kåkbrinken), a cannon barrel on the corner guards a medieval ❻ **rune stone.** (In case you can't read the old Nordic script, it says: "Torsten and Thorgun erected this stone in memory of their son.")

Continue farther down Prästgatan to Tyska Brinken and turn left. You will see the powerful brick steeple of the ❼ **German church** (Tyska Kyrkan). Its carillon has played four times a day since 1666. Think of the days when German merchants worked here. Today, Germans come to Sweden not to run the economy, but to enjoy its pristine nature (which is progressively harder to find in their crowded homeland).

• *Wander through the churchyard and out the back. Exit right onto Svartmangatan and follow it to the right, ending at an iron railing overlooking Österlånggatan.*

❽ **Viewpoint:** From this perch, survey the street below to the left and right. Notice how it curves. This marks the old shoreline. In medieval times, piers stretched out like fingers into the harbor. Gradually, as land was reclaimed and developed, these piers were extended, becoming lanes leading to piers farther away. Below you is a cute shop where elves can actually be seen making elves.

Walk right along Österlånggatan to ❾ **Järntorget**—a customs square in medieval times, and home of Sweden's first bank back in 1680 (the yellow building with the bars on the windows). A nearby Coop Nara supermarket offers picnic fixings. From here, Västerlånggatan—the eating, shopping, and commercial pedestrian mall of Gamla Stan—leads back across the island. You'll be there in a minute, but finish this walk by continuing out of the square (opposite where you entered) down Järntorgsgatan. Walk out into the traffic hell and stop on the ❿ **bridge** above the canal.

This is Stockholm's **lock,** where boats are raised a yard to sail from the sea into the lake. Nicknamed "the divorce lock," this is where captains and first mates learn to communicate under pressure and the public eye. Survey the view. Opposite Gamla Stan is the island of Södermalm—bohemian, youthful, artsy, and casual—with its popular view elevator. Moored on the saltwater side are the cruise ships, which bring thousands of visitors into town each day during the season. Many of these boats are bound for Finland. The old steamer *Patricia* (200 or so yards toward Södermalm) is a local favorite for raucous dining and dancing (see page 302). The towering white syringe is Gröna Lund's (amusement park) free-fall ride. The *Djurgården Färjan* sign marks the ferry that zips from here directly to Gröna Lund and Djurgården. The equestrian statue is Jean-Baptiste Bernadotte, the French nobleman invited to establish the current Swedish royal dynasty 200 years ago.

You could catch bus #2, which heads back downtown (the stop is just beyond Bernadotte, next to the waterfront). But better yet, linger longer in Gamla Stan—day or night, it's a lively place to enjoy. Västerlånggatan, Gamla Stan's main commercial drag, is a festival of distractions that keeps most visitors from seeing the historic charms of Old Town—which you just did. Now you can window-shop and eat (see "Eating," page 299). Or, if it's late, find some live music (see "Nightlife," page 293).

For more sightseeing, consider the other sights in Gamla Stan (see "Sights," below) or at the Royal Palace (see "Royal Palace," below). If you continue back up Västerlånggatan (always going straight), you'll pass the Parliament building and cross the water back over onto Norrmalm (where the street becomes Drottninggatan). This puts you back in Stockholm's modern, vibrant new town, with some worthwhile sights (see "Downtown Stockholm," page 282) and great shopping (see "Shopping," page 292).

SIGHTS

Gamla Stan

The best of Gamla Stan is covered in my self-guided walk, above. But here are a few ways to extend your time in the Old Town.

▲**Nobel Museum (Nobelmuseet)**—Opened in 2001 for the 100-year anniversary of the Nobel Prize, this wonderful little museum is thoroughly entertaining and creative. Portraits of all

700-plus prize winners hang from the ceiling—shuffling around the room like shirts at the dry cleaner's (miss your favorite, and he or she will come around again in three hours). Two video rooms run a continuous montage of quick programs (3-min bios of various winners in one, and 5-min films celebrating various intellectual environments—from Cambridge to Parisian cafés—in the other). The Viennese-style Café Satir is the place to get creative with your coffee...and sample the famous Nobel ice cream. All Nobel laureates who visit the museum are asked to sign the bottom of a chair in the café. Turn yours over and see who warmed your chair. And don't miss the lockable hangers, to protect your fancy, furry winter coat (60 kr; mid-May–mid-Sept daily 10:00–17:00, Tue until 20:00; off-season Tue–Sun 11:00–17:00, Tue until 20:00, closed Mon; on Stortorget in the center of Gamla Stan a block from the Royal Palace, tel.

08/5348-1800, http://nobelprize.org/nobelmuseum). The Swedish Academy, which awards the Nobel Prize for literature each year, is upstairs.

Parliament (Riksdaghuset)—For a firsthand look at Sweden's government, tour its Parliament buildings (free one-hour tours in English late June–Aug, usually Mon–Fri at 12:30 and 14:00, enter at Riksgatan 3a, call 08/786-4000 to confirm times). It's also possible to watch the Parliament in session.

Museum of Medieval Stockholm (Medeltidsmuseet)—While a bit grade-schoolish, this museum provides a good look at medieval Stockholm (free, Tue–Sun 11:00–16:00, Wed until 18:00, closed Mon except July–Aug, enter from park in front of Parliament, tel. 08/5083-1790, www.medeltidsmuseet.stockholm.se).

The Strömparterren park, with its café and Carl Milles statue of the *Sun Singer* greeting the day, is a pleasant place for a sightseeing break (pay WC in park, free WC in museum).

Royal Palace (Kungliga Slottet)

Although the royal family beds down at Drottningholm, this complex in Gamla Stan is still the official royal residence. The palace, designed in Italian Baroque style, was completed in 1754 after a fire wiped out the previous palace.

The changing of the guard and the awesome, don't-miss Royal Armory are the palace's highlights. The Royal Treasury is worth a look; the chapel is nice but no big deal; the Apartments of State are not much as far as palace rooms go; and you can skip Gustav III's Museum of Antiquities and the Museum of Three Crowns. The information booth in the semicircular courtyard (at the top, where the guard changes) gives out an explanatory brochure with a map marking the different entrances (main entrance is on the west side—away from the water—but the Royal Armory has a separate entrance). They also have a list of today's guided tours. In peak season, there are up to four different English tours a day—at the top of four successive hours (included in the admission)—allowing you to systematically cover the entire complex. Since the palace is used for state functions, it is sometimes closed to tourists.

▲▲**Military Parade and Changing of the Guard**—Starting at Nybroplan, Stockholm's daily military parade marches over Norrbro Bridge and up to the Royal Palace's outer courtyard, where the band plays and the guard changes (mid-May–Sept Mon–Sat at 11:45, Sun at 12:45). The performance is fresh and spirited, because the soldiers are visiting Stockholm just like you—and it's a chance for young soldiers from all over Sweden in every branch of the service to show their stuff in the big city. You can march with the band, or gather at the palace courtyard, where the band will arrive at about 12:15 (13:15 on Sun). The best place to stand is along the wall in the inner courtyard, near the palace information and ticket office. There are columns with wide pedestals for easy perching, as well as benches that people stand on to view the ceremony (arrive early). Generally, after the barking and goose-stepping formalities, the band shows off for an impressive 40-minute marching concert. Though the royal family now lives out of town at

Drottningholm, the palace guards are for real. If the guard by the cannon in the semicircular courtyard looks a little lax, try wandering discreetly behind him.

▲▲▲Royal Armory (Livrustkammaren)—The oldest museum in Sweden has the most interesting and best-displayed collection of medieval royal armor I've seen anywhere in Europe. The original 17th-century gear includes royal baby wear, outfits kings wore when they were killed in battle or assassinated, gowns representing royal fashion through the ages, and five centuries of royal Swedish armor—all wonderfully described in English. An added bonus is a basement lined with royal coaches (including coronation coaches)—well-preserved, richly decorated, and with evocative audioguide coverage (free, June–Aug daily 10:00–17:00; Sept–May Tue–Sun 11:00–17:00, Thu until 20:00, closed Mon; 20-kr audioguide is excellent—romantic couples can share it if they crank up the volume; 45-min tours June–Aug Mon–Fri at 13:00, Sat–Sun at 14:00; entrance at bottom of Slottsbacken at base of palace, tel. 08/5195-5544, www.lsh.se/livrustkammaren).

▲Other Royal Palace Museums—For the four museums below, you can enter through the main entrance and buy a 130-kr combo-ticket covering all of them (otherwise 90 kr apiece; mid-May–Aug daily 10:00–17:00; Sept–mid-May Tue–Sun 10:00–16:00, closed Mon; entirely closed for about a month in winter, usually in Jan; tel. 08/402-6130, www.royalcourt.se). Stockholm Card holders can go straight into each museum, bypassing the ticket office.

Royal Apartments: The stately palace exterior encloses 608 rooms (one more than Britain's Buckingham Palace) of glittering 18th-century Baroque and Rococo decor. Clearly the palace of Scandinavia's superpower, it's steeped in royal history. You'll walk the long halls through four sections: the Hall of State (with an exhibit of fancy state awards), the lavish Bernadotte Apartments (some fine Rococo interiors and portraits of the Bernadotte dynasty), the State Apartments (with rooms dating to the 1690s), and the Guest Apartments, where visiting heads of state still crash. Guided tours run daily in peak season (mid-May–mid-Sept at 11:00, 13:00, and 15:00).

Royal Treasury (Skattkammaren): Climbing down into the super-secure vault, you'll see 12 cases filled with fancy crowns, scepters, jeweled robes, and plenty of glittering gold. Nothing is explained, so get the 2-kr flier or take the guided tour at 14:00 (summer only).

Gustav III's Museum of Antiquities (Gustav III's Antikmuseum): In the 1700s, Gustav III traveled through Italy and brought home an impressive gallery of classical Roman statues. These are displayed exactly as they were in the 1790s. This was a huge deal for those who had never been out of Sweden (closed mid-Sept–mid-May).

Museum of Three Crowns (Museum Tre Kronor): This museum shows off bits of the palace from before a devastating 1697 fire. It's basically just more old stuff, interesting only to real history buffs (guided tours at 13:00 in summer).

▲**Royal Coin Cabinet and Swedish Economy Museum**—More than your typical royal coin collection, this is the best money museum I've seen in Europe. A fine exhibit tells the story of money from crude wampum to credit cards, and traces the development of the modern Swedish economy. Unfortunately, there aren't many English translations, which makes the included audioguide critical (free, daily July–Sept 9:00–17:00, Oct–June 10:00–16:00, Slottsbacken 6, tel. 08/5195-5300).

Downtown Stockholm

▲**Shoppers' Delight**—The modern center of Stockholm is not dedicated to recalling old kings, marveling at mementos of Stockholm's superpower days, or the preservation of old buildings; it's dedicated to shopping. Drottninggatan, the main pedestrian boulevard, cuts through town like a giant parade of commercialism. Festooned with sales banners blowing in the Nordic wind, the street is lined with human advertisements urging you to come in and try this or that.

For Old World shopping action, nip from Drottninggatan into the Hötorget market (outdoor square and indoor stalls, also see "Eating," page 299). Near an H&M department store (popular with my female staff for trendy and inexpensive Euro-fashions), Drottninggatan passes Sergels Torg. Underneath this square is a no-name but glitzy underground shopping area that leads the flow of shoppers into the Gallerian mall (impressive even to non-shoppers). To mall-hop to the Gallerian, follow signs through *Sergelgangen* to *Gallerian*. (Also see "Sergels Torg," below.)

Among a world of trendy shops, you'll find plenty of chic-yet-affordable little lunch bars, classy cafés for your *fika* (traditional

Swedish coffee-and-bun break, see sidebar on page 305), and even a spa (Alelsons Spa, 600 kr for 50-min Swedish massage, tel. 08/440-8080) providing an oasis of relaxation for stressed out shoppers.

At the Gallerian, you'll find Nordiska Kompaniet (NK), Sweden's leading department store (with a vast basement supermarket and lots of eateries). From here, it's an easy walk to Kungsträdgården, the "King's Garden Square," now entirely dedicated to commoners (ideally, shoppers; see "Kungsträdgården," below).

Waterside Walk—To be spritzed—not with perfume by sales girls (as in the shoppers' paradise listed above)—but by the sea, enjoy Stockholm's ever-expanding shoreline promenades. Tracing the downtown shoreline, while dodging in-line skaters and ice-cream trolleys rather than cars and buses, you can walk from Slussen in Gamla Stan all the way to the good ship *Wasa* in Djurgården. Perhaps the best stretch is Strandvägen (from Nybroplan to Djurgården). As you stroll, keep in mind that there's free fishing in central Stockholm, and the harbor waters are restocked every spring with 3,000 new fish. Locals tell of one lucky lad who pulled in a 35-kilo salmon.

▲**Kungsträdgården**—Five hundred years ago, this "King's Garden Square" was the private kitchen garden of the king, where he grew his cabbage salad. Today, this downtown people-watching center is considered Stockholm's living room, symbolizing the freedom-loving spirit of the people. While the English info board (20 yards to the statue king's immediate right) describes the garden as a private royal domain, the nearby giant clump of elm trees reminds locals that it's the people who rule now. In the 1970s, demonstrators chained themselves to these trees to stop the building of an underground station here. They prevailed, and today, locals enjoy the peaceful, breezy ambience of a tea house here instead. Watch the life-size game of chess and enjoy summer concerts at the bandstand. There's always something going on. Surrounded by the Sweden House, NK department store, a welcoming Volvo showroom (next to the TI, showing off the latest in Swedish car design), the harborfront, and tour boats, it's *the* place to feel Stockholm's pulse (but always ask first: *"Far jag kanna din puls?"*).

Kungsträdgården also throws huge parties. Restaurant Days is the "taste of Stockholm" festival for a week in early June, when restaurateurs show off and bands entertain all day. The beer flows freely, a rare public spectacle in Sweden. The Swedes even celebrate the Fourth of July here, with several days of festival events. The nearby Kungsträdgården T-bana station is famous as the best art station in town. The man at the turnstile is generally friendly to tourists who ask *snälla rara* (snel-lah rar-rah; pretty please) for permission to nip down the escalator to see the far-out design, proving to the gullible that Stockholm sits upon a grand, ancient civilization.

▲**Sergels Torg**—This square dominates the heart of modern Stockholm, between Kungsträdgården and the train station, and suggests that Moscow won the Cold War. The glassy tower glows at night, symbolic of Sweden's haunting northern lights. That and everything around you dates from the 1960s and 1970s. There's a huge discussion going on about what to do with the *"Platan"* ("the platter," as this below-street-level square is nicknamed)—so dated...

and so convenient for junkies. Enjoy the colorful, bustling underground mall, prowl through Åhléns department store, and dip into the Gallerian mall (described in "Shoppers' Delight," above). In the Kulturhuset, you'll find a library, Internet café, chessboards, art exhibits, a venue for new bands, and a café with foreign newspapers (Tue–Fri 11:00–18:00, Sat–Sun 11:00–16:00, closed Mon, tel. 08/5083-1508, www.kulturhuset.stockholm.se).

▲▲**City Hall (Stadshuset)**—The Stadshuset is an impressive mix of 8 million bricks, 19 million chips of gilt mosaic, and lots

of Stockholm pride. One of Europe's finest public buildings (built in 1923) and site of the annual Nobel Prize banquet, it's particularly enjoyable and worthwhile for its entertaining tours (60 kr, daily at 10:00 and 12:00, more in the summer, 300 yards behind station, bus #3 or #62, tel. 08/5082-9059, www.stockholm.se/stadshuset). Climb the 395-foot-tall **tower** (an elevator takes you halfway) for the best possible city view (20 kr, May–Sept daily 10:00–16:15, closed Oct–April). The City Hall's cafeteria, which you enter from the courtyard, serves complete lunches for 75 kr (Mon–Fri 11:00–14:00, closed Sat–Sun).

▲**Orientation Views**—For a bird's-eye perspective on this wonderful urban mix of water, parks, concrete, and people, consider these four viewpoints: **City Hall**'s tower (described above; view from tower pictured within this listing); the observatory in **Skansen**; the **Kaknäs Tower** (at 500 feet, once the tallest building

in Scandinavia; 30 kr, daily May–Aug 9:00–22:00, Sept–April 10:00–21:00, restaurant on 28th floor, east of downtown—bus #69 from Nybroplan or Sergels Torg, tel. 08/667-2105; view pictured on page 259); or the **Katarina elevator** (circa 1930s, ride 130 feet to the top; 5 kr, Mon–Sat 7:30–22:00, Sun 10:00–22:00, near Slussen T-bana stop—walk behind Katarinavägen toward Fjallgatan for grand city and harbor views).

▲**National Museum of Fine Arts**—Though mediocre by European standards, this 200-year-old museum is small, central, and user-friendly. Highlights include several works by Rembrandt

and Rubens; a fine group of Impressionists; art by the popular and good-to-get-to-know local Carl Larsson (who frescoed the entrance hall) and Anders Zorn; and a sizable collection of Russian icons. The middle floor is dedicated to design; one wing covers 1500–1700, the other 1900–2000. With thoughtful English descriptions, this exhibit walks you through the evolution of modern Swedish design: gracefully engraved glass from the 1920s, works from the Stockholm Exhibition of 1930, industrial design of the 1940s, Scandinavian Design movement of the 1950s, plastic chairs from the 1960s, modern furniture from the 1980s, and the Swedish new simplicity from the 1990s. If you'd like a private tour with the former museum director, rent the excellent audioguide (30 kr), which describes the top 13 works (free, Tue–Sun 11:00–17:00, Tue until 20:00, closed Mon, Södra Blasieholmshamnen, T-bana: Kungsträdgården, tel. 08/5195-4310, www.nationalmuseum.se).

Museum of Modern Art (Moderna Museet)—This bright, cheery, and free gallery on Skeppsholmen island is as far-out as can be, with Picasso, Braque, and lots of goofy Dada art (such as *Urinal* and *Goat with Tire*), as well as more contemporary stuff (free except for some temporary exhibitions, audioguide, fine bookstore, harborview café, Tue–Wed 10:00–20:00, Thu–Sun 10:00–18:00, closed Mon, walk or take bus #65, tel. 08/5195-5200, www .modernamuseet.se).

▲**Swedish Massage, Spa, and Sauna**—If you want to treat yourself to a Swedish spa experience with perhaps an authentic "Swedish massage," head for the elegant circa-1900 **Central-Badet Spa.** The regular 110-kr admission includes the use of a towel and bathrobe while you enjoy an extensive gym, "bubblepool," sauna, steam room, and an elegant Art Nouveau pool. A classic massage costs 650 kr per hour and includes the 110-kr admission (long hours, last entry 20:30, closed Sun in July, ages 18 and up, Drottninggatan 88, 10 min up from Sergels Torg, tel. 08/5452-1300, reservations at tel. 08/5452-1313). If you won't make it to Finland, enjoy a sauna here (for more info on saunas, see page 350 in Helsinki chapter). There are two saunas—one mixed, one not. Bring your towel into the sauna—not for modesty, but for hygiene (to separate your body from the bench). The steam room is mixed; bring two towels (one for modesty and the other to sit on). The pool is more for floating than for jumping and splashing. The leafy courtyard restaurant is a relaxing place to enjoy affordable, healthy, and light meals.

Stockholm's Djurgården

Four hundred years ago, Djurgården was the king's hunting ground. Now this entire lush island is Stockholm's fun center, protected as a national park. It still has a smattering of animal life among its biking paths, picnicking local families, art galleries, and various amusements. Of the three great sights on the island, the *Vasa* and Nordic museums are neighbors, and Skansen is a 10-minute walk away (or hop on any bus—they come every couple of minutes).

Getting There: Take bus #47 from the train station or Sergels Torg and get off at the Nordic Museum (also for the *Vasa* Museum), or continue on to the Skansen stop. In summer, you can also take a ferry from Nybroplan or Slussen (see "Getting Around Stockholm," page 269) or a tram from Nybroplan (daily in summer, weekends only in spring and fall). Walkers can enjoy the harborside Strandvägen promenade, which leads from Nybroplan directly to the island.

▲▲▲**Skansen**—This is Europe's original open-air folk museum, founded in 1891. It's a huge park gathering more than 150 historic buildings (homes, churches, shops, and schoolhouses) transplanted from all corners of Sweden.

Skansen was the first in what became a Europe-wide movement to preserve traditional architecture in open-air museums. Other languages have even borrowed the Swedish term "Skansen" (which originally meant "the Fort") to mean "open-air museum." Today, tourists still explore this

Stockholm's Djurgården

Swedish-culture-on-a-lazy-Susan, seeing folk crafts in action and wonderfully furnished old interiors (lively June–Aug before about 17:00, otherwise pretty dead).

In "Old Stockholm" (top of the escalator), shoemakers, potters, and glassblowers are busy doing their traditional thing in a re-created Old World Stockholm. The glassblowing demonstration here (daily 10:00–17:00) is as good as any you'll see in Sweden's glass country to the south. The rest of Sweden spreads out from Old Stockholm. Northern Swedish culture and architecture is in the north (top of park map) and southern Sweden's in the south (bottom of map).

Take advantage of the free map, and consider the 50-kr museum guidebook. With the book, you'll understand each building you duck into and even learn about the Nordic animals awaiting you in the zoo. Check the live crafts schedule at the information stand by the main entrance beneath the escalator to make a smart Skansen plan. Guides throughout the park are happy to answer your questions—but only if you ask them. The old houses come alive when you take the initiative to get information.

Kids love Skansen, especially its zoo (ride a life-size wooden

Dala-horse and stare down a hedgehog, or go on a feeding tour at 14:00), Lill' Skansen (a children's zoo), and mini-train and pony rides.

Cost and Hours: May–Sept 80 kr, May after 17:00 discounted to 30 kr; Oct–April to 50 kr. Open daily May 10:00–20:00, June–Aug 10:00–22:00, Sept 10:00–17:00, Oct–April 10:00–16:00, closed only on Christmas Eve. The historical buildings are open 11:00–17:00, some until 19:00 June–Aug, Oct–April 11:00–15:00 (only a few are open in winter). Tel. 08/5789-0005 for recorded info, or tel. 08/442-8000 (www.skansen.se). Gröna Lund, Stockholm's amusement park, is across the street.

Music: Skansen does great music. There's fiddling (30-min performances June–Aug nightly except Sun at 18:15), folk-dancing (Mon–Fri June–Aug at 19:00, also Sun at 14:30 and 16:00), and public dancing to live bands (nightly except Sun from 20:00, call for that evening's theme—big band, modern, ballroom, folk).

Eating at Skansen: While Skansen's main restaurant, **Solliden**, serves a big *smörgåsbord* lunch in a grand blue-and-white room (280 kr, daily 12:00–16:00 in summer) and the adjacent **Ekorren** cafeteria offers less-expensive self-service lunches with a view (60–70-kr daily specials), the most memorable meals are at the small folk food court on the main square, **Bollnastorget.** Here, among the duck-filled lakes, frolicking families, and peacenik local toddlers who don't bump on the bumper cars, kiosks dish up "Sami slow food" (smoked reindeer), waffles, hot dogs, and more. There are lots of picnic benches—Skansen encourages **picnicking.** The old-time **Stora Gungan Krog**, in Old Stockholm at the top of the escalator, is a cozy inn; their freshly baked cakes will tempt you (80–100-kr indoor or outdoor lunches—meat, fish, or veggie—with a salad-and-cracker bar, daily 11:00–17:00).

Aquarium: Admission to the aquarium is the only thing not covered on your Skansen ticket, but it is included on the Stockholm Card (aquarium entry-65 kr; mid-June–mid-Aug daily 10:00–18:00, July until 20:00; mid-Aug–mid-June Tue–Sun 10:00–16:30, closed Mon; tel. 08/660-1082).

▲▲▲*Vasa* **Museum (Vasamuseet)**—Stockholm turned a titanic flop into one of Europe's great sightseeing attractions. This glamorous but unseaworthy warship—top-heavy with an extra cannon deck—sank 20 minutes into her 1628 maiden voyage when a breeze caught the sails and blew her over. After 333 years at the bottom of Stockholm's harbor, she rose again from the deep with

the help of marine archaeologists. Rediscovered in 1956 and raised in 1961, this Edsel of the sea is today the best-preserved ship of its age anywhere—housed since 1990 in a brilliant museum. The masts perched atop the roof—best seen from a distance—show the actual height of the ship.

The *Vasa*, while not quite the biggest ship in the world, had the most firepower, with two fearsome decks of cannons. The statues draping the ship are all symbolic of the king's power. The lion on the magnificent prow is a reminder that Europe considered the Swedish king Gustavus Adolphus the "Lion from the North"—hoping he would save Protestants from the Catholics in the religious wars that engulfed much of 17th-century Europe. Painstakingly restored, 95 percent of the wood is original (modern bits are the brighter and smoother planks). Displays are well-described in English. Learn about the ship's rules (bread can't be older than eight years), why it sank (heavy bread?), how it's preserved (the ship, not the bread), and so on.

Cost, Hours, Location: 80 kr, daily mid-June–mid-Aug 8:30–18:00, off-season 10:00–17:00, winter Wed until 20:00, Galärvarvet, Djurgården, tel. 08/5195-4800, www.vasamuseet.se. The *Vasa* is on the waterfront immediately behind the stately brick Nordic Museum, a 10-minute walk from Skansen (see below). The museum also has a good café inside. To get from the Nordic Museum to the *Vasa* Museum, face the Nordic Museum and walk around to the right (going left takes you into a big dead-end parking lot).

Sightseeing Strategy: For a thorough visit, plan on spending an hour watching the 25-minute video and taking the 25-minute tour (in either order), then explore the boat and wander through the various exhibits. The English-subtitled video generally runs at the top of the hour. English tours run mid-June through late August at :30 past each hour from 9:30 to 17:30 (fewer tours off-season, call for times). Both the video and tour are included with your admission.

▲▲▲**Nordic Museum (Nordiska Museet)**—Built to look like a Danish Renaissance palace, this museum offers a fascinating peek at 500 years of traditional Swedish lifestyles. It's arguably more informative than Skansen. Take time to let the excellent 20-kr audioguide enliven the exhibits. Carl Milles' huge statue of Gustav Vasa, father of modern Sweden, overlooks the main gallery.

Highlights are on the top two floors. The middle floor (Level 3) holds the *Traditions* exhibit (showing and describing each old-time celebration of the Swedish year) and a section of exquisite table settings, folk costumes, and fancy fashions from the 18th through the 20th centuries. The top floor (Level 4) has an extensive Sami (Lapp) collection, old furniture, and an exhibit showing

Swedish living rooms over the last century; it provides an insightful look at today's Swedes, with—for instance—an intimate look at modern bedrooms (match photos of the owners with the various rooms).

Cost, Hours, Location: Free; late June–Aug daily 10:00–17:00; Sept–late June Mon–Fri 10:00–16:00, Sat–Sun 11:00–17:00; Djurgårdsvägen 6–16, at Djurgårdsbron, tel. 08/5195-6000, www.nordiskamuseet.se.

Gröna Lund—Stockholm's venerable and low-end Tivoli-type amusement park still packs in the local families and teens on cheap dates (60 kr, April–Sept daily 11:00–23:00, shorter hours off-season). It's a busy venue for local pop concerts.

▲**Thielska Galleriet**—If you liked the Larsson and Zorn art in the National Gallery and/or if you're a Munch fan, this charming mansion on the water at the far end of the Djurgården park is worth the trip (50 kr, Mon–Sat 12:00–16:00, Sun 13:00–16:00, bus #69 from train station, tel. 08/662-5884, www.thielska-galleriet.se).

▲**Biking the Garden Island**—In all of Stockholm, Djurgården is the natural place to enjoy a bike ride. There's a good and reasonable bike-rental place just over the bridge as you enter the island (see Djurgårdsbrons Sjöcafe in "Bike Rental," page 269), and a world of park-like paths and lanes with harbor vistas to enjoy.

Outer Stockholm

▲▲**Millesgården**—The home and garden of Sweden's greatest sculptor is dramatically situated on a steep slope running down to the water in Stockholm's upper-class suburb of Lidingö. Carl Milles' entertaining and provocative art was influenced by Rodin. The house dates from the 1920s; the extensive grounds have been turned into a museum. There's a classy café and a great picnic spot with views of Stockholm (80 kr, 15-kr English booklet explains art; mid-May–Sept daily 11:00–17:00; Oct–mid-May Tue–Sun 12:00–17:00, Thu until 20:00, closed Mon; tel. 08/446-7590, www.millesgarden.se). Catch the T-bana to Ropsten, then take bus #207 to the museum.

▲▲**Drottningholm Palace**—The queen's 17th-century summer castle and current royal residence has been called "Sweden's Versailles." Touring the palace, you'll see art that makes the point that Sweden's royalty is divine, and belongs with the gods. Beneath the clouds are the king and queen's earthly subjects...and you. Divine as Sweden's monarchs pretended to be, they were still on a budget: Test the "marble" doorways. (They warm to the touch, because they're stucco painted to look like marble.) You'll see three crowns on the Swedish coat of arms, a reminder of Sweden's aspiration to rule Norway and Denmark. The Room of War—with kings, generals, battle scenes, and bugle–like candleholders—is from the time when Sweden was a superpower (1600–1750). Of course, today's monarchs are figureheads ruled by a constitution. The royal family makes a point to be accessible and as "normal" as royalty can be (70 kr, May–Aug daily 10:00–16:30, Sept daily 12:00–15:30, Oct–April Sat–Sun only 12:00–15:30, call 08/402-6280 to reserve free-with-admission palace tours in English; offered June–Aug usually at 10:00, 12:00, 14:00, and 16:00; fewer off-season, www.royalcourt.se).

The 18th-century **Drottningholm Court Theater** (Drottningholms Slottsteater) somehow survived the ages—complete with its instruments, sound-effects machines, and stage sets. It's one of two such theaters remaining in Europe (the other is in Český Krumlov, Czech Republic). Visit it on a 30-minute guided tour (60 kr, May–Sept English theater tours normally depart half-past each hour, 11:30–16:30, no tours off-season, tel. 08/759-0406), or check their schedule for the rare opportunity to see perfectly authentic operas (about 25 performances each summer). Tickets for this popular time-tunnel musical and theatrical experience cost 165–600 kr and go on sale by phone, fax, or mail each March (see www.dtm.se).

Getting to Drottningholm: Reach the palace via a relaxing boat ride (125 kr round-trip, discount with Stockholm Card, 60 min, from City Hall), or take the T-bana to Brommaplan, where you can catch any 300-series bus to Drottningholm.

Sigtuna—This town, an old-time lakeside jumble of wooden houses and waffle shops, presents a fluffy, stereotyped version of Sweden in the olden days. You'll see a medieval lane lined with colorful tourist boutiques, cafés, a romantic park, waterfront promenade, old Town Hall, and rune stones. The TI can help you get oriented (tel. 08/5948-0650, http://sal.sigtuna.se/turism). If traveling to Uppsala (or Oslo) by car, Sigtuna is a short detour, good for a browse and an ice-cream cone, but little more. By public transport, it's probably not worth the tedious one-hour trip out (take the *pendeltåg* suburban train from Stockholm to Märsta and then change to bus #570, covered by Stockholm Card).

▲▲Archipelago (Skärgården)—Some of Europe's most scenic islands (24,000 of them!) surround Stockholm. If you cruise to Finland, you'll get a good dose of this island beauty. Otherwise, consider one of many half- or full-day trips from downtown Stockholm to the archipelago. Strömma

Kanalbolaget/Cinderella Båtarna ships leave from Nybroplan, while Waxholmsbolaget ships leave across from the Grand Hotel. For an island joyride without getting off the boat, consider the Stockholm Sightseeing company's 2.5-hour archipelago tour (see "Tours," page 271). And to enjoy a relaxing evening at sea, consider one of many good dinner cruises. The TI has a free archipelago mini-guidebook. For details, see www.waxholmsbolaget .se, www.strommakanalbolaget.com, or www.cinderellabatarna .com. Here are two of the most popular islands, with times and prices from Stockholm:

Vaxholm, with its well-preserved town mixing fishing huts and an old fortress, is the most popular destination (65 kr, 60 min, frequent departures throughout the day).

Grinda is a good, less-touristy, and lushly forested alternative to Vaxholm. Though a bit farther away, it offers perhaps the best package of classic archipelago scenery and a sleepy island port community (80 kr, 90 min).

SHOPPING

Modern design, glass, clogs, and wooden goods are popular targets for shoppers. There's a world of shopping temptations from the people's shopping boulevard, Drottninggatan, to Sergels Torg (see "Shoppers' Delight," page 282). Nordiska Kompaniet (NK, short for "no kronor left"), Stockholm's top-end department store, is located in an elegant early 20th-century building just across from the Sweden House. The classy Gallerian mall, across the street, stretches seductively from Sergels Torg nearly to Kungsträdgården. The Åhléns store, nearby at Sergels Torg, is less expensive than NK and has two cafeterias and a supermarket (see page 305). Designtorget, a store dedicated to contemporary Swedish design, sells the unique works of local designers for a commission (Mon–Fri 10:00–19:00, Sat 10:00–17:00, Sun 11:00–17:00, underneath Sergels Torg—enter from basement level of Kulturhuset).

For more on Swedish design, pick up the *Design Guide* flier at the TI (listing smaller stores throughout town with a flair for design). The trendy and exclusive shops (including Orrefors and Kosta) line Biblioteksgatan just off Stureplan.

Traditionally, stores are open weekdays from 10:00 to 18:00, Saturdays until 15:00, and closed on Sundays. Some of the bigger stores (such as NK and Åhléns) are open later on Saturdays and on Sunday afternoons (12:00–17:00).

For a *smörgåsbord* of Scanjunk, visit the Loppmarknaden, Northern Europe's biggest flea market, at the planned suburb of Skärholmen (free entry on weekdays, 15 kr on weekends when it's busiest, Mon–Fri 11:00–18:00, Sat 10:00–16:00, Sun 11:00–16:00,

T-bana: Skärholmen and walk across the square, tel. 08/710-0060). Hötorget, the produce market, also hosts a Sunday flea market (see page 304).

Visit Systembolaget, Sweden's state-run liquor store chain, before it disappears (rumor is that Sweden will soon follow Denmark's lead in liberalizing alcohol sales). For decades, Swedes have not been trusted to browse the wine and booze shelves on their own; only pictures are on display, and you have to order at the counter. One branch is on Gamla Stan at Lilla Nygatan 18, and another is on Norrmalm at Vasagatan 21 (both Mon–Wed 10:00–18:00, Thu–Fri 10:00–19:00, Sat 10:00–15:00, closed Sun).

NIGHTLIFE

Bars and Music in Gamla Stan—The street called Stora Nygatan, with several lively bars, has perhaps the most accessible and reliable place for good jazz in town: Stampen.

Stampen Jazz Bar has two venues: a tight, fun-loving saloon-like bar and a stone-vaulted cellar deep below. From Monday through Thursday, there's live jazz only in the saloon. On Friday and Saturday, they have bands in both the saloon and the cellar (100-kr cover and 50-kr beers, free blues Mon, doors open at 20:00, music at 21:00, free jam session Sat 14:00–18:00, closed Sun, Stora Nygatan 5, tel. 08/205-793, www.stampen.se).

Several other lively spots are within a block of Stampen on Stora Nygatan, including **Wirtstroms Irish Pub** (blues Tue–Sat 21:00-midnight, no cover, 50-kr beers, crowded old cellar under Irish pub, Stora Nygatan 13) and **O'Connells Irish Pub** (a sports bar at #21). Just beyond Gamla Stan, the good ship *Patricia* is rocking with live music and well-lubricated locals most nights (see page 302 for details).

Absolut Icebar Stockholm—If you just want to put on a heavy coat and drink a fancy vodka in a modern-day igloo, consider the fun if touristy Absolut Icebar, a bar literally made out of ice. Venture to the Nordic Sea Hotel, located at the central train station, and you'll get 40 minutes to sip your choice of vodka drinks in an ice glass, on an ice bar, in an ice room with ice windows (150 kr to get in, reservation required, Mon–Fri 12:00–24:00, Sun 12:00–22:00, Vasaplan 4, tel. 08/5056-3124, www.nordicseahotel.com).

Cinema—In Sweden, international movies are shown in their original language with Swedish subtitles. Swedish theaters charge more for longer films (85–110 kr, movies longer than 2 hours are the higher price), and tickets come with assigned seats (drop by to choose seats and buy a ticket, box offices generally open 11:00–22:00 daily). The Hötorget and Drottninggatan neighborhoods have many theaters.

SLEEPING

Peak season for Stockholm's hotels is business time—weeknights outside of summer vacation time. Rates drop by 30–50 percent in the summer (mid-June–mid-Aug) and on Friday and Saturday nights year-round. When I list two hotel rates, the first is the peak-season rate and the second is the summer/weekend rate. In summer, some hotels will discount their rates even further if business is slow; just ask politely if the hotel has any cheaper rooms.

Even in summer, Stockholm hotels are expensive. It's hard to find a normal double with bath for less than 1,000 kr. But Stockholm has plenty of money-saving deals for the savvy visitor willing to compromise a bit. Many places keep an odd misfit room (100 kr cheaper than the others) lashed to a bedpost in the attic, but will only tell you if you ask. Several backpacker places have a range of rooms, blurring the distinction between "hotel" and "hostel." Hotels here are so expensive that money-conscious travelers should consider doubles in hostels and rooms in simple hotels with shared bath—a respectable option in clean and wholesome Stockholm. Using Web sites and online booking services (including Expedia.com) can often snare you big savings, since many hotels allocate a baseline number of rooms at deep discounts to jumpstart their bookings.

There are other budget options. Plenty of people offer private accommodations (600–800-kr doubles). Stockholm's hostels are among Europe's best, offering good beds in simple but interesting places for about 250 kr per night. Each has helpful English-speaking staff, pleasant family rooms, and good facilities. Hosteling is cheapest when you're a member, provide your own

---

Sleep Code

(7 kr = about $1, country code: 46, area code: 08)
S = Single, **D** = Double/Twin, **T** = Triple, **Q** = Quad, **b** = bathroom, **s** = shower. Unless otherwise noted, all of my listings have non-smoking rooms and elevators, accept credit cards, and include big breakfast buffets. Everyone speaks English.

To help you sort easily through these listings, I've divided the rooms into three categories, based on the price for a standard double room with bath during high season:

$$$ **Higher Priced**—Most rooms more than 1,600 kr.
 $$ **Moderately Priced**—Most rooms between 800–1,600 kr.
  $ **Lower Priced**—Most rooms 800 kr or less.

sheets, and buy your own food for breakfast.

Through a program called **Stockholm à la Carte,** you can reserve off-peak (weekend and summer) hotel rooms and get a Stockholm à la Carte card thrown in for free. This includes free public transportation, and sightseeing discounts almost as good as the Stockholm Card (though not including the *Vasa* Museum). You can sign up for Stockholm à la Carte by phone or online (tel. 08/663-0080, www.destination-stockholm.com).

In Downtown Norrmalm, near the Train Station

$$$ **Freys Hotel** is a Scan-mod, four-star place, with 124 compact, smartly designed rooms on a quiet pedestrian street. While big, it works hard to be friendly and welcoming. It's well situated, located on a dead-end street across from the central train station. Its cool, candlelit breakfast room becomes a bar in the evening, popular for its selection of Belgian microbrews (Sb-1,700/895 kr, Db-1,900/1,290 kr, Bryggargatan 12, tel. 08/5062-1300, fax 08/5062-1313, www.freyshotels.com, freys@freyshotels.com). Check their Web site for summer specials.

$$$ **Central Hotel,** right across from the train station, is futuristic, with small, plush rooms and tight security (Sb-1,625/995 kr, Db-1,895/1,295 kr, extra bed-300 kr, garage-275 kr/day, Vasagatan 38, tel. 08/5662-0800, fax 08/247-573, www.profilhotels.se). There are often deep discounts for this hotel on Expedia.com.

$$$ **Rica Hotel Kungsgatan,** central but characterless, fills the top floors of a downsized department store with 270 rooms. If the starship *Enterprise* had a low-end hotel, this would be it. Save money by taking a room with no windows. Save even more by taking a room with no bed (Sb-1,650/920 kr, windowless Sb-1,195/720 kr, Db-1,900/1,345 kr, windowless Db-1,445/990 kr, Kungsgatan 47, tel. 08/723-7220, fax 08/723-7299, www.rica.se). The windowless rooms are the same size as others, extremely quiet, and well-ventilated. (I was kidding about rooms with no beds.)

$$ **Queen's Hotel,** a 10-minute walk from the station on a fine pedestrian street, is a bit rough around the edges but has a plush Old World lounge and a great location. The 32 rooms—18 with a private shower and toilet, 14 without private facilities—are scattered throughout an old apartment building and vary widely in amenities (S-795 kr, Sb-995/895 kr, D-850 kr, Db-1,100/995 kr, better Db-1,490/1,350 kr, extra bed-250 kr, Drottninggatan 71A, tel. 08/249-460, fax 08/217-620, www.queenshotel.se, info @queenshotel.se). The manager, Aron, promises a 10 percent discount to those who book directly with this book through 2007, so be sure to ask.

$ **City Backpackers** is central—a quarter-mile from the station—and open year-round. It's enthusiastically run, with

Stockholm Hotels

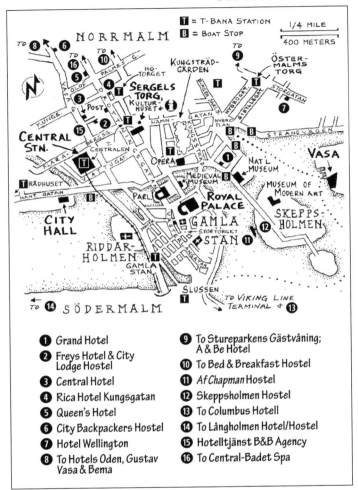

T = T-BANA STATION
B = BOAT STOP
1/4 MILE
400 METERS

NORRMALM

KUNGSTRÄD-GÅRDEN

ÖSTER-MALMS TORG

SERGELS TORG, KULTUR-HUSET

CENTRAL STN.

VASA

RÅDHUSET

CITY HALL

MEDIEVAL MUSEUM

NAT'L MUSEUM

MUSEUM OF MODERN ART

ROYAL PALACE

SKEPPS-HOLMEN

RIDDAR-HOLMEN

GAMLA STAN

SÖDERMALM

SLUSSEN

TO VIKING LINE TERMINAL

❶ Grand Hotel
❷ Freys Hotel & City Lodge Hostel
❸ Central Hotel
❹ Rica Hotel Kungsgatan
❺ Queen's Hotel
❻ City Backpackers Hostel
❼ Hotel Wellington
❽ To Hotels Oden, Gustav Vasa & Bema

❾ To Stureparkens Gästvåning; A & Be Hotel
❿ To Bed & Breakfast Hostel
⓫ Af Chapman Hostel
⓬ Skeppsholmen Hostel
⓭ To Columbus Hotell
⓮ To Långholmen Hotel/Hostel
⓯ Hotelltjänst B&B Agency
⓰ To Central-Badet Spa

100 beds and plenty of creativity (bunk in 8-bed room-210 kr, in quad-240 kr, bunk-bed D-560 kr, sheets-50 kr, free coffee and tea but no breakfast, laundry, free Internet access and Wi-Fi, movies, sauna, lockers, kitchen, shoes-off policy, Upplandsgatan 2A, tel. 08/206-920, fax 08/100-464, www.citybackpackers.se, info @citybackpackers.se).

$ City Lodge Hostel, new and well-run, is just a block in front of the central station on a quiet side street. It has a convivial lounge, kitchen, Internet access, and no curfew. It's a good value for Stockholm (beds in 16-bed dorm—175 kr, in 6-bed dorm—

230 kr, a few tiny bunk-bed doubles—550–700 kr, sheets-50 kr, reception open daily 9:00–20:00, Klara Norra Kyrkogata 15, tel. 08/226-630, www.citylodge.se, info@citylodge.se).

On Norrmalm, in Quieter Residential Areas

These options are in stately, elegant neighborhoods of five- and six-story turn-of-the-century apartment buildings. All are too far to walk from the station with luggage, but still in easy reach of downtown sights and close to T-bana stops.

$$$ Hotel Wellington, two blocks off Östermalmstorg square, is in a less-handy but charming part of town. It's modern and bright, with hardwood floors, 60 rooms, and a friendly welcome. While more expensive than the others, this hotel is a cut above in comfort (Db-2,330/1,600 kr, fill out their Choice Card and save 10 percent, mention this book when reserving and you might save a little more, Internet access, sauna, old-fashioned English bar; T-bana: Östermalmstorg, exit to Storgatan and walk toward big church to Storgatan 6; tel. 08/667-0910, fax 08/667-1254, www.wellington.se, cc.wellington@choice.se).

$$ Hotel Oden, a recently renovated 140-room place with all the comforts, is three T-bana stops from the train station (Sb-1,250/870 kr, Db-1,560/1,050 kr, extra bed-150 kr, sauna, Internet access, free coffee and tea in the evening; T-bana: Odenplan, exit in direction of Västmannagatan, Karlbergsvägen 24; tel. 08/457-9700, fax 08/457-9710, www.hoteloden.se). Some rooms come with a kitchenette for the same price (just request one).

$$ Hotel Gustav Vasa, a half block from Hotel Oden (and not as good), rents 42 rooms on several floors of a late-19th-century apartment building (S-695/595 kr, Sb-1,050/850 kr, Db-1,450/950 kr, T-bana: Odenplan, Västmannagatan 61, tel. 08/343-801, fax 08/307-372, www.gustavvasahotel.se, info@gustavvasahotel.se).

$$ Stureparkens Gästvåning, carefully run by Jan Lönnberg, is one floor of an apartment building converted into nine bright, clean, quiet, and thoughtfully appointed rooms. Only two rooms have a private bath (S-550 kr, D-895 kr, Db-995 kr, sprawling Db apartment-1,500 kr, extra bed-195 kr, 2-night minimum, kitchen; T-bana: Stadion, across from Stureparken at Sturegatan 58, take elevator to fourth floor; tel. 08/662-7230, fax 08/661-5713, www.stureparkens.nu, info@stureparkens.nu).

$$ Hotel Bema is a humble place that rents out 12 fine rooms for some of the best prices in town (twin Db-950/750 kr, bigger Db-1,050/850 kr, extra person-250 kr, breakfast in room, bus #65 from station to Upplandsgatan 13, tel. 08/232-675, www.hotelbema.se, hotell.bema@stockholm.mail.telia.com).

$$ At A & Be Hotel, with 12 homey rooms, the coffee's always on. The hotel fills the first floor of a grand old building in a residential section of town (S-540 kr, Ss-790 kr, Sb-840 kr, D-690 kr, Ds-890 kr, Db-990 kr, breakfast-50 kr, T-bana: Stadion or Östermalmstorg, Grev Turegatan 50, tel. 08/660-2100, fax 08/660-5987, www.abehotel.com, info@abehotel.com).

$ **Bed and Breakfast** is a tiny, woody, and easygoing independent hostel renting 39 cheap beds (195–220 kr per bunk in 4- to 10-bed rooms, tiny windowless S-390 kr, tiny windowless bunk bed D-530 kr, sheets-50 kr, kitchen, laundry, across the street from T-bana: Rådmansgatan, just off Sveavägen at Rehnsgatan 21, tel. & fax 08/152-838, www.hostelbedandbreakfast.com). From June to August, they also rent bunks in the nearby "Hole in the Ground," a 30-bed hall, for 135 kr a night.

On Gamla Stan and Skeppsholmen

These options are in the midst of sightseeing, a short bus or taxi ride from the train station. For the first two hotels, see the map on page 300. For the rest, see page 296.

$$$ **Rica Hotel Gamla Stan** offers rustic Old World elegance in the heart of Gamla Stan (a 5-min walk from Gamla Stan T-bana station). Its 51 small rooms are filled with chandeliers and hardwood floors (Sb-1,710/950 kr, Db-1,960/1,590 kr, 200 kr extra for larger room, Lilla Nygatan 25, tel. 08/723-7250, fax 08/723-7259, www.rica.se, info.gamlastan@rica.se).

$$$ **Lady Hamilton Hotel,** expensive and lavishly furnished, is shoehorned into Gamla Stan on a quiet street a block below the cathedral and Royal Palace. The centuries-old building has 34 small, plush rooms, and is filled with antiques and thoughtful touches (Db-2,350–2,550/1,700–1,900 kr, breakfast-140 kr, sauna, Storkyrkobrinken 5, tel. 08/5064-0100, fax 08/5064-0110, www.ladyhamiltonhotel.se, info@ladyhamiltonhotel.se).

$ *Af Chapman* **Hostel,** which likely will be closed through 2007 for a major renovation, is Europe's most famous youth hostel. After renovation, this 100-year-old cutter ship, permanently moored at Skeppsholmen island, will be open all year, with 140 beds in two- to 10-bed staterooms (lockout daily 11:00–15:00). The good ship has a rough, tight, and "bend your head, mate" clipper-ship ambience. Reception is at Skeppsholmen Hostel (see below).

$ **Skeppsholmen Hostel,** just ashore from the *Af Chapman* (above), has better facilities and smaller rooms (160 beds in 2- to 6-bed rooms plus one 17-bed dorm, no lockout during day; rates for both hostels: bunk in 3- to 10-bed room-245 kr, in 17-bed dorm-200 kr, D-500 kr, 45 kr less for hostel members, sheets-65 kr, breakfast-70 kr, laundry service, bus #65 from station or walk about 20 min, tel. 08/463-2266, fax 08/611-7155, www.stfchapman.com, info@chapman.stfturist.se).

On or near Södermalm

Södermalm is residential and hip, with Stockholm's best café and bar scene. You'll need to take the bus or T-bana to get here from the train station.

$$ Columbus Hotell—located in a 19th-century building that formerly housed a brewery, a jail, and a hospital—has 69 quiet rooms in the heart of Södermalm. Half of its rooms (first and second floors) have private facilities. Third-floor rooms have facilities down the hall (S-695 kr, Sb-1,250/950 kr, D-895 kr, Db-1,550/1,250 kr, T-1,095 kr, discounts on their Web site, no elevator; T-bana: Medborgarplatsen or bus #53 from train station to Tjärhovsplan, then a 5-min walk to Tjärhovsgatan 11; tel. 08/5031-1200, fax 08/5031-1201, www.columbushotell.se, columbus @columbushotell.se).

$$ Långholmen Hotel/Hostel is on Långholmen, a small island off of Södermalm that was transformed in the 1980s from Stockholm's main prison into a lovely park. Rooms are converted cells in the old prison building. You can choose between hostel- and hotel-standard rooms at many different price levels (hostel rooms: dorm bed-250 kr, D-585 kr, Db-685 kr, Q-1,000 kr, Qb-1,100 kr, 45-kr discount for hostel members, sheets-55 kr, breakfast-80 kr; hotel rooms: Sb-995–1,290/880 kr, Db-1,590/1,290 kr, extra bed-250 kr, includes breakfast; laundry room, kitchen, cafeteria, free parking, on-site swimming, T-bana: Hornstull, then walk 10 min down and cross small bridge to Långholmen island and follow hotel signs 5 min further, tel. 08/720-8500, fax 08/720-8575, www.langholmen.com).

Rooms in Private Homes

Stockholm's private rooms can be a deal in high season if you want to have an at-home experience. During hotels' weekend/summer discount periods, private rooms don't save you much over a hotel. Be sure to get the front-door security code when you call, as there's no intercom. Contact **Hotelltjänst,** a B&B booking agency (S-400 kr, D-600 kr, cash only, no breakfast, 2-night minimum; fully furnished apartments also available: 700 kr for one person, 900 kr for two; Nybrogatan 44, near train station, tel. 08/104-437, fax 08/213-716, www.hotelltjanst.com).

EATING

To save money, eat your main meal at lunch, when cafés and restaurants have 75-kr daily special plates *(dagens rätt)*. Most museums have handy cafés (with lots of turnover and therefore fresh food, 100-kr lunch deals, and often with fine views). Convenience stores

Gamla Stan Hotels and Restaurants

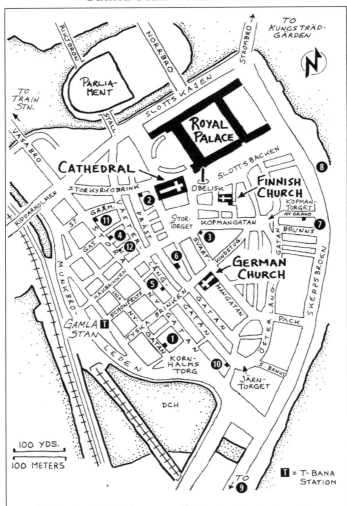

100 YDS.
100 METERS

T = T-BANA STATION

❶ Rica Hotel Gamla Stan
❷ Lady Hamilton Hotel
❸ Grillska Huset Cafeteria
❹ Hermitage Restaurant & Wirtstroms Irish Pub
❺ Glenfiddich Warehouse Restaurant & Bar
❻ Kryp In Restaurant

❼ Fem Små Hus Restaurant
❽ Pontus by the Sea & Brannvin
❾ To Patricia Rest. & Party Boat
❿ Konsum Supermarket
⓫ Stampen Jazz Club
⓬ O'Connells Irish Pub

serve gas station-style food (often with seats). Picnics are a great option—especially for dinner, when restaurant prices are highest.

In Gamla Stan

Most restaurants in Gamla Stan serve the 75-kr weekday lunch special mentioned above, which comes with a main dish, small salad, bread, and free tap water. Choose from Swedish, Asian, or Italian foods. Several popular places are right on Stortorget, the main square. Järntorget, at the far end, is another fun tables-in-the-square scene, and has a small Konsum supermarket for picnic shopping. Touristy places line Västerlånggatan. You'll find more romantic places hiding on side lanes. Here are my favorites (for locations, see the map on page 300):

Grillska Huset is a cheap and handy cafeteria run by Stockholms Stadsmission, a charitable organization for the poor. It's on the old square, with great indoor and outdoor seating (tranquil garden up the stairs and out back), fine daily specials (listed in Swedish only), a hearty salad bar, and a staff committed to helping others. You can feed the hungry (that's you) and help house the homeless at the same time. The 75-kr daily special—available Mon–Fri 11:00–14:00—gets you a hot plate, salad bar, and coffee (restaurant serves daily 11:00–18:00, 65-kr salad bar closes at 14:00, Stortorget 3, tel. 08/787-8605). They also have a fine little bakery.

Hermitage Restaurant serves tasty vegetarian food. Their daily special (only 70 kr, 85 kr after 15:00 and on weekends) buys a hot plate, salad, bread, and coffee (Mon–Sat 11:00–20:00, Sun 12:00–20:00, Stora Nygatan 11, tel. 08/411-9500).

Glenfiddich Warehouse Restaurant and Bar is popular for the 16 Swedish microbrews and long list of Scotch whisky it offers. But behind its long, classic bar is a small, elegant restaurant with a woody, noisy-yet-relaxed atmosphere. Under an Old World painted leather ceiling, the staff serves good Swedish cuisine (200-kr plates, 400-kr fixed-price meal, open from 16:30 daily, on the touristy strip in Gamla Stan at Västerlånggatan 68, tel. 08/791-9090).

Kryp In, a small, cozy restaurant tucked into a peaceful lane, has a stylish hardwood and candlelit interior and great sidewalk seating. They serve delicious, modern Swedish cuisine with a 345-kr three-course dinner. From June to August they have 120-kr weekend lunch specials (200–250 kr plates, Mon–Fri 17:00–23:00,

Sat 12:30–23:00, Sun 12:30–22:00, Prästgatan 17, tel. 08/208-841, reserve for dinner).

Fem Små Hus is a fancy Gamla Stan splurge, with candles leading you into a 16th-century cellar, where dressy diners are enjoying top-end modern Swedish cuisine (375- and 465-kr three-course meals, daily 17:00–24:00, Nygränd 10, tel. 08/108-775).

Royal *Smörgåsbord* at the Grand Hotel

To stuff yourself with all the traditional Swedish specialties (a dozen kinds of herring, salmon, reindeer, meatballs, lingonberries, and shrimp, followed by a fine table of cheeses and desserts) with a super harbor view, consider splurging for Stockholm's best *smörgåsbord* at the Grand Hotel's dressy **Grand Veranda Restaurant.** The Grand Hotel, where royal guests and Nobel Prize winners stay, faces the harbor across from the palace (380 kr, tap water is free, other drinks extra, nightly 18:00–22:00, Sat–Sun also 13:00–16:00, May–Sept also Mon–Fri 12:00–15:00, reservations necessary, no shorts, Södra Blasieholmshamnen 8, tel. 08/679-3586). Pick up their English flier for a good explanation of the proper way to enjoy this grand buffet.

Eating on the Water

Pontus by the Sea is a classy restaurant with a long, covered, and heated veranda offering grand harbor views. Pontus is well-respected for its modern mix of French and Swedish cuisine. Half the place is a sofas-on-the-harbor cocktail lounge. Call to reserve a harborside table (daily from 17:00 until late, Tullhus 2, tel. 08/202-095).

Brannvin Restaurant serves traditional and modern Swedish meals on a heated veranda with a harbor view (70–120-kr lunch specials, 125–240-kr dinner plates, Mon–Sat 12:00–21:30, closed Sun, Tullhus 2, tel. 08/225-755).

Patricia **Restaurant and Party Boat** is a fun, raucous place to enjoy a basic Swedish meal surrounded by good-time Swedes. The menu on this old steamer is a fun-loving surf-and-turf mix, with 200-kr plates and a 99-kr lobster feed on Wednesday nights. The boat has one deck packed with dinner tables, a bar on the top deck, and two dance zones below: one that's a *schlager* pop bar and dance floor, and the other that's a late-night disco (free, with music from 21:00). The boat really rocks with live music on weekends. Consider having dinner or going late just for drinks and dancing (Wed–Sun from 17:00 until late, gay night on Sun, closed Mon–Tue, 200 yards past Djurgården boat dock, near Slussen at Stadsgårdskajen 152, tel. 08/743-0570, www.patricia.st).

Djurgårdsbrons Sjöcafe is a simple bike-rental hut that serves basic plates in a great, casual waterfront setting with tables on a

Savoring a Swedish *Smörgåsbord*

The *smörgåsbord* is probably the only well-known Swedish (and Scandinavian) culinary tradition. While Swedes celebrate with food for holidays and other festive occasions, travelers can sample the smörgåsbord any time of year. Good smörgåsbord opportunities are at the Grand Hotel in Stockholm and Oslo, and on the overnight boats between Stockholm and Helsinki or Copenhagen and Oslo.

"Smörgåsbord" translates to something like "bread and butter table." It has evolved over the centuries to the elaborate spread seen today. A modern smörgåsbord is best served with an ice-cold shot of vodka or Sweden's other local fire waters: *brännvin* or *aquavit*, spirits distilled from grains or potatoes and flavored with herbs and spices. (Try a shot along with your meal.)

Here are seven simple steps to a *smaklig* (tasty) smörgåsbord:

1. Browse the buffet before you begin, so you can budget your stomach space. Think of the smörgåsbord as a four- to six-course meal.

2. Don't overload your plate. Instead, make several trips, taking a fresh plate and cutlery each time. To signal the waiter that you're finished with each round, lay your fork and knife side-by-side on the plate. If you're getting up but not are finished with your plate, place your fork and knife (in the shape of an *X*) on the plate.

3. Begin with the herring dishes, along with boiled potatoes and *knäckebröd* (Swedish crisp bread).

4. Next, sample the other fish dishes (warm and cold) and more potatoes. *Gravlax* is salt-cured salmon flavored with dill, served along with a sweet mustard sauce *(gravlax senap)*.

5. Move on to salads, egg dishes, and various cold cuts. Don't forget more potatoes and *knäckebröd*.

6. Now for the meat dishes—it's meatball time! Pour on some gravy as well as a spoonful of lingonberry sauce, and load up on more potatoes. Other roast meats and poultry may also tempt you.

7. Still hungry? Load up on cheese, fruit, desserts, cakes, custards, and coffee.

   Smaklig måltid! Enjoy your meal!

dock (plates from 100 kr, daily, just over Djurgårdsbron Bridge, tel. 08/661-4488). This is a handy stop after your Skansen or *Vasa* visit.

Dinner Cruises: Several ships sail nightly from Strandvägen, offering three-course dinners during a scenic 2.5- to 5-hour cruise (425 kr regardless of which trip you choose, drinks extra, departing daily 17:30 and 19:00, tel. 08/5871-4000, www .strommakanalbolaget.com).

On Norrmalm

At the Royal Opera House: The Operakällaren, one of Stockholm's most exclusive restaurants, runs a little "hip pocket" restaurant called **Backfickan** on the side, specializing in traditional Swedish quality cooking at reasonable prices. It's ideal for someone eating out alone or for anyone wanting an early dinner (they serve daily specials from 12:00 all the way up to 20:00). Sit inside—at tiny private sidetables or at the big counter with the locals—or, in good weather, grab a table on the sidewalk. Choose from two to four different daily specials (about 110–150 kr) or pay 170–220 kr for main dishes from their regular menu (Mon–Sat 12:00–23:30, closed Sun, on the inland side of Royal Opera House, tel. 08/676-5809).

At or near Hötorget: Hötorget ("Hay Market") now feeds people instead of horses. This vibrant outdoor produce market, just two blocks from Sergels Torg, is a fun place to picnic-shop. The outdoor market closes at 18:00, and many merchants put their unsold produce on the push list (earlier closing and more desperate merchants on Sat). **Hötorgshallen,** next to Hötorget (in the basement under the modern cinema complex), is a colorful indoor food market with an old-fashioned bustle, plenty of exotic and ethnic edibles, and—in the tradition of food markets all over Europe—some great little eateries. The best is **Kajsas Fisk Restaurang,** hiding behind the fish stalls. Owner Monica dishes out delicious fish soup to little Olivers who can hardly believe they're getting... more. For 75 kr, you get a big bowl of her hearty soup (includes one refill), plus a simple salad, bread and crackers, butter, and water. They also do 70–85-kr daily fish specials (Mon–Fri 11:00–18:00, Sat 11:00–15:00, closed Sun, Hötorgshallen 3, tel. 08/207-262).

Kungshallen, an 800-seat indoor food court across the street from Hötorget, has 14 eateries—mostly chain restaurants and fast-food counters, including Chinese, sushi, pizza, Greek, and Mexican (daily 9:00–23:00).

Restaurang Drottninggatan is a busy place with tables perfectly positioned for people-watching on the busy pedestrian boulevard (hearty 100–200-kr plates, daily, Drottninggatan 67, tel. 08/227-522).

Near Sergels Torg: The many modern shopping malls and

Fika: **Sweden's Coffee Break**

Swedes drink more coffee per capita than just about any other country in the world. The Swedish coffee break—or *fika*—is a ritual. Fika is to Sweden what teatime is to Britain. The typical fika is a morning or afternoon break in the workday, but can happen any time, any day. It's the perfect opportunity (and excuse) for tourists to take a break as well.

Fika-fare is coffee with a snack—something sweet or savory. Your best bet is a *kanelbulle,* a Swedish cinnamon bun. These can be found nearly everywhere coffee is sold, including just about any café or *konditori* (bakery) in Stockholm. A coffee (usually with a refill) and a cinnamon bun in a café will cost you about 30 kr. But at Pressbyran, the Swedish convenience stores found all over town, you can satisfy your fika-fix for 15 kr by getting a coffee and bun to go. Grab a park bench or waterside perch, relax, and enjoy.

---

department stores around Sergels Torg all have appealing-if-pricey eateries catering to the needs of hungry local shoppers. **Åhléns** department store has a Hemköp supermarket in the basement (Mon–Fri 8:00–21:00, Sat–Sun 10:00–21:00) and two fine cafeterias upstairs with 79-kr daily specials—Swedish on the second floor (Mon–Sat 10:00–17:00, Sun 11:00–17:00) and Italian on the fourth floor (Mon–Fri 11:00–19:30, Sat 11:00–18:30, Sun 11:00–17:30).

In Östermalm: **Saluhall,** on Östermalmstorg square (near recommended Hotel Wellington), is a great old-time indoor market with plenty of fun eateries (Mon–Fri 9:30–18:00, Sat 9:30–14:00, closed Sun). Upstairs, the **Örtagården** vegetarian restaurant serves a 75-kr buffet weekdays until 16:30, and a larger 125-kr buffet evenings and weekends (Mon–Sat 10:30–21:00, closed Sun, Nybrogatan 31, tel. 08/662-1728).

TRANSPORTATION CONNECTIONS

By Bus

Unless you have a railpass, long-distance buses are cheaper than trains and preferable on some routes, such as from Stockholm to Oslo or Kalmar. Buses usually take longer, but have more predictable pricing, shorter ticket lines, and student discounts. Swebus is the largest operator (tel. 020-021-8218, www.swebusexpress.se); Säfflebussen also has lots of routes, including to Oslo (www.safflebussen .se). It's worth knowing about discount offers: buy tickets at least 24 hours ahead for Swebus discounts; Säfflebussen cuts ticket prices on low-demand days and times.

From Stockholm by Bus to: **Copenhagen** (2/day, 9–16 hrs, 540–640 kr), **Oslo** (7/day, 7–12 hrs, 400–600 kr), **Kalmar** (3/day, 6 hrs, 260 kr).

By Train

The easiest and cheapest way to book train tickets is online at

www.sj.se. Simply select your journey and pay for it with a credit card. When you arrive at the train station, print out your tickets at a self-service ticket kiosk (bring your purchase confirmation code). You can also buy tickets at a ticket window in a train station, but this comes with long lines and a five percent surcharge. For timetables and prices, check the Web, call 0771/757-575, or use one of the self-service ticket kiosks. (Tourists can't purchase tickets on the phone or at a kiosk, however; this requires a locally issued credit card.)

As with airline tickets, Swedish train ticket prices vary with demand. I've listed the base price for each destination, but ask for the *"Just nu"* ("Just now") fare, which can earn you up to a 60 percent discount if you book far enough in advance.

For railpass holders, seat reservations are required on express (X2000) and overnight trains, and recommended on some other trains (to Oslo, for example). Second-class seat reservations to Copenhagen cost 62 kr (143 kr in first class). If you have a railpass, the only way you can make a seat reservation is by going to a ticket window in a train station (not online, by phone, or at self-service ticket kiosks).

From Stockholm by Train to: Copenhagen (almost hourly, 5.5 hrs on X2000 high-speed train, most with a transfer at Malmö Central Station, 1,100 kr, reservation required; overnight service departs at 23:05 and requires a change in Malmö at 6:42; all trains stop at Copenhagen airport before terminating at central station), **Oslo** (2/day, 8–9 hrs, with a change in Göteborg and likely also Halden; plus a direct 8.75-hour night train that doesn't run every night). For details on travel to Växjö or Kalmar, see the South Sweden chapter, page 310.

By Boat

The boat companies run shuttle buses from the train station to coincide with each departure; check for details when you buy your ticket.

From Stockholm to: Helsinki and Tallinn (daily/nightly boats, 16 hrs, see Helsinki and Tallinn chapters), **Turku** (daily/nightly boats, 11 hrs).

By Plane

To Helsinki and Tallinn: The boat trip to Helsinki or Tallinn takes 16 hours. Though less romantic, flying is faster, and inexpensive now that many low-fare airlines (such as www.flysnowflake .com) are offering flights across the Baltic. For flights from Stockholm to Helsinki, also check www.blue1.com; to Tallinn, also visit www.flynordic.com and www.estonian-air.com. When comparing prices between boats and planes, remember that the boat fare includes a night's lodging.

Route Tips for Drivers

Stockholm to Oslo: It's a 7.75-hour drive from Stockholm to Oslo. Årjäng, just before the Norwegian border, is a good place for a rest stop. At the border, change money at the little TI kiosk (on right side). Pick up the Oslo map and *What's on in Oslo*, and consider buying your Oslo Card here.

Near Stockholm: Uppsala

Uppsala is a compact city with a cathedral and university that win Sweden's "oldest/largest/tallest" awards. If you're not traveling anywhere else in Sweden other than Stockholm, Uppsala makes a pleasant day trip. But if you're short on time, Uppsala is not worth sacrificing time in Stockholm or a boat trip to the archipelago. To reach Uppsala, take the train from Stockholm's central station (1–3/hr, 40 min, 48–64 kr, buy tickets at ticket windows). If you visit, allow the better part of a day, including the trip out and back. During summer vacations, the town is very quiet.

Tourist Information: The TI has free maps and sightseeing info (mid-June–Aug Mon–Fri 10:00–18:00, Sat 10:00–15:00, Sun 12:00–16:00; Sept–mid-June closed Sun, Fyristorg 8, tel. 018/727-4800, fax 018/132-895, www.uppland.nu).

Arrival in Uppsala: From the train station, walk straight out the front door, go three blocks, and you'll reach the river. Turn right and walk to the second bridge. Just across the bridge is the TI; the university and cathedral are behind it. To your right, on the train station side of the river, is the bustling shopping zone. In the middle of the shopping zone is Storatorget, the main square.

SIGHTS

▲▲**Uppsala Cathedral**—One of Scandinavia's largest, most historic cathedrals, it has a fine Gothic interior, with the tomb of King Gustav Vasa at the very end. The building was completed in 1453; the spires and interior decorations are from the 19th century.

Inside, pick up the 10-kr leaflet explaining each chapel, and ask about a guided tour in English (late June–mid-Sept usually Mon–Sat at 11:00 and 14:00, Sun at 16:00; church entry free, daily 8:00–18:00).

University—Scandinavia's first university was founded here in 1477. Linnaeus and Celsius are two famous grads. Directly across from the cathedral is the **Gustavianum,** the university's oldest surviving building and now a museum (40 kr, Tue–Sun 10:00–16:00, closed Mon). Inside, the anatomy theater is thought-provoking. Its only show was a human dissection. Up the hill is **Carolina Rediviva,** Uppsala University's library. Off the entry hall, a small exhibit of treasured old books includes the sixth-century Silver Bible, named for its silver-ink writing in the extinct Gothic language (20 kr, mid-May–Aug Mon–Fri 9:00–17:00, Sat 10:00–17:00, Sun 11:00–16:00; free Sept–mid-May Mon–Fri 9:00–20:00, Sat 10:00–17:00, closed Sun). Most other university buildings are closed to non-students.

Near the University: **Uppland Museum** (Upplandsmuseet), a regional history museum with prehistoric bits and folk-art scraps, is on the river by the waterfall, near the TI (free, Tue–Sun 12:00–17:00, closed Mon). Uphill from the university library are the **botanical gardens** and museum named after Linnaeus, and the 16th-century **Uppsala Castle,** which houses an art museum and runs slice-of-castle-life tours (60 kr, daily June–late Aug at 13:00 and 15:00, entry only possible with a tour, tel. 018/727-2485).

▲**Gamla Uppsala**—This site, which gives historians goosebumps even on a sunny day, includes nine large royal burial mounds circled by a walking path with English descriptions. Fifteen hundred years ago, when the Baltic Sea was higher and it was easy to sail all the way to Uppsala, the pagan Swedish kings had their capital here. The attractive Visitors Center gives a good overview

of early Swedish history and displays items found in the mounds (50 kr, May–Aug daily 11:00–17:00; Sept–April Wed and Sat–Sun 12:00–15:00, closed Mon–Tue and Thu–Fri; guided tours available in summer, tel. 018/239-300, www.raa.se/gamlauppsala). The venerable Gamla Uppsala church dates to the 12th century (free, daily

April–Sept 9:00–18:00, Oct–March 9:00–16:00).

Gamla Uppsala is great for picnics, or you can recharge at the half-timbered Odinsborg café, which serves sandwiches, mead, and a 150-kr all-you-can-eat buffet lunch (in summer daily 12:00–18:00, tel. 018/323-525). To reach Gamla Uppsala from downtown Uppsala, go to the bus stop at Vaksalagatan 7–13 (a block and a half from Storatorget, the main square) and take bus #2, marked "Gamla Uppsala," to the last stop (20 kr, pay driver, runs every 40 min). Allow two or three hours for your visit, including the time it takes to bus there and back.

EATING

Eateries abound along the river and in the business district. Riverside **Kung Kral,** near the cathedral, has 90-kr weekday lunch specials, 125–220-kr main dishes, and outdoor seating in a little square. Ask about their five-shot sampler of Swedish firewater (St. Persgatan 4, Mon–Fri 11:30–22:00, Sat 12:00–22:00, Sun 13:00–22:00, tel. 018/125-090). You can pack a picnic and enjoy one of Uppsala's parks or join the locals down on the boardwalk along the river, below St. Olov's Bridge. For picnic fixings, stop by **Hemkop,** a grocery located on the ground floor of Åhléns department store, on Storatorget.

SOUTH SWEDEN

Växjö and Kalmar

Outside of Stockholm, the southeastern province of Småland is the most interesting region in Sweden. More Americans came from this area than any other part of Scandinavia, and the emigration center in Växjö tells the story well. Between Växjö and Kalmar is Glass Country, a 70-mile stretch of forest sparkling with glassworks that welcome guests to tour and shop. Historic Kalmar has a rare Old World ambience and the most magnificent medieval castle in Scandinavia. From Kalmar, you can cross one of Europe's longest bridges to hike through the Stonehenge-like mysteries of the strange island of Öland.

Planning Your Time

By train, on a three-week Scandinavian trip, I'd skip this area in favor of the direct, high-speed train from Copenhagen to Stockholm, or the night train from Malmö (just over the Øresund Bridge from Copenhagen) to Stockholm. Side-trips from Stockholm to Helsinki and Tallinn merit more time than this part of Sweden does.

But if you're driving or have extra time, the sights described in this section are an interesting way to spend a couple of days. While I'm not so hot on the Swedish countryside (OK, blame my Norwegian heritage), you can't see only Stockholm and say you've seen Sweden. Växjö and Kalmar give you the best possible dose of small-town Sweden. (I find Lund and Malmö, both popular side-trips from Copenhagen, relatively dull. And I'm not old or sedate enough to find a sleepy boat trip along the much-loved Göta Canal appealing.)

South Sweden

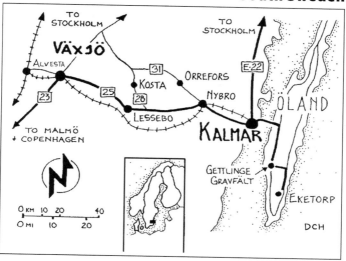

Drivers can spend three days getting from Copenhagen to Stockholm this way:

Day 1: Leave Copenhagen after breakfast, drive over the bridge to Sweden and on to Växjö, tour Växjö's House of Emigrants, drive into Glass Country, tour Kosta glassworks, and arrive in Kalmar in time for dinner.

Day 2: Spend the day in Kalmar touring the castle and Kalmar County (Läns) Museum, and browsing through its people-friendly old center.

Day 3: 8:00-Begin five-hour drive north along the coast to Stockholm; 10:30-Break in Västervik; 12:00-Stop in Söderköping for picnic lunch and a walk along the Göta Canal; 13:30-Continue drive north; 16:00-Arrive in Stockholm.

Shorten your stops on Day 3 and you'll arrive in Stockholm in time to make the overnight boat to Tallinn or Helsinki. This is an especially good plan on Sunday through Wednesday in the off-season, when boat fares are cheaper. You can see Stockholm on the way back.

Växjö

A pleasant but sleepy town of 75,000, Växjö (VEK-hwuh) is in the center of Småland. The town center is compact and pedestrian-friendly; the train station, main square, and two important museums are all within two blocks of each other. An enjoyable three-mile path encircles its nearby lake. A farmer's market enlivens the otherwise too-big main square on Wednesday and Saturday mornings. Train travelers not interested in glass can make this a convenient three-hour stopover en route to Kalmar.

Tourist Information: Upon arrival, pick up a map at the train station information desk and you won't need to trek over to the TI, several blocks away in the town library (mid-June–Aug Mon–Fri 9:30–18:00, Sat–Sun 10:00–14:00, closed Sun in late June and late Aug; Sept–mid-June Mon–Fri 9:30–16:30, closed Sat–Sun; free Internet access, Västra Esplanaden 7, tel. 0470/41410, www.turism .vaxjo.se).

Internet Access: The Everlast Internet café, near the train station, has better hours and more computers than the TI (30 kr/hr, June–mid-Aug Mon–Sat 12:00–20:00, Sun 13:00–20:00, shorter hours off-season, Sandgärdsgatan 12).

SIGHTS AND ACTIVITIES

▲▲**House of Emigrants (Utvandrarnas Hus)**—If you have Swedish roots, this tidy museum and archive is really exciting. Even if you don't, it's an interesting stop. The permanent "Dream of America" exhibit tells the story of the "American Fever" that burned in Sweden from the 1850s to the 1920s. In 1900, Chicago was the second-largest Swedish town in the world. Back then, one in six Swedes lived in the US (40 kr, May–Aug Mon–Fri 9:00–17:00, Sat–Sun 11:00–16:00; Sept–April Tue–Fri 9:00–16:00, Sat 11:00–16:00, closed Sun–Mon, tel. 0470/20120, www.swemi.se). Minnesota Day, the second Sunday in August, is a real hoot, as thousands of Minnesotans storm Växjö; it caps a larger festival that starts on Thursday evening. The Liv Ullmann movie about the massive Swedish migration, *The Emigrants,* and its sequel, *The New Land,* make for great pre-trip viewing.

Upstairs is an excellent library and genealogical research center. You're welcome to take a peek. Swedish-American roots-seekers (10,000 a year come from the US) are welcome. First, visit their Web site and make reservations (www.swemi.se). Then print out their research form and send it in with $60 in cash, and they'll get started on researching your family's history in preparation for your arrival (research center services: 150 kr/half-day, 200 kr/day, May–Aug Mon–Fri 9:00–16:00, closed Sat–Sun; Sept–April Tue–Fri 9:00–16:00, closed Sat–Mon).

▲**Swedish Glass and Smålands Museum**—This instructive museum offers a good look at the glass industry (bottom floor), plus exhibits on local forestry and prehistory upstairs (40 kr, Mon–Fri 10:00–17:00, Sat–Sun 11:00–17:00; Sept–May closed Mon, uphill from House of Emigrants, www.smalandsmuseum.se).

Domkyrka—Växjö's striking brick-red church features some fine sacred art—in glass, of course. The thoughtfully written 15-kr brochure describes it well (entry-60 kr, daily 9:00-17:00, www .svenskakyrkanivaxjo.se). The church offers **concerts** on many Thursday evenings in summer (late June–mid-Aug at 20:00).

Linnéparken—This peaceful park, beside the cathedral, is dedicated to the great Swedish botanist Carl von Linné (a.k.a. Carolus Linnaeus). It has an arboretum, lots of well-categorized perennials, and a children's playground.

Swimming—From the House of Emigrants you can look across the lake to the town's modern swimming hall (Simhall), a five-minute walk away (65-kr base price includes sauna; extra if you want to tan, use the exercise room, or rent a towel or locker; call for open-swim hours, tel. 0470/41204).

SLEEPING

As elsewhere in Scandinavia, hotels charge less on Friday and Saturday nights and from late June through early August. When I list two hotel rates, the first is the peak-season rate and the second is the summer/weekend rate.

$$$ Elite Stadshotell is a biggish, modern, business-class hotel with all the comforts. It's in a royal setting on the town's main square (Sb-1,295/695 kr, Db-1,495/845 kr, summer and weekend rates can stretch during slow times, no free parking, a block in front of train station at Kungsgatan 6, tel. 0470/13400, fax 0470/44837, www.elite.se).

$$ Hotell Värend is well-worn but comfortable, inexpensive, and six blocks from the train station along Kungsgatan (24 rooms, Sb-850/550 kr, Db-950/795 kr, Tb-950/795 kr, non-smoking,

---

Sleep Code

(7 kr = about $1, country code: 46, area code: 0470)
S = Single, **D** = Double/Twin, **T** = Triple, **Q** = Quad, **b** = bathroom, **s** = shower. All of these hotels accept credit cards and include breakfast.

To help you sort easily through these listings, I've divided the rooms into three categories, based on the price for a standard double room with bath during high season:

$$$ **Higher Priced**—Most rooms 1,000 kr or more.
$$ **Moderately Priced**—Most rooms between 600–1,000 kr.
$ **Lower Priced**—Most rooms 600 kr or less.

elevator, parking, a block beyond N. Esplanaden at Kungsgatan 27, tel. 0470/776-700, fax 0470/36261, www.hotellvarend.se, info @hotellvarend.se). If driving, follow *Centrum* signs into town from the freeway. At the Royal Corner Hotel, turn left; 200 yards later, at the first light, turn right onto N. Esplanaden, then left onto Kungsgatan.

$$ Hotel Esplanad, nearby, is a bit more modest, with 23 cheaper rooms with shared bath (S-470/350 kr, Sb-720/470 kr, D-570/520 kr, Db-850/670 kr, parking, N. Esplanaden #21A, tel. 0470/22580, fax 0470/26226, www.hotell-esplanad.com). From the train station, walk five blocks up Klostergatan and turn left on N. Esplanaden.

$ *Hostel:* Växjö's fine hostel is near a lake two miles out of town. It's difficult to reach by public transport (200 kr/bed in 2- to 4-bed rooms, D-400 kr, 45-kr discount for members, breakfast-50 kr, reservations required in summer, office open daily 8:00–10:00 & 17:00–20:00, tel. 0470/63070, fax 0470/63216, www .vaxjovandrarhem.nu).

EATING

After-hours Växjö is not very exciting. Consider livening things up by dining out. Elegant **Lagerlunden,** the restaurant in Elite Stadshotell, has 100-kr lunch specials and dinner specials for 150-250 kr (Mon–Fri 11:30–14:00 & 18:00–24:00, Sat 18:00–24:00, closed Sun year-round and for lunch in July). A younger crowd stands in line to see and be seen at **PM,** with good modern cuisine and nice outdoor tables (80-kr lunch specials, dinners from 150 kr, Mon–Sat 11:30–23:00, probably later Fri–Sat, closed Sun, Storgatan 24 at corner of Västergatan, tel. 0470/700-444).

If you're looking to save money, or if it's a Sunday—when other restaurants are closed—visit one of downtown Växjö's dozen or so Asian restaurants and kebab-and-pizza-shops. Of these, **Ali Baba's** is a cut above (Mon–Thu 10:00–22:00, Fri–Sat 12:00–24:00, Sun 12:00–22:00, Sandgärdsgatan 10). **La Gondola,** serving Swedish, Chinese, Thai, and Greek food, is engagingly multinational (Mon–Thu 11:00–22:00, Fri–Sat 12:00–23:00, Sun 12:00–22:00, Storgatan 33).

For groceries, visit the **ICA supermarket** at the corner of Sandgärdsgatan and Klostergatan, one block from the train station (Mon–Fri 8:00–20:00, Sat 8:00–17:00, Sun 11:00–17:00), or **Konsum,** 500 yards from the train station (daily 7:00–22:00).

TRANSPORTATION CONNECTIONS

From Växjö by Train to: Copenhagen 5/day, 3 hrs), **Stockholm** (every 2 hrs, 3.5 hrs, change in Alvesta), **Kalmar** (12/day, 70 min). See the Stockholm chapter (page 264) for information on taking trains in Sweden. Växjö does not have good long-distance bus connections.

Between Växjö and Kalmar

▲▲**Kingdom of Crystal (Glasriket)**—This is Sweden's Glass Country. Frankly, these glassworks *(glasbruk)* cause so much excitement because of the relative rarity of anything else thrilling in Sweden, outside of greater Stockholm. The helpful *Glasriket/ Kingdom of Crystal* brochure (available at any TI) describes the many glassworks that welcome the public with tours and demonstrations. It's an ever-changing scene. Kosta and Orrefors are the most famous places to visit. The Glasriket Pass (95 kr, good for discounts on tours, special events, and exhibitions, sold at glassworks and local TIs) is worthwhile only if you're visiting several glass houses or plan on joining one of the special "Hyttsill" dinners at the glass school. For more information, see www.glasriket.se.

Though there are buses from Växjö to Kosta, the glassworks aren't worth the time and trouble unless you have a car. Train travelers should instead take a careful look at the glass exhibit in the Växjö Museum and then go straight to Kalmar. The drive from Växjö to Kalmar is a 70-mile joy—light traffic with endless forest and lake scenery punctuated by numerous glassworks. The driving time between Växjö and Kosta is 45 minutes; it's another 45 minutes between Kosta and Kalmar.

Kosta boasts the oldest of the *glasbruks,* dating back to 1742. Today, the glassworks are a thriving tourist and shopping center. Watch the glassblowers in action for 20 kr, or for free with a 95-kr *Glasriket* pass (early July–early Aug daily 10:00–16:00; Kosta's shop hours: Mon–Fri 10:00–19:00, Sat–Sun 10:00–17:00, shorter hours off-season; tel. 0478/34500, www.kostaboda.se). Tours start in the historic and glass exhibition rooms, then go to the actual blowing room, where guides are constantly narrating the ongoing work. Tours are free in summer, but off-season you'll have to call in advance to reserve a guided tour in English, and pay an extra fee. You can visit the exhibition hall, blowing room, and, of course, the shop for free all year.

Visitors show the most enthusiasm in the shopping hall, where crystal "seconds" (with tiny bubbles or sets that don't quite match) and discontinued models are sold at good prices. This is duty-free shopping, and they'll happily mail your purchases home. In town, follow signs for Glasbruk.

Orrefors has the most famous of the several renowned glassworks in Glass Country. Tours go twice daily in English at 11:45 and 13:45 (53 kr, free with 95-kr *Glasriket* pass, call to confirm tour times, tel. 0481/34195). Most visitors just observe the work from platforms (20 kr, glassblowing action late May–late Aug Mon–Sat 10:00–15:45, longer hours and open Sun 12:00–16:00 in July). Like Kosta, their shop sells nearly perfect crystal seconds at deep discounts (Mon–Fri 10:00–19:00, Sat–Sun 10:00–17:00, www.orrefors .se). Don't miss the dazzling museum (open same hours as shop).

Transjö Glashytta offers a much different experience. Set up in an old converted farm 10 minutes south of Kosta, this tiny glassworks does expensive but fine art pieces (daily, usually 11:00–17:00, but call ahead, tel. 0478/50700).

Lessebo Paper Mill (Handpappersbruk)—The town of Lessebo has a 300-year-old paper mill that's kept working for visitors to enjoy. If you've never seen handmade paper produced, this mill is worth a visit. Get the English-language brochure (25 kr, Mon–Fri 8:00–16:30, closed Sat–Sun, shorter hours outside of summer; English-language tours at 9:30, 10:30, 13:00, and 14:15 in summer; mill makes paper Mon–Fri 7:00–11:30 & 12:30–15:00—otherwise it's open but dead, tel. 0478/47691). By car, Lessebo is an easy stop between Växjö and Kosta. Just after the Kosta turnoff, you'll see a black-and-white Handpappersbruk sign.

Kalmar

Kalmar feels formerly strategic and important. In its day, the town was the gateway to Sweden—back when the Sweden/Denmark border was just a few miles to the south. Today, it's a bustling small city of 60,000, with 7,000 students in its university and maritime academy. It's now the gateway to the holiday island of Öland. Kalmar's salty old center, fine castle, and busy waterfront give it a wistful sailor's charm. The town is great on foot or by bike.

History students remember Kalmar as the place where the treaty establishing the Kalmar Union was signed. This 1397 "three crowns" treaty united Norway, Sweden, and Denmark and created a huge kingdom. But the union, which was dominated by Denmark, lasted only about a hundred years. When Gustav Vasa came to power in 1523, it was dissolved, and even the European Union hasn't been able to reunify the Scandinavian Peninsula since. Kalmar town was originally next to the castle, but after a huge fire in 1647 it was entirely rebuilt on the nearby island of

Kvarnholmen. There it was encircled by giant Baroque earthworks and bastions, parts of which still survive.

ORIENTATION

Tourist Information

Look for the TI in a modern building by the small-boat harbor, 200 yards from the train station past the end of the tracks. They have helpful brochures and maps of town, and sell a 30-kr brochure, *A Walk around Kalmar*, outlining the town's historical sights, the Old Town, park, and castle (late June–early Aug Mon–Fri 9:00–21:00, Sat–Sun 10:00–17:00; early June and late Aug Mon–Fri 9:00–19:00, Sat–Sun 10:00–16:00; Sept–May Mon–Fri 9:00–17:00, closed Sat–Sun; Internet access–40 kr/hr, tel. 0480/417-700, fax 0480/417-720, www.kalmar.se/turism). They'll book you a room anywhere in Sweden for a 50 kr fee. The building is the Kalmar Maritime Academy. It's built to look like a ship, and its bridge simulator inside is used for training future sailors.

Arrival in Kalmar

Arriving at the combined bus and train station couldn't be easier. Get a reservation for your departure at the station (lockers available). The main, modern area of town (Kvarnholmen) is dead ahead; bikes are to your left; the TI to your right; and the castle behind you.

Helpful Hints

Bike Rental: Kalmar, with its cheery lanes, surrounding parks, and brisk harborfront, makes for happy biking. **Team Sportia,** a big sport shop near the station, rents fine bikes for 100 kr per day (Mon–Fri 10:00–18:00, Sat 10:00–15:00, closed Sun; leaving station, turn left on Stationsgatan and walk 300 yards to roundabout; Södra Vägen 2, tel. 0480/21244). The TI's *Vasa Stigen* flier outlines a pleasant bike/hike past the castle and around the Stensö Peninsula.

SIGHTS

▲▲**Kalmar Castle (Kalmar Slott)**—This moated castle is one of Europe's great medieval experiences. The stark exterior, cuddled by a lush park, houses a fine Renaissance palace interior, which is the work of King Gustav Vasa (r. 1523–1560) and his sons.

Approaching the castle, you'll walk up steps made of Catholic gravestones into the central courtyard, where you'll buy your ticket. Then away you'll go on a circular route through faded but grand halls alive with Swedish history and well-described in

English. The fine architectural details were mostly painted onto the walls—a necessary cost-saving measure in relatively poor Northern Europe. Kalmar Castle was a royal hub until 1658, when the Swedish frontier shifted south and the castle lost its strategic importance (75 kr, June–Aug daily 10:00–17:00, until 18:00 in July; May and Sept daily 10:00–16:00, Oct Sat–Sun 11:00-15:30, Nov–March open only Sat–Sun 11:00–16:00 on second weekend of month, tel. 0480/451-491, www.kalmarslott.kalmar.se). English-language tours are worthwhile for the goofy medieval antics of Sweden's kings (included in admission price, 45 min, offered daily late June–mid-Aug usually at 11:30 and 15:30, reconfirm times by phone or on Web site). Check out the eerie exhibit on the women's prison ("Codex"); find the book with English-language descriptions. Walk around the ramparts. The castle lawn cries out for a picnic.

▲**Krusenstiernska Gården**—Two hundred yards from the castle, this relaxed, kid-friendly garden, with its breezy café selling traditional homemade cakes, is a treat (free, May–Aug Mon–Fri 10:00–18:00, Sat–Sun 12:00–17:00; closed off-season, Stora Dammgatan 11, tel. 0480/411-552). On weekday afternoons, take a guided tour of an early-19th-century upper-middle-class home, which is lovingly cluttered with old family photos, toys, and Gustavian-style furniture. A helpful English-language leaflet gives a room-by-room inventory (tours-25 kr, hourly June–Aug Mon–Fri 13:00–16:00, Sat–Sun 13:00–15:00). Walk the lanes between the garden and the train station. Before the fires in the 1600s, this area was the center of Kalmar. Now it's a toy village of colorfully painted wooden homes, tidy yards, and perfect fences.

▲**Kalmar Town**—Today, downtown Kalmar is on the island of Kvarnholmen. Find lively Larmtorget, near the train station, and then stroll the Storgatan pedestrian street to the main square, Stortorget, and the biggest Baroque church in Sweden. It was built in the 17th century in a grand style befitting a European power. The area beyond Östra Vallgatan (the old eastern wall of the city) has a pleasant park, small swimming beach, and the last remaining *Klapphus* in Kalmar. In the mid-1800s, there were four of these small, wooden buildings—used for washing laundry—at the seaside. Today the *Klapphus* is still used for washing rugs and carpets; take a peek inside and see if anyone is at work. The quieter lanes and Lilla Torget street have fine, old wooden homes. The surviving ramparts mark the old harbor line. The 20th-century extension is filled with parked cars and a modern shopping center.

▲▲**Kalmar County (Läns) Museum**—The third level of this fine harborfront museum displays salvage from the royal ship *Kronan*, which exploded and sank in a battle near Kalmar in 1676. Lots of interesting soggy bits and rusted pieces giving a here's-the-buried-

Kalmar

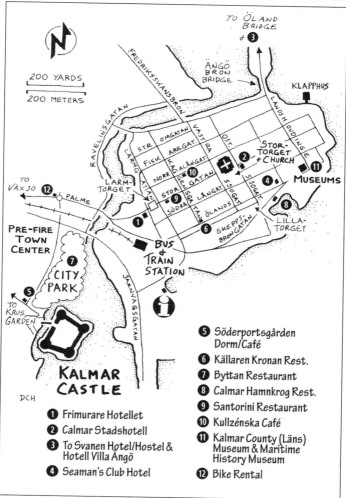

N

200 YARDS
200 METERS

TO ÖLAND BRIDGE

❸

ÄNGÖ BRON BRIDGE

KLAPPHUS

FREDRIKSSKANSBRON

RAVELINSGATAN

LARMGATAN

STR OMGATAN

FISK AREGAT

VASTRA

OST

LANDSHOVDINGE

STOR-TORGET + CHURCH

❷

❶❶ MUSEUMS

NORR KALANGAT

❶⓿ GATAN

STOR SÓTRAN

SÓDRA

LÁNGAT

ÓLANDS

SJÓGAT

SJÓGAT

❹

❽

TO VÄXJÖ ❶❷ PALME

LARM-TORGET

❶

LILLA-TORGET

PRE-FIRE TOWN CENTER

CITY PARK ❼

❺

TO KRUS-GARDEN

JÄRNVÄGSGATAN

BUS & TRAIN STATION

❻ SKEPPS-BRONGATAN

ℹ

KALMAR CASTLE

DCH

❶ Frimurare Hotellet
❷ Calmar Stadshotell
❸ To Svanen Hotel/Hostel & Hotell Villa Ängö
❹ Seaman's Club Hotel

❺ Söderportsgården Dorm/Café
❻ Källaren Kronan Rest.
❼ Byttan Restaurant
❽ Calmar Hamnkrog Rest.
❾ Santorini Restaurant
❶⓿ Kullzénska Café
❶❶ Kalmar County (Läns) Museum & Maritime History Museum
❶❷ Bike Rental

treasure thrill are well-described in English. (For maximum info, borrow the *Kronan* English-language booklet.) This exhibit gives a much more intimate look at life at sea than Stockholm's grander *Vasa* Museum. See the excellent 12-minute film about the ship. The fourth level is worth a quick look for its exhibit on Jenny Nyström (an early-1900s Kalmar artist who gained fame for her cute Christmas illustrations featuring elves and pixies) and a tiny café serving light lunches. The second level has an exhibition on medieval, pre-fire Kalmar. From the museum's door, you can see the distant half of the long bridge leading to the island of Öland (50 kr, late June–mid-Aug daily 10:00–18:00; mid-Aug–late June Mon–Fri 10:00–16:00, Sat–Sun 11:00–16:00, Skeppsbrogatan 51, tel. 0480/451-370, www.kalmarlansmuseum.se).

Maritime History Museum (Sjöfartsmuseum)—This humble little three-room exhibit behind the Kalmar County Museum is a jumble of model boats, charts, and paraphernalia interesting only if you sail or speak Swedish (30 kr, mid-June–mid-Sept daily 11:00–16:00; in off-season only open Sun 12:00–16:00, Södra Långgatan 81, tel. 0480/15875).

▲**Island of Öland**—The island, 90 miles long and only eight miles wide, is a pleasant local resort known for its birds, windmills, flowers, beaches, and prehistoric sights. Sweden's king and queen have their summer home on Öland. Public transportation is miserable, so the island is worthwhile only if you have a car and three extra hours. Until recently, the bridge from Kalmar to the island was Europe's longest (free, 3.7 miles).

A 60-mile circle south of the bridge will give you a good dose of the island's windy rural charm. **Gettlinge Gravfält** (just off the road about 10 miles up from the south tip) is a wonderfully situated, boat-shaped, Iron Age graveyard littered with monoliths and overseen by a couple of creaky old windmills. It offers a commanding view of the windy and mostly treeless island. Farther south is the **Eketorp Prehistoric Fort,** a reconstructed fifth-century stone fort that, as Iron Age forts go, is fairly interesting. Several evocative huts and buildings are filled with what someone imagines may have been the style back then, and the huge rock fort is surrounded by strange, runty, piglike creatures, which were common in gardens 1,500 years ago. A sign reads: "For your convenience and pleasure, don't leave your children alone with the animals" (70 kr, late June–late Aug daily 10:00–18:00; cheaper off-season: 50 kr, late Aug–late June 10:00–17:00; free English-language tours usually daily May–Aug at 14:00, tel. 0485/662-000).

SLEEPING

(8 kr = about $1, country code: 46, area code: 0480)
The TI can nearly always find you a room in a private home (400–500 kr per double, 40 kr per person for sheets, 50 kr fee per booking, no breakfast). They can also get you special last-minute discounts on fancy hotels.

$$$ Frimurare Hotellet fills a grand, old building overlooking a fine square. While quite large, it has soul and is warmly run by Marianne, her daughter Linda, and a disarmingly friendly staff. Rich public areas, broad hardwood halls, chandeliers, and pilasters give it 19th-century elegance. Rooms have been thoughtfully renovated and provide modern comfort (Sb-900 kr, Db-1,110 kr, about 300 kr less on weekends and mid-June–late Aug, these rates promised with this book in 2007, family rooms at same price as doubles, non-smoking, free sauna, bike rental-50 kr/day, 50 yards in front of train station facing square at Larmtorget 2, tel. 0480/15230, fax 0480/85887, www.frimurarehotellet.com).

$$$ **Calmar Stadshotell,** more expensive and impersonal, is by the big church on Stortorget (Sb-1,095 kr, Db-1,295 kr, about 300 kr less on weekends and mid-June–late Aug, non-smoking rooms, Stortorget 14, tel. 0480/496-900, fax 0480/496-910, www .profilhotels.se, calmarstadshotell@profilhotels.se).

$$ **Svanen,** a 15-minute walk or short bus ride from the center in the Ängö neighborhood, is a new breed of budget hotel with a mix of nicer hotel rooms with private bath, cheaper rooms with shared bath, and hostel beds. All guests have access to laundry and kitchen facilities, a TV room, Internet access (60 kr/hr), and a sauna (hotel: S-540 kr, Sb-625–765 kr depending on size, D-655 kr, Db-760-865 kr, includes sheets and breakfast; hostel: 195 kr per bed in 2–6 bed rooms, sheets-50 kr, no member discount, breakfast-60 kr; reception open daily 7:30–21:00, Rappegatan 1, tel. 0480/25560, fax 0480/88293, www.hotellsvanen.se). You'll see a blue-and-white hotel sign and a hostel symbol at the edge of town on Ängöleden street, a mile from the train station. Catch bus #402 at the station to Ängöleden (2–3/hr, 5 min, 20 kr, pay driver) or a take a taxi for about 70 kr. They rent canoes for exploring the small bays around Kalmar (100 kr/half-day, 170 kr/day).

$$ **Hotell Villa Ängö,** a five-minute walk from Svanen, is a big, old house by the sea, with a peaceful garden and nine homey ground-floor rooms. Manager Barbro lives around the corner and practically lets the place run itself, leaving the door open and the key waiting for you in the door. She neither uses e-mail nor speaks much English (S-350 kr, Sb-400 kr, D-500 kr, Db-600 kr, basement sauna, Baggensgatan 20, tel. 0480/85415). Follow the same directions as for Svanen, then turn from Rappegatan onto Baggensgatan and go five blocks.

$$ **Söderportsgården,** a university dorm with 35 simple yet classy rooms, welcomes tourists from mid-June through mid-August. It's idyllically located across from the entrance to Kalmar Castle (S-520 kr, D-600 kr, Db-745 kr, Tb-1,025 kr, Qb-1,290 kr, includes sheets and breakfast, Slottsvägen 1, tel. & fax 0480/12501, www.soderportsgarden.se).

$ The **Seaman's Club (Sjöfartsklubben)** is a historic home, built as a girls' school in 1820, now used as a student dormitory by the maritime academy during the school year, and open to tourists from mid-June through mid-August. It has 13 cheap hostelesque rooms, harbor views, and a lazy garden just five blocks from the train station (S-250 kr, D-350 kr, T-450 kr, Q-550 kr, sheets-50 kr, no breakfast, kitchen privileges, lively common room, reception open same hours as TI, Ölandsgatan 45, at corner of Proviantgatan, near the Kalmar County Museum, tel. 0480/10810).

EATING

Kalmar has a surprising number of good dining options for a small city. For lunch, look for the *dagens rätt* (daily special) for 65–85 kr, which gets you a main dish, salad, bread, and usually coffee or a soft drink. Many restaurants in Kalmar offer fixed-price menus at dinner.

Byttan, in a landmark 1930s functionalist building in the city park, offers fine dining (or just a coffee break) with views of the castle (85-kr lunch special Mon–Fri 11:30–14:00, main dishes-125–205 kr; open Mon–Fri 11:30–22:00, Sat 13:00–23:00, Sun 11:00–20:00, you'll pass it as you walk to the castle, tel. 0480/16360).

Källaren Kronan, open only for dinner, is an elegant candle-lit cellar restaurant with tables under stone arches. They serve old-time Swedish dishes as well as modern cuisine and have good-value specials (entrées-165–195 kr; fixed-price meals: two courses-195 kr, three courses-220 kr, three veggie courses-150 kr; Tue–Fri 18:00–23:00, Sat 12:00–23:00, Sun 17:00–22:00, closed Mon, two blocks from train station at Ölandsgatan 7, tel. 0480/411-400).

Calmar Hamnkrog is *the* place for a dressy harborview meal among the Swedish sailing set (90-kr lunch specials and three-course dinners for 250 kr, Mon–Fri 11:30–14:00 & 18:00–22:00, Sat 18:00–22:00, closed Sun, call ahead to reserve window seating, Skeppsbrogatan 30, tel. 0480/411-020, www.calmarhamnkrog.se).

Santorini, in the pedestrian zone, is a comfy Greek–Italian restaurant with 65-kr lunch specials, 80–120-kr pastas, and 189-kr three-course dinners (Mon–Thu 11:00–22:00, Fri–Sat 12:00–23:00, Sun 13:00–21:00, Storgatan 10, tel. 0480/87087).

Cafés: For a quick, light lunch or afternoon snack, visit the café in **Söderportsgården,** across from the walkway to the castle, or the smaller café inside the castle itself. In the downtown pedestrian zone, cozy antique-filled **Kullzénska Café,** with cakes and sandwiches, is larger than it looks (Mon–Fri 10:00–18:30, Sat 10:00–15:30, Sun 12:00–16:30, Kaggensgatan 26 at the corner of Norra Långgatan, go up the stairs).

Supermarkets: There's an **ICA** in the harborside shopping complex (Mon–Fri 8:00–20:00, Sat 8:00–18:00, Sun 11:00–18:00). In the pedestrian district, there's a **Konsum** in the Kvasten mall at the corner of Kaggensgatan and Storgatan (Mon–Fri 9:00–20:00, Sat 9:00–18:00, Sun 11:00–18:00).

TRANSPORTATION CONNECTIONS

From Kalmar by Train to: Växjö (12/day, 70 min), **Copenhagen** (5/day, 4 hrs), **Stockholm** (3/day, faster route is 4.5 hrs with a transfer in Alvesta; longer route through Linköping takes 6 hrs).

By Bus to Stockholm: The bus to Stockholm is much cheaper and not that much slower than the train (3/day, 6 hrs, 250 kr, 10 percent discount if you buy your ticket a day in advance).

Route Tips for Drivers

Kalmar to Copenhagen: See "Route Tips for Drivers" at the end of the Near Copenhagen chapter.

Kalmar to Stockholm: Leaving Kalmar, follow E-22 *Lindsdal* and *Nörrköping* signs. The Kalmar–Stockholm drive is 230 miles and takes nearly six hours. Sweden did a cheap widening job, paving the shoulders of the old two-lane road to get 3.8 lanes. Still, traffic is polite and sparse. There's little to see, so stock the pantry, set the compass on north, and home in on Stockholm.

Make two pleasant stops along the way. **Västervik** is 90 miles north of Kalmar, with an 18th-century core of wooden houses (3 miles off the highway, *Centrum* signs lead you to the harbor). Park on the waterfront near the great little smoked-fish market (Mon–Sat).

Söderköping is just right for a lunch on the **Göta Canal** stop. Stay on E-22 past where you'd think you'd exit for the town center, then turn right at the Kanalbåtarna/Slussen. Look for the *Kanal P* signs leading to a handy canalside parking lot. From there, walk along the canal into the action.

Sweden's famous Göta Canal consists of 190 miles of canals cutting the country in half, with 58 locks *(slussen)* working up to a summit of 300 feet. It was built 150 years ago, with more than seven million 12-hour man-days (60,000 men working about 22 years) at a low ebb in the country's self-esteem—to show her industrial might. Today it's a lazy three- or four-day tour, which shows Sweden's zest for good living. Take just a peek at the Göta Canal over lunch, in the medieval town of Söderköping.

The TI on Söderköping's Rådhustorget (a square about a block off the canal) has good town and Stockholm maps, a walking brochure, and canal information. On the canal is the Kanalbutiquen, a yachters' laundry (40 kr, wash and dry, open daily), shower, shop, and WC, with idyllic picnic grounds just above the lock. From the lock, stairs lead up to the Utsiktsplats pavilion (commanding view).

From Söderköping, E-22 takes you to Nörrköping. Follow E-4 signs through Nörrköping, past a handy rest stop, and into

Stockholm. The Centrum is clearly marked. (Viking's ferry terminal for Helsinki is in Södermalm; Silja's is northeast of town in Ropsten—see ferry terminal info in beginning of Helsinki chapter, page 337.)

FINLAND

FINLAND

(Suomi)

 From medieval times to 1809, Finland was part of Sweden. City fires have left little standing from this period, but Finland still has a sizeable Swedish-speaking minority, bilingual street signs, and close cultural ties to Sweden.

In 1809, Sweden lost Finland to Russia. Under the next century of relatively benign Russian rule, Finland began to industrialize, and Helsinki grew into a fine and elegant city. Still, at the beginning of the 1900s, the rest of Finland was mostly dirt-poor and agricultural, and its people were eagerly emigrating to northern Minnesota. (Read Toivo Pekkanen's *My Childhood* to learn about the life of a Finnish peasant in the early 1900s.)

In 1917, Finland and the Baltic states won their independence from Russia, fought brief but vicious civil wars, and then enjoyed two decades of prosperity...until the secret Nazi–Soviet pact of August 1939 assigned them to the Soviet sphere of influence. When Russia invaded, only Finland resisted successfully, its white-camouflaged ski troops winning the Winter War against the Soviet Union in 1939–1940 and holding off the Russians in the Continuation War from 1941 to 1944.

After World War II, Finland was made to suffer for having fought against one of the Allied Powers. The Finns were forced to cede Karelia (eastern Finland) to the USSR, to accept Soviet naval bases on Finnish territory, and to pay huge reparations to the Soviet government. Still, Finland's bold, trend-setting modern design and architecture blossomed, and it built up successful timber, paper, and electronics industries. All through the Cold War, Finland teetered between the West and the Soviet Union, trying to be part of Western Europe's strong economy while treading lightly and making nice with her giant neighbor to the east. The collapse of the Soviet Union has done to Finland what a good long sauna might do to you.

When Moscow's menace vanished, so did about 20 percent of Finland's trade. After a few years of adjustment, Finland is on an upswing now. Many Finns used to move to Sweden (where they are the biggest immigrant group), looking for better jobs in

Finland

Stockholm. Some still nurse an inferiority complex, thinking of themselves as poor cousins to the Swedes. But now Finland is the most technologically advanced country in Europe. Home to the giant mobile-phone company Nokia, Finland has more mobile-phone numbers than fixed ones, and ranks fourth among European nations—ninth globally—in the number of Internet users per capita. Finns are counting on their membership in the European Union and the euro zone to cement the strength of their economy.

We think of Finland as Scandinavian, but it's better to call it "Nordic." Technically, the Scandinavian countries are Denmark, Sweden, and Norway—all constitutional monarchies with closely related languages. Add Iceland, Finland, and maybe Estonia—former Danish or Swedish colonies that speak separate languages—and you have the "Nordic countries." Iceland, Finland, and Estonia are republics, not monarchies. In 1906, Finnish women were the first in Europe to vote, and today 40 percent of the Finnish parliament—as well as the Finnish president—is female.

Finland is known as a nation of few words; Finns value silence, yet are easily approachable. Tourists are not considered a headache to the locals the way they are in places like Paris and Munich. Compared to Sweden or Denmark, Finland has not attracted many immigrants, and fewer of the service workers you will deal with come from elsewhere.

Finnish is a difficult-to-learn Finno-Ugric language originating east of Russia's Ural Mountains; its only related European

Finland Almanac

Official Name: Republic of Finland.

Population: Finland is home to 5.2 million people (40 per square mile). The majority are Finnish in descent (93.4 percent). Other ethnicities include Swedish (6 percent), Russian, Estonian, Roma, and Sami (less than 1 percent each). The official languages are Finnish, spoken by 92 percent, and Swedish, spoken by 5 percent. Small minorities speak Sami and Russian. Finland is 84 percent Lutheran, 1 percent Greek Orthodox, 1 percent other Christian, and nearly 14 percent unaffiliated.

Latitude and Longitude: 64°N and 26°E, similar latitude to Nome, Alaska.

Area: 130,600 square miles (almost the size of Montana).

Geography: Finland is bordered by Russia to the east, Sweden and Norway to the north, the Baltic Sea to the west, and Estonia to the south. Much of Finland is flat and covered with forests, with the Lapland region extending north of the Arctic Circle. Finland is home to thousands of lakes and encompasses nearly as many islands: It has 187,800 lakes and 179,500 islands the last time I counted.

Biggest City: Helsinki is the capital of Finland and has a population of 562,000; 1.4 million people live in the Helsinki urban area, or nearly one in four Finns.

Economy: Finland's Gross Domestic Product is $163 billion and its per capita GDP is $31,208. Manufacturing, timber, engineering, electronics, and telecommunications are its chief industries, with cell phones among its top exports.

Currency: €1 (euro) = about $1.20.

Government: Finland has both a president, responsible for foreign policy, and a prime minister, who with the 200-member Parliament (Eduskunta) is responsible for domestic legislation. President Tarja Halonen was re-elected to a second six-year term in January 2006. Matti Vanhanen was named prime minister in June 2003.

Flag: The Finnish flag is white with a blue cross.

The Average Finn: The average Finn is 41 years old, has 1.73 children, and will live to be 78.

languages are Estonian (closely) and Hungarian (distantly). Finland is officially bilingual, and 5 percent of the country's population speaks Swedish as a first language. You'll notice that Helsinki is called *Helsingfors* in Swedish. Helsinki's street signs list places in both Finnish and Swedish. Nearly every educated young person speaks effortless English—the language barrier is just a road turtle.

The only essential word needed for a quick visit is *kiitos* (KEY-toes)—that's "thank you," and locals love to hear it. *Kippis* (keep-peace) is what you say before you down a shot of Finnish vodka or cloudberry liqueur *(lakka)*.

HELSINKI

The next best thing to being in Helsinki is getting there. Europe's most enjoyable cruise, from Stockholm to Helsinki, starts with dramatic archipelago scenery, a setting sun, and a royal *smörgåsbord* dinner. Dance until you drop and sauna until you drip. Budget travel rarely feels this hedonistic. Seventeen hours after you depart, it's "Hello, Helsinki."

The Cruise from Stockholm to Helsinki

Two fine and fiercely competitive lines, Viking and Silja, connect the capitals of Sweden and Finland. Each line offers state-of-

the-art ships with luxurious *smörgåsbord* meals, reasonable cabins, plenty of entertainment (discos, saunas, gambling), and enough duty-free shopping to sink a ship. Of the two, Viking has the reputation as the party boat. Silja is considered more elegant (but still has its share of sometimes irritating and noisy passengers).

The Pepsi and Coke of the Scandinavian cruise industry vie to outdo each other with bigger and fancier boats. The ships are big—at 56,000 tons, nearly 200 yards long, and with 2,700 beds, they're the largest (and cheapest) luxury hotels in Scandinavia. Many other shipping lines buy their boats used from Viking and Silja.

Which line is best? You could count showers and compare *smörgåsbords*, but both lines go overboard to win the loyalty of the nine million duty free–crazy Swedes and Finns who make the

Sailing the Baltic Sea

trip each year. Eurail and Eurail Selectpasses cover deck passage only on the Silja line (trip uses up one flexi-day); cabins cost extra.

Scanrail passes get you a 50 percent discount on deck passage on both Silja and Viking (doesn't use up a flexi-day); cabins cost extra, but Silja also applies the 50 percent discount to the cheapest four-passenger cabin. Viking has an older, less luxurious fleet, but caters better to low-budget travelers, selling cheap *ekonomi* cabins (shower down the hall) and allowing passengers to pay for deck passage only and sleep for free on chairs, sofas, and under the stars or stairs. Viking's fares for standard passage are only slightly lower than Silja's, but students, seniors, and railpass holders can score discounts.

Cruise Schedules

Both Viking and Silja sail nightly from Stockholm and Helsinki. In both directions, the boats leave about 16:30–17:30 and arrive the next morning around 9:30–10:00. Both companies also sail daily between Stockholm and Turku, Finland. For exact schedules, see www.vikingline.fi and www.silja.com.

   Scenery: During the first few hours out of Stockholm, your ship passes through the *skärgården* (archipelago). The third hour features the most exotic island scenery—tiny islets with cute red huts and happy people. I'd have dinner at the first sitting (shortly after departure) and be on deck for sunset.

Time Change: Finland is one hour ahead of Sweden. Sailing from Stockholm to Helsinki, operate on Swedish time until you're ready to go to bed, then reset your watch. Morning schedules are Finnish time (and vice versa when you return). The cruise-schedule flier in English makes this clear (pick it up as you board).

Cost

Fares vary by season and by day of the week. Mid-June to mid-August is most crowded and expensive (with prices the same regardless of day). During the off-season, Friday prices are about double the regular fare; try to avoid travel on a Friday.

In summer, a one-way ticket per person for the cheapest bed that has a private bath (in a below-sea-level, under-car-deck "C" quad) costs about €60. Couples will pay a total of about €180–225 for the cheapest double room (with bath) that's above the car deck. Friday is most expensive. Fares drop about 25 percent off-season for departures Sunday through Wednesday. Each ship offers a whale of a *smörgåsbord* dinner for an extra €32 and a big breakfast for €10. Reserving your meals in advance knocks about 10 percent off the cost and the hassle of hustling for a reservation after you board. Try to reserve a specific table in advance, too (window seats go quickly).

Round-trip cruise fares (across and back on successive nights, leaving you access to your bedroom throughout the day) generally cost little more than a one-way trip. In peak season, couples can share the cheapest double cabin round-trip for about €220–260. The drawback is that this leaves you with only a few hours on land. But you can get the round-trip fare on non-successive nights if you book a hotel through the cruise line for every intervening night—if it fits your schedule, this is a good deal (especially on Thu departures off-season).

The fares are cheap because locals sail to shop and drink duty- and tax-free. It's a huge operation—mostly for locals. The boats are filled with about 45 percent Finns, 45 percent Swedes, and 10 percent cruisers from other countries. The average passenger spends as much on booze and duty-free items as for the boat fare. The boats now make a midnight stop in the Åland Islands, a part of Finland that's exempt from European Union membership, to preserve the international nature of the trip and maintain the duty-free status.

Reservations

Call the cruise line direct in Scandinavia to reserve your crossing. *For summer or weekend sailings, reserve well in advance.* The

Helsinki Harbor

Swedish reservations numbers are tel. 46-8/222-140 (Silja) and tel. 46-8/452-4000 (Viking). In Helsinki, call 358-9/18041 (Silja) or 358-9/12351 (Viking). You can pay by credit card and pick up your ticket at the terminal (arrive one hour before departure) or pick them up early at the city office (in Stockholm, Viking's is at Cityterminalen and Silja's is at Kungsgatan 2; in Helsinki, Viking's is at Mannerheimintie 14 and Silja's is at Mannerheimintie 2). Operators speak English. Any travel agent in Scandinavia can also sell you a ticket (with a small booking fee). You may save money by booking online. Visit Viking at www.vikingline.fi to be directed to an online sales agent. You can book directly through Silja at www.silja.com.

Terminals

Locations: In Stockholm, Viking Line ships moor at Stadsgården on Södermalm. To get there from Stockholm's bus station, take Viking's shuttle bus (30 kr) to the dock or public bus #53 to the Londonviadukten stop.

Silja Line's harbor is northeast of the center. You can walk to the terminal from the Gärdet T-bana station (about 10 min), but it's easier to catch the Silja shuttle bus (25 kr) from the bus station.

In Helsinki, both lines are perfectly central, on opposite sides of the main harbor, a 10-minute walk from the center. See the Helsinki map above for details.

Terminal Buildings: These are well-organized, with cafés, lockers, tourist information desks, lounges, and phones. Remember, 2,000 passengers come and go with each boat. Customs is a snap. Boats open 90 minutes before departure, and you must have checked in by 15 minutes before departure.

Parking: Both lines offer safe and handy parking in Stockholm. Ask for details when you reserve your ticket.

Onboard Services

Meals: While ships have cheap, fast cafeterias as well as classy, romantic restaurants, they are famous for their *smörgåsbord* dinners. Board the ship hungry. Dinner is self-serve in two sittings, one at about 18:00, the other a couple hours later. Pay for both the dinner buffet (€32) and breakfast buffet (€10) when you buy your ticket (you'll save 10 percent). If you board without a reservation, go to the restaurant and make one. Make sure to reserve your table, not just your meal; window seats are highly sought after. Pick up the *How to Eat a Smörgåsbord* brochure. The key is to take small portions and pace yourself. The price includes free beer, wine, soft drinks, and coffee. Of course, you can also bring a picnic and eat it on deck.

Sauna: Each ship has a sauna, which costs about €5 extra. Reserve a time upon boarding. Saunas on Silja are half price or even free in the morning (for those with a cabin towel). Silja also offers massage on board from 15:00 to 22:00, for an extra fee. Reserve immediately upon boarding.

Banking: Ships take euros and Swedish kronor, and just about every vendor or shop also accepts credit cards. Each boat has a handy exchange desk on board with acceptable rates. None of the boats has an ATM, but all terminals have ATMs and exchange windows.

Tourist Info on Board: Boats generally offer racks of *Stockholm* or *Helsinki This Week* magazines. Grab a copy for some practical bedtime reading.

Options

Tallinn: You can visit Tallinn as a day trip from Helsinki, or Helsinki as a day trip from Tallinn, or you can make a triangle trip: Stockholm–Helsinki–Tallinn–Stockholm, or vice versa. See the Tallinn chapter for details on the Helsinki–Tallinn and Stockholm–Tallinn crossings.

Turku: Both Viking and Silja also sail from Stockholm to Turku in Finland, a shorter crossing (11 hours, departing daily at about 8:00–9:00 and 20:00–21:00). Turku is two hours from Helsinki by bus or train. The boats are usually smaller, with less cruise-ship excitement. The cheaper fare saves you enough to pay for the train trip from Turku to Helsinki.

Helsinki

Helsinki is the only European capital with no medieval past. In 1746, Sweden built a huge fortress on an island outside its harbor. The town of Helsinki was founded to supply the fortress. After taking over Finland in 1809, the Russians decided to move its capital and university closer to St. Petersburg—from Turku to Helsinki. They hired a young German architect, Carl Ludwig Engel, to design new public buildings for Helsinki and told him to use St. Petersburg as a model. This is why the oldest parts of Helsinki (around Market Square and Senate Square) feel so Russian—stone buildings in yellow and blue pastels with white trim and columns. Hollywood used Helsinki for the films *Gorky Park* and *Dr. Zhivago*, because filming in Russia was not possible during the Cold War.

Though the city was part of the Russian Empire in the 19th century, most of its residents still spoke Swedish, which was the language of business and culture. In the mid-1800s, Finland began to industrialize. The Swedish upper class in Helsinki expanded the city, bringing in the railroad and surrounding the old Russian-inspired core with neighborhoods of four- and five-story apartment buildings, including some Art Nouveau masterpieces. Meanwhile, Finns moved from the countryside to Helsinki to take jobs as industrial laborers. The Finnish language slowly acquired equal status with Swedish, and eventually Finnish speakers became the majority in Helsinki.

Since downtown Helsinki didn't exist until the 1800s, it was more consciously designed and laid out than other European capitals. With its many architectural overleafs and fine Neoclassical and Art Nouveau buildings, Helsinki often turns guests into students of urban design and planning. In bookstores, look for the two concise guides to Helsinki architecture by Jonathan Moorhouse. Katajanokka, Kruununhaka, and Eira are good walking neighborhoods for architecture buffs.

Helsinki can be windy and cold, but it's worth the chill.

Planning Your Time

On a three-week trip through Scandinavia, Helsinki is worth at least the time between two successive nights on the cruise ship—about seven hours. To do the city justice, two days is ideal.

For a quick one-day visit, start with the two-hour Hello Helsinki bus tour that meets the boat at the dock. Then take my self-guided walking tour through the compact city center from the harbor—enjoying Helsinki's ruddy harborfront market and getting goose bumps in the churches—to the National Museum of Finland. In the afternoon, dive into Finnish culture in the open-air folk museum or take a boat tour of the harbor. Enjoy a cup of coffee at Café Kappeli before reboarding. Sail away while sampling another *smörgåsbord* dinner.

ORIENTATION

(Helsinki's area code: 09; from outside Finland: 358-9)
Helsinki's natural gateway is its harbor, where ships from Stockholm and Tallinn dock. At the top of the harbor is Market

Square (Kauppatori), an outdoor food and souvenir bazaar. Nearby are two towering, can't-miss-them landmarks: the white Lutheran Cathedral and the brick Uspenski Cathedral.

Helsinki's grand pedestrian boulevard, the Esplanade, begins right at Market Square, heads up past the TI, and ends after a few blocks in the central shopping district. The broad, traffic-filled Mannerheimintie, a bustling avenue that veers north through town past the train and bus stations, begins at the far end of the Esplanade. For a do-it-yourself orientation to town along this route, follow my "Welcome to Helsinki" self-guided walk on page 341. The "Tram #3T Tour" (page 344) also provides a good drive-by introduction to the main sights.

Tourist Information

There are two TIs: a main TI on Market Square, and a small branch at the train station. The friendly, energetic **main TI** offers great service and is fun to graze through. It's located a half-block inland from Market Square, on the right just past the fountain, at the corner of the Esplanade and Unioninkatu (May–Sept Mon–Fri 9:00–20:00, Sat–Sun 9:00–18:00; Oct–April Mon–Fri 9:00–18:00, Sat–Sun 10:00–16:00; Internet access, tel. 09/169-3757, www.visithelsinki.fi). Pick up the city map, the public-transit map, *Helsinki on Foot* (six well-described walking tours with maps), the monthly *Helsinki This Week* magazine (lists sights, hours, and events), and *City* magazine (good, opinionated restaurant listings, geared for the younger crowd). Ask for the brochure on the scenic #3T tram and go over your sightseeing plans.

The tiny **train-station TI**, which consists of a one-person desk inside the Helsinki Expert office, provides many of the same services and publications as the main TI and has similar hours.

Helsinki Expert: This private service sells the Helsinki Card (see below), ferry tickets, and transport passes, and also makes hotel bookings. They have one branch in the train station hall, and another occupying the back desks in the main TI on Market Square. They always know about wild bargains, like luxury-hotel clearance deals that cost only €20 more than the cheapies. There's a €5 fee for walk-in hotel reservations (e-mail and phone reservations are free), and ferry bookings cost €7 (hours of branch at main TI: June–Aug Mon–Fri 9:00–19:00, Sat–Sun 9:00–17:00; Sept–May Mon–Fri 9:00–17:00, Sat 10:00–16:00, closed Sun; branch at train station has similar hours, tel. 09/2288-1500, fax 09/2288-1599, www.helsinkiexpert.fi).

Helsinki Card: If you're planning to do a lot of sightseeing in Helsinki, this card can be a good deal (€29/24 hours, €42/48 hours, €53/72 hours). It includes free entry to sights; free use of buses, trams, and the ferry to Suomenlinna; an orientation bus tour—normally €23—for €11; and a 72-page booklet (sold at Helsinki Expert, most hotels, and ferry ports, www.helsinkicard.com).

Arrival in Helsinki

By Ferry: Helsinki has five ferry terminals *(terminaali)*—see map on page 333 and the color map in the front of this book. The Olympia and Makasiini terminals are on the west side (to the left as you face inland) of the main harbor. The Katajanokka and Kanava terminals are on the east side (right) of the main harbor. Most Silja Line boats use the Olympia terminal; most Viking boats use the Katajanokka terminal. The Makasiini and Kanava terminals are mostly for fast boats to Tallinn. Trams stop near all the main-harbor terminals. The Länsi terminal, in Helsinki's western harbor, is for large car ferries to Tallinn and is inconvenient to reach by public transportation (take a taxi).

By Train and Bus: The train station, an architectural landmark, is near the top of the Esplanade, a 15-minute walk from Market Square. Local buses leave from both sides of the building, trams stop out front, and the subway runs underneath. The newly built long-distance Kampii bus station is two blocks away, on the other side of Mannerheimintie; ticket windows are on the ground floor, with bus platforms below.

By Plane: To get between the airport and downtown Helsinki, take the Finnair bus (€5.20, downtown terminus is platform 30 at Elielinaukio on west side of train station, 3/hr, 35-min trip) or public bus #615 (€3.40, pay driver, Helsinki Card and Tourist Ticket not valid, downtown terminus is platform #10 at Rautatientori on east side of train station, 2–4/hr, 45-min trip, also stops at Hakaniemi). Or take the Yellow Line door-to-door shared van service (€20 for 1–2 people, €28 for 3–4 people, €40 for 5–6 people, tel. 0600-555-555, www.airporttaxi.fi). Cabs run €30.

Helpful Hints

Time: Finland and Estonia are one hour ahead of Sweden and the rest of Scandinavia.

Money: Euro collectors, take note: Finland has taken its one- and two-cent coins out of circulation. All cash transactions are rounded to the nearest five cents. Collectors can pay €3 for €0.03 in Finnish small change at coin shops (such as Moneta on Unioninkatu).

Telephones: Finding international phone cards in Helsinki is challenging. Unlike the rest of Europe, Finland does not use 00 as its international access code. It is 999, or another 900 number, depending on which service you're using.

Internet Access: These places are handy: main **TI** (three free but often busy terminals); **National Museum of Finland** (six ignored and free terminals in its superb second-floor information center); **Mbar Café** (€5/hr, 10 terminals, Mon–Sat 9:00–24:00, Sun 12:00–22:00, in Lasipalatsi complex, Mannerheimintie 22–24, enter on Salomonkatu and go to the back) and **Library 10** (12 free terminals in post office across from train station, Mon–Thu 10:00–22:00, Fri–Sun 12:00–18:00, pick up free visitors card from desk and ask for a time slot, often a wait, Elielinaukio 2G).

Bike Rental: Try **Greenbike** (€13/day, €20/24 hrs, daily 10:00–20:00, Bulevardi 32, tel. 050/404-0400, www.greenbike.fi).

Getting Around Helsinki

In compact Helsinki, you won't need to use public transportation as much as in Stockholm.

By Bus and Tram: With the public-transit route map (available at the TI) and a little mental elbow grease, the buses and trams  are easy, giving you Helsinki by the tail. Single tickets are good for an hour of travel (€2.20 from automatic vending machines at larger stops, or from driver). The Tourist Ticket (€6 for 24 hours of unlimited travel) pays for itself if you take three or more rides; longer versions are also available (€12/72 hrs, €18/120 hrs). The single subway line uses the same tickets but is not useful for most visitors (www.hkl.fi). Public transportation is covered by the Helsinki Card.

Tram #3T makes the rounds of most of the town's major sights in an hour. It runs every 10 minutes in a confusing but convenient figure-eight route; tram #3B follows the same route in the opposite direction. Either buy a single ticket—good for one hour—and stay on the tram for the circuit, or get the Tourist Ticket, allowing you to hop off to tour a sight, then catch a later tram. The TI promotes tram #3T as a self-guided tour and has a helpful explanatory brochure (available at TI and often on board). The tram's sightseeing route is described on page 344.

In summer, the antique red **Pub Tram** makes a 50-minute circle through the city while its passengers get looped on the beer for sale on board (€7, leaves on the hour mid-May–mid-Aug Tue–Sat 14:00–20:00 from in front of Fennia building, no trams Sun–Mon, Mikonkatu 17, across from train-station tower).

TOURS

▲▲▲**Orientation Bus Tour**—Fast, very good 105-minute, €23 introductory tours leave daily from three points: Silja Terminal (live guide in Swedish and English, departs after ship arrives at 10:30), Viking Terminal (recorded in 11 languages, departs after ship arrives at 10:45), and downtown (recorded, departs from Esplanade Park at the corner of Fabianinkatu and the Esplanade— summer at 10:00, 11:00, 12:00, 13:00 and 14:00; winter at 11:00 only). Take advantage of discounts (€3 off when booked on your ship or on the Web at www.helsinkiexpert.fi; 10:00 and 14:00 downtown departures are free with Helsinki Card; 11:00, 12:00, and 13:00 downtown departures are half-price with Helsinki Card). Tickets can also be purchased from the driver, or by phone at tel. 09/2288-1600.

These bus tours give a good city overview with a look at all the important buildings, from the newly remodeled Olympic Stadium to Embassy Row. A 10-minute stop at the Sibelius Monument is long enough, but 10 minutes is rushed at the "Church in the Rock" (Temppeliaukio). You'll learn strange facts, such as how they took down the highest steeple in town during World War II so that the Soviet bombers flying in from Estonia couldn't see their target.

Harbor Tours—Several boat companies compete for your attention along Market Square, offering 90-minute, €12–16 cruises around the waterfront roughly hourly from 10:00 to 18:00 in summer. The narration is slow moving—often tape-recorded and in as many as four languages. Taking the ferry out to Suomenlinna and back gets you onto the water for much less money (see page 337; €4.40, covered by Helsinki Card and Tourist Ticket). But if the weather's good and you're looking for something one step above a snooze in the park...then all aboard.

Local Guides—**Helsinki Expert** can arrange a private guide (book at least three days in advance, €165/3 hours, tel. 09/2288-1222). Or you can book my favorite guide direct (local schoolteacher

Helsinki at a Glance

▲▲▲**Temppeliaukio Church** Awe-inspiring, copper-topped 1969 "Church in the Rock." **Hours:** Mon–Sat 10:00–17:00, Thu–Fri until 20:00, Sun 12:00–17:30.

▲▲**Lutheran Cathedral** Green-domed, 19th-century Neoclassical masterpiece. **Hours:** June–Aug Mon–Sat 9:00–24:00, Sun 12:00–24:00; Sept–May Mon–Sat 9:00–18:00, Sun 12:00–18:00.

▲▲**Uspenski Cathedral** Orthodoxy's most prodigious display in Western Europe. **Hours:** May–Sept Mon–Sat 9:30–16:00, Sun 12:00–15:00; Oct–April Tue–Fri 9:30–16:00, Sat 9:30–14:00, Sun 12:00–15:00, closed Mon.

▲▲**National Museum of Finland** The scoop on Finland, featuring folk costumes, an armory, czars, and thrones; the prehistory exhibit is best. **Hours:** Tue–Wed 11:00–20:00, Thu–Sat 11:00–18:00, Sun 11:00–18:00, closed Mon.

▲▲**Seurasaari Open-Air Folk Museum** Island museum with 100 historic buildings from Finland's farthest corners. **Hours:** June–Aug daily 11:00–17:00; late May and early Sept Mon–Fri 9:00–15:00, Sat–Sun 11:00–17:00.

▲▲**Suomenlinna Fortress** Helsinki's harbor island, sprinkled with picnic spots, museums, and military history. **Hours:** Daily May–Aug 10:00–18:00, Sept–April 10:00–16:00.

▲**Senate Square** Consummate Neoclassical square, with Lutheran Cathedral. **Hours:** Always open.

▲**Sibelius Monument** Stainless-steel sculptural tribute to Finland's greatest composer. **Hours:** Always open.

Kiasma Modern-art museum. **Hours:** Tue and Sun 10:00–17:00, Wed–Sat 10:00–20:30, closed Mon.

Hanne Calonius, €100/3 hours, hanne.calonius@edu.hel.fi, tel. 09/684-8564).

Meet the Finns: Citysherpa is an innovative free service that matches volunteer local guides and foreign visitors with the same interests. Helsinki residents place "personals" on their Web site (http://hs.fi/citysherpa), such as "Music lover wants to show you his favorite disc shops and flea markets," "Long-distance runner wants to run together through beautiful parks," and "Father and daughter want to show city to middle-aged couples or families."

SELF-GUIDED WALK

Welcome to Helsinki

Start at the obelisk in the center of **Market Square,** the harborfront market. This is the **Czarina's Stone,** with its double-headed eagle of imperial Russia. It was the first public monument in Helsinki, designed by Carl Engel and erected in 1835 to celebrate the visit by Czar Nicholas and Czarina Alexandra. Step over the chain and climb to the top step for a clockwise spin tour:

The big, red **Viking ship** and white **Silja ship** are each floating hotels for those making the 40-hour Stockholm–Helsinki round-trip. The brown-and-tan brick building is the old market hall. A number of harbor cruise boats vie for your business. The trees mark the beginning of Helsinki's grand promenade, the Esplanade. Hiding in the leaves is the venerable iron-and-glass Café Kappeli. The yellow building across from the trees is the TI. From there, a string of Neoclassical buildings face the harbor. The blue-and-white **City Hall** building was designed by Engel in 1833 as the town's first hotel (built to house the Czar and Czarina). The Lutheran Cathedral is hidden from view behind this building. Next is the **Swedish Embassy** (flying the blue-and-yellow Swedish flag and designed to look like Stockholm's Royal Palace). Then comes the **Supreme Court** and, in the far corner, Finland's **Presidential Palace.** Standing proud, and reminding Helsinki of the Russian behemoth to its east, is the Orthodox **Uspenski Cathedral.**

Explore the colorful **outdoor market**—part souvenirs and crafts, part fruit and veggies, part fish and snacks (Mon-Sat roughly 6:30–18:00, tourist stalls only on Sun). Then, with your back to the water, walk left to the **fountain,** *Havis Amanda,* designed by Ville Vallgren and unveiled here in 1908. The fountain has become the symbol  of Helsinki, the city known as the "Daughter of the Baltic." The voluptuous figure, modeled after the artist's Parisian mistress, was a bit too racy for the conservative town, and Vallgren had trouble getting paid. But as artists often do, Vallgren had the last laugh: For more than a hundred years now, the city budget office (above the Sasso restaurant across the street) has seen only her backside.

Helsinki

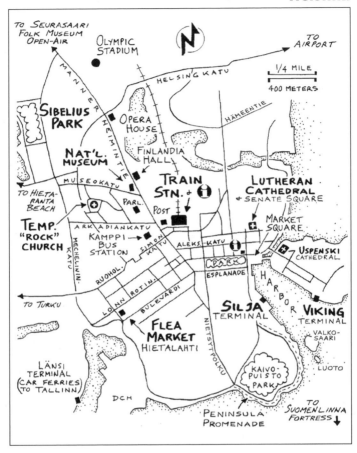

Across the street on the right, you'll see the **TI.** Next door is the delightful **Jugendsalen,** built in Art Nouveau style in 1904, originally as the lobby of a bank. It's now a city information office for locals. Though not a TI, the Jugendsalen does have brochures on Helsinki in a calm environment, plus temporary art and history exhibits celebrating the city's many charms (Mon–Fri 9:00–16:00, Sun 11:00–17:00, closed Sat, closed Sun in late June–July, Pohjoisesplanadi 19).

Make a one-block detour up Unioninkatu (noteworthy shops listed in "Shopping," page 353) to the Neoclassical **Senate Square** (page 345) and **Lutheran Cathedral** (page 347).

Backtrack to the TI. In the park across the street is my favorite café in Northern Europe, **Café Kappeli.** If you've got some time, dip into this old-fashioned, gazebo-like oasis of coffee, pastry, a €7 salad bar, and relaxation. In the 19th century, this was a popular hangout for local intellectuals and artists. Today the café offers romantic tourists waiting for their ship a great €3-cup-of-coffee memory. The bandstand in front hosts nearly daily music and dance performances in summer.

Behind Café Kappeli stretches the **Esplanade,** Helsinki's top shopping boulevard, sandwiching a park in the middle (another Engel design from the 1830s). The grandiose street names Esplanadi and Bulevardi, while fitting today, must have been bombastic and almost comical in rustic little 1830s Helsinki. Informative signs (in English) explain Esplanade Park's background and its many statues.

The north side (with the TI) is interesting for window-shopping, people-watching, and sun-worshipping. You'll pass several stores specializing in Finnish design. At #35, Gamla Passage leads to a courtyard hopping with bars and live music at night (see "Nightlife," page 355). Farther up on the right, at #39, is the huge **Academic Bookstore** (Akateeminen Kirjakauppa), designed by Alvar Aalto, with an extensive map and travel section, periodicals, English books, and Café Aalto (bookstore and café open Mon–Fri 9:00–21:00, Sat 9:00–18:00, closed Sun).

Finally, you'll come to the prestigious **Stockmann department store**—Finland's Harrods. Stockmann is the biggest, best,

and oldest department store in town, with a great gourmet supermarket in the basement (see listing in "Shopping," page 353). Just beyond is the main intersection in town: the Esplanade and Mannerheimintie. Nearby you'll see the famous *Three Blacksmiths* **statue.** (Locals say, "If a virgin walks by, they'll strike the anvil." It doesn't work. I tried.) Across the street, the Old Student Hall is decorated with mythic Finnish heroes.

The Stockmann's entrance facing the *Three Blacksmiths* is one of the city's most popular meeting points. Everyone is Finland knows exactly what it means when you say: "Let's meet under the Stockmann's clock." Across the tracks from the clock is a **tram #3T** stop (see "Tram #3T Tour," below).

Things spread out from here, but if you want to stay on foot, more remains to be seen within a short walk. Two blocks away, through a busy shopping center, is the harsh (but serene) architecture of the **train station** (by Eliel Saarinen, 1916). The four people on the facade symbolize peasant farmers with lamps coming into the Finnish capital. Wander around inside. Continuing past the post office and the equestrian statue (of Field Marshal Carl Mannerheim), return to Mannerheimintie, which leads to the large, white **Finlandia Hall,** another Aalto masterpiece. Across the street is the excellent little **National Museum of Finland** (looks like a church; see page 349), and a few blocks behind that is the sit-down-and-wipe-a-tear, beautiful "Church in the Rock," **Temppeliaukio** (see page 348). Sit. Enjoy the music. It's a wonderful place to end this walk. Welcome to Helsinki.

If you want to continue on to the **Sibelius Monument,** in a lovely park setting (see page 348), take bus #24 (direction Seurasaari) from nearby Arkadiankatu street. (The same ticket is good for your return trip.) Ride it to the end of the line for the bridge to Seurasaari Island and Finland's open-air folk museum. From there, bus #24 returns to the top of the Esplanade.

SELF-GUIDED TRAM TOUR

Tram #3T Tour

Of Helsinki's many tram routes, #3T seems made-to-order for a tourists' joyride (rated ▲▲). As you make the hour-long loop, you can hop on and off to visit the sights, or just relax and take in the workaday city most visitors miss (one-hour ticket-€2.20, Tourist Ticket-€6/24 hours, free with Helsinki Card).

There are two convenient places to hop on: at **Market Square** (near the fountain, across from the TI); or in front of the clock at **Stockmann department store** on Mannerheimintie. At most stops an electronic sign displays the minutes until the next two trams arrive (#3T goes one way, while #3B does this route in reverse).

Pick up the flier on-board that charts your loop and explains the sights you'll pass. Here are a few things to look for:

If you get on at Market Square, you'll first pass **Senate Square** (Lutheran Cathedral), and then head up the city's Fifth Avenue-type main shopping drag, **Aleksanterinkatu.**

Your next stop is the Stockmann's clock and *Three Blacksmiths* statue. At the **Lasipalatsi** stop, the big commercial Glass Palace (on the left) is pure 1930s functionalism. Across the street (on the right) is **Kiasma,** Helsinki's museum of contemporary art, with its equestrian statue of Field Marshal Carl Mannerheim (later Finland's sixth president). Behind the main post office is the **train station.**

Next you'll see the new **Parliament** building (near the tram, on the right) with the old one behind it (a box on the hill, circa 1930).

At the stop for the **Natural History Museum** (closed until 2008), look for the green dome of **Temppeliaukio,** the "Church in the Rock," up one block on the right and accessible from the Sammonkatu stop. From here you pass the **Helsinki School of Economics** (classes taught in Finnish and Swedish), and cross a trendy neighborhood with fine 1920s apartments. Young couples start out here, move to the suburbs when they have their kids, and return as empty nesters.

Later you pass the **Opera House** and the 1952 **Olympic Stadium** on the right. The next stop is **Linnanmäki,** Helsinki's low-end, Tivoli-like amusement park (on the right, open daily until late), by far the most visited sight in town.

Next you enter a working-class neighborhood. Its football fields are frozen into ice rinks for hockey in winter. You'll pass the striking stone **Kallio Church** (on your right) and stop at **Hakaniemi Market,** a big indoor/outdoor market (on your left). Crossing a saltwater inlet, you pass the **Botanical Gardens** (on the right) and then return to the town center, stopping at the train station with its striking architecture.

Finally, you loop south through a neighborhood of fine cafés, shops, embassies, and Art Nouveau buildings. After stopping at the old market hall, the #3T circle is complete—you're back at Market Square.

SIGHTS

Central Helsinki

▲**Senate Square**—Once a town square with a church and City Hall, this square's original buildings were burned in 1808 during Swedish/Russian fighting. Later, after Finland became a grand duchy of the Russian Empire, the czar sent in architect Carl Engel (a German who had lived and worked in St. Petersburg) to give the place some Neo-class. The result: the finest Neoclassical square in Europe.

Survey Senate Square from the top of the Lutheran Cathedral steps. The Senate building (now the Prime Minister's office) is on your left. The small, blue, stone building with the slanted mansard roof in the far-left corner, from 1757, is one of just two pre-Russian-conquest buildings remaining in Helsinki. On the right, the line of once-grand Russian administration buildings now houses the **university** (36,000 students, 60 percent women). Symbolically (and physically), the university and government buildings are connected via the cathedral, and both use it as a starting point for grand ceremonies.

The **statue** in the center of the square honors Russian Czar Alexander II. While he wasn't popular in Russia (he was assassinated), he was well-liked by the Finns. That's because he gave Finland more autonomy in 1853 and never pushed the

Central Helsinki

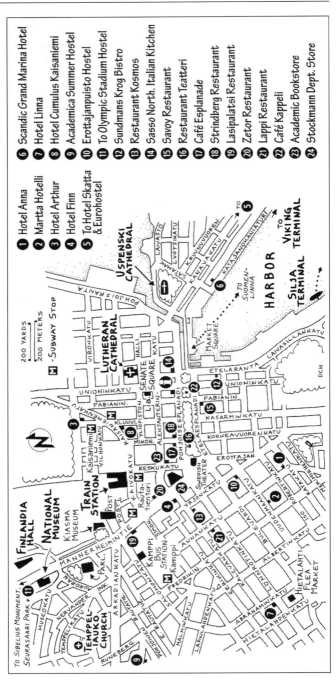

1 Hotel Anna
2 Martta Hotelli
3 Hotel Arthur
4 Hotel Finn
5 To Hotel Skatta & Eurohostel
6 Scandic Grand Marina Hotel
7 Hotel Linna
8 Hotel Cumulus Kaisaniemi
9 Academica Summer Hostel
10 Erottajanpuisto Hostel
11 To Olympic Stadium Hostel
12 Sundmans Krog Bistro
13 Restaurant Kosmos
14 Sasso North. Italian Kitchen
15 Savoy Restaurant
16 Restaurant Teatteri
17 Café Esplanade
18 Strindberg Restaurant
19 Lasipalatsi Restaurant
20 Zetor Restaurant
21 Lappi Restaurant
22 Café Kappeli
23 Academic Bookstore
24 Stockmann Dept. Store

"Russification" of Finland. The statue shows him holding the Finnish constitution, which he supported. It defined internal independence and affirmed autonomy.

The huge staircase leading up to the cathedral is a popular meeting (and tanning) spot in Helsinki. This is where students gather...and romances are born. Café Engel (opposite the cathedral at Aleksanterinkatu 26) is a fine place for a light lunch or cake and coffee. The café's winter lighting seems especially designed to boost the spirits of glum, daylight-deprived Northerners. The **Helsinki City Museum** is around the corner at Sofiankatu 4, with thorough descriptions in English (€4, free on Thu, open Mon–Fri 9:00–17:00, Sat–Sun 11:00–17:00, www.helsinkicitymuseum.fi).

The **National Library,** in its fine purpose-built Neoclassical building, is immediately to the left as you face the cathedral. It's free, open to the public, and worth a look (Mon–Fri 9:00–20:00, Sat 9:00–16:00, closed Sun, www.library.helsinki.fi). In czarist times, the National Library received a copy of every book printed in the Russian Empire. With all the chaos Russia suffered throughout the 20th century, a good percent of its Slavic texts were destroyed. But Helsinki, which enjoyed relative stability, claims to have the finest collection of Slavic books in the world.

▲▲**Lutheran Cathedral**—With its prominent green dome and the 12 apostles overlooking the city and harbor, this church is Carl

Engel's masterpiece. Finished in 1854, the interior is pure architectural truth. Open a pew gate and sit, surrounded by the saints of Protestantism, to savor Neoclassical nirvana. Physically, this church is perfectly Protestant—austere and unadorned—with the emphasis on preaching (prominent pulpit) and music (huge organ). Statuary is limited to the local Reformation big shots: Martin Luther, Philip Melanchthon (Luther's Reformation sidekick), and the leading Finnish Reformer, Mikael Agricola. A follower of Luther at Wittenberg, Agricola brought the Reformation to Finland. He also translated the Bible into Finnish, and is considered the father of the modern Finnish language. Agricola's Bible is to Finland what the Luther Bible is to Germany, and the King James Bible is to the English-speaking world (free, June–Aug Mon–Sat 9:00–24:00, Sun 12:00–24:00; Sept–May Mon–Sat 9:00–18:00, Sun 12:00–18:00, on Senate Square).

▲▲**Uspenski Cathedral**—This Orthodox cathedral, built in 1868 when Finland belonged to Russia, hovers above Market Square and faces the Lutheran Cathedral as Russian culture faces

Europe's. The uppermost "onion dome" represents the "sacred heart of Jesus," while the smaller ones represent the hearts of the 12 apostles. The cathedral's interior is a potentially emotional icon experience. Its rich images are a stark contrast to the sober Lutheran Cathedral. While commonly called the "Russian church," the cathedral is actually Finnish Orthodox, answering to the patriarch in Constantinople (Istanbul). Much of eastern Finland (the Karelia region) is Finnish Orthodox. The cathedral's Orthodox Mass, with candles,

incense, icons in action, and timeless music (human voices only—no instruments), is beautiful (free, May–Sept Mon–Sat 9:30–16:00, Sun 12:00–15:00; Oct–April Tue–Fri 9:30–16:00, Sat 9:30–14:00, Sun 12:00–15:00, closed Mon, Kanavakatu 1).

▲▲▲**Temppeliaukio Church**—Another great example of church architecture (from 1969), this "Church in the Rock" was blasted out of solid rock and capped with a copper-and-skylight dome. It's normally filled with live or recorded music and awestruck visitors. Grab a pew. Gawk upward at a 13-mile-long coil of copper ribbon. Look at the bull's-eye and ponder God. Forget your camera. Just sit in the middle, ignore the crowds, and be thankful for peace. Under your feet is an air-raid shelter that can accommodate 6,000 people (free, Mon–Sat 10:00–17:00, Thu–Fri until 20:00, Sun 12:00–17:30; sometimes closes for special events and concerts, Lutherinkatu 3, tel. 09/2340-5920). The church is at the top of a hill in a residential neighborhood about a 15-minute walk north of the bus station (or take tram #3T or #3B to Sammonkatu stop). You can attend the English-language Lutheran service (Sun at 14:00) or one of many concerts.

▲**Sibelius Monument**—Six hundred stainless-steel pipes—built on solid rock as is so much of Finland—shimmer in a park to honor

Finland's greatest composer, Jean Sibelius. The artist, Eila Hiltunen, was forced to add a bust of the composer's face to silence critics of her otherwise abstract work. Bus #24 stops here (25 min until the next bus, or catch a quick glimpse on the left from the bus) on its way to the Seurasaari Open-Air Folk Museum. City orientation bus tours stop here for 10 minutes—long enough. The #3T tram, which runs more frequently, stops a few blocks away.

▲▲National Museum of Finland (Suomen Kansallismuseo)—
This pleasant, easy-to-handle collection (covering Finland's
story from A to Z, with good English descriptions) is in a grand
building designed by three of Finland's greatest architects in the
early 1900s. The Neoclassical furniture, folk costumes, armory,
and portraits of Russia's last czars around an impressive throne
are interesting, but the highlight is the "Prehistory of Finland"
exhibit, Finland's largest permanent archaeological collection.
Following the clear English-language descriptions, you'll learn
how Stone, Bronze, and Iron Age tribes of Finland lived (€6, free
Tue 17:30–20:00, covered by Helsinki Card; Tue–Wed 11:00–
20:00, Thu–Sat 11:00–18:00, Sun 11:00–18:00, closed Mon; peaceful second-floor info center with Internet access, Mannerheimintie
34, tel. 09/4050-9544, www.kansallismuseo.fi). The museum café,
with a tranquil outdoor courtyard, has light meals and Finnish
treats such as lingonberry juice and reindeer quiche.

Finlandia Hall (Finlandia-Talo)—Alvar Aalto's most famous
building in his native Finland means little to the non-architect

without a tour (€6, many days at
14:00 in summer, 30 min, call ahead
to check times; hall information
shop open July–Aug Mon–Fri 9:00–
16:00, Sat–Sun 12:00–16:00; Sept–
June Mon–Fri 9:00–16:00, closed
Sat–Sun, Mannerheimintie 13e, tel.
09/40241, www.finlandia.hel.fi). To
see the building from its best angle,
view it from the seaside parking lot, not the street—where nearly
everyone who looks at the building thinks, "So what?"

Kiasma—Finland's museum of contemporary art, designed by
American architect Steven Holl, doesn't have a permanent collection, but you can ask at the TI or check online to find out what's
showing (€8, covered by Helsinki Card, Tue and Sun 10:00–17:00,
Wed–Sat 10:00–20:30, closed Mon, Mannerheiminaukio 2, near
train station, www.kiasma.fi).

Concerts—Concerts in Helsinki's churches, including Kallio
Church with its magnificent new organ, can be excellent. Ask at
the TI, check their daily events board, and keep an eye out for
posters. Many venues post listings in *Helsinki This Week* magazine.

Outer Helsinki

A weeklong car trip up through the Finnish lakes and forests to
Mikkeli and Savonlinna would be relaxing, but you can actually
enjoy Finland's green-trees-and-blue-water scenery without leaving Helsinki. Here are three great ways to get out and go for a
walk on a sunny summer day.

Sauna

Finland's vaporized fountain of youth is the sauna—Scandinavia's answer to support hose and face-lifts. A traditional sauna is a wood-paneled room with wooden benches and a wood-fired stove topped with rocks. The stove is heated blistering hot. Undress entirely before going in. Lay your towel on the bench, and sit or lie on it (for hygienic reasons). Ladle water from the bucket onto the rocks to make steam. Choose a higher bench for hotter temperatures.

The famous birch branches are always available for slapping. Finns claim this enhances circulation and say the chlorophyll released with the slapping opens your sinuses while emitting a refreshing birch aroma. (Follow the lead of the locals around you—tourists merrily flagellating themselves can be really annoying.) Let yourself work up a sweat, then, just before bursting, go outside to the shower for a Niagara of liquid ice. Suddenly your shower stall becomes a Cape Canaveral launch pad, as your body scatters to every corner of the universe. A moment later you're back together and can re-enter the steam room and

Seurasaari Open-Air Folk Museum

Inspired by Stockholm's Skansen, also on a lovely island on the edge of town, this is a collection of one hundred historic buildings from every corner of Finland. Rated ▲▲, it's wonderfully furnished and gives rushed visitors an opportunity to sample the far reaches of Finland without leaving the capital city. The €1.20 map or the helpful €6 guidebook provide needed information if you're not taking a tour (free park entry, €5 to enter buildings, covered by Helsinki Card, June–Aug daily 11:00–17:00; late May and early Sept Mon–Fri 9:00–15:00, Sat–Sun 11:00–17:00, tel. 09/4050-9660, www.seurasaari.fi). Check their Web site to confirm the times for English tours (free with €5 entry ticket, 60 min, mid-June–mid-Aug, generally at 15:00). Off-season, when the buildings are closed, the place is empty and not worth the trouble. To reach the museum, ride bus #24 (from the top of the Esplanade, 2/hr) to the end (note departure times for your return) and walk across the quaint footbridge.

There's a café in the center of the island; you're welcome to bring a picnic. The separate Tomtebo café, with the sprawling front yard at the mainland end of the bridge to Seurasaari, has great repeat as necessary. Only rarely will you feel so good. The Finnish Sauna Society's informative Web site details the history of saunas and sweat baths (www.sauna.fi).

Your hostel, hotel, or the ship you came to Finland on may have a sauna. Ask them when they heat it, and whether it's semi-public (separate men's and women's hours, pay per person) or for private use (book and pay for a 45- to 60-minute time slot, and save money by bringing a group of friends, either mixed or same-sex). Public saunas are a dying breed these days, because most Finns have private saunas in their homes or cabins. But some public saunas survive in rougher, poorer neighborhoods.

For a good, traditional wood-heated sauna with a coarse and local crowd, try the **Kotiharjun Sauna.** While there are no tourists and no English signs, the guy at the desk speaks English and can help: pay €8 plus €2 for a towel, find a locker, strip (keep the key on your wrist), and head for the steam. Cooling off is nothing fancy, just a bank of cold showers. A woman in a fish-cleaner's apron will give you a wonderful scrub with Brillo pad-like mitts for €6. Regulars relax with beers on the sidewalk just outside (Tue–Fri 14:00–22:00, Sat 13:00–21:00, closed Sun–Mon, last entry two hours before closing; men–ground floor, women–upstairs; massage-€20/30 min, €30/hr; 200 yards from Sörnäinen subway stop, Harjutorinkatu 1, tel. 09/753-1535).

homemade cakes and hosts occasional folk-dance performances in summer (June–Aug daily 11:00–18:00, closed off-season; performances-€8, generally on Sun; folk-dance info: tel. 09/484-511 or 09/484-234, www.kolumbus.fi/seurasaarisaatio).

Suomenlinna Fortress

The island guarding Helsinki's harbor served as a strategic fortress for three countries: Finland, Sweden, and Russia. Rated ▲▲, it's now a popular park with several museums and a Visitors Center about five minutes on foot from the boat dock. Pick up a free Suomenlinna mini-newspaper and a brochure (with map) at the Helsinki TI, ferry terminal, or at the Visitors Center.

The fortress was built by the Swedes with French financial support in the mid-1700s to counter Russia's rise to power. (Peter the Great had built his new capital, St. Petersburg, on the Baltic and was eyeing the West.) Named Sveaborg—fortress of Sweden—the fortress was Sweden's military pride and joy. With five miles of walls and hundreds of cannons, it was the second strongest fort of its kind in Europe after Gibraltar. Helsinki, a small peasant community of 1,500 people before 1750, soon became a boom town supporting this grand "Gibraltar of the North."

The fort, built by more than 15,000 workers, was a huge investment and stimulated lots of innovation. In the 1760s it had the world's biggest and most modern dry dock. In 1790 a decisive Swedish naval victory was launched from Sveaborg, costing Russia 9,500 men and 60 boats. But in 1809 the Russians took the "invincible" fort without a fight—by siege—a huge and cheap military gift.

Don't miss the Suomenlinna Museum within the Visitors Center, where the complete story is presented in a fascinating "multi-vision" show. Also on the island are a toy museum and several military museums. Suomenlinna has 1,000 permanent residents, is home to Finland's Naval Academy, and is most appreciated by locals for its fine scenic strolls. The island is large—actually, it's four islands connected by bridges—and you and your imagination get free run of the fortifications and dungeon-like chambers. When it's munch-time, you'll find a half-dozen cafés and plenty of picnic opportunities.

Cost, Hours, and Information: Visitors Center—free, daily May–Aug 10:00–18:00, Sept–April 10:00–16:00; Suomenlinna Museum—€5, covered by Helsinki Card, same hours as Visitors Center; 25-min "multi-vision" show on the island's history on the half-hour, last showing at 17:00; pick up English translation of exhibits by entrance; smaller museums-€3–4 each, open summer only; tel. 09/684-1880, www.suomenlinna.fi.

Tours: Consider a 60-minute English-language tour (€6, covered by Helsinki Card, depart Visitors Center daily June–Aug at 11:00 and 14:00).

Getting There: Catch a ferry to Suomenlinna from Market Square. Walk past the higher-priced excursion boats to the public HKL ferry (€4.40 round-trip, free with Helsinki Card and Tourist Ticket, 15-min trip, 2–3/hr in summer—generally at :00, :20, and :40, but pick up schedule to confirm, nearly hourly in winter).

Peninsula Promenade

For a breezy, salty seaside walk, consider this promenade around the Kaivopuisto Park peninsula. Allow 90 minutes for a leisurely pace. From Market Square, wander past the old brick market hall and Silja Terminal (with its huge ship likely at the dock) and follow the shoreline pedestrian path. The first island you come to, Valkosaari, hosts the local yacht club—NJK—the oldest in Scandinavia, with a classy restaurant (daily 17:00–24:00). The next island, Luoto, is home to the posh Palace Kämp by the Sea restaurant (with shuttle boat service). During a typical winter the bay freezes (18 inches is strong enough to allow cars to drive to the islands—in the past there was even a public bus route that extended to an island during the winter). The fortress island of Suomenlinna is in the distance. The hill you're circling (on the right) is home to several embassies; ahead, Ursula Café, with its fine harbor views, is good for a coffee break.

Around the corner, the next island, Uunisaari, belonged to the military until the 1980s. Its unique plant life (much studied by local students) is believed to have hitched a ride all the way to Finland from Siberia on the boots of Russian soldiers. The odd-looking pier nearby is a station for washing rugs (those are not picnic tables). Saltwater brightens the rag rugs traditionally made by local grandmas. While American men put on aprons and do the barbeque, Finnish men wash the carpets. After the scrub, the rugs are sent through big mechanical wringers and hung on nearby racks to dry in the wind. The posted map shows 11 such stations scattered around Helsinki. Buy an ice cream at the nearby stand and watch the action (best in the morning).

In the distance, beyond its massive shipyards, looms Helsinki's big new port, hosting 270 cruise ships a year. From here you can follow Neitsytpolku street back to the town center, keeping an eye out for fun Art Nouveau buildings.

Near Helsinki

Porvoo, the second-oldest town in Finland, has wooden architecture that dates from the Swedish colonial period. This coastal town can be reached from Helsinki by bus (one hour) or by excursion boat from Market Square.

Turku, the historic capital of Finland, is a two-hour bus or train ride from Helsinki. Overall, Turku is a pale shadow of Helsinki, and there is little reason to make a special trip. It does have a handicraft museum in a cluster of wooden houses (the only part of town to survive a devastating fire in the early 1800s), an old castle, a fine Gothic cathedral, and a market square. Viking and Silja boats sail from Turku to Stockholm every morning and evening, passing through the especially scenic Turku archipelago.

Naantali, a cute, commercial, well-preserved medieval town with a quaint harbor, is an easy bus ride from Turku (4/hr, 20 min).

SHOPPING

The Esplanade: The Esplanade is capped by the enormous, sprawling **Stockmann** department store (Mon–Fri 9:00–21:00, Sat 9:00–18:00, Sun 12:00–18:00, closed Sun in winter, Aleksanterinkatu

52B, www.stockmann.fi). The street is lined with smaller stores ideal for window-shopping. Keep an eye out for sleek Scan-design gifts. Consider the purses, scarves, clothes, and fabrics from **Marimekko,** the well-known Finnish fashion company (sold in several shops along the Esplanade including #14, www.marimekko .fi). Fans of Tove Jansson's Moomin children's stories won't want to miss the **Moomin Shop,** at #33 in the Kämp Galleria (Mon–Fri 10:00–19:00, Sat 10:00–17:00, closed Sun). Bookworms enjoy the impressive **Academic Bookstore** just before Stockmann (#39). The **Artek Store** (#18) was founded by designers Alvar and Elissa Aalto and showcases the Aalto-friendly, modern, and practical style that is standard in Finnish homes today. For less glamorous shopping needs, visit the mall above and around the bus station.

Market Square: This harborfront square is packed not only with fishmongers and producers, but also with stands selling Finnish souvenirs and more refined crafts (roughly Mon–Fri 6:30–18:00, Sat 6:30–16:00, summer only Sun 10:00–16:00). Sniff the stacks of trivets, made from cross-sections of juniper twigs—an ideal, fragrant, easy-to-pack gift for the folks back home (they smell even nicer when you set something hot on them).

Flea Market: If you brake for garage sales, Finland's biggest flea market, the outdoor **Hietalahti Market,** is worth the 15-minute walk from the harbor or a short ride on tram #6 from Mannerheimintie (June–Aug Mon–Fri 8:00–14:00, Sat 8:00–15:00, Sun 10:00–16:00; less action and closed Sun in off-season). The stalls in the adjacent red-brick indoor market specialize in antiques. In the distance, notice the shipyard—birthplace of many of the world's luxury cruise ships.

Unioninkatu Street: This short street (connecting the market with the Lutheran Cathedral) is lined with a fun variety of popular shops. **Kiseleffin Talo,** a top-end handicraft market, is a collection of 20 special boutiques with excellent handicrafts, popular for small, typically Finnish gifts (Mon–Fri 10:00–18:00, Sat 10:00–16:00, Sun 11:00–16:00, at Unioninkatu 27 and Aleksanterinkatu 28).

Kalevala Jewelry sells quality made-in-Finland jewelry at Unioninkatu 25. While modern in feel, it's clearly inspired by archeological finds from ancient Finn and Sami tombs. Traditional costumes in the back show how folkloric people would have sported their jewels (12 percent VAT refunds, tel. 0207-611-380).

G-Boutique sells designer furs at Unioninkatu 27. I enjoy just popping in to see men sitting nervously while their ladies swing through the racks of Finland's top furs (tel. 09/602-682). The shop's slogan, "Finnish fur for sure," is blissfully ignorant of the politically incorrectness of it all (www.furs.fi).

Fishermen head next door where the **Schroder Sport Shop** shows off its famous selection of popular Finnish-made Rapala fishing lures—ideal for the fisherfolk on your gift list.

Across the street, at **Neuhaus Chocolate Café** (#32), manager Roger Alfa is a connoisseur of euro coins and can explain what happened to the local pennies. **Moneta,** next door (also #32), is a real coin shop.

NIGHTLIFE

While it's easy to make friends in a bar, anything alcoholic is expensive. For the latest on hot nightspots, read the English insert of *City* magazine that lists the "best" of everything in Helsinki.

A good bet for a drink, live music (generally jazz), and lots of fun-seeking locals (young and old) is **Michelle Terrace,** where three lively bars share a courtyard. The boomer-friendly scene hops almost nightly through the summer (Gamla Passage, enter at Aleksanterinkatu 46 or at #35 off the Esplanade). Wednesday, called "little Friday" here, is livelier than other work nights.

For cheap fun, Hietaranta Beach and the park on Suomenlinna island are where the local kids hang out (and even skinny-dip) at 22:00 or 23:00. Helsinki is one of Europe's safest cities after dark.

SLEEPING

The rack rate (highest rate) for a standard hotel doubles starts at about €160, but you rarely need to pay this much. You have three basic money-saving options: modest but comfortable smaller hotels; discounted big-hotel rooms in summer and on weekends; and unusually comfortable hostels and student dorms that rent plenty of twin-bedded rooms. Also remember that some of the cheapest beds in Helsinki are on the cruise ships to Stockholm.

Most large Helsinki hotels have a two-tiered pricing system: weekend discounts on Friday and Saturday nights, and higher rack rates the rest of the week. From late June to early August, you get the weekend discount every day of the week. A few hotels extend the weekend discount to Sunday nights as well. When two prices are listed, the first is for weeknights, the second for weekends and summer.

Business-class hotels play a complicated game of price discrimination with computer programs that tell them exactly how much to charge for a room based on demand. They often jumpstart things by offering a number of deeply discounted rooms to those

Sleep Code

(€1 = about $1.20, country code: 358)
S = Single, **D** = Double/Twin, **T** = Triple, **Q** = Quad, **b** = bathroom,
s = shower. Unless otherwise noted, credit cards are accepted
and breakfast is included.

To help you sort easily through these listings, I've divided
the rooms into three categories, based on the full (non-week-
end) price for a standard double room with bath:

$$$ Higher Priced—Most rooms €150 or more.
  $$ Moderately Priced—Most rooms between €80–150.
    $ Lower Priced—Most rooms €80 or less.

who book long in advance on the Web. My listings will save you
money when the hotel is busy, but you'll likely do better with a
Web booking when it's quiet.

All places listed have elevators and accept credit cards. Unless
otherwise noted, breakfast is included.

Helsinki Expert's hotel booking service, with branches at the
TI and the train station, can reserve you a hotel bed for a €5 fee
and always knows where the best deals are (see page 336).

Central Hotels

$$$ Hotel Anna is comfortable and feels like home. Its 64 rooms
are efficiently run as a fundraiser for the Finnish Free Church.
For more air in the rooms, ask at the desk for a key to open the
windows (Sb-€120, superior Sb-€135, Db-€160, superior Db-€175,
junior suite-€205, extra bed-€15, book by e-mail and ask for a Rick
Steves discount—generally 10 percent off business rate and 25 per-
cent for summer and weekends, non-smoking rooms, elevator; 4
blocks south of the top of the Esplanade, Annankatu 1; tel. 09/616-
621, fax 09/602-664, www.hotelanna.fi, info@hotelanna.fi).

$$$ Martta Hotelli, in a modern building, rents 44 charm-
ing rooms and serves breakfast on a sixth-floor terrace. It's a good
value run by an organization you can't help but enjoy supporting:
a Finnish society dedicated to homemaking and gardening (Sb-
€98/€75, small head-to-toe twin Db-€130/€85, full Db-€155/€95,
suite-€170/€130, Tb-€150/€100, weekend rates also valid Sun night,
non-smoking rooms, sauna, Uudenmaankatu 24, tel. 09/618-7400,
fax 09/618-7401, www.marttahotelli.fi, info@marttahotelli.fi).

$$ Hotel Arthur, a five-minute walk from the train station
on a quiet street, is well-worn and run by the YMCA, with 160
forgettable industrial-strength rooms (S-€52/€37, Sb-€94/€73,
D-€68/€61, small twin Db-€114/€92, nicer Db-€134/€108,

extra bed-€20, weekend rates also valid Sun night, non-smoking rooms, Vuorikatu 19, tel. 09/173-441, fax 09/626-880, www
.hotelarthur.fi).

$$ Hotelli Finn is wonderfully central, stowed quietly on the sixth floor of an office building at the top of the Esplanade. While its carpets are frayed and stained, its 27 simple, comfy rooms—half with private showers, all with toilet and sink—are a good choice when other places are charging rack rates (S-€55, Sb-€65, D-€65, Db-€80, Tb-€97, Qb-€115, small breakfast served in room-€6, Kalevankatu 3B, tel. 09/684-4360, fax 09/6844-3610, www
.hotellifinn.fi, hotelli.finn@kolumbus.fi).

$$ Hotel Skatta is an old sailors' hotel (from May–Oct, it's half-booked by Nordic Jet Line for their staff). It has a salty, street-level lounge, and 23 rooms quietly stowed away on the sixth and seventh floors. Though a bit institutional, it's clean, well-run, has refreshingly straight pricing, and is just two blocks from the Katajanokka ferry terminal along the #4 tram line (Sb-€65, Db-€80, extra bed-€10, breakfast-€5, all Db are twins, great gym and sauna in basement for guests—fun if you're looking for a sailor, Internet access, call well in advance, Linnankatu 3, tel. 09/659-233, fax 09/631-352, www.hotelskatta.com).

$ Omena Hotelli (Apple Hotel) will be the newest budget hotel in town when it opens in 2007 with €55 rooms that sleep up to four people. Omena's hotels are entirely automated: You book on the Web, they bill you, and you receive a room access code. Check their Web site for location and details on the Helsinki opening (tel. 20/428-2119, www.omena.com).

Expensive Hotels with Great Weekend Deals

On Friday and Saturday nights and from late June to early August, even Helsinki's more expensive hotels have great deals on doubles. Hotels set aside a certain number of rooms at great prices for those who book long in advance. Prices get even better for non-refundable hotel rooms. These Web-based savings can save you a bundle.

$$$ Scandic Grand Marina, a huge four-star hotel right between the Katajanokka and Kanava terminals, discounts its €232 doubles to €100 or less (Katajanokanlaituri 7, tel. 09/16661, fax 09/664-764, www.scandic-hotels.com/grandmarina, grandmarina@scandic-hotels.com). Reserve well in advance on their Web site, and save even more with their free Hilton club card.

$$$ Hotel Linna, with 48 modern rooms behind a striking Art Nouveau facade, discounts its €210 doubles to €116 (Lönnrotinkatu 29, tel. 010/344-4100, fax 010/344-4101, www
.palace.fi, linna@palace.fi).

$$$ Hotel Cumulus Kaisaniemi, with 101 rooms, is big and without soul, but it's right near the train station (Sb-€143/€89,

Db-€175/€112, ask for quieter room on back side, Kaisaniemenkatu 7, tel. 09/172-881, fax 09/605-379, www.cumulus.fi, kaisaniemi .cumulus@restel.fi).

Hostels

Helsinki's hostels are unusually comfortable. While they offer €3 discounts for those with hostel cards, all ages are welcome with or without a hostel membership. Eurohostel and Academica are more like budget hotels than hostels.

$ Eurohostel is a modern hostel 200 yards from the Katajanokka ferry terminal or a 10-minute walk from Market Square. The more expensive rooms are newly renovated and come with TVs (255 beds, S-€39–42, D-€47–52, T-€70–78, family room with up to 4 kids under age 15-€57–64, shared twins or triples-€24–26 per person, includes sheets, breakfast-€6.30, free morning sauna, evening sauna-€5, private lockable closets, handy tram #4 stop around the corner, Linnankatu 9, tel. 09/622-0470, fax 09/655-044, www.eurohostel.fi). It's packed with facilities, including a laundry room, a members' kitchen with unique refrigerated safety-deposit boxes for your caviar and beer, a restaurant, and plenty of good budget-travel information. While generally fully booked in advance, they release no-show beds at 18:00.

$ Academica Summer Hostel is a university dorm used as a hostel from June through August. Finnish university students have it good—rooms are hotel-quality with private baths and kitchenettes, though all doubles have twin beds. Guests can have a morning sauna and use the swimming pool for free. It's a 10-minute walk from the train station; from the harbor, take tram #3T to the Kauppakorkeakoulu stop (250 rooms, Sb-€40–55, old Db-€60, renovated Db-€75, Tb-€75, Qb-€90, prices include sheets and breakfast; hostel beds in shared 2–4 bed rooms cost €18 per person plus €6 for breakfast and €5 if you need sheets; between Mechelininkatu and Runeberginkatu at Hietaniemenkatu 14, tel. 09/1311-4334, fax 09/441-201, www .hostelacademica.fi, hostelacademica@hyy.fi).

$ Erottajanpuisto is a small, quiet, friendly, older—and therefore slightly ramshackle—hostel in a great location on the third floor of a 19th-century apartment building in the center of town. It has an inviting lounge, a kitchen, and 15 rooms with four to eight beds apiece (dorm bed-€22.50, S-€46, D-€60, T-€78, Q-€100, includes sheets, breakfast-€5, no elevator, Uudenmaankatu 9, tel. 09/642-169, fax 09/680-2757, www.erottajanpuisto.com, info @erottajanpuisto.com).

$ Olympic Stadium Hostel (Stadionin Retkeilymaja) is big, crowded, and impersonal. Its 162 beds are a last resort (€16 per bed in 9- or 12-bed rooms, sheets-€5, breakfast-€6, tel. 09/477-8480, www.stadionhostel.com, info@stadionhostel.fi). Take tram #3T or #7A from downtown to the Aurora Hospital stop.

EATING

Helsinki is filled with restaurants serving everything from traditional Finnish and Russian food to nouvelle cuisine in modern, bright interiors. In 2007 a new law is expected to make Finland's restaurants entirely smoke-free.

Restaurants are a good value for lunch. Finnish companies get a tax break if they distribute lunch coupons (worth €8) to their employees. It's no surprise that most downtown Helsinki restaurants offer weekday lunch specials that cost exactly the value of the coupon.

Dressy Splurge Dinners

Sundmans Krog Bistro is sedate and Old World but not folk-loric, filling an old merchant's mansion facing the harbor. As the less fussy and more affordable little sister of an adjacent, posh, Michelin-rated restaurant, quality is assured. A rare and memorable extra is their Baltic herring buffet—featuring pickled, creamed, and grilled herring with potatoes and all the toppings—€12 as a starter, €17 as a main course. The €18 lunch special (Mon–Fri 11:00–15:00) includes the herring buffet and a daily fish dish (entreés-€20–25, three-course "Helsinki" dinner-€46, daily 11:00–21:30, Etelaranta 16, tel. 09-6226-4120).

Restaurant Kosmos serves dependable Helsinki cuisine in a big, square dining hall that takes you back to the days between the wars. Their cuisine is specifically Helsinki—with a stress on fish and Baltic herring—with a Russian twist. Locals appreciate the ambience maintained by three generations of the Hepolampi family. Their fun printed history traces the restaurant's 75 years, from a haven for strong drinks, to a hangout for the 1950s intelligentsia, to today's best traditional Finnish cuisine. You're likely to sit next to a local celebrity—and not know it (daily three-course dinner special-€38, hearty entreés-€20–25, Mon–Fri 11:30–24:00, Sat 16:00–24:00, closed Sun, Kalevankatu 3, tel. 09/647-255).

Sasso Northern Italian Kitchen is a trendy spot for top-end Italian. It faces but ignores the harbor (pastas-€18, entreés-€20, four-course dinner special-€52, Mon–Sat from 16:30, closed Sun; across from Market Square and the harbor at the end of the Esplanade, Pohjoisesplanadi 17; tel. 09/1345-6240).

Savoy Restaurant, where locals go for a special occasion, is expensive, formal, and drenched in Alvar Aalto design. Everything—from the chairs and lampshades to the doors—is 1937 original. The food is pure Scandinavian. While the terrace offers a great eighth-floor rooftop view, the interior is where you'll experience the classic Finnish atmosphere (three-course meal-€72, five-course meal-€89, Mon–Fri 18:00–24:00, closed Sat and Sun, Etelaesplanadi 14, tel. 09/684-4020).

Venerable Esplanade Cafeterias with Fancy Upstairs Restaurants

Highly competitive cafés and restaurants line the sunny north side of the Esplanade—most offering enticing lunch salads and light meals in their cafés (with fine sidewalk seating), plush sofas for cocktails in their bars, and fancy restaurant dining upstairs. Most are open daily 10:00–22:00.

At **Restaurant Teatteri,** the Wine & Deli section is a hit with locals for its great salad bar (crispy base, you choose which two meats or extras to add, €8 with bread, Caesar salad option, too). Their cocktail bar—trendy with office workers yet comfortable for baby-boomer tourists—has fine park-side seating (indoors and out). The restaurant upstairs is classically modern Finnish in decor with nicely presented international dishes and a jazzy feel (fun tapas selection—3, 6, or 9 on a plate, €20 to €25 entreés; facing Café Esplanade at the top of Esplanade park, Pohjoisesplanadi 2, tel. 09/681-1130).

Café Esplanade, across from Restaurant Teatteri, competes head-on with an equal €8 salad bar (add your two favorite extras to the base). The cafeteria line is lined with temptations, including famous cinnamon rolls. Sit outside and enjoy the Parisian-style sidewalk setting. Their bistro in back is fast, affordable, and popular with locals for a light meal (€9 lunch specials, Pohjoisesplanadi 37, tel. 09/665-496).

Strindberg is also popular (at the corner of Mikonkatu). Downstairs is an elegant cafeteria with outdoor and indoor tables great for people-watching (sandwiches and salads, €6–8). The upstairs cocktail lounge—with big sofas and bookshelves, giving it a den-like coziness—attracts the after-work office crowd. Also upstairs, the inviting restaurant has huge entreés for €15–25 with fish, meat, pasta, and vegetarian options. Consider their "classics" list (reservations smart—a must for a window seat overlooking the Esplanade, Pohjoisesplanadi 33, tel. 09/681-2030).

Functional Eating

Lasipalatsi, the renovated, rejuvenated 1930s Glass Palace, houses a trendy upstairs restaurant and cheaper downstairs café across

Mannerheimintie from the train station. The café (with a youthful terrace on the square out back) offers soup, salad bar, bread, and coffee for €7.50 at lunch, plus €4 sandwiches and €4 cakes. Upstairs, the restaurant takes pride in its functionalist architecture (soups, pastas, and salads for €7–15, traditional Finnish entreés for €15–26, very long café hours, restaurant open Mon–Fri 11:00–24:00, Sat from 12:00, Sun 18:00–23:00, across from post office at Mannerheimintie 22–24, tel. 09/612-6700).

Theme Dining: Tractors and Lapp Cuisine

Zetor, the self-proclaimed *traktor* restaurant, mercilessly lampoons Finnish rural culture and cuisine (while celebrating it deep down). Sit next to a cow-crossing sign at a tractor-turned-into-a-table, in a "Finnish Western" atmosphere reminiscent of director Aki Kaurismäki's movies. Main dishes run €10–16 and include reindeer, elk stew, smoked herring, and less exotic fare—sure to leave you with fun memories (Sun–Fri 15:00–24:00, Sat 11:00–24:00; 200 yards north of Stockmann department store, across street from McDonald's at Mannerheimintie 3–5; reserve for Fri and Sat, tel. 09/666-966, www.ravintolazetor.fi).

Lappi Restaurant is a fine place for Lapp cuisine, with an entertaining menu and creative decor that has you thinking you've traveled north and lashed your reindeer to the hitchin' post. The friendly staff serves tasty Sami dishes in a snug and very woody atmosphere (€15–30 dinner plates; Mon–Fri 17:00–22:30, Sat–Sun 13:00–22:30; mid-Aug–mid-June also Mon–Fri 12:00–17:00; reservations a must after 19:00, off Bulevardi at Annankatu 22, tel. 09/645-550, www.lappires.com).

Fun Harborfront Market Eateries and Picnics

Helsinki's delightful and vibrant **Market Square** is magnetic any time of day...but especially at lunchtime. This really is the most memorable, casual, quick—and cheap—lunch place in town. A half-dozen tents (erected to shield diners from bird bombs—more problematic with bird flu concerns) serve fun food on paper plates (lunch only). Kahvipaikka Snellman is a hit for its meat pies (€3) and pastries called "apple pigs" (€2.50). It's not unusual for the Finnish president to stop by here with visiting dignitaries. There's a crepe place, a couple of cheap indoor eateries (including a sushi bar) in the red-brick indoor market, and at the far end—my favorites—several salmon grills (€8 for a good meal). The only real harborside dining in this part of town is picnicking. While these places provide picnic tables, you can also have it foil-wrapped to go and grab benches right on the water down near Uspenski Cathedral.

In **supermarkets,** buy the semi-flat bread (available dark or light) that Finns love—every slice is a heel. Finnish liquid yogurt is also a treat (sold in liter cartons). Karelian pasties—filled with rice or mashed potatoes—make a good snack. There's a good, big supermarket at Lönnrotinkatu and Annankatu (Mon–Fri 8:00–21:00, Sat 8:00–18:00, June–Aug also Sun 12:00–21:00), and an upscale one beneath the Stockmann department store (Aleksanterinkatu 52B).

TRANSPORTATION CONNECTIONS

From Helsinki, it's easy to get to **Turku** (hourly, 2 hrs) or **St. Petersburg, Russia,** by either bus or train. To St. Petersburg, the bus is slower and cheaper (3/day, 9 hrs, about €30–45, less for students) than the train (2/day, 6 hrs, €51, no student discount). Travelers to Russia need a visa and should not wait until Helsinki to plan their trip (see www.russianembassy.org). For train info, visit www.vr.fi. For bus info in English, consult www.matkahuolto.fi.

By Boat from Helsinki to: Stockholm (Silja and Viking lines sail nightly; see beginning of this chapter for details), **Tallinn** (ferries and—in summer only—fast boats travel the 50 miles many times a day; see the Tallinn chapter for details). See "Arrival in Helsinki," page 337, for terminal locations.

ESTONIA

ESTONIA

(Eesti)

Estonians are related to the Finns and have a similar history—first Swedish domination, then Russian (1710–1918), and finally independence after World War I. In 1940, Estonians were at least as affluent and as advanced as the Finns, but they could not preserve their independence from Soviet expansion during World War II. As a result, Estonia sank into a 50-year communist twilight from which it is still emerging. In 2004, Estonia took a significant step forward when it was invited to join the European Union. By 2009, it expects to switch from the krooni to the euro.

One problematic legacy of the Soviet experience is Estonia's huge Russian population. Most Estonian Russians' parents and grandparents were brought to Estonia in the 1950s and 1960s to work in now-defunct factories in Tallinn and in the northeastern cities. Twenty-five percent of Estonia's population is now Russian. Making Russians feel at home in Estonia while building a distinctly Estonian culture and identity is one of independent Estonia's biggest challenges. Estonia will always face both west, across the Baltic, and east, into the Russian hinterlands.

EU membership seemed like a natural next step to many Estonians. They already thought of themselves as part of the Nordic world. Language, history, religion, and twice-hourly ferry departures connect Finns and Estonians. It's only 50 miles between Helsinki and Tallinn, and an overnight boat ride to Stockholm. Finns visit Tallinn to eat, drink, and shop more cheaply than at home. While some Estonians resent how Tallinn becomes a Finnish nightclub on summer weekends, most people on both sides are happy to have friendly new neighbors.

Younger Estonians speak English—it's the first choice these days at school. Estonian is similar to Finnish, and equally difficult. Only a million people speak Estonian worldwide. Two useful phrases to know are *"Tänan"* (TAN-on; "Thank you") and *"Terviseks!"* (TEAR-vee-sex; "Cheers!"). The farther you go beyond the touristy zones, the more you see that Russian is still Estonia's

Estonia Almanac

Official Name: Eesti Vabariik—the Republic of Estonia—or simply Estonia.

Population: Estonia is home to 1.3 million people (77 per square mile). Three in four are of Estonian heritage and about one-quarter are of Russian descent, with smaller minorities of Ukranians, Belarusians, and Finns. About 70 percent speak the official language—Estonian—and more than 30 percent speak Russian. The majority of Estonians are unaffiliated with any religion. About 14 percent are Lutheran and 13 percent are Orthodox.

Latitude and Longitude: 59°N and 26°E, similar latitude to Juneau, Alaska.

Area: 17,500 square miles, about the size of New Hampshire and Vermont combined.

Geography: Between Latvia and Russia, Estonia borders the Baltic Sea and Gulf of Finland. It includes more than 1,000 islands and islets, the largest of which are Saaremaa and Hiiumaa.

Biggest City: The capital of Estonia, Tallinn, has 400,320 people (505,000 in the metropolitan area).

Economy: Estonia's transition to a free-market economy has included joining the World Trade Organization and the European Union. It has a Gross Domestic Product of $22 billion and a per-capita GDP of $16,700. Its three major trading partners are Finland, Sweden, and Germany, which accounts for its strengths in electronics and telecommunications.

Currency: Thirteen Estonian krooni (kr) = about $1.

Government: Estonia is a constitutional democracy, with a president elected by parliament (Toomas Ilves, since October 2006), and a prime minister (Andrus Ansip, since April 2005). The 101-member parliament (Riigikogu) is elected by popular vote every four years.

Flag: The pre-1940 Estonian flag was restored in 1990. It has three equal horizontal bands with blue at the top, black in the middle, and white on the bottom.

The Average Estonian: The average Estonian is 39 years old, has 1.4 children, and will live to be 72.

Estonia

main second language. If you know some Russian, use it. It's the mother tongue of more than 40 percent of Tallinners (many of whom have no intention of learning Estonian).

TALLINN

Stepping off the boat in Tallinn, you feel that you've traveled further culturally than you have throughout the rest of Scandinavia. Tallinn's Nordic Lutheran culture and language connect it with Stockholm and Helsinki, but two centuries of Tsarist Russian rule and 45 years in the Soviet Union have blended in a distinctly Russian flavor. Like Prague and Kraków, Tallinn has modernized at an astounding rate since the fall of the Soviet Union in 1991. Yet it has beautifully preserved the Old World ambience within its walled town center. Colorfully painted medieval houses share cobbled lanes with blocky, communist-style buildings...and everything is enlivened with Estonians thoroughly enjoying their freedom.

If you're pondering a cultural detour on your Nordic vacation, Tallinn and Helsinki are the logical choices—both are quite different from the "core" Scandinavian countries, and both are easily reached on a night cruise from Stockholm (or a quick flight from Stockholm or just about anywhere). Tallinn is much cheaper than Helsinki, with great restaurants and good shopping. It's also more challenging. Why not give yourself a couple of extra days and do both as a triangular side-trip from Stockholm?

Sailing from Stockholm to Tallinn

Tallink's ships leave Stockholm at 18:00 every evening and arrive in Tallinn at 11:00 the next morning. Return trips leave Tallinn at 18:00 and arrive in Stockholm at 10:00. All times are local; Tallinn is an hour ahead of Stockholm.

Fares vary by the day and season—highest on Friday nights and from July 1 to August 15; lowest on Sunday through Wednesday nights the rest of the year. I've given high/low prices

Helsinki/Tallinn Connections

Company	Ship Type	Helsinki Terminal	Helsinki Phone #
Tallink	Ferries and fast boats	Länsi	09/228-311
Linda Line	Fast boats	Makasiini	09/668-9700
Nordic Jet Line	Fast boats	Kanava	09/681-770
Silja	Fast boats	Makasiini	09/18041
Eckerö Line	Ferries	Länsi	09/228-8544
Viking	Ferries	Katajanokka	09/12351

Note: Finland's country code is 358 (drop initial zero of area code when calling Finland internationally).

here in Swedish currency (8 kronor = about $1). A one-way berth in a four-person cabin with a private bath costs 425/265 kronor on the *Regina Baltica*, 545/370 kr on the *Victoria*. Round-trip prices cost only a little more: 530/330 kr on the *Regina Baltica*, 680/460 kr on the *Victoria*. The two legs of a round-trip don't have to be on successive days (unlike the Stockholm–Helsinki ferries), and the price depends on both the outbound and return days of the week. Couples can rent a cabin for themselves for roughly four times the per-person prices above.

Breakfast is 80 kr, and the *smörgåsbord* dinner is 200 kr. Reserve your meal (and even, if possible, your table) when you buy your ticket. The boats have exchange offices with acceptable rates for your leftover cash.

Reserve by calling either the Stockholm reservations line (tel. 46-8/666-6001) or the Estonian booking number (tel. 372/640-9808). Unfortunately, they cannot take your credit-card number over the phone; they'll send you a form to mail or fax back. Pick up your tickets at the port on the day of departure or at their downtown office (Klarabergsgatan 31 in Stockholm). Online booking is possible only in Swedish and for entire cabins (www.tallink.se).

In Stockholm, Tallink ships leave from the Frihamnen harbor. To get from downtown Stockholm to Frihamnen harbor, take the shuttle bus from the main station (25 kr, leaves at about 15:30, check times when buying ticket), or take public bus #1 (marked Frihamnen) from Kungsgatan to the end of the line (30 kr, 3–6/hr, 25 min). In Tallinn, the Tallink ships dock at Terminal D.

Speeding Between Helsinki and Tallinn

From April to October, four different companies offer **fast boats** that link Helsinki and Tallinn (2/hr, 90–100 min, first departure

Company	Tallinn Terminal	Tallinn Phone #	Web site
Tallink	Ferries: A; Fast boats: D	640-9808	www.tallink.ee, www.tallink.se
Linda Line	Linnahall	699-9333	www.lindaline.ee
Nordic Jet Line	C	613-7000	www-eng.njl.fi
Silja	D	611-6661	www.silja.fi
Eckerö Line	B	631-8606	www.eckeroline.fi
Viking	A	666-3966	www.vikingline.fi

Note: Estonia's country code is 372.

about 7:00, last about 21:30). You can reserve in advance by phone or online, or buy tickets from a travel agency (such as the Helsinki Expert office in the TI—see below), but it's rarely necessary. Fast-boat trips may be canceled in stormy weather (in which case you'll be put on a bigger, slower boat).

Fares run €20–45 one-way (evening departures from Helsinki and morning departures from Tallinn are cheapest). Round-trips start at about €35 if you come back with the same company. Linda Line, which uses small hydrofoils, is the fastest (only 90 min, 45-pound luggage limit). The Tallink, Nordic Jet, and Silja fast boats take cars and tolerate bad weather the best.

Big **car ferries** also run year-round between Helsinki and Tallinn (7/day, 3.5 hours, cheaper at €15–20 one-way, €23 round-trip, student and senior discounts) and come with great *smörgåsbord* buffets (expect €10 extra for breakfast, €20 for dinner). Foot passengers prefer the Viking ferries, which depart from central Helsinki. The Tallink and Eckerö Line ferries use Helsinki's Länsi terminal (no problem for drivers, but hard to reach by public transit).

The helpful **Helsinki Expert** desk in the Helsinki TI sells tickets (€7 fee per booking) and posts a sheet clearly explaining departures and costs. The TI in Tallinn posts a list but does not sell tickets. The chart in this chapter lists the names, ship types, phone numbers, terminals, and Web sites for the main ferry operators. Web sites have all the latest information, and most allow online booking. Tallinn and Helsinki each have five different ferry terminals; make sure you know which one your boat leaves from (for descriptions of Helsinki's terminals, see page 372; for Tallinn's, see "Arrival in Tallinn," below).

Helsinki Expert also sells €149 day-trip **tours to Tallinn** that give you fast round-trip boat crossings, transfers, a three-hour bus and walking tour, lunch, and an hour or so to wander and shop. But Tallinn is accessible enough for most travelers to do it on their own—it's cheaper and more fun to just buy boat tickets and follow my "Welcome to Tallinn" self-guided walk, below.

Tallinn

Among Nordic medieval cities, there's none nearly as well-preserved as Tallinn. Its mostly intact city wall includes 26 watchtowers, each topped by a pointy red roof. Baroque and choral music ring out in its old Lutheran churches. I'd guess Tallinn has more restaurants, cafés, and surprises per capita and square inch than any city in this book—and the fun is affordable on nearly any budget.

Tallinn is busy cleaning up the mess left by the communist experiment. New shops, restaurants, and hotels are bursting out of old buildings. The city changes so fast, even locals can't keep up. The Old Town is getting a lot of tourist traffic now, so smart shopping is wise. You'll eat better for half the price by seeking out places that cater to locals.

The city was a medieval stronghold of the Baltic trading world. In the 19th and early 20th centuries, Tallinn industrialized and expanded beyond its walls. Architects encircled the Old Town, putting up broad streets of public buildings, low, Scandinavian-style apartment buildings, and single-family wooden houses. After 1945, Soviet planners ringed the city with stands of now-crumbling concrete high-rises where many of Tallinn's Russian immigrants settled.

Tallinn's Old Town is a fascinating package of pleasing towers, ramparts, facades, *striptiis* bars, churches, shops, and people-watching. It's a rewarding detour for those who want to spice their Scandinavian travels with an ex-Soviet twist.

Planning Your Time

On a three-week tour of Scandinavia, Tallinn is certainly worth a day. Get oriented with either the official walking tour or my "Welcome to Tallinn" self-guided walk (see both below). Check concert schedules if you'll be around for the evening.

Day-Trippers: Whether arriving from Helsinki or Stockholm, hit the ground running by following my self-guided walk right from the ferry terminal. Enjoy the best restaurant you can afford in the Old Town for lunch. Then spend the afternoon shopping and browsing (or out at the open-air museum, if you're into folk history). Remember to bring a jacket (it can be chilly even on sunny summer days).

ORIENTATION

(13 Estonian krooni = about $1)

Almost everything of interest to tourists is in Tallinn's walled Old Town, an easy 15-minute walk from the ferry terminals where most visitors land (see "Arrival in Tallinn," below). The Old Town is divided into two parts (historically, two separate towns): the upper town, Toompea, and the lower town, with Town Hall Square. It's all surrounded by a remarkably intact medieval wall, and within that wall, another wall separates the two towns.

Town Hall Square (Raekoja plats) marks the heart of the medieval lower town. The TI and nearly everything of sightseeing and edible interest is nearby. Pickpockets have become a problem in the more touristy parts of the Old Town, so keep valuables in your money belt.

Tourist Information

The hardworking, English-speaking **TI** has maps, concert listings, and free brochures. It also sells *Tallinn This Week* and the Tallinn Card—see below (Mon–Fri 9:00–20:00, Sat–Sun 10:00–18:00, closes an hour or two earlier off-season, a block off Town Hall Square at Kullassepa 4, tel. 645-7777, www.tourism.tallinn.ee, turismiinfo@tallinnlv.ee).

Travelers' Tent is a creative service offered by young people for young visitors in a tent set up in the park immediately in front of the TI. While its future is in doubt, if it's there in 2007 it will be a handy source for backpacker info, youthful tours, bike rental, and cheap accommodations, with longer hours than the TI. Their map (free, but give a donation) is packed with fun tips to enjoy Tallinn down, dirty, and cheap.

Tallinn in Your Pocket is the best city guidebook on Tallinn (35 kr, on sale all over town, on ships, at airport newsstands, and at the TI). It has complete restaurant, hotel, and sight listings that go far beyond what's listed in this book, plus a rare Old Town map listing all of the tiny streets (for pre-trip planning, use the online edition at www.inyourpocket.com).

Tallinn Card: This card, sold at the TI, airport, ports, and big hotels, gives you free use of public transport and entry to museums (130 kr/6 hrs, 350 kr/24 hrs, 400 kr/48 hrs, 450 kr/72 hrs, includes good info booklet, www.tallinn.ee/tallinncard). From the 24-hour level up, it also includes the 2.5-hour bus and walking tour (see "Tours," below).

Arrival in Tallinn

By Boat: If you have no luggage, just walk 15 minutes into the center of town—just follow signs to city center and set your sights on the spire in the distance (or follow my "Welcome to Tallinn" walk, below). The zone between the port and town is a sprawling, car-friendly commercial zone—the first stop for many Finns bargain-hunting for booze, cigarettes, and clothing. With luggage, it's best to grab a cab (see taxi advice under "Getting Around Tallinn," below). Public transport from the port area is mediocre; buses and trams can bring you to the area around the Hotel Viru, but not into the Old Town (bus #2 stops at Terminals A and D, 2/hr).

Tallinn has four terminals lettered A through D, and a fifth terminal called Linnahall (used only by the fast Linda Line boat). Terminals A, B, and C are clustered together; Terminal D is a 10-minute walk to the east (and is the farthest from the Old Town), and the Linnahall terminal is a 10-minute walk to the west. Each terminal offers baggage storage. Find out which terminal you're leaving from so that you don't miss your return boat.

By Plane: The airport is close to town and has a small info desk (www.tallinn-airport.ee, tel. 372/605-8888). A taxi to the Old Town should cost less than 150 kr (confirm price first, see taxi advice under "Getting Around Tallinn," below). Public bus #2 connects the airport and the center of the Old Town (runs from curb in front of the arrivals area to near Hotel Viru, and continues on to the ferry terminals (2/hr, single tickets cost 10 kr from kiosks, 15 kr from driver). To get to the Old Town, ride six stops to "Likma."

Helpful Hints

Currency Exchange: About 13 Estonian krooni (kr) equal $1. The kroon is permanently tied to the euro (15.65 krooni = €1), but euros are rarely accepted, and if they are, don't expect a good exchange rate. Plenty of exchange offices compete to change your leftover Swedish kronor and euros, but skip them if you can—banks have the best rates. A bank near the TI is **SEB** (Mon–Fri 9:00–16:30, closed Sat–Sun, Harju 13). ATMs are everywhere, including at the ferry terminals and the airport. Credit cards are widely accepted.

Telephones: Estonian phone numbers are seven digits with no area codes. Tallinn numbers begin with 6, and mobile phones (more expensive to call) begin with 5. Phone cards for public booths are sold at kiosks around town (in 50-kr and 100-kr denominations).

Internet Access: In the Old Town, several places advertise Internet access. The **Apollo Bookstore** has three terminals upstairs in a cool cafe. The top floor (A5) at the **Kaubamaja** department

Tallinn

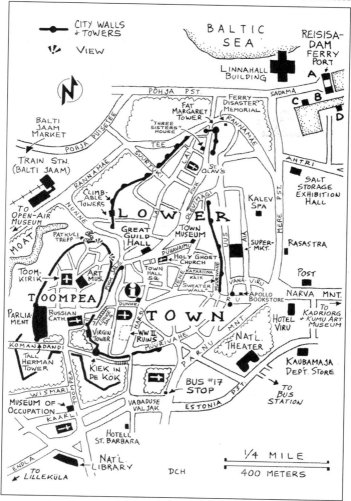

store charges a straight 35 kr per hour (daily 9:00–21:00, in far building of Viru shopping center). Many hotels offer free Internet access in their lobbies and some have Wi-Fi.

Travel Agency: While nothing exceptional, **Mainedd Travel Agency** (on Town Hall Square) is as good as any. It's handy and sells tickets to all boats for no extra fee (Mon–Fri 9:30–17:30, closed Sat–Sun, Raekoja plats 18, tel. 644-4744).

Train Station: While Tallinn has a sleepy and cute little train station, few tourists will use it. The station, a 10-minute walk across the busy highway from the Old Town, is adjacent to the big, cheap Hotel Shnelli and the colorful farmers market.

Laundry: Pesumaja will do your laundry for you for 67 kr per load; drop off before noon for same-day service (Mon–Fri 8:00–20:00, Sat–Sun 11:00–19:00, Pärnu maantee 48, across from Kosmos stop of tram lines #3 or #6, or walk 10 min from Vabaduse väljak).

Local Guide: Antonio Salto is a good local guide (antonio.villacis @luukku.com).

Getting Around Tallinn

If you're just exploring the Old Town and surrounding areas, your feet are all you need. Take a bus, tram, or trolley if you're sleeping outside of the Old Town, or if you're going to Kadriorg (palace), the Kumu Art Museum, the open-air folk museum, or the airport. (The bus from the boat terminal stops several blocks away from the Old Town behind Viru Hotel.)

One ticket, valid for a single ride on any type of public transport, costs 10 kr from a kiosk at a bus stop or 15 kr when purchased from the driver. If you'll be shuttling around town a lot, you can save by purchasing a packet of 10 tickets for 80 kr from a kiosk, or by buying a transit pass (1-day pass/40 kr, 3-day pass/80 kr, sold at newsstands). The Tallinn Card covers public transportation (described in "Tourist Information," above). For more information, see www.tourism.tallinn.ee.

Taxis in Tallinn are expensive and quick to rip off tourists. Until they get regulated and honest, I'd try to avoid them. Any pick-up in the Old Town comes with a steep minimum charge, so you'll save a bit by walking away from the tourist center and into the real world. There's no consistency in the taxi business here—each of the countless companies is free to charge what they like. You'll see the prices listed on their doors. If you've just arrived at the airport or the ferry port, it may be hard to avoid taking a cab. The cabbies who flag *you* down ("Taxi?"), and have run-down-looking cars or offer strip-club brochures, are likely into creative income augmentation. Thankfully, the city is cracking down on these guys.

TOURS

Bus and Walking Tour—This thoroughly enjoyable 2.5-hour tour of Tallinn comes in two parts: first by bus, then on foot (250 kr, covered by Tallinn Card—except 6-hr version of card, tour in English and Finnish, April–Oct daily departures from Hotel Viru at 10:30, 12:30, and 15:00—free shuttles leave harbor terminals about 30 minutes beforehand).

SELF-GUIDED WALK

Welcome to Tallinn

This walk, worth ▲▲▲, explores the "two towns" of Tallinn. The city once consisted of two feuding medieval towns separated by a wall. The upper town—on the hill, called Toompea—was the seat of government ruling Estonia. The lower town was an autonomous Hanseatic trading center filled with German, Danish, and Swedish merchants who hired Estonians to do their menial labor.

Two steep, narrow streets—the "Long Leg" and the "Short Leg"—connect Toompea and the lower town. This walk explores both towns, going up the short leg and down the long leg. From the ferry terminal, start with #1. For the complete tour, those already in town can walk out to Fat Margaret Tower and start at #1, or just pick up the tour from #5 (Town Hall Square) and wander down Pikk Street (covering sights #1, #2, #3, and #4 in reverse).

❶ To Fat Margaret Tower and Start of Walk: From the ferry terminal, hike toward the tall tapering spire, go through a small

park, and enter the Old Town through the archway by the squat Fat Margaret Tower. Just outside the tower on a bluff overlooking the harbor is a broken black arch, a memorial to several hundred people who perished in 1994 when the *Estonia* passenger ferry sank during its Tallinn-Stockholm run. The details remain murky, and conspiracy theorists still think Sweden sank it. (The boat sank very quickly; Sweden has never allowed any divers to explore the remains, and now there's talk of entombing it in concrete, leading some to believe the incident involved some kind of nuclear material-related mischief.)

Fat Margaret Tower guarded the entry gate of the town (in medieval times, the sea came much closer to this point than it does today). The relief above the gate is Swedish, dating from the 16th century, when Sweden took Estonia from Germany. (The paltry Estonian Maritime Museum in the tower is open Wed–Sun 10:00–18:00.)

Just inside the gate is the merchant's home, nicknamed the "Three Sisters" (on right with your back to the sea), a textbook example of a merchant home/warehouse/office from the 15th-century Hanseatic Golden Age. The charmingly carved door evokes the wealth of Tallinn's merchant class back then.

• *Head up Pikk (which means "long") street.*

Tallinn Walking Tour

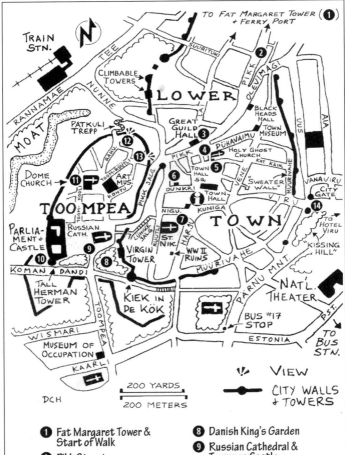

1 Fat Margaret Tower & Start of Walk

2 Pikk Street

3 Great Guild Hall

4 Church of the Holy Ghost

5 Town Hall Square

6 The Wheel Well

7 St. Nicholas' (Niguliste) Church

8 Danish King's Garden

9 Russian Cathedral & Toompea Castle

10 Tall Hermann Tower

11 Dome Church (Toomkirik)

12 Patkuli Viewpoint

13 Kohtuotsa Viewpoint

14 Viru Gate & End of Walk

❷ **Pikk Street:** This street, the medieval merchants' main drag leading from the harbor up into town, is lined with interesting buildings—many were warehouses complete with cranes on the gables. You'll pass St. Olav's Church (Oleviste kirik), notable for what was once the tallest spire in Scandinavia. Its plain whitewashed interior is skippable, though climbing 234 stairs up the tower rewards you with a great view (35 kr, daily 10:00–18:00).

The ministry of police (at Pikk 59) was, before 1991, the sinister local headquarters of the KGB. "Creative interrogation methods" were used in here. Locals well knew that "from here started the road of suffering," as Tallinn's troublemakers were sent to Siberian gulags.

Farther up Pikk, the fine hall of the Black Heads Society (at #26) dates from 1440. For 500 years, until Hitler called Germans home in 1930s, this was the German merchants' club. Today, it's a concert venue. Its namesake "black head" is the head of St. Mauritius, an early Christian martyr beheaded in Switzerland (A.D. 200). Reliefs decorating the building recall Tallinn's Hanseatic glory days.

Architecture fans enjoy several fanciful facades (including the boldly Art Nouveau #18, and the colorful, eclectic facade across the street).

❸ **Great Guild Hall:** Pikk, home to the big-shot merchants, feels Germanic because it once was. The Great Guild Hall was the epitome of wealth, with its wide (and therefore highly taxed) front. Its charming little Estonian History Museum offers a chronological sweep, including Viking and Crusades and foreign lords, with lots of artifacts on one easy floor (worth the 15 kr and 15 min, see "Sights," page 381).

Across the street, at #16, the famous Maiasmokk ("Sweet Tooth") coffee shop, which was the sweetest place in town during Soviet days, remains a fine spot for a cheap coffee-and-pastry break (see "Eating," page 390).

❹ **Church of the Holy Ghost (Pühavaimu kirik):** Sporting a great clock from 1633, the church is worth a visit. The plaque on the wall is in Estonian and Russian. Before 1991, things were designed for "inner tourism" (within the USSR). This church retains its 14th-century design. The old flag of Tallinn in back, the same as today's Danish flag, recalls the 13th-century Danish rule. The Danes sold Tallinn to Germany, which lost it to the Swedes, who lost it to the Russians until it won independence in 1991. The windows are mostly from the 1990s (suggested 10-kr donation, Pühavaimu 2, tel. 644-1487).

• *From the church, tiny Saiakang lane (meaning "white bread"—bread, cakes, and pies have been sold here since medieval times) leads to Town Hall Square.*

❺ **Town Hall Square (Raekoja plats):** A marketplace through the centuries, this is the natural springboard for Old Town explorations. The cancan of fine old buildings is a reminder that this was the center of the autonomous lower town, a merchant city of Hanseatic traders. Once the scene of bad people chained to pillories for public humiliation and knights showing off in chivalrous tournaments, today it's full of Scandinavians savoring the cheap beer, children singing on the bandstand, and cruise-ship groups listening to their guides. (While you'll see few Americans early and late, the old center is inundated with them throughout midday, sticking close to their well-scrubbed, young local guides.)

The 15th-century Town Hall (Raekoda) dominates the square; it's now a museum and climbing the tower earns a commanding view (see "Sights," page 382). On the opposite side of the square, across from #12 in the corner, the pharmacy (Raeapteek) dates from 1422 and claims—as do many—to be Europe's oldest. While still a functioning pharmacy, the decor goes back to medieval times, and welcomes guests with painted ceiling beams, English descriptions, and long-expired aspirin (Mon–Fri 9:00–17:00, closed Sat–Sun). The Town Hall Square is ringed by touristy restaurants—Kehrwieder Cafe, next to the pharmacy, has the widest selection of coffee drinks. The TI is a block away (behind City Hall).

• *Facing the Town Hall, head right up Dunkri street one block to the well.*

❻ **The Wheel Well:** The well is named for the "high-tech" wheel, a marvel that made fetching water easier. Most of the Old Town's buildings are truly old, dating from the 15th- and 16th-century boom-time. Decrepit before the 1991 fall of the USSR, Tallinn is newly-affluent and quickly being revitalized.

❼ **St. Nicholas' (Niguliste) Church:** This church served the German merchants and knights that lived in this neighborhood 500 years ago. The Russians bombed it in World War II: In one terrible night, on March 9, 1944, Tallinn was hit, and the area around this church—once a charming district, dense with medieval buildings—was flattened. Beyond the church, some ruins remain.

• *From the church, turn right and climb the steep, cobbled, Lühike jalg (Short Leg Lane). Passing through the gate, notice the original oak door, one of two gates through the wall separating the two cities. This passage is still the ritual meeting point of the mayor and prime minister whenever there is an important agreement between town and country. Circle left of the Russian church to the garden overlooking the wall.*

❽ **Danish King's Garden:** Stand in the former garden of the Danish king. The imposing wall once had 46 towers—the stout round tower way ahead is nicknamed "Kiek in de Kök" (Peek in the Kitchen). It was situated so that "peek" is exactly what guards could do. (It's now a museum; see "Sights," page 382.)

Tallinn is famous among Danes as the birthplace of their flag. According to legend, the Danes were losing a battle here. Suddenly, a white cross fell from heaven and landed in a pool of blood. The Danes were inspired and went on to win. To this day, their flag is a white cross on a red background.

• *Walk toward the pink palace and look at the Russian Orthodox church.*

❾ Russian Cathedral and Toompea Castle: The Alexander Nevsky Cathedral was built here in 1900 over the grave of a legendary Estonian hero. It was a crass attempt to flex Russian cultural muscles during a period of Estonian national revival. Step inside for a whiff of Russian Orthodoxy; more than a quarter of Tallinn's population is ethnic Russian. Cross the street to the pink palace—an 18th-century addition that Russia built onto the Toompea Castle. Today, it's the Estonian Parliament building, flying the Estonian flag—the flag of both the first (1918–1940) and second (1991–present) Estonian republics. (Locals say they were always independent...just occupied—first by Nazis, and then by Russians.) Notice the Estonian seal: three lions for three great battles in Estonian history, and oak leaves for strength and stubbornness. Ancient pagan Estonians, who believed spirits lived in oak trees, would walk through forests of oak to toughen up.

• *Step left across the parking lot, around the palace, and into the park to see the...*

❿ Tall Hermann Tower: This tallest tower of the castle wall is a powerful symbol here. For 50 years, while Estonian flags were hidden in cellars, the Soviet flag flew from Tall Hermann. In 1987, as the USSR was unraveling, the Estonians proudly and defiantly replaced the red Soviet flag here with their own black, white, and blue flag.

In 1988, 400,000 patriots—imagine...a third of all Estonians—gathered at the festival song grounds outside Tallinn to sing national songs. In 1989, the people of Latvia, Lithuania, and Estonia held hands to make "the Baltic Chain"—a human chain that stretched 360 miles from Tallinn to Vilnius in Lithuania. Finally, in 1991, Estonia declared its freedom.

• *Backtrack and go uphill, passing the Russian church on your right. Climb Toom-Kooli street to the...*

⓫ Dome Church (Toomkirik): Estonia is ostensibly Lutheran, but few Tallinners go to church. Most churches double as concert venues or museums. Enter Toomkirik (Tue–Sun 9:00–17:00, closed Mon, www.eelk.ee/tallinna.toom). It's a textbook example of simple Northern European Gothic, built in the 13th century during Danish rule. Once the church of Tallinn's wealthy, it's littered with medieval coats of arms, each representing a rich merchant family and carved by local masters—the smaller the coat of arms, the older the family. The floor is paved with tombstones. Leaving the church, turn left. Pass the slanted tree and the big green Estonian Art Museum on your right, and go down cobbled Rahukohtu lane, where a glimpse of the ramshackle 1980s survives. Local businesses are moving their offices here and sprucing up the neighborhood.

• *Pass under the yellow Patkuli Vaateplats arch and belly up to the grand viewpoint.*

⑫ Patkuli Viewpoint: Survey the scene. On the far left, the Neoclassical facade of the executive branch of Estonia's government enjoys the view. Below you, a bit of the old moat survives. The *Group* sign marks Tallinn's tiny train station, and the clutter of stalls behind that is the rustic market. In the distance, ferries shuttle to and from Helsinki (just 50 miles away). Beyond the lower town's medieval wall and towers stands the green spire of

St. Olav's Church, once 98 feet taller and, locals claim, the world's tallest tower in 1492. Beyond that is the 985-foot-tall TV tower (famously fast Japanese elevators zip visitors to a café for grand views). During Soviet domination, Finnish TV was responsible for giving Estonians their only look at Western lifestyles. Imagine: In the 1980s, many locals had never seen a banana or pineapple—except on TV.

• *Go back through the arch, turn immediately left down the narrow lane, turn right, take the first left, and pass through the trees to another viewpoint.*

⑬ Kohtuotsa Viewpoint: On the far left is the busy cruise port and the skinny white spire of the Church of the Holy Ghost; the spire to its right is the 16th-century Town Hall spire. On the far right is the tower of St. Nicholas' Church. Visually trace Pikk

street, Tallinn's historic main drag, which leads from Toompea down the hill (below you from right to left), through the gate tower, past the Church of the Holy Ghost (and Town Hall Square), and out to the harbor. The undesirable part of this city of 400,000 is the clutter of Soviet-era apartment blocks in the distant horizon. The nearest

skyscraper (white) is Hotel Viru, in Soviet times the biggest hotel in the Baltics, and infamous as a clunky, dingy slumber mill. This walk ends there.

• *From the viewpoint, descend to the lower town. Go out and left down Kohtu, past the Finnish Embassy (on left). Back at the Dome Church, the slanted tree points the way, left down Piiskopi (Bishop's Street). At the onion domes, turn left again and follow the old wall down Pikk jalg (Long Leg Street) into the lower town. Wander back to Town Hall Square (Raekoja plats).*

⓮ **To Viru Gate and End of Walk:** Cross through the square (left of the Town Hall's tower) and go downhill (passing the kitschy medieval Olde Hansa Restaurant, with its bonneted waitresses and merry men). Continue straight down Viru street toward Hotel Viru (the blocky white skyscraper in the distance). Viru street is old Tallinn's busiest and kitschiest shopping street. Just past the strange and modern wood/glass/stone mall, Müürivahe street leads left along the old wall. This is a colorful and tempting gauntlet of women selling handmade knitwear (although anything with images and bright colors is likely machine-made). Beyond the sweaters, Katariina Käik, a lane with top-notch local artisan shops, leads left. Back on Viru street, the golden arches lead to the medieval arches—Viru Gate—that mark the end of old Tallinn. Outside the gates (at Viru 23), an arch leads into the Bastion Gardens, a tangle of antique, quilt, and sweater shops that delight shoppers, and the fine Apollo bookstore (with Internet access and a fine little café upstairs). Opposite Viru 23, above the flower stalls, is a small park on a piece of old bastion known as the Kissing Hill (come up here after dark and you'll find out why). Just beyond is Hotel Viru and the real world.

(Note: If you started this tour at #5, Town Hall Square, you can pick up the part you missed by walking along the park outside the walls toward the ferry terminal, arcing left until you hit the memorial to the doomed *Estonia* passenger ferry outside Fat Margaret Tower.)

SIGHTS

In or near the Old Town

Tallinn has dozens of small museums, most suitable only for specialized tastes (complete listings in *Tallinn in Your Pocket*). The following museums are the ones I'd make an effort to see.

Town Hall (Raekoda)—This building facing Town Hall Square is now a fine museum with exhibits on the town's administration and history, good views, and a surprisingly interesting bit on the story of limestone (35 kr, covered by Tallinn Card, July–Aug Mon–Sat 10:00–16:00, closed Sun, Sept–June by appointment only, tel. 645-7900, www.tallinn.ee/raekoda). The tower, which rewards visitors with a wonderful city view, is accessed around the corner (25 kr, covered by Tallinn Card, June–Aug daily 11:00–18:00, closed rest of year).

Kiek in de Kök—The "Peek in the Kitchen" tower, now a museum, mixes medieval cannons and charts left over from the Livonian wars (floors 3–5) with modern photography exhibits (floors 1, 2, and 6, 25 kr, good English descriptions, Tue–Sun 10:30–18:00, closed Mon, tel. 644-6686).

Tallinn City Museum (Tallinna Linnamuuseum)—This museum features Tallinn history from 1200 to the 1950s, fully described in English (35 kr, Wed–Mon 10:30–17:30, closed Tue, Vene 17, at corner of Pühavaimu, tel. 644-6553).

Estonian History Museum—Located in the Great Guild Hall, the museum tells the story of the country in a chronological sweep, including Vikings, Crusades, foreign lords, and lots of artifacts on one easy floor (15 kr, good English descriptions, Thu–Tue 11:00–18:00, closed Wed, Pikk 17, tel. 641-1630, www.eam.ee).

▲▲Museum of Occupation (Okupatsioonide Muuseum)—Newly opened with funding from a wealthy Estonian-American, this compact museum tells the history of Estonia under Nazi and Soviet occupation from 1939 to 1991. It's organized around seven TV monitors screening documentary films in English and Estonian, each focusing on a different time period. In the basement by the WCs is a collection of Soviet-era statues of communist leaders (10 kr, Tue–Sun 11:00–18:00, closed Mon, Toompea 8, at corner of Kaarli puiestee, tel. 668-0250, www.okupatsioon.ee).

Outer Tallinn

▲Kadriorg—This seaside park and cute, pint-sized summer residence, a 10-minute tram ride from Tallinn, was built by Peter the Great for Czarina Catherine after Russia took over Tallinn in 1710. Occupying Peter's palace, the **Foreign Art Museum** (Väliskuunsti Muuseum) has a very modest Russian and Western European collection in a pretty building with pleasant gardens out back (45 kr, Tue–Sun 10:00–17:00, closed Mon year-round and Tue in Oct–April, tel. 606-6400). The mansion on the far side of the gardens is the local White House (although it's pink)—home of Estonia's president. The park, which runs north down to the sea, is delightful for a stroll or picnic. Trams #1 and #3 take 10 minutes to go east from the center of Tallinn to Kadriorg, the end of the line (where the tram makes a U-turn, stopping 200 yards from Kadriorg, 400 yards from the Kumu Art Museum).

▲▲Kumu Art Museum—This main building of the Art Museum of Estonia opened in 2006. It's the first time Estonia's art has been properly displayed all together, and is the biggest cultural and sightseeing news of the decade for Tallinn. With a striking building designed by Finnish architect, Pekka Vapaavuori, it houses the very best of Estonian art through the ages (although little survives from before the last century). The collection was established with the modern state of Estonia in 1919; however, much of the collection was destroyed in World War II. From 1945 to 1991, the purchasing policies for the collection

were subservient to the dominant ideology—many of the key works could only be added after 1991.

Estonian art evolved along with the basic European art styles against the background of the nation's history. The permanent exhibition is shown in three parts: The third floor features classic art up until World War II. The fourth floor is "Difficult Choices," an exhibit devoted to art from the last half of the 20th century (fascinating for its Soviet influence and post-war socialist realism). And the top floor (fifth) features contemporary art (more fun than most contemporary collections). The Kumu also always has stimulating temporary exhibits (75 kr, May–Sept Tue–Sun 11:00–18:00, until 21:00 on Thu, closed Mon; Oct–April Wed–Sun 11:00–18:00, closed Mon–Tue; trendy café, tram #1 or #3 to the end of the line, 200 yards behind Kadriorg, at end of Weizenbergi street, tel. 602-6000, www.ekm.ee).

▲Open-Air Museum (Vabaõhumuuseum)—As in every Nordic country, Estonians salvaged farm buildings, windmills, and an old church from rural areas and transported them to Rocca al Mare, a park-like setting just outside of town. The park's Kolu tavern serves traditional dishes (30 kr, May–Sept daily 10:00–17:00, grounds stay open until 20:00; Oct–April buildings closed but grounds and tavern open daily 10:00–17:00; take bus #21 from train station to Rocca al Mare stop, tel. 654-9100, www.evm.ee). The audioguide is necessary to help you visualize life in the old houses.

SHOPPING

With so many Scandinavian tourists coming to Tallinn, the Old Town is full of trinkets, but it is possible to find quality stuff.

The **"Sweater Wall"** is a great place to buy sweaters and woolens. Find the stalls under the wall on Müürivahe street (near the corner of Viru street, described in "Welcome to Tallinn" self-guided walk, above). Butter knives and juniper-wood trivets are a good value here. From there, explore **Katariina Käik,** a small alley between Müürivahe and Vene streets, which has several handicraft stores and workshops selling pieces that make nice souvenirs.

Diele Gallerii sells good postcards, and displays work by Estonian artists (Vanaturu kael 3, just below Town Hall Square). Look around for Navitrolla's animal-themed prints (vaguely reminiscent of *Where the Wild Things Are*), or visit his gallery at Pikk jalg 7 (www.navitrolla.ee).

Apollo Bookstore has a fine English selection (Mon–Fri 10:00–20:00, Sat 10:00–19:00, Sun 11:00–17:00, better for general English books, Viru 23).

The **Mere Art Market** is just outside of the Old Town (north of Viru street at Mere puiestee 1), and is a lively little handicrafts market selling mostly clothing and cloth goods (daily 9:00–17:00).

Balti Jaam Market, Tallinn's bustling traditional market, is behind the train station, and has little of touristic interest besides

wonderful photo ops. It's a great time-warp scene (look for the Jaama Turg gate, daily 8:00–18:00). Just outside the market at the end of the train station is a no-name diner (open 24/7) with a bustling stainless-steel kitchen cranking out traditional dishes—the cheapest hot food in town. While you won't see or hear a word of English here, the glass case displays the various offerings and prices (meals-35 kr, soups-20 kr, dirt-cheap-yet-wonderful savory pancakes). Unfortunately, this area is dangerous after dark.

ENTERTAINMENT

Music: The TI has a list of concerts and tickets available (generally about 120 kr). Tallinn has a dense schedule of Baroque, Renaissance, and choral music performances, especially during the annual Old Town Days, generally the first weekend in June (May 31-June 3 in 2007, www.tourism.tallinn.ee). Choral singing became a symbol of the struggle for Estonian independence after the first Estonian Song Festival in 1869 (still held every 5 years—next one in 2009). Even outside of festival times, you'll find performances in Tallinn's churches and concert halls (advertised on posters around town). Tickets are usually available at the door. Hortus Musicus is one of Estonia's best classical ensembles.

Estonia's three best modern choral composers and arrangers are Arvo Pärt, Veljo Tormis, and Erkki-Sven Tüür. Other Estonian groups have also put out a lot of good CDs. A good music shop is on the ground floor of the Kaubamaja department store (daily 9:00–21:00, behind Hotel Viru).

Swimming: The **Kalev Spa,** recently opened in 2006, is Estonia's largest and newest spa. Many Finns come here on fitness packages, but simply enjoying the huge pool is lots of fun (daily 8:00–22:30, pool and spa 80 kr for 90 min before 16:00; 120 kr for 90 min after 16:00; at the edge of the Old Town, Aia 18, tel. 649-3300, www.kalevspa.ee).

SLEEPING

Tallinn has a great choice of hotels. There are some bargains, even in the Old Town, but even more if you're willing to stay a short walk or bus ride away. Summer is high season (Tallinn has more leisure than business travelers), and prices almost always drop from October to April. I've listed high-season prices here. Use a taxi to get to your hotel when you arrive, and then figure out public transportation later.

In the Old Town

$$$ Barons Hotel, central and upscale in a beautiful Art Nouveau former bank building with a 1912 "oldest still-working elevator in Estonia," has 34 unremarkable rooms (Sb-2,200 kr, Db-2,700 kr, free Internet access, Suur-Karja 7, tel. 699-9700, fax 699-9710, www.baronshotel.ee).

$$$ Baltic Hotel Imperial is a fine four-star hotel that feels like a chain (and is), with 32 small modern rooms and a generally spacious, very professional brick ambience (Db-2,400 kr, extra bed-350 kr, Nunne 14, tel. 627-4800, fax 627-4801, www.baltichotelgroup.com, imperial@baltichotelgroup.com).

Sleep Code

(13 kr = about $1, country code: 372)
S = Single, **D** = Double/Twin, **T** = Triple, **Q** = Quad, **b** = bathroom, **s** = shower. Credit cards are accepted and breakfast is included unless otherwise noted. Many hotels (especially the bigger ones) have cheaper deals on their Web sites, and offer individuals only the inflated rack rates, as the bulk of their business comes from agencies.

To help you sort easily through these listings, I've divided the rooms into three categories, based on the full price for a standard double room with bath:

$$$ **Higher Priced**—Most rooms 1,500 kr or more.
$$ **Moderately Priced**—Most rooms between 750–1,500 kr.
$ **Lower Priced**—Most rooms 750 kr or less.

$$$ Kalev Spa Hotel rents 100 modern, bright, and tidy rooms in a big six-story hotel that opened in 2006 behind Estonia's largest and newest spa. While lots of Finns come here on fitness packages, those with no interest in fitness are entirely welcome (Sb-1,500 kr, small Db-1,700 kr, big Db-1,900 kr, prices include unlimited use of pool and spa facilities, request a shower rather than a bath to get a bigger room, check online for lower rates, at the edge of the Old Town, behind the big modern swimming pool complex at Aia 18, tel. 649-3300, fax 649-3301, www.kalevspa.ee, kalevspa@kalevspa.ee).

$$ Meriton Old Town Hotel, extremely mod and comfy yet wearing an Old World jacket, sits grandly for a hotel in its category at the tip of the Old Town, not far from the ferry terminals. Most of its tight doubles have twin beds and showers (41 rooms, Sb-1,100 kr, Db-1,326 kr, non-smoking, elevator, free Internet access, Lai 49, tel. 614-1300, fax 614-1311, www.meritonhotels.com, oldtown @meritonhotels.com).

$$ Hotel Shnelli, a big new "efficiency hotel" adjacent to the sleepy little train station (in a neighborhood that's a bit seedy at night) and a 10-minute walk from the Old Town, rents 100 Ikea-mod rooms (Sb/Db-970 kr overlooking tracks or 1,190 kr looking toward Old Town, triple windows, silent station, no views either way—go with the cheap rooms, family room-1,600 kr, extra bed-330 kr, request sixth or seventh floor for air-con, Toompuiestee 37, tel. 631-0100, fax 631-0101, www.gohotels.ee, reservations @gohotels.ee).

Tallinn Hotels and Restaurants

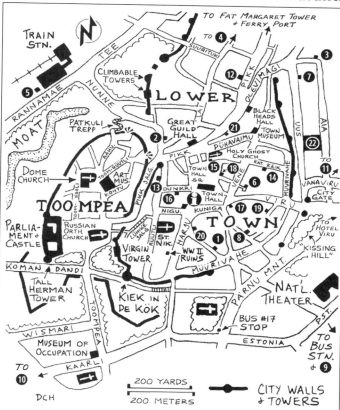

1. Barons Hotel &
   St. Patrick's Pub 1
2. Baltic Hotel Imperial
3. Kalev Spa Hotel
4. To Meriton Old Town Hotel
5. Hotel Shnelli
6. Villa Hortensia &
   Chocolaterie
7. Old House Guest-
   house & Hostel
8. Hostel Vana Tom
9. To Hotell G9 & Eesti
   Maja Restaurant
10. To Valge Villa & Tihase B&B
11. To Rasastra B&B Agency

12. Hell Hunt Pub
13. Von Krahli Baar, Vanaema
    Juures & Rest. Aed
14. Controvento Rist. Pizzeria
15. Balthasar Garlic Rest.
16. Beer House
17. Olde Hansa & Peppersack
    Restaurants
18. Troika Restaurant
19. Must Lammas Restaurant
20. Rest. Bakuu &
    Pegasus Café
21. Maiasmokk Café & Pastries
22. Rimi Supermarket

$$ Villa Hortensia, in a ramshackle courtyard tucked away from the Vene shopping street, rents six cozy rooms with kitchen-ettes above a trendy little café. The three twin-bed rooms and one double-bed room are furnished sparsely with beds in a sleeping loft. The "deluxe" room comes with a double bed and a small balcony. The apartment is on two floors, with a double bed upstairs and a fold-out sofa bed in the living room. Creatively run by jewelry designer Jaan Pärn, this is a good choice for a home-away-from-home in the heart of the Old Town. Jaan's jewelry shop, across the courtyard, serves as the reception (Sb-600 kr, Db-800 kr, deluxe Db-1,200 kr, Estonian-chic apartment-2,000 kr for 3 to 6 people, no breakfast, no elevator, 50 yards off the corner of Vene and Viru streets at Vene 6, look for *Master's Courtyard* and *Chocolaterie* signs, tel. 504-6113, jaan.parn@mail.ee, www.jpgoldart.ee).

$ Old House Guesthouse and Hostel, well-run and in a peaceful location halfway between Town Hall Square and the ferry terminals, has a mix of charming dorms (3-, 4-, or 6-bed rooms) with kitchen facilities, and guesthouse rooms with break-fast and a shared bath (18 rooms, dorm bed-310 kr, S-450 kr, D-650 kr, offsite apartments-950 to 1,500 kr, free parking, Uus 22, tel. 641-1464, fax 641-1604, www.oldhouse.ee, info@oldhouse.ee). The manager, Christian, promises a 10 percent discount in 2007 for those booking directly with this book.

$ Hostel Vana Tom, well-run and centrally located two blocks off the Town Hall Square, has cheap hostel beds, along with some doubles (60 beds, densely packed 9- to 15-bed triple-bunk rooms-235 kr per bunk; simple, sinkless, but decent D-640 kr; T-830 kr, Q-1,065 kr, showers down the hall, next-day laundry service, Väike-Karja 1, tel. 631-3252, www.hostel.ee). Try to ignore the harmless little *striptiis* bar upstairs.

$ Hotell G9 is a great value if you don't mind being on the other side of Hotel Viru a few blocks out of the Old Town. This is an oasis of simple, practical comfort on the third floor of a drab office building. All but two of its 23 rooms have twin beds (Sb-550–650 kr, Db-670–750 kr, extra bed-180 kr, no break-fast, Gonsiori 9; set back from street at intersection of Maneeži, Gonsiori, and Reimann streets; tel. 626-7100, fax 626-7102, www .hotelg9.ee, hotelg9@hot.ee). Try Šeš-Beš, a good Azerbaijani res-taurant on the ground floor.

Near the Ferry Terminals

If you're cruising in, these two places are almost too convenient—right next to Terminals A/B/C and D, respectively, but without any Old Town character.

$$ Express Hotel is a few steps from Terminals A/B/C, close to the Linnahall terminal, and a short walk from the Old

Town. It's a modern Motel 6–type place—cheery, excellent prices, and plenty comfortable. Each of the well-designed 163 rooms is the same (Sb or Db-1,070 kr, extra bed-390 kr, children under 16 sleep free on sofa beds, request a non-smoking floor, elevator, free Internet access, Sadama 1, tel. 667-8700, fax 667-8800, www .revalhotels.com, expresstallinn@revalhotels.com). Rooms can be stuffy in summer as windows don't open very far and there's no air-conditioning.

$$ City Hotel Portus is in an utterly charmless location right across from Terminal D. Its motto is "young at heart" and the theme is rock and roll, with Muzak and posters throughout. While it's perfectly comfortable, there's little reason to stay here unless you're arriving or leaving from Terminal D at odd hours (107 rooms, Sb/Db-1,049 kr, extra bed-350 kr, check online for lower rates, Uus-Sadama 23, tel. 680-6600, fax 680-6601, www .tallinnhotels.ee).

In Lilleküla

Lilleküla is a quiet, green, and peaceful residential area of single-family houses, small Soviet-era apartment blocks, and barking dogs. For a clearer understanding of Estonian life, stay here. You'll save money without sacrificing comfort. The downside: It's a 15-minute, 10-kr bus ride into the center. To get to Lilleküla by bus from the center, go to Vabaduse väljak (see Tallinn overview map, page 373) and board bus #17 or #17a from the stop across the street from the Palace Hotel (3/hr, can also board by Estonia Theater).

$$ Valge Villa ("White Villa"), a homey guest house set in a great garden run by Anne and Andres Vahtra and their family, does everything right and is worth the high-for-a-guest-house price. Its 10 rooms are spacious and well-furnished (Sb-780 kr, Db-880 kr, small suite-990 kr, larger suite-1,170 kr, suite-apartments-1,600 kr, extra bed-300 kr, kids under 12 stay free in same room, every fifth night free, stay 7 nights and pay for 5, free Internet access and Wi-Fi, bikes-225 kr/day, sauna-300 kr, laundry service-120 kr; take bus #17 or #17a to Räägu stop, or trolleybus #2, #3, or #4 to Tedre stop; Kännu 26/2, between Rästa and Räägu streets, tel. & fax 654-2302, www.white-villa.com).

$ At Tihase B&B, young, English-speaking Ivo Roosi rents two funky, double-bed spare rooms in his bachelor pad (he lives upstairs), plus a backyard cottage with a private bath and a sauna. Complete with a garden and a tabby cat, this is a fun real-people experience. It's a Scandinavian-style red wooden house with white trim (S-400 kr, D-600 kr, Db-700 kr, 50–100 kr less off-season, cash or PayPal only, free Internet access and Wi-Fi, sauna-250 kr, take bus #17 or #17a to Hauka stop, Tihase 6A, tel. 683-1775, mobile 511-9541, www.tihase.ee, tihase@tihase.ee). Ivo does one-day countryside car tours tailored to your interests (from 550 kr per person), and can pick you up at the ferry terminal for 125 kr or the airport for 200 kr.

Rooms in Private Homes

$ Rasastra Bed & Breakfast agency, run by English-speaking Ms. Urve Susi, coordinates a network of families around town (and throughout the Baltics) who rent out spare rooms and entire apartments. Reserve in advance online, especially if you want to stay in the Old Town (S-330 kr, D-550 kr, T-700 kr; apartments with sitting room, bedroom, kitchen, and private bathroom average 900 kr; breakfast-50 kr). The office, which has an array of TI booklets and maps, is at Mere puiestee 4, near Hotel Viru; follow the signs one flight up the stairs of the red—not brown—brick building (daily 9:30–18:00, tel. & fax 661-6291, www.bedbreakfast.ee, rasastra @online.ee). Drop by the office first to pay and pick up the address, and then get settled in. You might be be staying alone or with a family. Expect little English and to share the family bathroom.

EATING

Restaurants in Tallinn are cheap, plentiful, and usually good. Visiting Scandinavians gorge themselves on inexpensive food. Few restaurants have non-smoking sections. Most accept credit cards.

Unless you got bad service, round up by 5–10 percent when paying your bill.

A few years ago it was hard to find authentic local cuisine, but now it seems Estonian food is trendy—a hot and hearty Northern mixture of meat, potatoes, root vegetables, mushrooms, bread, and soup. Pea soup is a local specialty.

A typical pub snack is Estonian garlic bread *(küüslauguleivad)*—deep-fried strips of dark rye bread smothered in garlic and served with a dipping sauce. Estonia's Saku beer is good, cheap, and on tap at most eateries. Try the nutty, full-bodied Tume variety.

Pubs in the Old Town

Young Estonians eat well and affordably at pubs. Soup, a main dish, and a beer will run you about 120 kr ($10). At lunch on weekdays, look for the *päeva praad* (dish of the day—meat, veggies, and a starch) for as little as 35–40 kr. In some pubs, you go to the bar to look at the menu, order, and pay. Then you find a table, and they'll bring your food out when it's ready.

Hell Hunt Pub ("The Gentle Wolf") attracts a mixed expat and local crowd with its tasty food (lunch special-39 kr, soups-40–50 kr, main dishes-65–95 kr, daily 12:00–very late, Pikk 39, tel. 681-8333). This place, known as the first Western-style pub to open after 1991, offers inviting pub conviviality inside, and rustic courtyard seating across the street.

St. Patrick's Pub 1, though not especially Irish, has good pub food in a medieval atmosphere (weekday lunch special until 18:00-37 kr, main dishes-60–100 kr, Sun–Thu 11:00–2:00 in the morning, Fri–Sat 11:00–4:00 in the morning, Suur-Karja 8, tel. 631-4801). Note that there are two other less atmospheric branches of this pub, so check the address before you go.

Von Krahli Baar serves cheap, hearty Estonian grub, such as potato pancakes *(torud)* stuffed with mushroom or shrimp (50 kr, half-portion-35 kr), in a tiny courtyard and a dark, beer-stained bar that doubles as a center for Estonia's alternative theater scene (daily 12:00–23:00, Rataskaevu 10/12, a block uphill from Town Hall Square, near Wheel Well, tel. 626-9096). It originated as the bar of a theater that expanded to become a restaurant, so you'll feel like you're eating backstage with the stagehands.

Restorant Aed, a new place, calls itself "the embassy of pure food." While not vegetarian, it is passionate about serving organic and healthy food, with a woody, romantic ambience (tasty dinners from 150–200 kr, Mon–Sat 12:00–22:00, closed Sun, Rataskaevu 8, tel. 626-9088).

Controvento Ristorante Pizzeria is a hit with locals for its serious Italian cuisine. Enjoy the interior, which is old and rustic yet classy, or sit outside on a quiet cobbled lane (pizza and pasta-100 kr, daily 12:00–22:30, on the handicraft-filled Katariina Käik lane which you enter at Vene 12, tel. 644-0470).

Balthasar Garlic Restaurant is pretty touristy, but it's worth considering if you like dining on lots of garlic in rustic Old World elegance with a second-floor view overlooking Town Hall Square. This creaky open-beam palace features cuisine that is "European with a passion for garlic" (200–300 kr-main courses, daily 12:00–23:00, call to reserve a window-view table, on Town Hall Square opposite the City Hall at Raekoja plats 11, tel. 627-6400).

The **Beer House** is best described as a sprawling and boisterous Tyrolean Hooters. Billing itself as the "home of the living beer," this big, modern, and sloppy beer hall brews its respected beer on site and serves hearty portions with waitresses just aching to slap-dance (main dishes-100–200 kr, long hours daily, vast indoor section, cute garden out back and street-side tables out front, live music Fri–Sat from 21:00, a block above Town Hall Square at Dunkri 5).

Traditional Dining in the Old Town

The Old Town is full of restaurants packed with atmosphere and traditionally dressed servers. Dine under medieval arches, in candlelit restaurants, or at tables outside in good weather. Most offer stick-to-your-ribs Estonian fare as well as more modern options. My favorite is the first one.

Vanaema Juures ("Grandma's Place"), a small cellar restaurant, serves homey, candlelit, traditional Estonian meals, such as pork roast with sauerkraut and horseradish. This is your best bet for local cuisine, and dinner reservations are strongly advised. No tacky medieval stuff here—just good food in a pleasant ambience, where you expect your waitress to show up with her hair in a bun and wearing granny glasses (main dishes-125–200 kr, Mon–Sat 12:00–22:00, Sun until 18:00, Rataskaevu 10, tel. 626-9080).

Medieval Cuisine: Two restaurants just below Town Hall Square specialize in recreating medieval food (from the days before the arrival of the potato and tomato from the New World). They are each grotesquely touristy, complete with gift shops to buy your souvenir goblet. And both have street seating where you'll get all the tourists but none of the atmosphere.

Olde Hansa, filling three creaky old floors and outdoor tables with tourists, candle wax, and scurrying medieval waitresses, has gotten quite expensive, with most main dishes approaching 200 kr (daily 11:00–24:00, music circulates nightly after 18:00, a belch below Town Hall Square at Vana turg 1, reserve in advance, tel. 627-9020).

Peppersack, across the street, has a grand dining room, with stained glass and wooden beams, as well as a more casual and quiet grill downstairs. The menu is for meat lovers, with medieval names for the 140–250-kr dishes (daily 12:00–23:00, reservations advised, Viru tänav 2, tel. 646-6900).

Russian Food: As over a third of the local population is enthusiastically Russian (often with no interest in even learning to speak Estonian), there are plenty of places serving cuisine from the former Soviet Union. You choose—Russian, Georgian, or Azerbaijani.

Troika is my choice for Russian food. Right on Town Hall Square, with folkloric-costumed waitstaff, they serve *bliny* (pancakes) for 69–96 kr, *pelmeni* (dumplings) for 55–82 kr, and main dishes for 110–180 kr. Sit in the upstairs tavern (more casual), out on Town Hall Square, or down in the cellar restaurant. There's generally a strumming guitarist playing after 19:00 (daily 12:00–23:00, Raekoja plats 15, tel. 627-6245).

Must Lammas is plain and elegant, focusing on just plain tasty Caucasian food from Georgia, Armenia, and Azerbaijan (main dishes-100–220 kr, Mon–Sat 12:00–23:00, Sun until 18:00,

Sauna 2, tel. 644-2031).

Restoran Bakuu, the choice of visiting Russians, is your chance to eat good Azerbaijani cuisine. The interior is simple—as you might expect in Azerbaijan—or sit outside on the small terrace (main dishes-100–150 kr, daily 11:00–24:00, a block from the TI at Harju 7, tel. 699-9680).

More Eateries

Eesti Maja ("Estonian House"), six blocks from the touristy Old Town, fills a basement in a dreary modern building. It serves very traditional Estonian food in a nationalistic environment. Estonian diaspora publications are on sale and photos of the Estonian army decorate the walls. The 75-kr weekday lunch buffet includes soup and dessert (buffet Mon–Fri 11:00–15:00, main dishes-120–170 kr, daily 11:00–23:00, outside Old Town behind Hotel Viru; downstairs at Lauteri 1 by the corner of Rävala puiestee; tel. 645-5252).

Maiasmokk ("Sweet Tooth") café and pastry shop, founded in 1864, is the grande dame of Tallinn cafés—ideal for dessert or breakfast. Even through the Soviet days, this was *the* place for a good pastry. Point to what you want from the selection of classic local pastries at the pastry counter, and sit down for breakfast or coffee on the other side of the shop or at their fine outdoor seating on the nearby square. Everything's very cheap (Mon–Sat 8:00–21:00, Sun 10:00–19:00, Pikk 16, across from church with old clock). They also have a marzipan shop (separate entrance).

The **Chocolaterie** at Vene 6 has scrumptious fresh pralines, sandwiches, coffee, and a lovely courtyard.

Breakfast: **Pegasus** is a trendy café with an extensive breakfast menu, from porridge to a full fry (Mon–Sat 8:00–11:00, closed Sun, across the square from the TI at Harju 1, tel. 631-4040).

Supermarkets: The **Rimi** supermarket at Aia 7 is on the edge of the Old Town, a few blocks from Hotel Viru (daily 9:00–22:00). Another supermarket is in the basement of the big shopping center directly behind Hotel Viru.

TRANSPORTATION CONNECTIONS

The bus is usually the best way to travel by land from Tallinn. The bus station *(autobussijaam)* is a few stops outside Town Hall Square on bus #2, or a short taxi ride.

From Tallinn to: Riga (9 buses/day, 6 hrs, no train option), **Vilnius** (3 buses/day, 10 hrs), **St. Petersburg** (5 buses/day, 9 hrs), **Moscow** (take the overnight train or fly). Americans and Canadians need a passport and a visa to travel to Russia (see www .russianembassy.org). For the latest bus and train schedules, consult *Tallinn in Your Pocket.*

APPENDIX

Let's Talk Telephones

Here's a primer on making phone calls in Europe. For information specifics on Scandinavia, see "Telephones" in the Introduction.

Making Calls Within a European Country: About half of all European countries use area codes (like we do in most of the US); the other half uses a direct-dial system without area codes.

To make calls within a country that uses a direct-dial system (Denmark, Norway, Estonia, Belgium, the Czech Republic, France, Italy, Poland, Portugal, Spain, and Switzerland), you dial the same number whether you're calling across the country or across the street.

In countries that use area codes (such as Finland, Sweden, Austria, Britain, Croatia, Germany, Hungary, Ireland, the Netherlands, Slovakia, and Slovenia), you dial the local number when calling within a city, and you add the area code if calling long-distance within the country.

Making International Calls: You always start with the international access code—011 if you're calling from America or Canada, or 00 from Europe. Finland is the only exception: When calling from Finland, first dial 999, or another 900 number, depending on which phone service you're using.

After dialing the international access code of the country you're in, then dial the country code of the country you're calling (see "Country Codes" chart).

What you dial next depends on the phone system of the country you're calling. If the country uses area codes, drop the initial 0 of the area code, then dial the rest of the number.

Countries that use direct-dial systems (no area codes) vary in how they're accessed internationally by phone. For instance, if you're making an international call to Denmark, Norway, Estonia,

European Calling Chart

Just smile and dial, using this key:
AC = Area Code, LN = Local Number.

European Country	Calling long distance within ...	Calling from the US or Canada to ...	Calling from a European country to ...
Austria	AC + LN	011 + 43 + AC (without the initial zero) + LN	00 + 43 + AC (without the initial zero) + LN
Belgium	LN	011 + 32 + LN (without initial zero)	00 + 32 + LN (without initial zero)
Britain	AC + LN	011 + 44 + AC (without initial zero) + LN	00 + 44 + AC (without initial zero) + LN
Croatia	AC + LN	011 + 385 + AC (without initial zero) + LN	00 + 385 + AC (without initial zero) + LN
Czech Republic	LN	011 + 420 + LN	00 + 420 + LN
Denmark	LN	011 + 45 + LN	00 + 45 + LN
Estonia	LN	011 + 372 + LN	00 + 372 + LN
Finland	AC + LN	011 + 358 + AC (without initial zero) + LN	999 + 358 + AC (without initial zero) + LN
France	LN	011 + 33 + LN (without initial zero)	00 + 33 + LN (without initial zero)
Germany	AC + LN	011 + 49 + AC (without initial zero) + LN	00 + 49 + AC (without initial zero) + LN
Greece	LN	011 + 30 + LN	00 + 30 + LN
Hungary	06 + AC + LN	011 + 36 + AC + LN	00 + 36 + AC + LN
Ireland	AC + LN	011 + 353 + AC (without initial zero) + LN	00 + 353 + AC (without initial zero) + LN
Italy	LN	011 + 39 + LN	00 + 39 + LN

European Country	Calling long distance within ...	Calling from the US or Canada to ...	Calling from a European country to ...
Netherlands	AC + LN	011 + 31 + AC (without initial zero) + LN	00 + 31 + AC (without initial zero) + LN
Norway	LN	011 + 47 + LN	00 + 47 + LN
Poland	LN	011 + 48 + LN (without initial zero)	00 + 48 + LN (without initial zero)
Portugal	LN	011 + 351 + LN	00 + 351 + LN
Slovakia	AC + LN	011 + 421 + AC (without initial zero) + LN	00 + 421 + AC (without initial zero) + LN
Slovenia	AC + LN	011 + 386 + AC (without initial zero) + LN	00 + 386 + AC (without initial zero) + LN
Spain	LN	011 + 34 + LN	00 + 34 + LN
Sweden	AC + LN	011 + 46 + AC (without initial zero) + LN	00 + 46 + AC (without initial zero) + LN
Switzerland	LN	011 + 41 + LN (without initial zero)	00 + 41 + LN (without initial zero)
Turkey	AC (if no initial zero is included, add one) + LN	011 + 90 + AC (without initial zero) + LN	00 + 90 + AC (without initial zero) + LN

- The instructions above apply whether you're calling a land line or mobile phone.
- The international access codes (the first numbers you dial when making an international call) are 011 if you're calling from the US or Canada, or 00 if you're calling from anywhere in Europe (except Finland, where it's 999).
- To call the US or Canada from Europe, dial 00, then 1 (the country code for the US and Canada), then the area code and number. In short, 00 + 1 + AC + LN = Hi, Mom!

the Czech Republic, Italy, Portugal, or Spain, simply dial the international access code, country code, and phone number. But if you're calling Belgium, France, Poland, or Switzerland, drop the initial 0 of the phone number.

Country Codes

After you've dialed the international access code (011 if you're calling from America or Canada, or 00 from Europe—except in Finland, where you'll dial 999 or another 900 number), dial the code of the country you're calling.

Austria—43	Italy—39
Belgium—32	Morocco—212
Britain—44	Netherlands—31
Canada—1	Norway—47
Croatia—385	Poland—48
Czech Rep.—420	Portugal—351
Denmark—45	Slovakia—421
Estonia—372	Slovenia—386
Finland—358	Spain—34
France—33	Sweden—46
Germany—49	Switzerland—41
Gibraltar—350	Turkey—90
Greece—30	US—1
Ireland—353	

US Embassies

If you lose your passport, here's whom to contact:

Denmark: Dag Hammarskjölds Allé 24, Copenhagen, tel. 33 41 71 00, www.usembassy.dk

Estonia: Kentmanni 20, Tallinn, tel. 668-8100, www.usemb.ee

Finland: Itäinen Puistotie 14B, Helsinki, tel. 09/616-25701, www.usembassy.fi

Norway: Henrik Ibsens Gate 18, Oslo, tel. 22 44 85 50, ext. 8941/8715/8894, www.usa.no

Sweden: Dag Hammarskjölds Väg 31, Stockholm, tel. 08/783-5300, www.usemb.se

Festivals and Public Holidays in 2007

This is a partial list of events in Scandinavia. Many event dates hadn't been set at the time this book went to print. For more information, contact the Scandinavian National Tourist Office in the US (tel. 212/885-9700, www.goscandinavia.com, info @goscandinavia.com) and check these Web sites: www.visitdenmark .com, www.visitnorway.com, www.visit-sweden.com, www.finland -tourism.com, www.whatsonwhen.com, and www.festivals.com.

2007

JANUARY
S	M	T	W	T	F	S
	1	2	3	4	5	6
7	8	9	10	11	12	13
14	15	16	17	18	19	20
21	22	23	24	25	26	27
28	29	30	31			

FEBRUARY
S	M	T	W	T	F	S
				1	2	3
4	5	6	7	8	9	10
11	12	13	14	15	16	17
18	19	20	21	22	23	24
25	26	27	28			

MARCH
S	M	T	W	T	F	S
				1	2	3
4	5	6	7	8	9	10
11	12	13	14	15	16	17
18	19	20	21	22	23	24
25	26	27	28	29	30	31

APRIL
S	M	T	W	T	F	S
1	2	3	4	5	6	7
8	9	10	11	12	13	14
15	16	17	18	19	20	21
22	23	24	25	26	27	28
29	30					

MAY
S	M	T	W	T	F	S
		1	2	3	4	5
6	7	8	9	10	11	12
13	14	15	16	17	18	19
20	21	22	23	24	25	26
27	28	29	30	31		

JUNE
S	M	T	W	T	F	S
					1	2
3	4	5	6	7	8	9
10	11	12	13	14	15	16
17	18	19	20	21	22	23
24	25	26	27	28	29	30

JULY
S	M	T	W	T	F	S
1	2	3	4	5	6	7
8	9	10	11	12	13	14
15	16	17	18	19	20	21
22	23	24	25	26	27	28
29	30	31				

AUGUST
S	M	T	W	T	F	S
			1	2	3	4
5	6	7	8	9	10	11
12	13	14	15	16	17	18
19	20	21	22	23	24	25
26	27	28	29	30	31	

SEPTEMBER
S	M	T	W	T	F	S
						1
2	3	4	5	6	7	8
9	10	11	12	13	14	15
16	17	18	19	20	21	22
23/30	24	25	26	27	28	29

OCTOBER
S	M	T	W	T	F	S
	1	2	3	4	5	6
7	8	9	10	11	12	13
14	15	16	17	18	19	20
21	22	23	24	25	26	27
28	29	30	31			

NOVEMBER
S	M	T	W	T	F	S
				1	2	3
4	5	6	7	8	9	10
11	12	13	14	15	16	17
18	19	20	21	22	23	24
25	26	27	28	29	30	

DECEMBER
S	M	T	W	T	F	S
						1
2	3	4	5	6	7	8
9	10	11	12	13	14	15
16	17	18	19	20	21	22
23/30	24/31	25	26	27	28	29

Jan 26-Feb 4	Winter Jazz Festival (www.vinterjazz.dk), Odense, Denmark
Mid-Feb	"Frozen Waterfall" Winter Arts Festival (theater, music; www.vinterspillene.no), Lillehammer, Norway
April 1	Hat Festival (spring festival), Bergen, Norway
Before Easter	Easter Festival (theater, concerts), Bergen, Norway
April 8	Easter, Scandinavia
April 27–May 1	Ole Blues Festival, Bergen, Norway
End of April	Maritime Festival, Bergen, Norway
April 30	Walpurgis Night (bonfires, choirs), Sweden

May 1	May Day (parades, some closures), Scandinavia
May 9–13	Stavanger International Jazz Festival ("MaiJazz"; www.maijazz.no), Stavanger, Norway
May 15	St. Hallvard's Day (theater, concerts), Oslo, Norway
May 4	Common Prayer Day (businesses closed), Denmark
Mid-May	Flower Festival, Copenhagen, Denmark
May 17	Constitution Day (parades, closures), Norway
End of May	International Festival (theater, music, dance), Norway
End of May	Swinging Jazz Festival, Copenhagen, Denmark
End of May	Dragon Boat Festival (Chinese boat races), Bergen, Norway
May 31–June 3	Old Town Days (music), Tallinn, Estonia
June 1–30	Taste of Stockholm (outdoor food vendors; www.smakapastockholm.se), Stockholm, Sweden
June 5	Constitution Day (businesses closed), Denmark
June 6	National Day (parades), Sweden
June 6	Archipelago Boat Day (steamboat parade), Stockholm, Sweden
June 14–17	Norwegian Wood Rock Music Festival (www.norwegianwood.no), Oslo, Norway
Early June	Wooden Boats Festival, Stavanger, Norway
Mid-June	Medieval Festival ("Middelalderfestival"; www.middelalderbyen.no), Oslo, Norway
Mid-June–Mid-Aug	Fløyen Concert Festival (classical music), Bergen, Norway
Solstice	Midsummer Eve (celebrations, bonfires), Scandinavia
Late June–Aug	Hans Christian Andersen Festival, Odense, Denmark
July 5–8	Roskilde Festival (music and theater, www.roskilde-festival.dk), Roskilde, Denmark
July 6–15	Copenhagen Jazz Festival (www.jazzfestival.dk), Copenhagen, Denmark

July 4	Fourth of July festivities, Stockholm, Sweden
Mid-Late July	International Jazz Festival (www.jazzfest .dk), Århus, Denmark
Late July	Cutty Sark Tall Ship Race, Bergen, Norway
Early Aug	Water Festival (10 days), Stockholm, Sweden
Mid-Aug	Emigration Festival, Växjö, Sweden
Aug 11–19	Chamber Music Festival, Oslo, Norway
Aug 14–20	Jazz Festival (www.oslojazz.no), Oslo, Norway
Aug 6–12	International Chamber Music Festival (www.icmf.no), Stavanger, Norway
Late Aug	Seafood Festival, Oslo, Norway
Late Aug	International Chamber Music Festival, Bergen, Norway
Aug 17–Sept 2	Helsinki Festival (music, dance, film, theater; www.helsinkifestival.fi), Helsinki, Finland
Aug 31-Sept 9	Århus Festival (music, dance, theater; www.aarhusfestuge.dk), Århus, Denmark
Sept 15–18	DølaJazz Festival (www.dolajazz.no), Lillehammer, Norway
Late Sept	Folk Festival, Odense, Denmark
Oct 1	Rain Festival (raincoat and umbrella parade), Bergen, Norway
Early Oct–Nov	Art Festival (jazz, dance), Bergen, Norway
Early-Mid-Oct	Contemporary Music Festival, Oslo, Norway
Early Nov	Autumn Jazz Festival, Copenhagen, Denmark
Mid-Nov–Dec 23	Christmas Fair (Tivoli Garden), Copenhagen, Denmark
Dec 6	Independence Day (candlelit windows), Finland
Dec 13	St. Lucia Day (festival of lights), Sweden
Dec 25	Christmas, Scandinavia

Metric Conversion (approximate)

1 inch = 25 millimeters	32° F = 0° C
1 foot = 0.3 meter	82° F = about 28° C
1 yard = 0.9 meter	1 ounce = 28 grams
1 mile = 1.6 kilometers	1 kilogram = 2.2 pounds
1 centimeter = 0.4 inch	1 quart = 0.95 liter
1 meter = 39.4 inches	1 square yard = 0.8 square meter
1 kilometer = 0.62 mile	1 acre = 0.4 hectare

Climate Chart

The first line is average low temperature, the second line is average high temperature, and the third line is the number of days with no rain. For information on more destinations, check www.worldclimate.com.

	J	F	M	A	M	J	J	A	S	O	N	D

DENMARK • Copenhagen

J	F	M	A	M	J	J	A	S	O	N	D
29°	28°	31°	37°	45°	51°	56°	56°	51°	44°	38°	33°
37°	37°	42°	51°	60°	66°	70°	69°	64°	55°	46°	41°
14	15	19	18	20	18	17	16	14	14	11	12

ESTONIA • Tallinn

J	F	M	A	M	J	J	A	S	O	N	D
14°	12°	19°	32°	41°	50°	54°	52°	48°	39°	30°	19°
25°	25°	32°	45°	57°	66°	68°	66°	59°	50°	37°	30°
12	12	18	19	19	20	18	16	14	14	12	12

FINLAND • Helsinki

J	F	M	A	M	J	J	A	S	O	N	D
17°	15°	20°	30°	40°	49°	55°	53°	46°	37°	30°	23°
26°	25°	32°	44°	56°	66°	71°	68°	59°	47°	37°	31°
11	10	17	17	19	17	17	16	16	13	11	11

NORWAY • Oslo

J	F	M	A	M	J	J	A	S	O	N	D
19°	19°	25°	34°	43°	50°	55°	53°	46°	38°	31°	25°
28°	30°	39°	50°	61°	68°	72°	70°	60°	48°	38°	32°
16	16	22	19	21	17	16	17	16	17	14	14

SWEDEN • Stockholm

J	F	M	A	M	J	J	A	S	O	N	D
26°	25°	29°	37°	45°	53°	57°	56°	50°	43°	37°	32°
30°	30°	37°	47°	58°	67°	71°	68°	60°	49°	40°	35°
15	14	21	19	20	17	18	17	16	16	14	14

Temperature Conversions: Fahrenheit and Celsius

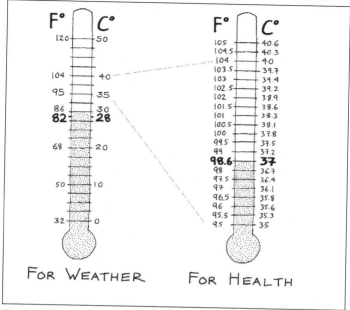

FOR WEATHER   FOR HEALTH

Europe takes its temperature using the Celsius scale, while we opt for Fahrenheit. For weather, remember that 28°C is 82°F—perfect. For health, 37°C is just right.

Numbers and Stumblers

- Europeans write a few of their numbers differently than we do. 1 = ⅂ , 4 = ⅄ , 7 = ⅂ . Learn the difference or miss your train.
- Throughout Europe, dates appear as day/month/year, so Christmas is 25/12/07.
- Commas are decimal points and decimals are commas. A dollar and a half is $1,50, and there are 5.280 feet in a mile.
- When pointing, use your whole hand, palm down.
- When counting with fingers, start with your thumb. If you hold up your first finger to request one item, you'll probably get two.
- What Americans call the second floor of a building is the first floor in Europe.
- Europeans keep the left "lane" open for passing on escalators and moving sidewalks. Keep to the right.

Making Your Hotel Reservation

Most hotel managers know basic "hotel English." Faxing or e-mailing are the preferred methods for reserving a room. They're more accurate than telephoning and much faster than writing a letter. Use this handy form for your fax or find it online at www.ricksteves.com/reservation. Photocopy and fax away.

One-Page Fax

To: _____ @ _____
               hotel   *fax*

From: _____ @ _____
                 name   *fax*

Today's date: _____ / _____ / _____
                    day   *month*   *year*

Dear Hotel _____ ,
Please make this reservation for me:

Name: _____

Total # of people: _____ # of rooms: _____ # of nights: _____

Arriving: _____ / _____ / _____   My time of arrival (24-hr clock): _____
               day   *month*   *year*   (I will telephone if I will be late)

Departing: _____ / _____ / _____
                 day   *month*   *year*

Room(s): Single _____ Double _____ Twin _____ Triple _____ Quad _____

With: Toilet _____ Shower _____ Bath _____ Sink only _____

Special needs: View _____ Quiet _____ Cheapest _____ Ground Floor _____

Please fax, mail, or e-mail confirmation of my reservation, along with the type of room reserved and the price. Please also inform me of your cancellation policy. After I hear from you, I will quickly send my credit-card information as a deposit to hold the room. Thank you.

_____

Signature

_____

Name

_____

Address

_____

City   *State*   *Zip Code*   *Country*

_____

E-mail Address

INDEX

Travel smart...carry on!

The latest generation of Rick Steves' carry-on travel bags is easily the best—benefiting from two decades of on-the-road attention to what really matters: maximum quality and strength; practical, flexible features; and no unnecessary frills. You won't find a better value anywhere!

Rick Steves' Convertible Carry-On

This is the classic "back door bag" that Rick Steves lives out of for three months every summer. It's made of rugged, water-resistant 1000-denier nylon. Best of all, it converts easily from a smart-looking suitcase to a handy backpack with comfortably-curved shoulder straps and a padded waistbelt.

This roomy, versatile 9" x 21" x 14" bag has a large 2500 cubic-inch main compartment, plus three outside pockets (small, medium and huge) that are perfect for often-used items. And the cinch-tight compression straps will keep your load compact and close to your back—not sagging like a sack of potatoes.

Wishing you had even more room to bring home souvenirs? Pull open the full-perimeter expando-zipper and its capacity jumps from 2500 to 3000 cubic inches. When you want to use it as a suitcase or check it as luggage (required when "expanded"), the straps and belt hide away in a zippered compartment in the back. Choose from five great traveling colors: black, navy, blue spruce, evergreen or merlot.

Rick Steves' 21" Roll-Aboard

At 9" x 21" x 14" our sturdy 21" Roll-Aboard is rucksack-soft in front, but the rest is lined with a hard ABS-lexan shell to give maximum protection to your belongings. We've spared no expense on moving parts, splurging on an extra-long button-release handle and big, tough inline skate wheels for easy rolling on rough surfaces.

Wishing you had even more room to bring home souvenirs? Pull open the full-perimeter expando-zipper and its capacity jumps from 2500 to 3000 cubic inches.

Rick Steves' 21" Roll-Aboard features exactly the same three-outside-pocket configuration and rugged 1000-denier nylon fabric as our Convertible Carry-On, plus a full lining and a handy "add-a-bag" strap.

Choose from five great traveling colors: black, navy, blue spruce, evergreen or merlot.

For great deals on a wide selection of travel goodies, begin your next trip at the Rick Steves Travel Store!

Visit the Rick Steves Travel Store at
www.ricksteves.com

Start your trip at
www.ricksteves.com

Rick Steves' Web site is packed with over 3,000 pages of timely travel information. It's also your gateway to getting FREE monthly travel news from Rick— and more!

Free Monthly European Travel News

Fresh articles on Europe's most interesting destinations and happenings. Rick will even send you an e-mail every month (often direct from Europe) with his latest discoveries!

Timely Travel Tips

Rick Steves' best money-and-stress-saving tips on trip planning, packing, transportation, hotels, health, safety, finances, hurdling the language barrier...and more.

Travelers' Graffiti Wall

Candid advice and opinions from thousands of travelers on everything listed above, plus whatever topics are hot at the moment (discount flights, packing tips, scams...you name it).

Rick's Annual Guide to European Railpasses

The clearest, most comprehensive guide to the confusing array of railpass options out there, and how to choo-choose the railpass that best fits your itinerary and budget. Then you can order your railpass (and get a bunch of great freebies) online from us!

Great Gear at the Rick Steves Travel Store

Enjoy bargains on Rick's guidebooks, planning maps and TV series DVDs, and on his custom-designed carry-on bags, roll-aboard bags, day packs and light-packing accessories.

Rick Steves Tours

This year more than 10,000 lucky travelers will explore Europe on a Rick Steves tour. Learn more about our 25 different one-to-three-week itineraries, read uncensored feedback from our tour alums, and sign up for your dream trip online!

Rick on Radio and TV

Download free podcasts of our weekly *Travel with Rick Steves* public radio show; read the scripts and see video clips from public television's *Rick Steves' Europe*.

Respect for Your Privacy

Ordering online from us is secure. When you buy something from us, join a tour, or subscribe to Rick's free monthly travel news e-mails, we promise to never share your name, information, or e-mail address with anyone else. You won't be spammed!

Have fun raising your Travel I.Q. at
www.ricksteves.com

Rick Steves

More *Savvy.* More *Surprising.* More *Fun.*

COUNTRY GUIDES 2007

Croatia & Slovenia
England
France
Germany & Austria
Great Britain
Ireland
Italy
Portugal
Scandinavia
Spain
Switzerland

CITY GUIDES 2007

Amsterdam, Bruges & Brussels
Florence & Tuscany
Istanbul
London
Paris
Prague & The Czech Republic
Provence & The French Riviera
Rome
Venice

BEST OF GUIDES

Best of Eastern Europe
Best of Europe

As the #1 authority on European travel, Rick gives you inside information on what to visit, where to stay, and how to get there—economically and hassle-free.

www.ricksteves.com

PHRASE BOOKS & DICTIONARIES

French
French, Italian & German
German
Italian
Portuguese
Spanish

MORE EUROPE FROM RICK STEVES

Easy Access Europe
Europe 101
Europe Through the Back Door
Postcards from Europe

RICK STEVES' EUROPE DVDs

All 43 Shows 2000-2005
Britain
Eastern Europe
France & Benelux
Germany, The Swiss Alps & Travel Skills
Ireland
Italy
Spain & Portugal

PLANNING MAPS

Britain & Ireland
Europe
France
Germany, Austria & Switzerland
Italy
Spain & Portugal

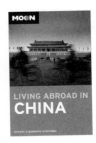

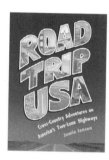

CREDITS

Researcher

Sonja Groset
Sonja, whose immigrant parents are from Sweden and Norway, loves returning to her Scandinavian roots each summer, whether to spend time with relatives or to run the Stockholm Marathon. She's worked for Rick Steves for 10 years—researching guidebooks, leading tours, and designing Web pages for www.ricksteves.com.

IMAGES

Location	Photographer
Front color matter: Copenhagen–Nyhavn	Sonja Groset
Front color matter: Fjord	Cameron Hewitt
Denmark: Copenhagen's Højbro Plads	Rick Steves
Copenhagen: Nyhavn	Cameron Hewitt
Near Copenhagen: Frederiksborg Castle	David C. Hoerlein
Central Denmark: Ærøskøbing	Rick Steves
Jutland: Danish Countryside	Rick Steves
Norway: Sognefjord	Rick Steves
Oslo: Vigeland Sculpture Garden	Rick Steves
Norway in a Nutshell: Aurland	Sonja Groset
More on the Sognefjord: Balestrand	Cameron Hewitt
Gudbrandsdal Valley and Jotunheimen Mountains: Maihaugen Open-Air Folk Museum	Rick Steves
Bergen: Bryggen	Cameron Hewitt
South Norway: South Norway Port Town	Rick Steves
Sweden: Stockholm	Cameron Hewitt
Stockholm: Drottningholm Palace	Rick Steves
South Sweden: Kalmar Castle	Rick Steves
Finland: Helsinki's Lutheran Cathedral	Cameron Hewitt
Helsinki: Helsinki Harbor	Cameron Hewitt
Estonia: Tallinn	Cameron Hewitt
Tallinn: Old Town Square	Cameron Hewitt

Rick Steves' Guidebook Series

Country Guides

Rick Steves' Best of Europe
Rick Steves' Best of Eastern Europe
Rick Steves' Croatia & Slovenia (new in 2007)
Rick Steves' England
Rick Steves' France
Rick Steves' Germany & Austria
Rick Steves' Great Britain
Rick Steves' Ireland
Rick Steves' Italy
Rick Steves' Portugal
Rick Steves' Scandinavia
Rick Steves' Spain
Rick Steves' Switzerland

City and Regional Guides

Rick Steves' Amsterdam, Bruges & Brussels
Rick Steves' Florence & Tuscany
Rick Steves' Istanbul (new in 2007)
Rick Steves' London
Rick Steves' Paris
Rick Steves' Prague & the Czech Republic
Rick Steves' Provence & the French Riviera
Rick Steves' Rome
Rick Steves' Venice

Rick Steves' Phrase Books

French
German
Italian
Spanish
Portuguese
French/Italian/German

Other Books

Rick Steves' Europe Through the Back Door
Rick Steves' Europe 101: History and Art for the Traveler
Rick Steves' Easy Access Europe
Rick Steves' Postcards from Europe
Rick Steves' European Christmas

(Avalon Travel Publishing)

AVALON
publishing group incorporated

Avalon Travel Publishing
1400 65th Street, Suite 250
Emeryville, CA 94608

Avalon Travel Publishing is an Imprint of Avalon Publishing Group, Inc.

Printed in the USA by Worzalla. First printing January 2007.

ISBN(10) 1-56691-822-7
ISBN(13) 978-1-56691-822-0
ISSN 1084-7206

Thanks to my wife, Anne, for making home my favorite travel destination. Thanks also to Thor, Hanne, Geir, Hege, and Kari-Anne, our Norwegian family.

In loving memory of Berit Kristiansen, whose house was my house for 20 years of Norwegian travel.

For the latest on Rick's lectures, guidebooks, tours, public radio show, and public television series, contact Europe Through the Back Door, Box 2009, Edmonds, WA 98020, 425/771-8303, fax 425/771-0833, www.ricksteves.com, rick@ricksteves.com.

Europe Through the Back Door Managing Editor: Risa Laib
ETBD Editors: Cathy McDonald, Gretchen Strauch, Jennifer Madison Davis, Jennifer Hauseman (Senior Editor)
Avalon Travel Publishing Editor and Series Manager: Madhu Prasher
Avalon Travel Publishing Project Editor: Patrick Collins
Copy Editor: Jennifer Malnick
Proofreader: Pamela Vevea
Indexer: Carl Wikander
Production & Typesetting: Holly McGuire, Patrick David Barber
Research Assistance: Sonja Groset, Jennifer Madison Davis, David C. Hoerlein
Interior Design: Amber Pirker, Jane Musser, Laura Mazer
Cover Design: Kari Gim, Laura Mazer
Maps and Graphics: David C. Hoerlein, Laura VanDeventer, Lauren Mills, Barb Geisler, Mike Morgenfeld
Photography: Cameron Hewitt, Sonja Groset, Rick Steves, Ian Watson, David C. Hoerlein
Front Matter Color Photos: p. i, Copenhagen, Denmark, © Sonja Groset; p. iv, Fjords, Norway, © Cameron Hewitt
Cover Photos: front image, Helsinki Harbor © Rick Steves; back image: Aerial view of Bergen © Cameron Hewitt